Dynamite Entertainment Presents

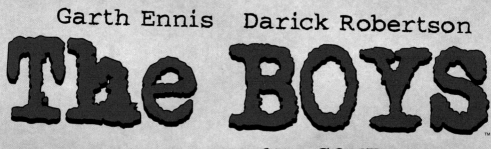

Garth Ennis Darick Robertson

The BOYS™

volume two: GET SOME

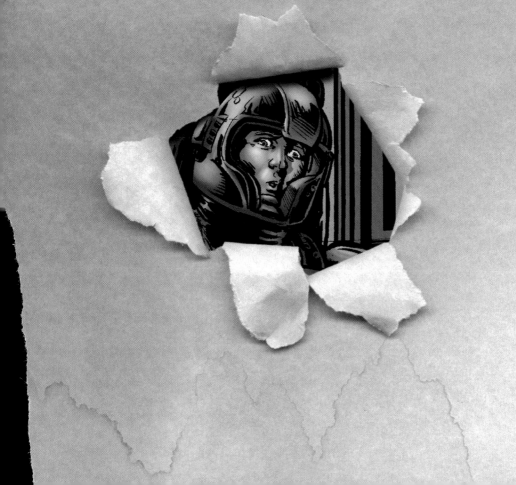

THE BOYS™

CASE FILE

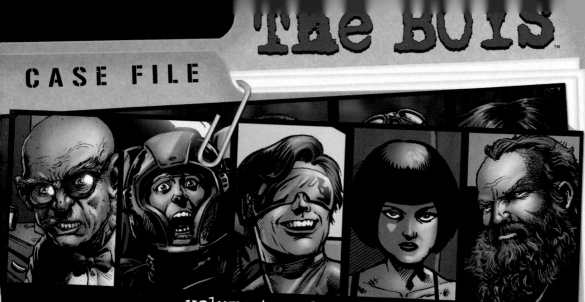

volume two: GET SOME

Written by:
GARTH ENNIS

Illustrated by:
DARICK ROBERTSON
& PETER SNEJBJERG

Additional inks by:
RODNEY RAMOS

Lettered by:
SIMON BOWLAND

Colored by:
TONY AVIÑA

Cover by:
DARICK ROBERTSON
& TONY AVIÑA

The Boys Created By: ENNIS & ROBERTSON

Collects issues seven through fourteen of The Boys, originally published by Dynamite Entertainment.

Trade Design By: JASON ULLMEYER

DYNAMITE ENTERTAINMENT®

To find a comic shop in your area, call the comic shop locator service toll-free 1-888-266-4226

QUANTITY PURCHASES: Companies, professional groups, clubs, and other organizations may qualify for sp terms when ordering quantities of this title. For information, direct your inquiry to the Special Sales Departme

For media rights, foreign rights, promotions, licensing, and advertising: marketing@dynamiteentertainment.co

Printed in Canada.

First Printing
SOFTCOVER ISBN-10: 9-133305-68-1 ISBN-13: 9-789133-305688
10 9 8 7 6 5 4 3 2 1

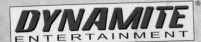

For Nicky Barrucci
and Joe Rybandt

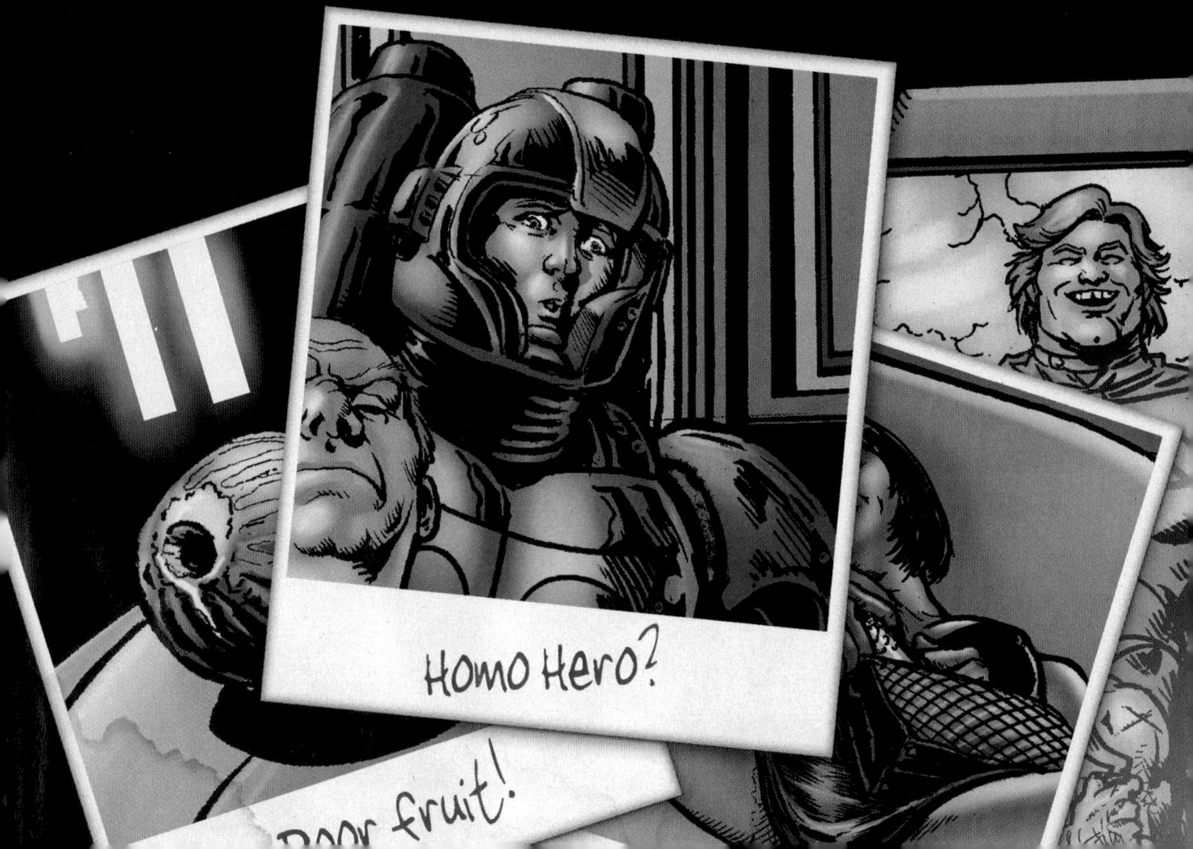
Homo Hero?
fruit!

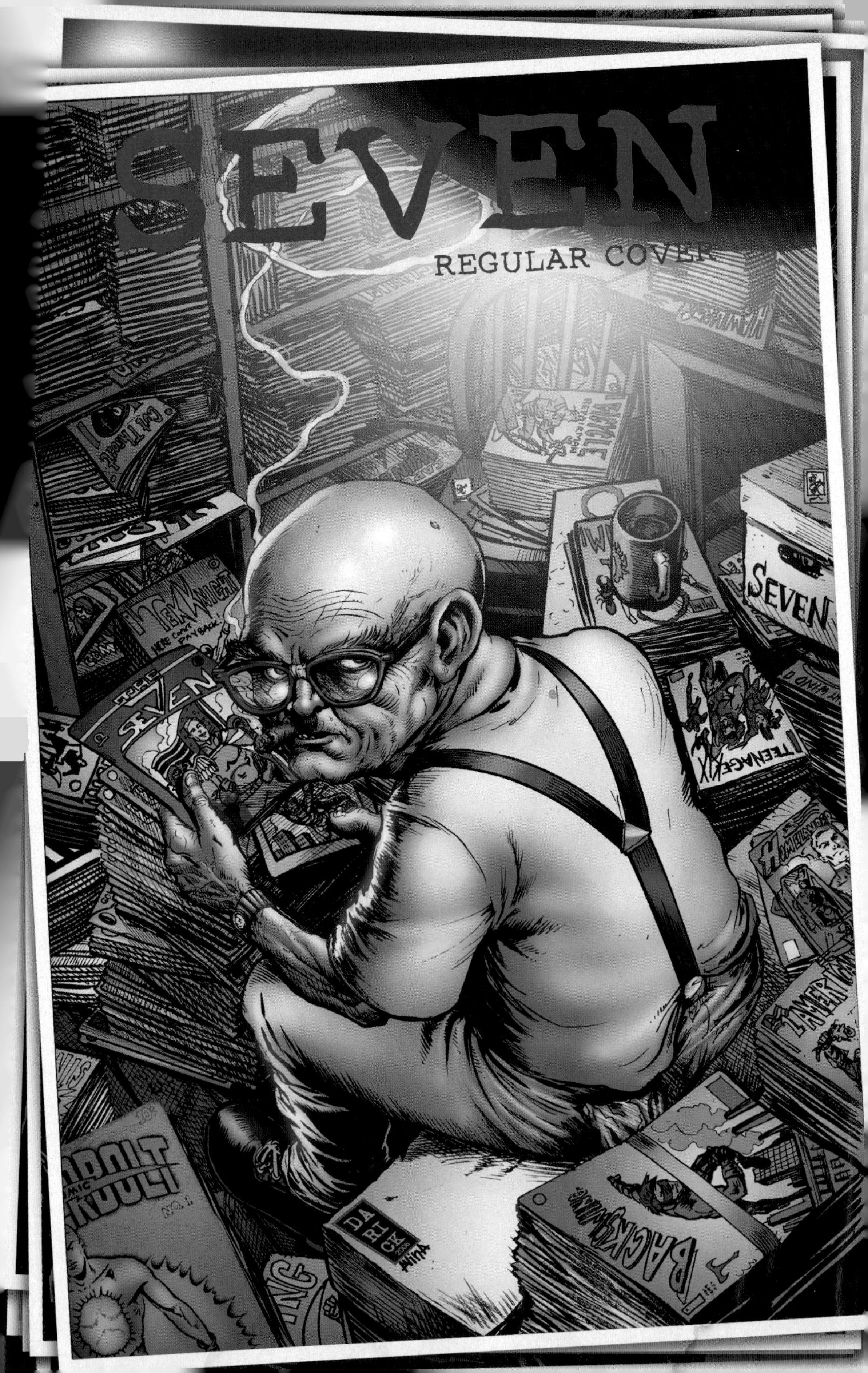
SEVEN
REGULAR COVER
SEVEN
THE SEVEN
HERE COMES PAYBACK!
TEENAGE
BACKSTABBING
NO. 1

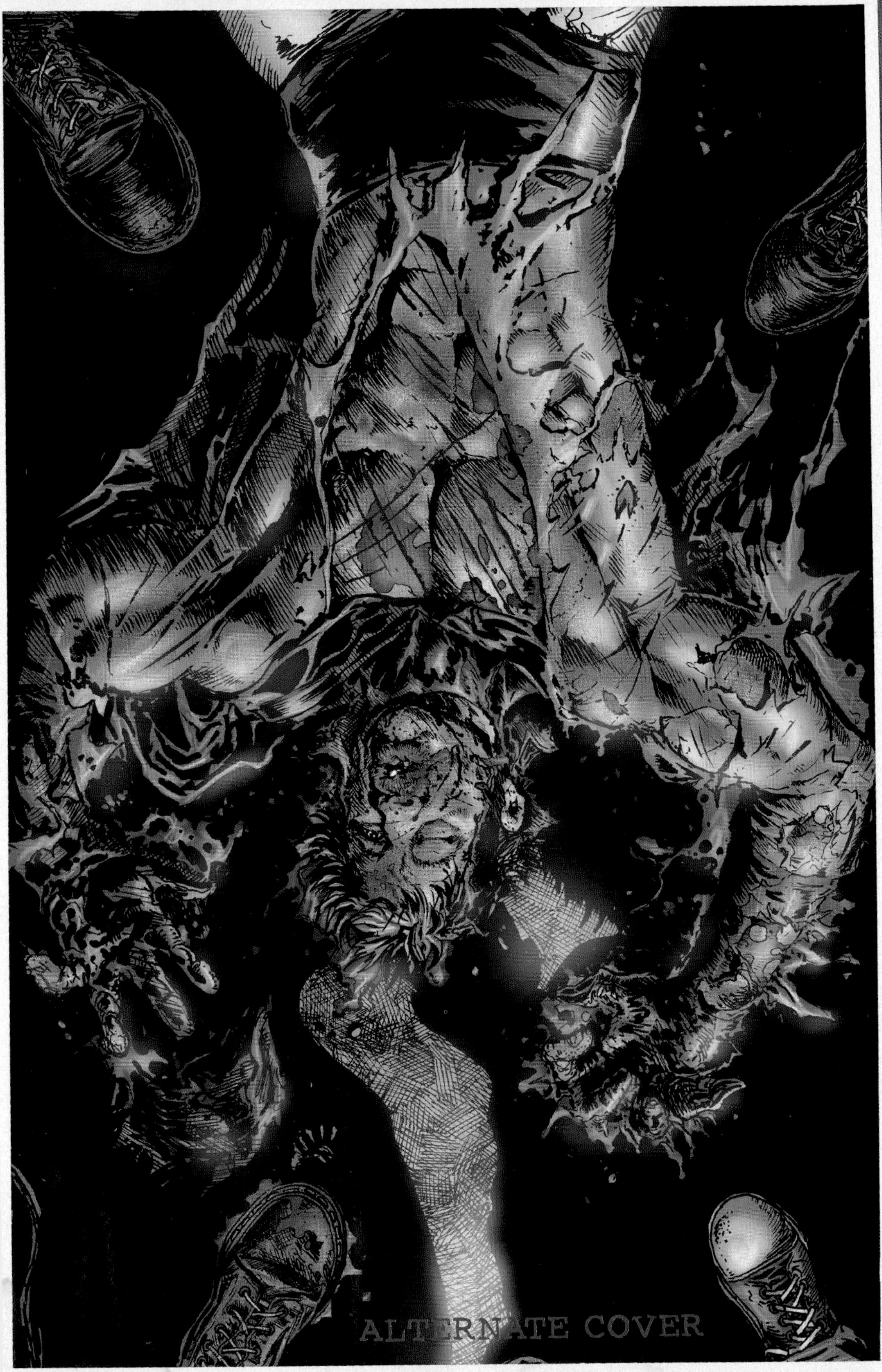
ALTERNATE COVER

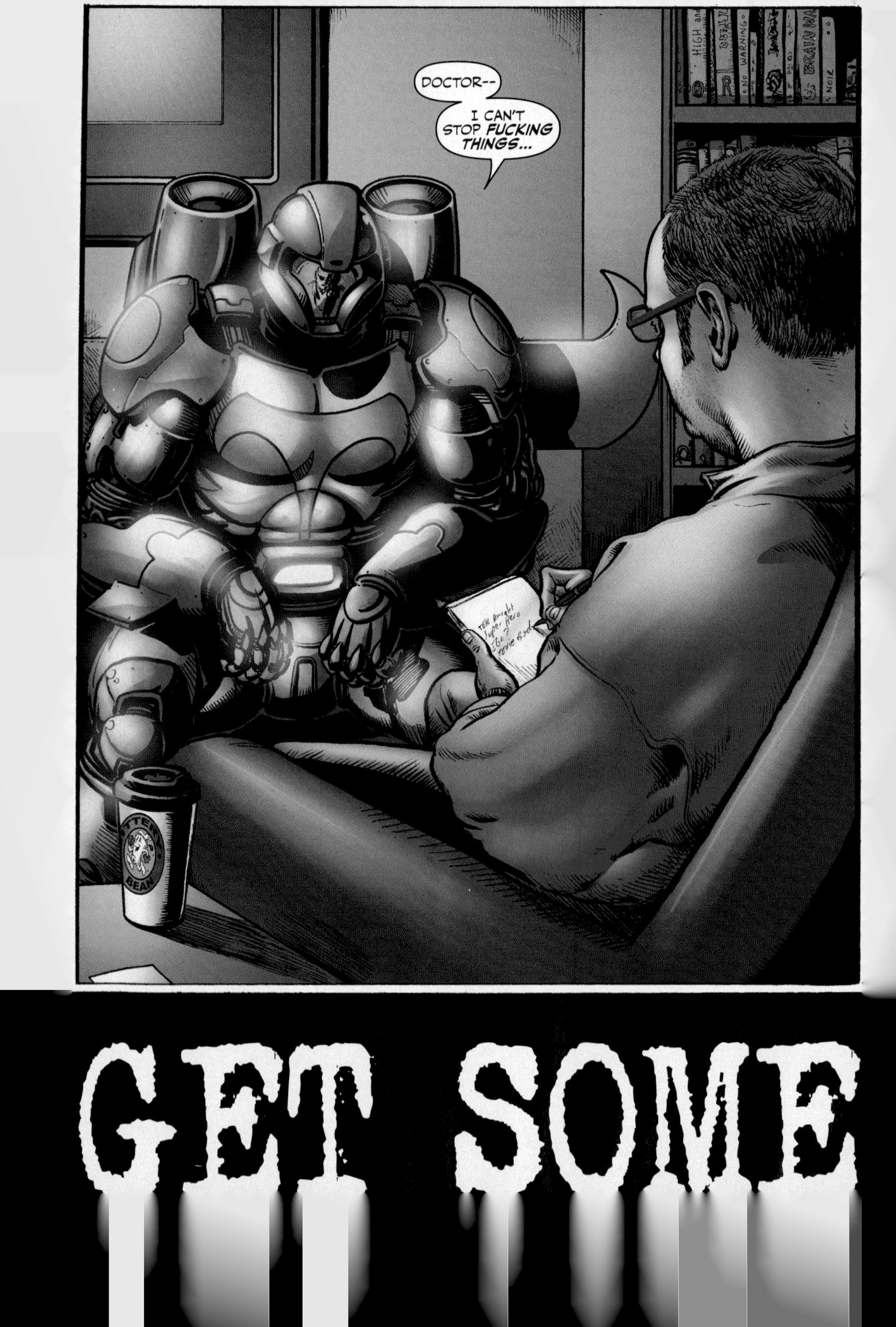
DOCTOR--
I CAN'T STOP FUCKING THINGS...

GET SOME

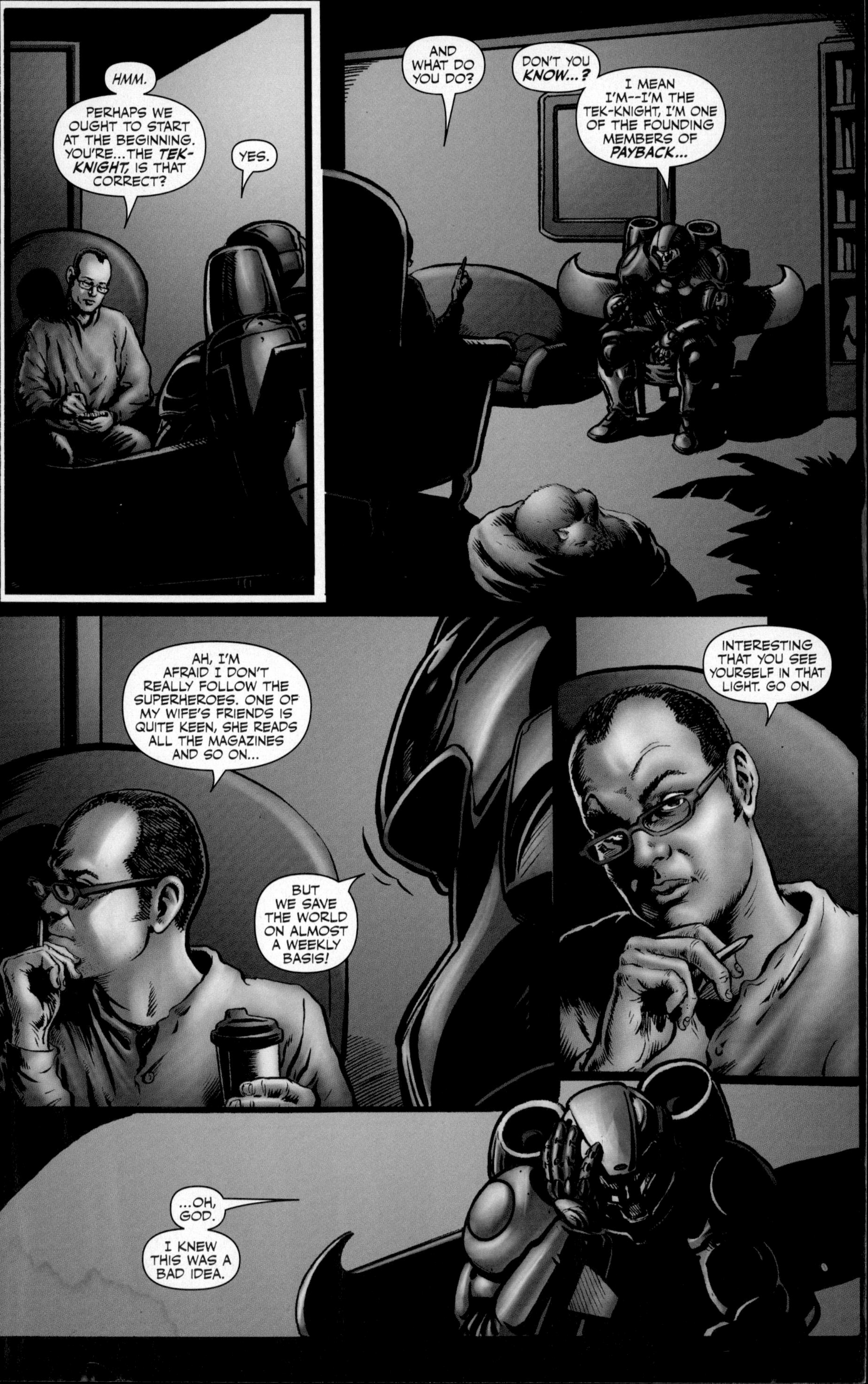
HMM.
PERHAPS WE OUGHT TO START AT THE BEGINNING. YOU'RE...THE *TEK-KNIGHT,* IS THAT CORRECT?
YES.
AND WHAT DO YOU DO?
DON'T YOU *KNOW...?*
I MEAN I'M--I'M THE TEK-KNIGHT, I'M ONE OF THE FOUNDING MEMBERS OF *PAYBACK...*
AH, I'M AFRAID I DON'T REALLY FOLLOW THE SUPERHEROES. ONE OF MY WIFE'S FRIENDS IS QUITE KEEN, SHE READS ALL THE MAGAZINES AND SO ON...
BUT WE SAVE THE WORLD ON ALMOST A WEEKLY BASIS!
INTERESTING THAT YOU SEE YOURSELF IN THAT LIGHT. GO ON.
...OH, GOD.
I KNEW THIS WAS A BAD IDEA.

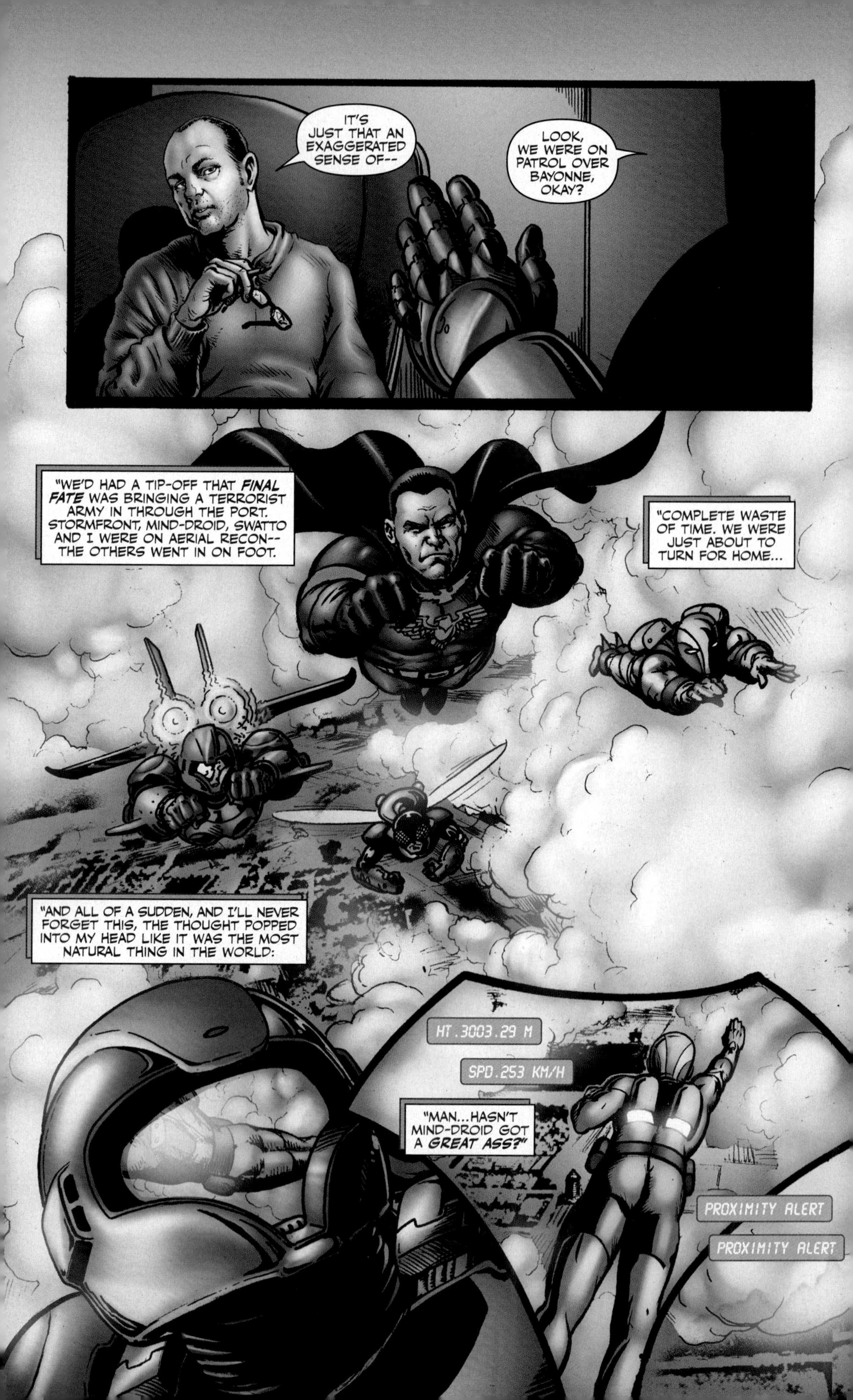
IT'S JUST THAT AN EXAGGERATED SENSE OF--
LOOK, WE WERE ON PATROL OVER BAYONNE, OKAY?
"WE'D HAD A TIP-OFF THAT *FINAL FATE* WAS BRINGING A TERRORIST ARMY IN THROUGH THE PORT. STORMFRONT, MIND-DROID, SWATTO AND I WERE ON AERIAL RECON-- THE OTHERS WENT IN ON FOOT.
"COMPLETE WASTE OF TIME. WE WERE JUST ABOUT TO TURN FOR HOME...
"AND ALL OF A SUDDEN, AND I'LL NEVER FORGET THIS, THE THOUGHT POPPED INTO MY HEAD LIKE IT WAS THE MOST NATURAL THING IN THE WORLD:
HT.3003.29 M
SPD.253 KM/H
"MAN...HASN'T MIND-DROID GOT A *GREAT ASS?*"
PROXIMITY ALERT
PROXIMITY ALERT

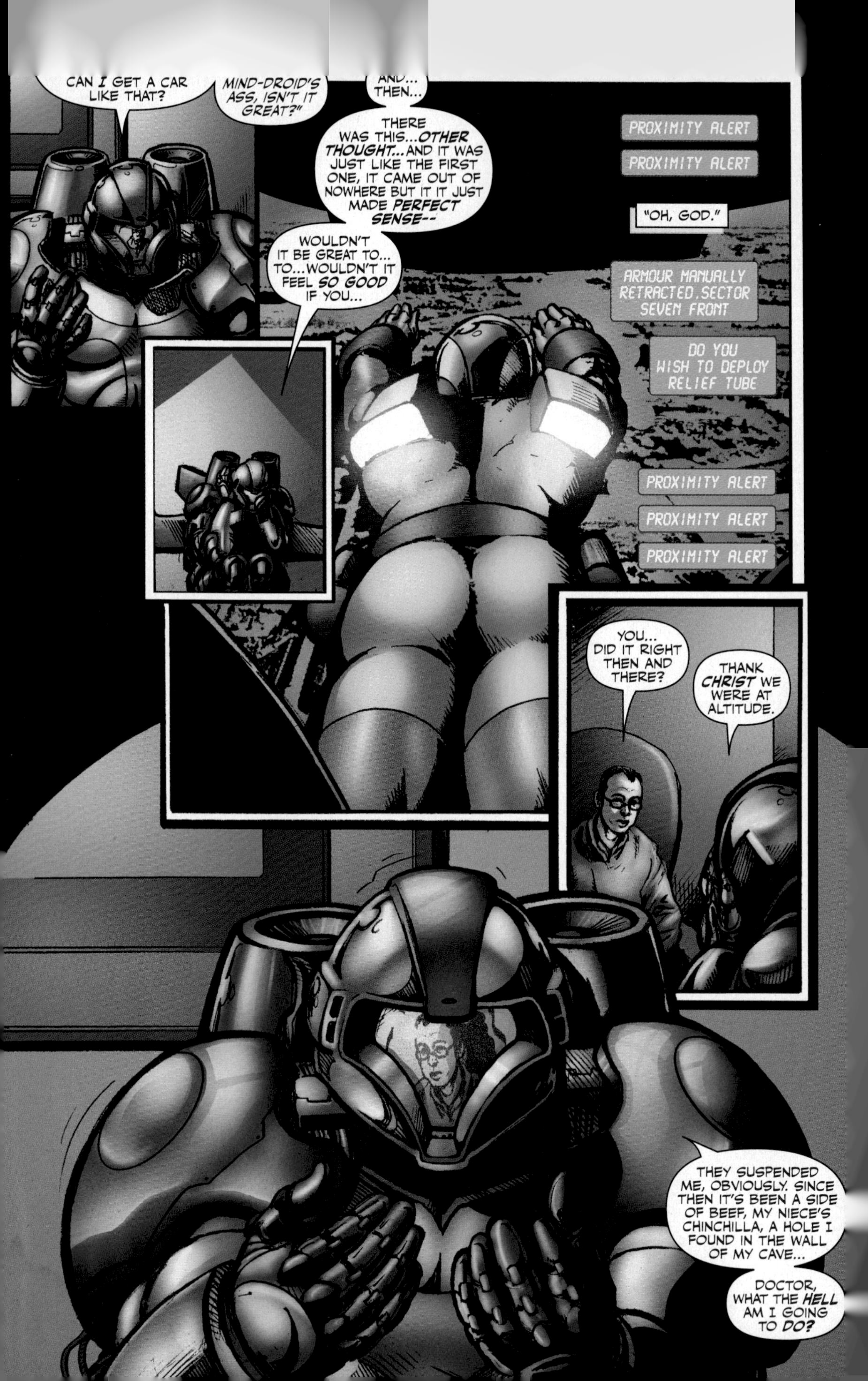

CAN I GET A CAR LIKE THAT?
MIND-DROID'S ASS, ISN'T IT GREAT?"
AND... THEN...
THERE WAS THIS...OTHER THOUGHT...AND IT WAS JUST LIKE THE FIRST ONE, IT CAME OUT OF NOWHERE BUT IT IT JUST MADE PERFECT SENSE--
WOULDN'T IT BE GREAT TO... TO...WOULDN'T IT FEEL SO GOOD IF YOU...
PROXIMITY ALERT
PROXIMITY ALERT
"OH, GOD."
ARMOUR MANUALLY RETRACTED. SECTOR SEVEN FRONT
DO YOU WISH TO DEPLOY RELIEF TUBE
PROXIMITY ALERT
PROXIMITY ALERT
PROXIMITY ALERT
YOU... DID IT RIGHT THEN AND THERE?
THANK CHRIST WE WERE AT ALTITUDE.
THEY SUSPENDED ME, OBVIOUSLY. SINCE THEN IT'S BEEN A SIDE OF BEEF, MY NIECE'S CHINCHILLA, A HOLE I FOUND IN THE WALL OF MY CAVE...
DOCTOR, WHAT THE HELL AM I GOING TO DO?

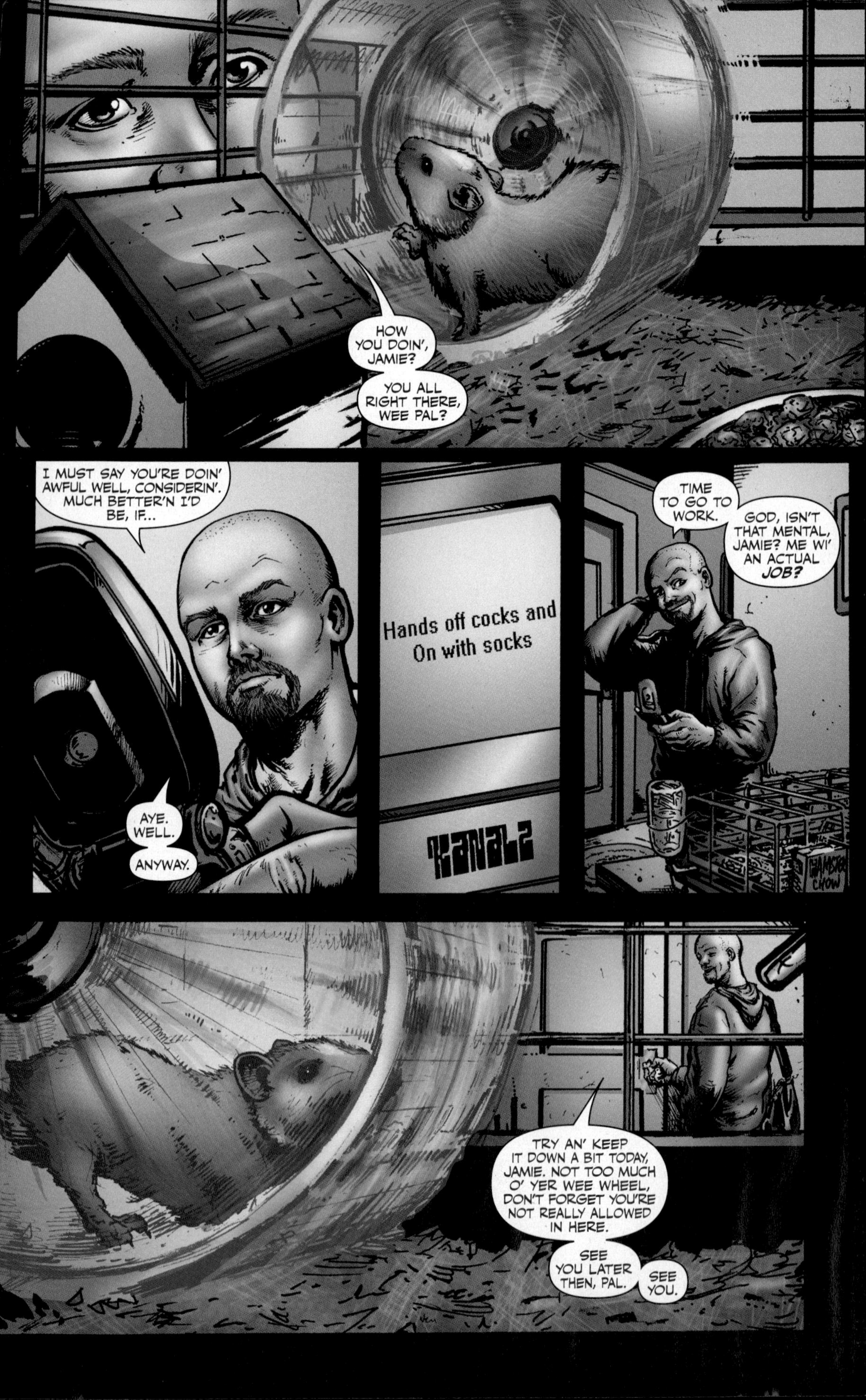

HOW YOU DOIN', JAMIE?
YOU ALL RIGHT THERE, WEE PAL?
I MUST SAY YOU'RE DOIN' AWFUL WELL, CONSIDERIN'. MUCH BETTER'N I'D BE, IF...
AYE. WELL.
ANYWAY.
Hands off cocks and On with socks
KANAL2
TIME TO GO TO WORK.
GOD, ISN'T THAT MENTAL, JAMIE? ME WI' AN ACTUAL *JOB?*
HAMSTER CHOW
TRY AN' KEEP IT DOWN A BIT TODAY, JAMIE. NOT TOO MUCH O' YER WEE WHEEL, DON'T FORGET YOU'RE NOT REALLY ALLOWED IN HERE.
SEE YOU LATER THEN, PAL.
SEE YOU.

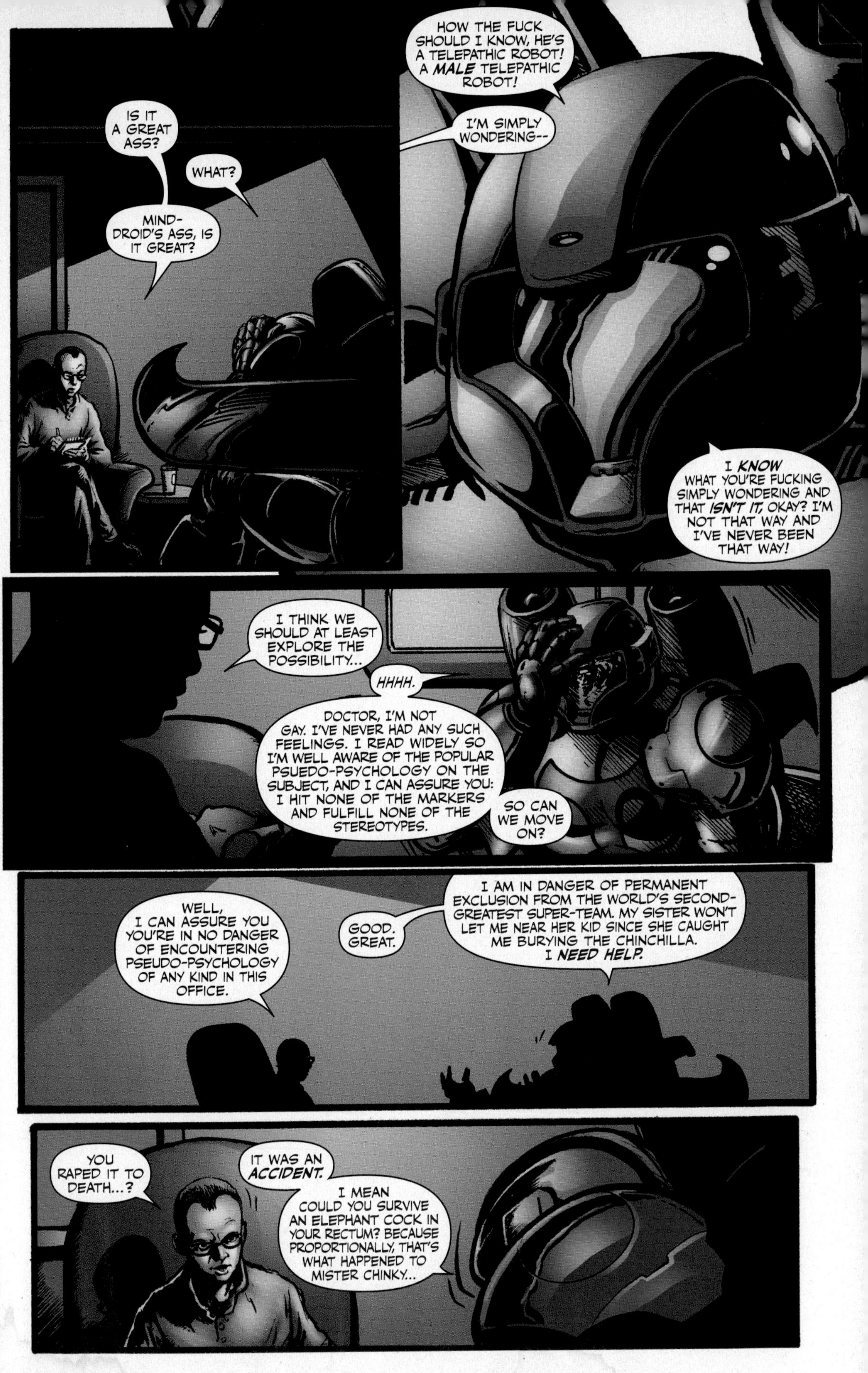
HOW THE FUCK SHOULD I KNOW, HE'S A TELEPATHIC ROBOT! A MALE TELEPATHIC ROBOT!
IS IT A GREAT ASS?
WHAT?
MIND-DROID'S ASS, IS IT GREAT?
I'M SIMPLY WONDERING--
I KNOW WHAT YOU'RE FUCKING SIMPLY WONDERING AND THAT ISN'T IT, OKAY? I'M NOT THAT WAY AND I'VE NEVER BEEN THAT WAY!
I THINK WE SHOULD AT LEAST EXPLORE THE POSSIBILITY...
HHHH.
DOCTOR, I'M NOT GAY. I'VE NEVER HAD ANY SUCH FEELINGS. I READ WIDELY SO I'M WELL AWARE OF THE POPULAR PSUEDO-PSYCHOLOGY ON THE SUBJECT, AND I CAN ASSURE YOU: I HIT NONE OF THE MARKERS AND FULFILL NONE OF THE STEREOTYPES.
SO CAN WE MOVE ON?
WELL, I CAN ASSURE YOU YOU'RE IN NO DANGER OF ENCOUNTERING PSEUDO-PSYCHOLOGY OF ANY KIND IN THIS OFFICE.
GOOD. GREAT.
I AM IN DANGER OF PERMANENT EXCLUSION FROM THE WORLD'S SECOND-GREATEST SUPER-TEAM. MY SISTER WON'T LET ME NEAR HER KID SINCE SHE CAUGHT ME BURYING THE CHINCHILLA. I NEED HELP.
YOU RAPED IT TO DEATH...?
IT WAS AN ACCIDENT.
I MEAN COULD YOU SURVIVE AN ELEPHANT COCK IN YOUR RECTUM? BECAUSE PROPORTIONALLY, THAT'S WHAT HAPPENED TO MISTER CHINKY...

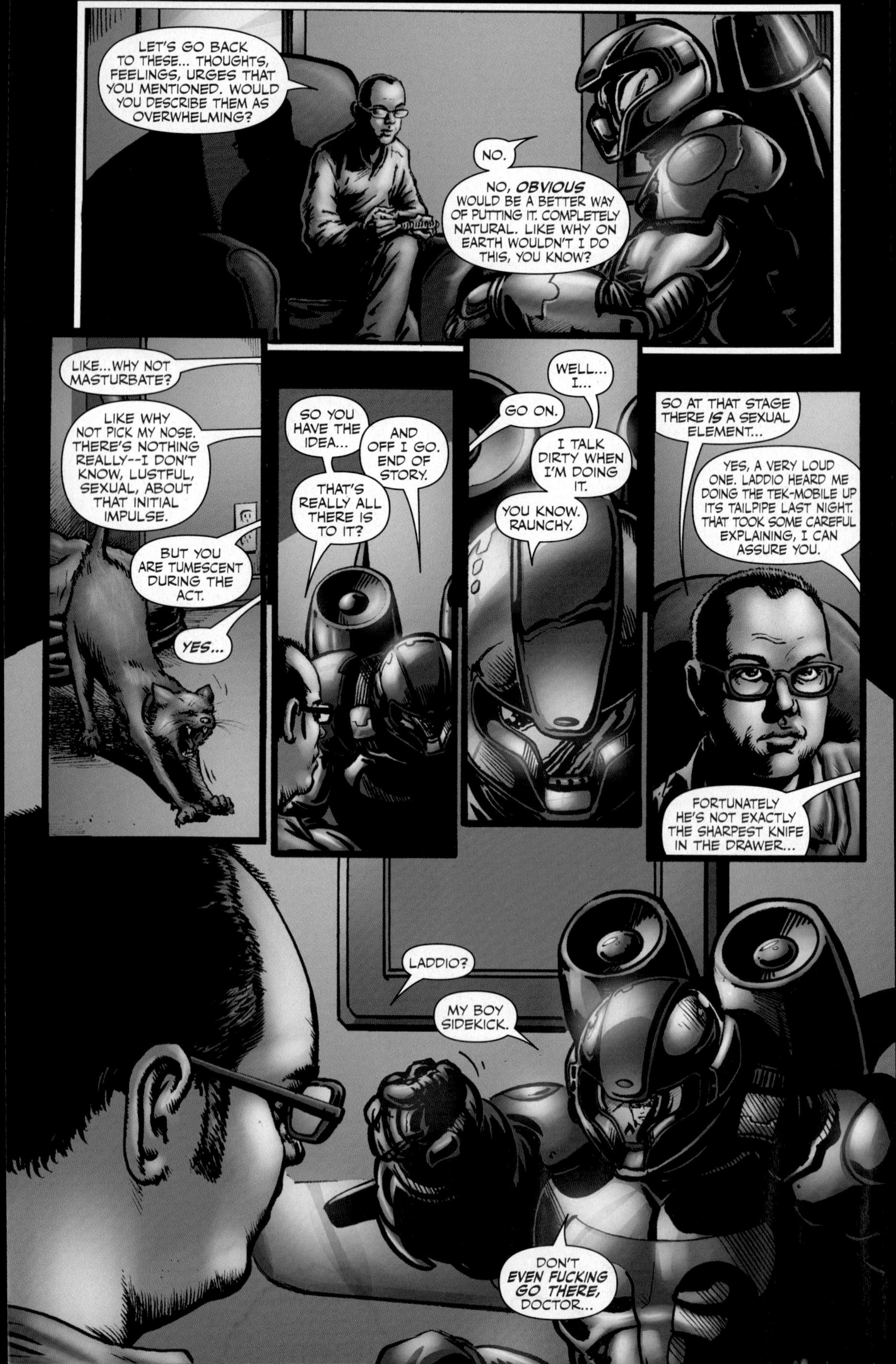
LET'S GO BACK TO THESE... THOUGHTS, FEELINGS, URGES THAT YOU MENTIONED. WOULD YOU DESCRIBE THEM AS OVERWHELMING?
NO.
NO, *OBVIOUS* WOULD BE A BETTER WAY OF PUTTING IT. COMPLETELY NATURAL. LIKE WHY ON EARTH WOULDN'T I DO THIS, YOU KNOW?
LIKE...WHY NOT MASTURBATE?
LIKE WHY NOT PICK MY NOSE. THERE'S NOTHING REALLY--I DON'T KNOW, LUSTFUL, SEXUAL, ABOUT THAT INITIAL IMPULSE.
BUT YOU ARE TUMESCENT DURING THE ACT.
YES...
SO YOU HAVE THE IDEA...
AND OFF I GO. END OF STORY.
THAT'S REALLY ALL THERE IS TO IT?
WELL... I...
GO ON.
I TALK DIRTY WHEN I'M DOING IT.
YOU KNOW. RAUNCHY.
SO AT THAT STAGE THERE *IS* A SEXUAL ELEMENT...
YES, A VERY LOUD ONE. LADDIO HEARD ME DOING THE TEK-MOBILE UP ITS TAILPIPE LAST NIGHT. THAT TOOK SOME CAREFUL EXPLAINING, I CAN ASSURE YOU.
FORTUNATELY HE'S NOT EXACTLY THE SHARPEST KNIFE IN THE DRAWER...
LADDIO?
MY BOY SIDEKICK.
DON'T *EVEN FUCKING GO THERE,* DOCTOR...

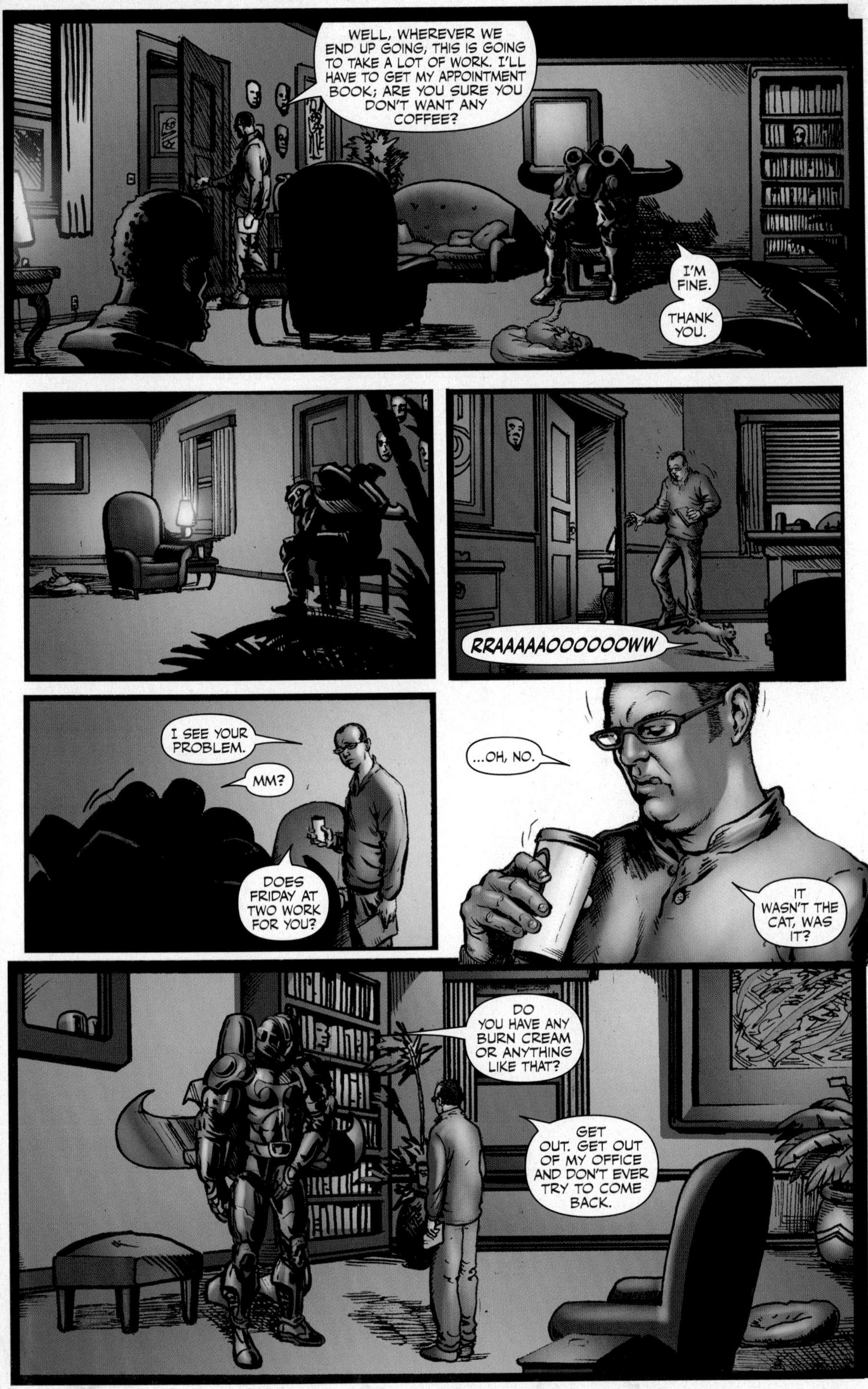
WELL, WHEREVER WE END UP GOING, THIS IS GOING TO TAKE A LOT OF WORK. I'LL HAVE TO GET MY APPOINTMENT BOOK; ARE YOU SURE YOU DON'T WANT ANY COFFEE?
I'M FINE.
THANK YOU.
RRAAAAAOOOOOOWW
I SEE YOUR PROBLEM.
MM?
DOES FRIDAY AT TWO WORK FOR YOU?
...OH, NO.
IT WASN'T THE CAT, WAS IT?
DO YOU HAVE ANY BURN CREAM OR ANYTHING LIKE THAT?
GET OUT. GET OUT OF MY OFFICE AND DON'T EVER TRY TO COME BACK.

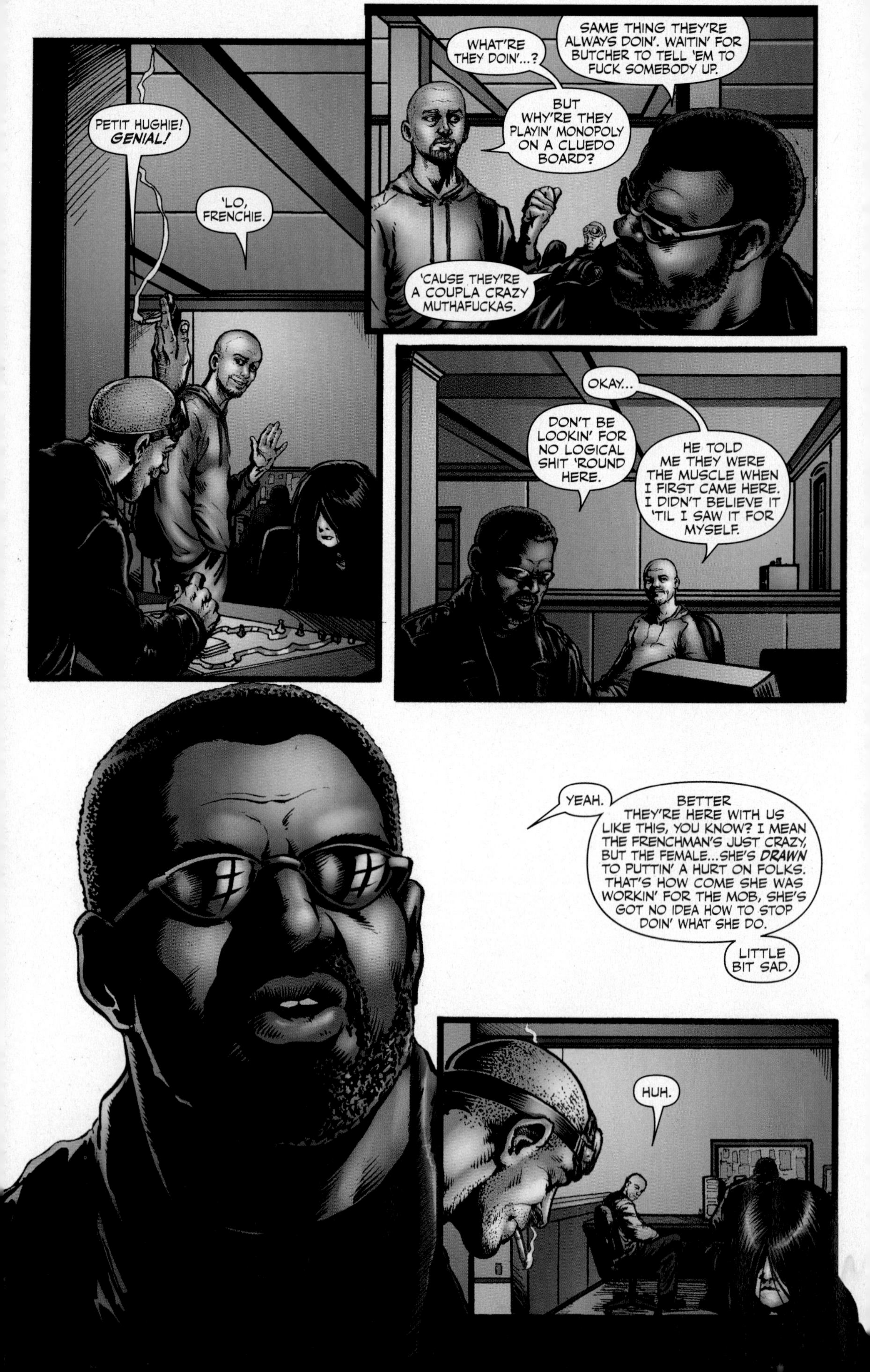
PETIT HUGHIE! *GENIAL!*
'LO, FRENCHIE.
WHAT'RE THEY DOIN'...?
SAME THING THEY'RE ALWAYS DOIN'. WAITIN' FOR BUTCHER TO TELL 'EM TO FUCK SOMEBODY UP.
BUT WHY'RE THEY PLAYIN' MONOPOLY ON A CLUEDO BOARD?
'CAUSE THEY'RE A COUPLA CRAZY MUTHAFUCKAS.
OKAY...
DON'T BE LOOKIN' FOR NO LOGICAL SHIT 'ROUND HERE.
HE TOLD ME THEY WERE THE MUSCLE WHEN I FIRST CAME HERE. I DIDN'T BELIEVE IT 'TIL I SAW IT FOR MYSELF.
YEAH.
BETTER THEY'RE HERE WITH US LIKE THIS, YOU KNOW? I MEAN THE FRENCHMAN'S JUST CRAZY, BUT THE FEMALE...SHE'S *DRAWN* TO PUTTIN' A HURT ON FOLKS. THAT'S HOW COME SHE WAS WORKIN' FOR THE MOB, SHE'S GOT NO IDEA HOW TO STOP DOIN' WHAT SHE DO.
LITTLE BIT SAD.
HUH.

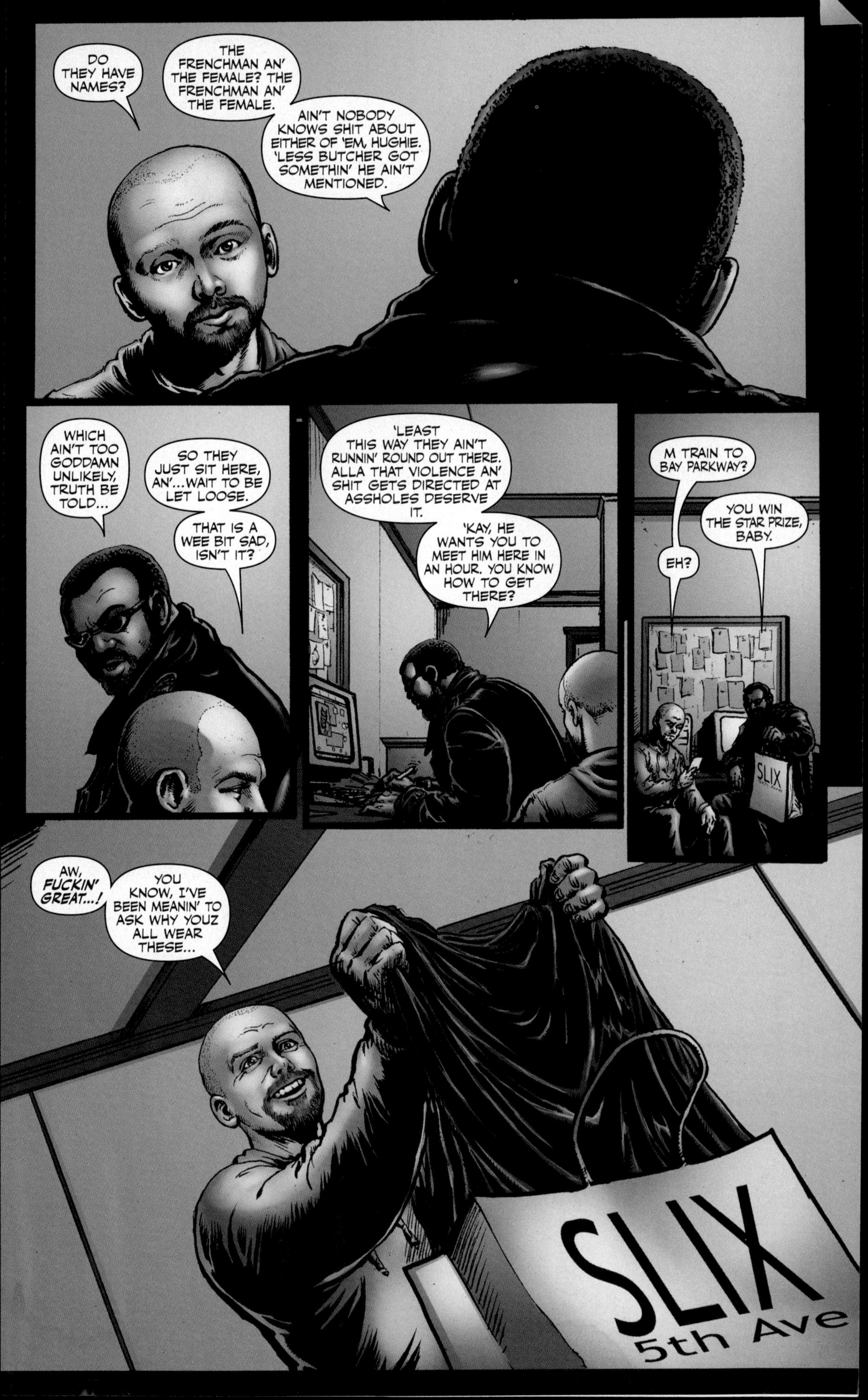
DO THEY HAVE NAMES?
THE FRENCHMAN AN' THE FEMALE? THE FRENCHMAN AN' THE FEMALE.
AIN'T NOBODY KNOWS SHIT ABOUT EITHER OF 'EM, HUGHIE. 'LESS BUTCHER GOT SOMETHIN' HE AIN'T MENTIONED.
WHICH AIN'T TOO GODDAMN UNLIKELY, TRUTH BE TOLD...
SO THEY JUST SIT HERE, AN'...WAIT TO BE LET LOOSE.
THAT IS A WEE BIT SAD, ISN'T IT?
'LEAST THIS WAY THEY AIN'T RUNNIN' ROUND OUT THERE. ALLA THAT VIOLENCE AN' SHIT GETS DIRECTED AT ASSHOLES DESERVE IT.
'KAY, HE WANTS YOU TO MEET HIM HERE IN AN HOUR. YOU KNOW HOW TO GET THERE?
M TRAIN TO BAY PARKWAY?
EH?
YOU WIN THE STAR PRIZE, BABY.
SLIX 5th Ave
AW, FUCKIN' GREAT...!
YOU KNOW, I'VE BEEN MEANIN' TO ASK WHY YOUZ ALL WEAR THESE...
SLIX
5th Ave

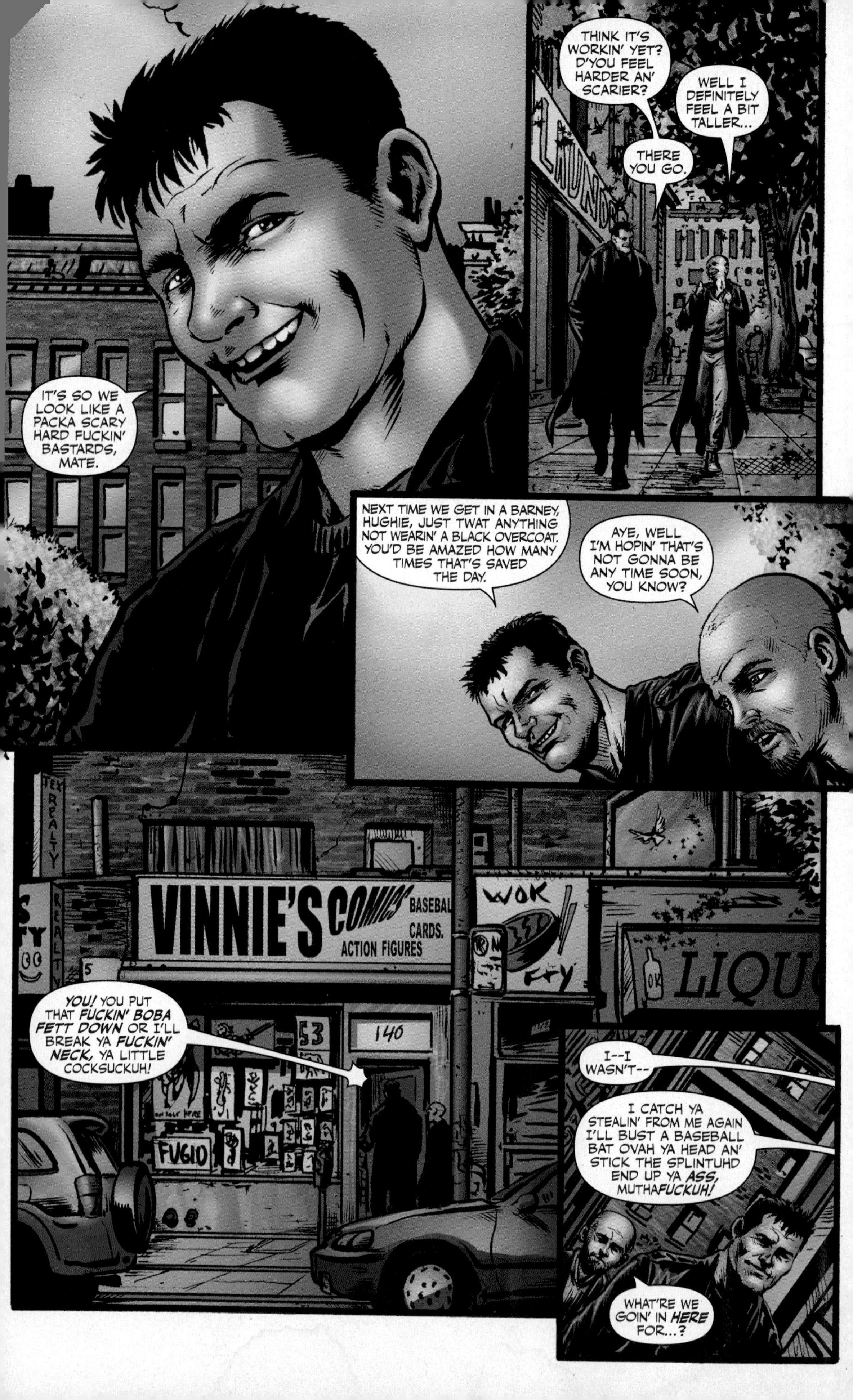
IT'S SO WE LOOK LIKE A PACKA SCARY HARD FUCKIN' BASTARDS, MATE.
THINK IT'S WORKIN' YET? D'YOU FEEL HARDER AN' SCARIER?
WELL I DEFINITELY FEEL A BIT TALLER...
THERE YOU GO.
LAUNDR
NEXT TIME WE GET IN A BARNEY, HUGHIE, JUST TWAT ANYTHING NOT WEARIN' A BLACK OVERCOAT. YOU'D BE AMAZED HOW MANY TIMES THAT'S SAVED THE DAY.
AYE, WELL I'M HOPIN' THAT'S NOT GONNA BE ANY TIME SOON, YOU KNOW?
TEX REALTY
VINNIE'S COMICS BASEBALL CARDS. ACTION FIGURES
WOK Fry
LIQU
140
53
FUGIO
YOU! YOU PUT THAT FUCKIN' BOBA FETT DOWN OR I'LL BREAK YA FUCKIN' NECK, YA LITTLE COCKSUCKUH!
I--I WASN'T--
I CATCH YA STEALIN' FROM ME AGAIN I'LL BUST A BASEBALL BAT OVAH YA HEAD AN' STICK THE SPLINTUHD END UP YA ASS, MUTHAFUCKUH!
WHAT'RE WE GOIN' IN HERE FOR...?

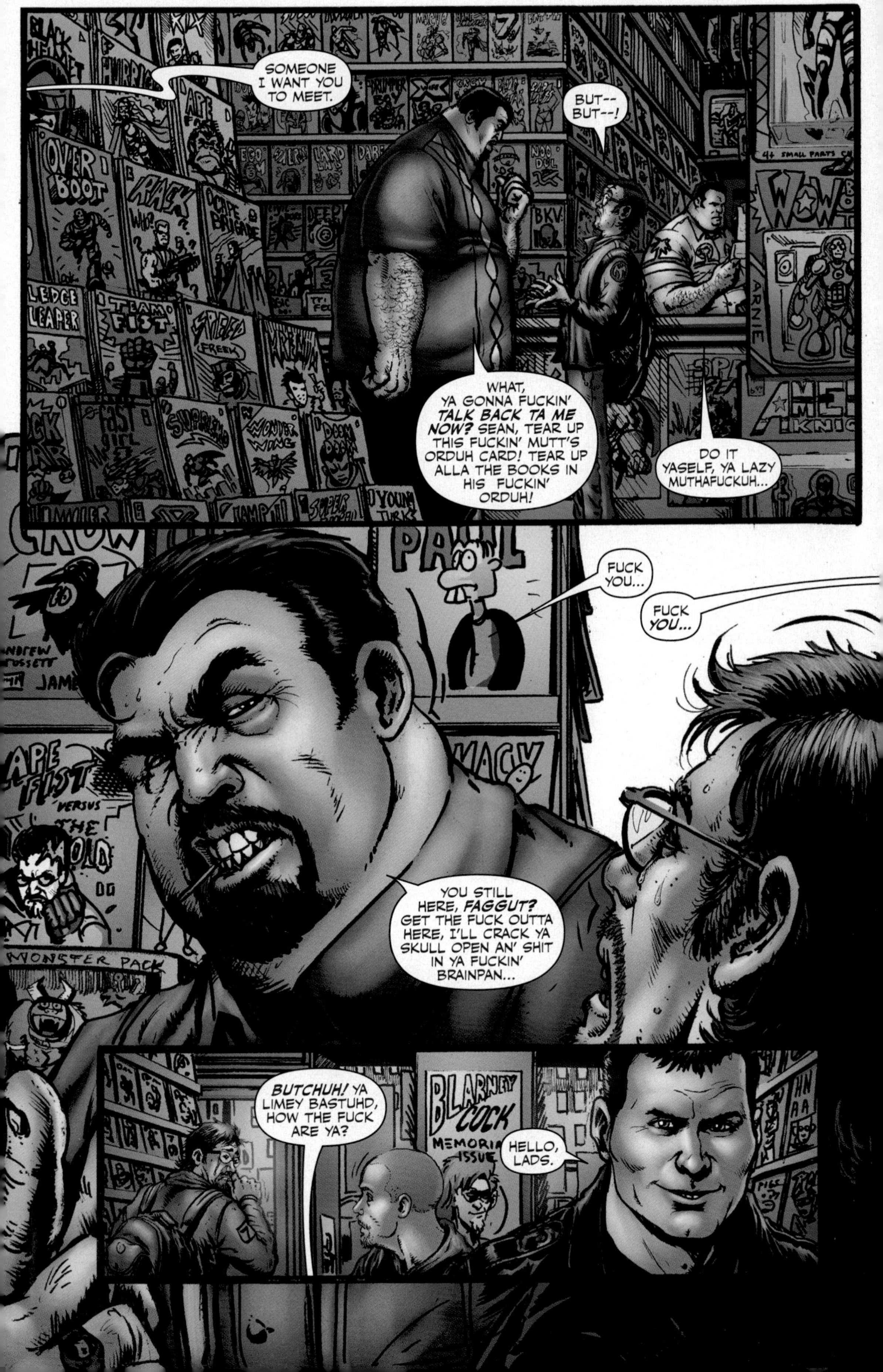
SOMEONE I WANT YOU TO MEET.
BUT-- BUT--!
WHAT, YA GONNA FUCKIN' *TALK BACK TA ME NOW?* SEAN, TEAR UP THIS FUCKIN' MUTT'S ORDUH CARD! TEAR UP ALLA THE BOOKS IN HIS FUCKIN' ORDUH!
DO IT YASELF, YA LAZY MUTHAFUCKUH...
FUCK YOU...
FUCK *YOU...*
YOU STILL HERE, *FAGGUT?* GET THE FUCK OUTTA HERE, I'LL CRACK YA SKULL OPEN AN' SHIT IN YA FUCKIN' BRAINPAN...
BUTCHUH! YA LIMEY BASTUHD, HOW THE FUCK ARE YA?
HELLO, LADS.

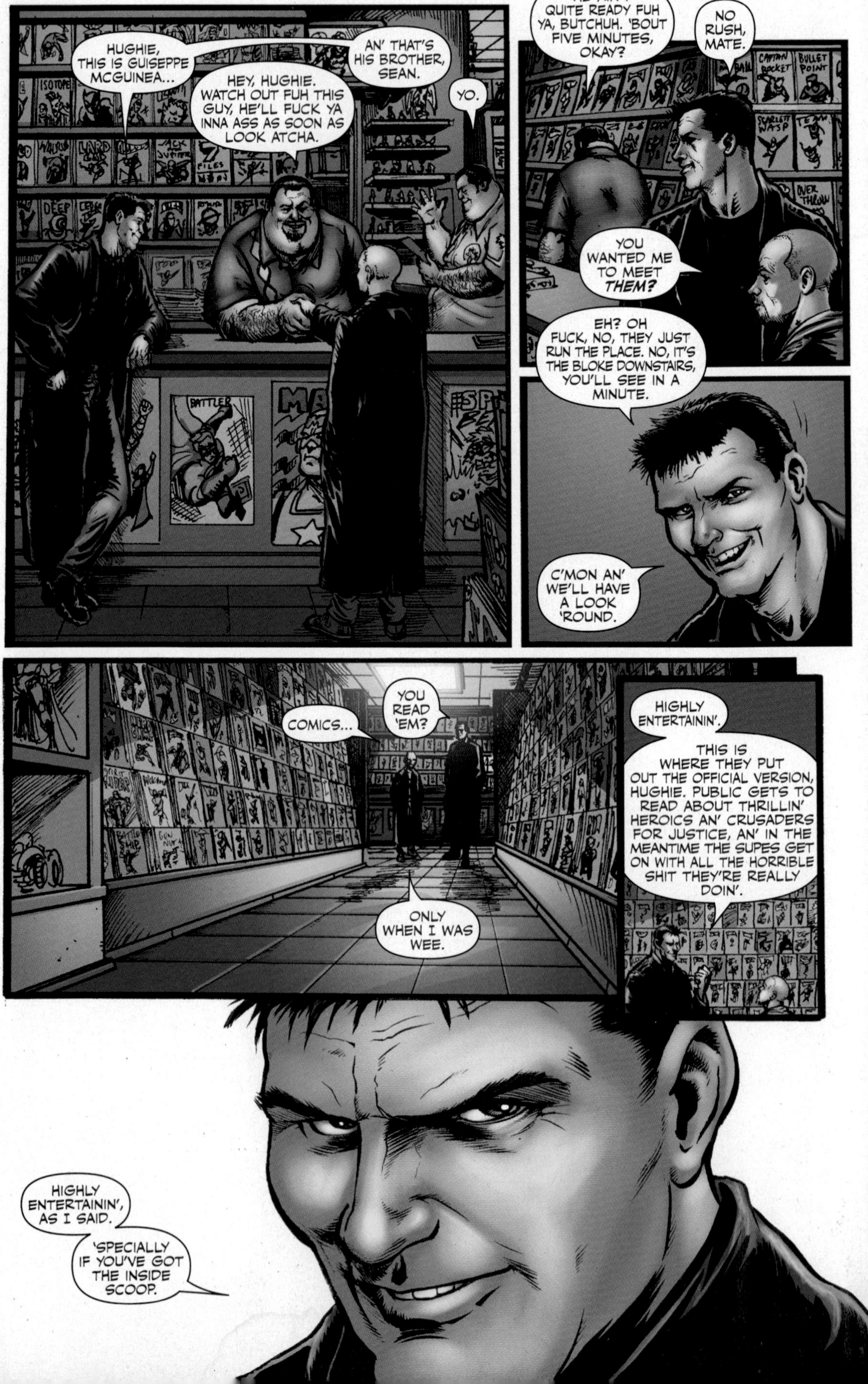
HUGHIE, THIS IS GUISEPPE MCGUINEA...
AN' THAT'S HIS BROTHER, SEAN.
HEY, HUGHIE. WATCH OUT FUH THIS GUY, HE'LL FUCK YA INNA ASS AS SOON AS LOOK ATCHA.
YO.
HE AIN'T QUITE READY FUH YA, BUTCHUH. 'BOUT FIVE MINUTES, OKAY?
NO RUSH, MATE.
YOU WANTED ME TO MEET *THEM?*
EH? OH FUCK, NO, THEY JUST RUN THE PLACE. NO, IT'S THE BLOKE DOWNSTAIRS, YOU'LL SEE IN A MINUTE.
C'MON AN' WE'LL HAVE A LOOK 'ROUND.
COMICS...
YOU READ 'EM?
ONLY WHEN I WAS WEE.
HIGHLY ENTERTAININ'.
THIS IS WHERE THEY PUT OUT THE OFFICIAL VERSION, HUGHIE. PUBLIC GETS TO READ ABOUT THRILLIN' HEROICS AN' CRUSADERS FOR JUSTICE, AN' IN THE MEANTIME THE SUPES GET ON WITH ALL THE HORRIBLE SHIT THEY'RE REALLY DOIN'.
HIGHLY ENTERTAININ', AS I SAID.
'SPECIALLY IF YOU'VE GOT THE INSIDE SCOOP.

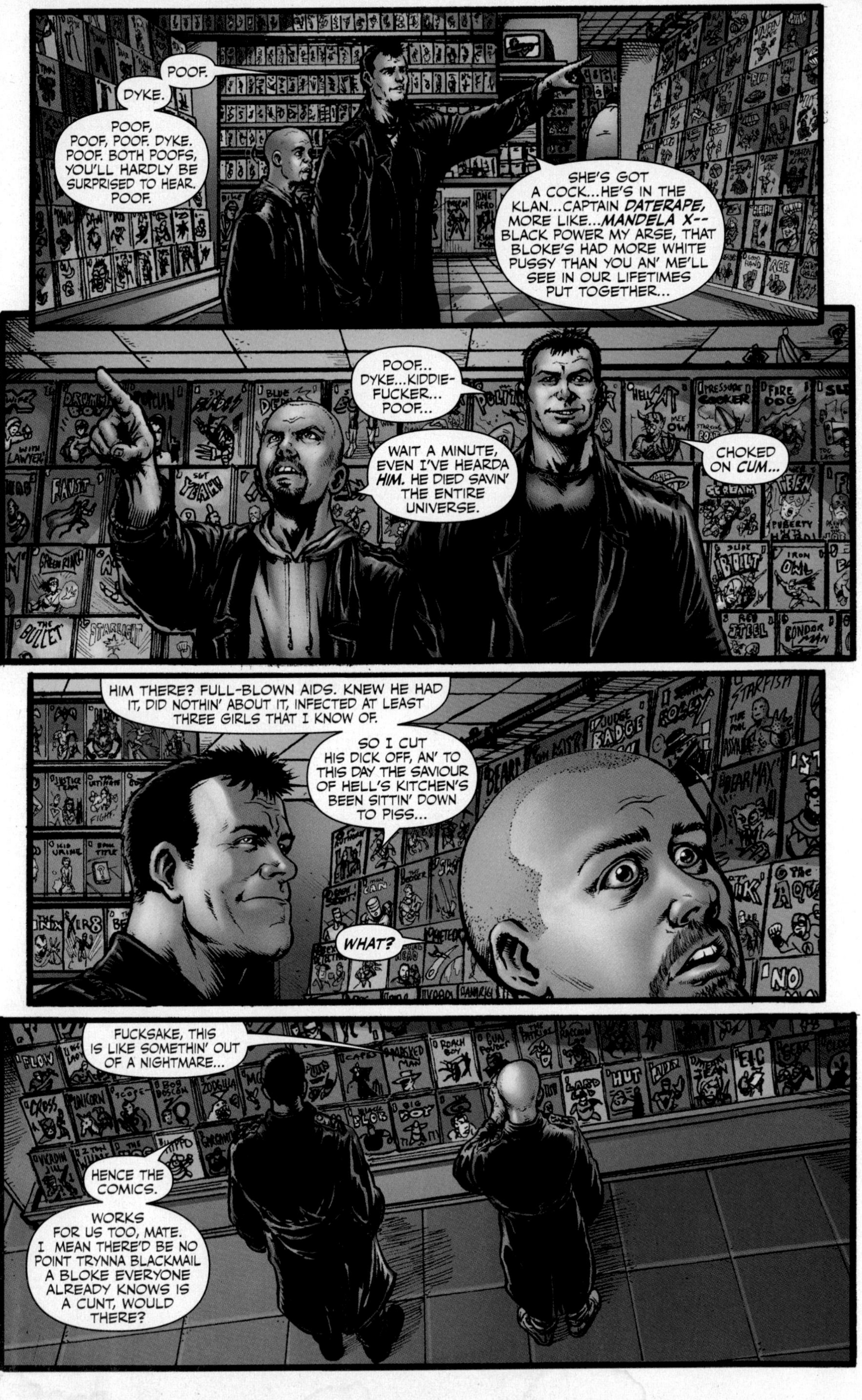
POOF.
DYKE.
POOF, POOF, POOF. DYKE. POOF. BOTH POOFS, YOU'LL HARDLY BE SURPRISED TO HEAR. POOF.
SHE'S GOT A COCK...HE'S IN THE KLAN...CAPTAIN DATERAPE, MORE LIKE...MANDELA X--BLACK POWER MY ARSE, THAT BLOKE'S HAD MORE WHITE PUSSY THAN YOU AN' ME'LL SEE IN OUR LIFETIMES PUT TOGETHER...
POOF... DYKE...KIDDIE-FUCKER... POOF...
WAIT A MINUTE, EVEN I'VE HEARDA HIM. HE DIED SAVIN' THE ENTIRE UNIVERSE.
CHOKED ON CUM...
HIM THERE? FULL-BLOWN AIDS. KNEW HE HAD IT, DID NOTHIN' ABOUT IT, INFECTED AT LEAST THREE GIRLS THAT I KNOW OF.
SO I CUT HIS DICK OFF, AN' TO THIS DAY THE SAVIOUR OF HELL'S KITCHEN'S BEEN SITTIN' DOWN TO PISS...
WHAT?
FUCKSAKE, THIS IS LIKE SOMETHIN' OUT OF A NIGHTMARE...
HENCE THE COMICS.
WORKS FOR US TOO, MATE. I MEAN THERE'D BE NO POINT TRYNNA BLACKMAIL A BLOKE EVERYONE ALREADY KNOWS IS A CUNT, WOULD THERE?

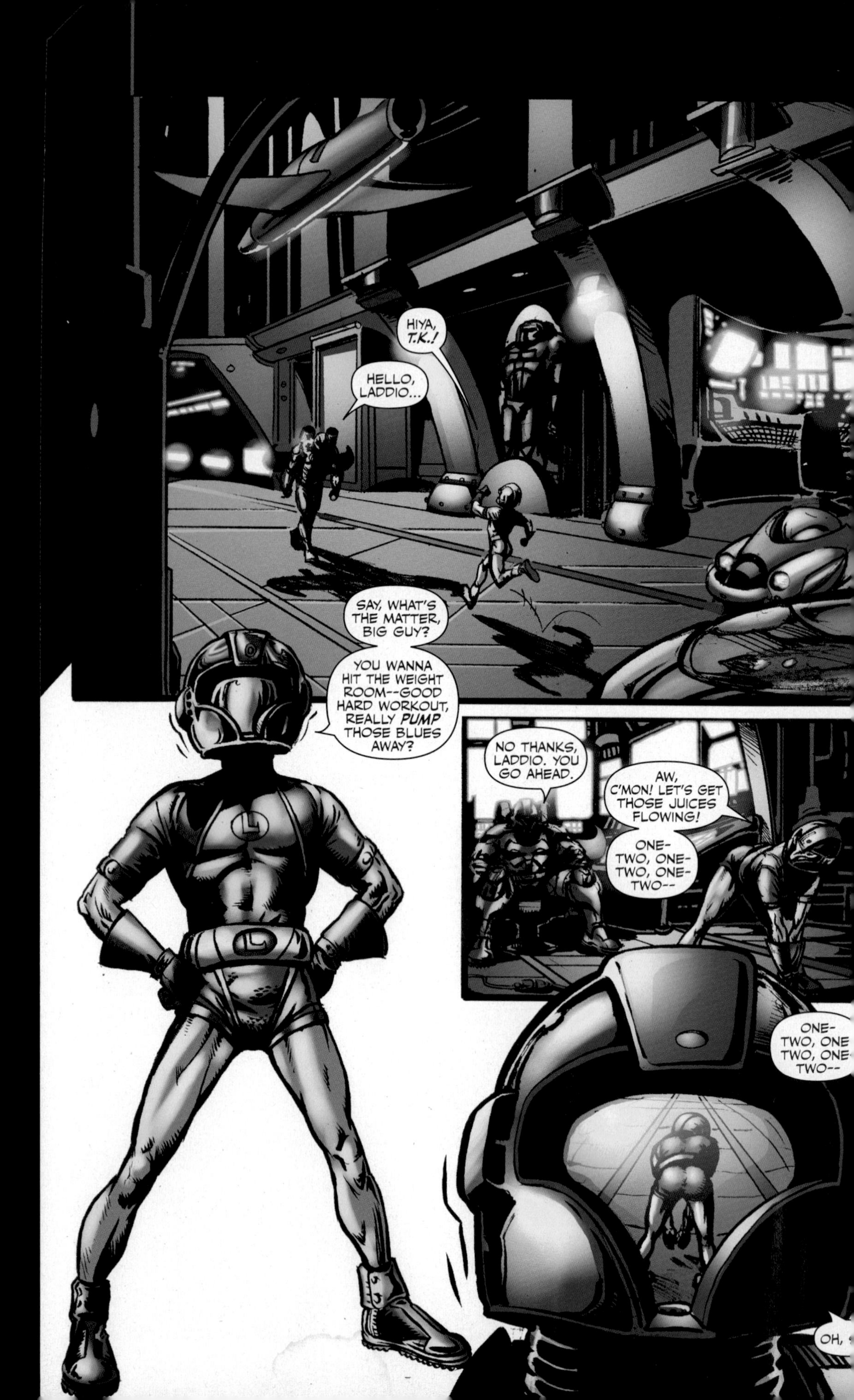
HIYA, T.K.!
HELLO, LADDIO...
SAY, WHAT'S THE MATTER, BIG GUY?
YOU WANNA HIT THE WEIGHT ROOM--GOOD HARD WORKOUT, REALLY PUMP THOSE BLUES AWAY?
NO THANKS, LADDIO. YOU GO AHEAD.
AW, C'MON! LET'S GET THOSE JUICES FLOWING!
ONE-TWO, ONE-TWO, ONE-TWO--
ONE-TWO, ONE TWO, ONE-TWO--

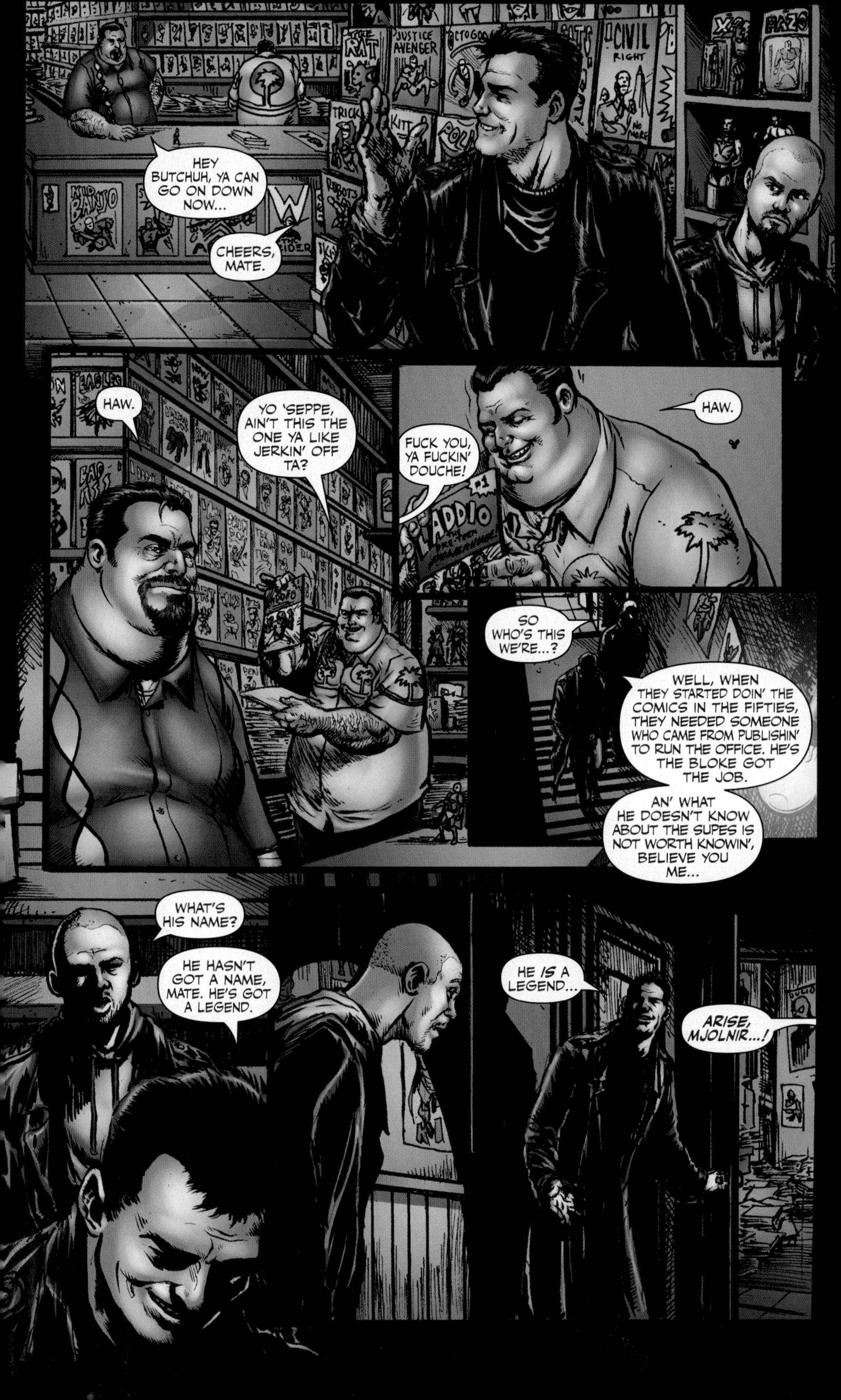

HEY BUTCHUH, YA CAN GO ON DOWN NOW...
CHEERS, MATE.
HAW.
YO 'SEPPE, AIN'T THIS THE ONE YA LIKE JERKIN' OFF TA?
FUCK YOU, YA FUCKIN' DOUCHE!
HAW.
SO WHO'S THIS WE'RE...?
WELL, WHEN THEY STARTED DOIN' THE COMICS IN THE FIFTIES, THEY NEEDED SOMEONE WHO CAME FROM PUBLISHIN' TO RUN THE OFFICE. HE'S THE BLOKE GOT THE JOB.
AN' WHAT HE DOESN'T KNOW ABOUT THE SUPES IS NOT WORTH KNOWIN', BELIEVE YOU ME...
WHAT'S HIS NAME?
HE HASN'T GOT A NAME, MATE. HE'S GOT A LEGEND.
HE *IS* A LEGEND...
ARISE, MJOLNIR...!

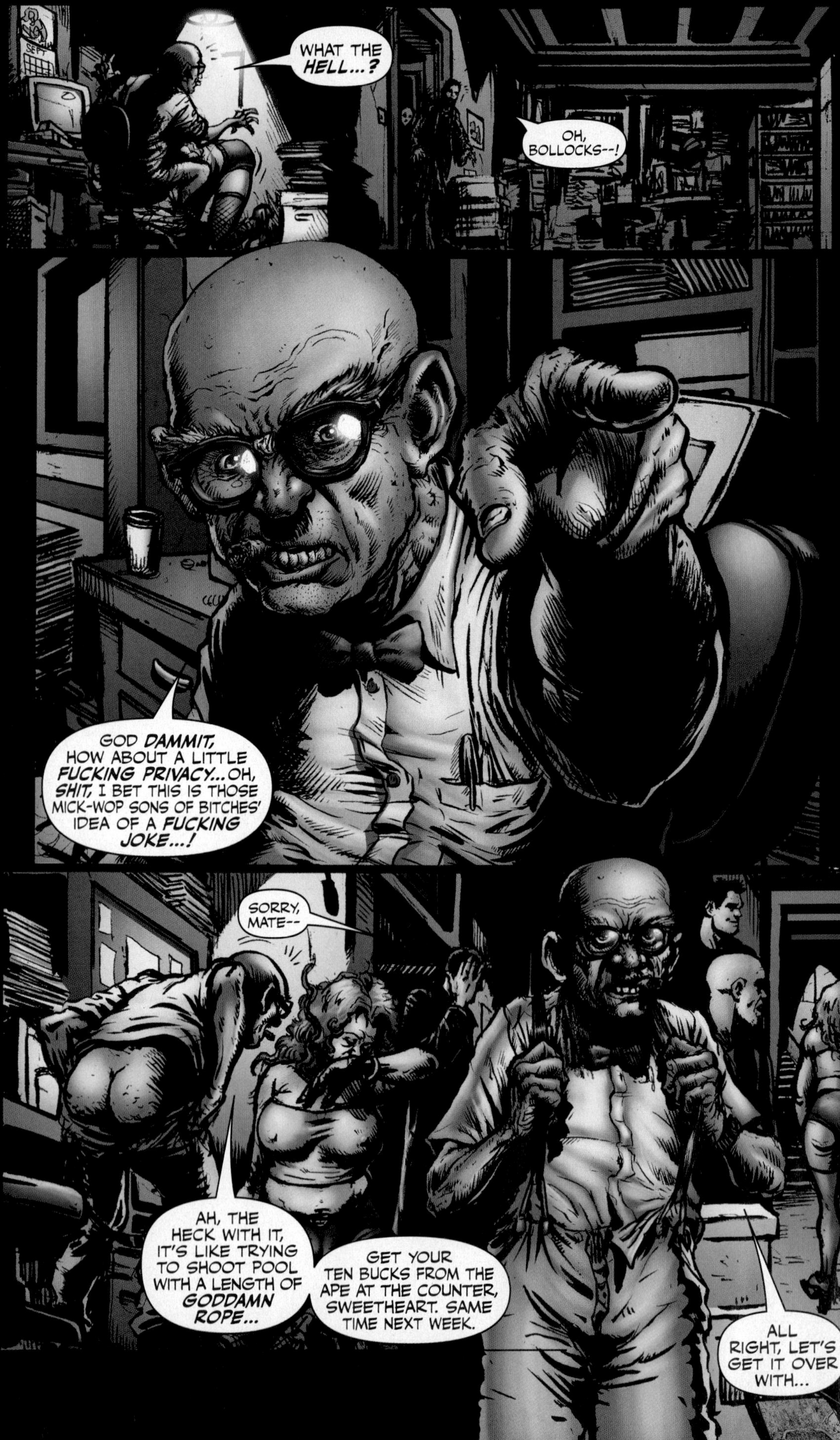
WHAT THE HELL...?
OH, BOLLOCKS--!
GOD DAMMIT, HOW ABOUT A LITTLE FUCKING PRIVACY...OH, SHIT, I BET THIS IS THOSE MICK-WOP SONS OF BITCHES' IDEA OF A FUCKING JOKE...!
SORRY, MATE--
AH, THE HECK WITH IT, IT'S LIKE TRYING TO SHOOT POOL WITH A LENGTH OF GODDAMN ROPE...
GET YOUR TEN BUCKS FROM THE APE AT THE COUNTER, SWEETHEART. SAME TIME NEXT WEEK.
ALL RIGHT, LET'S GET IT OVER WITH...

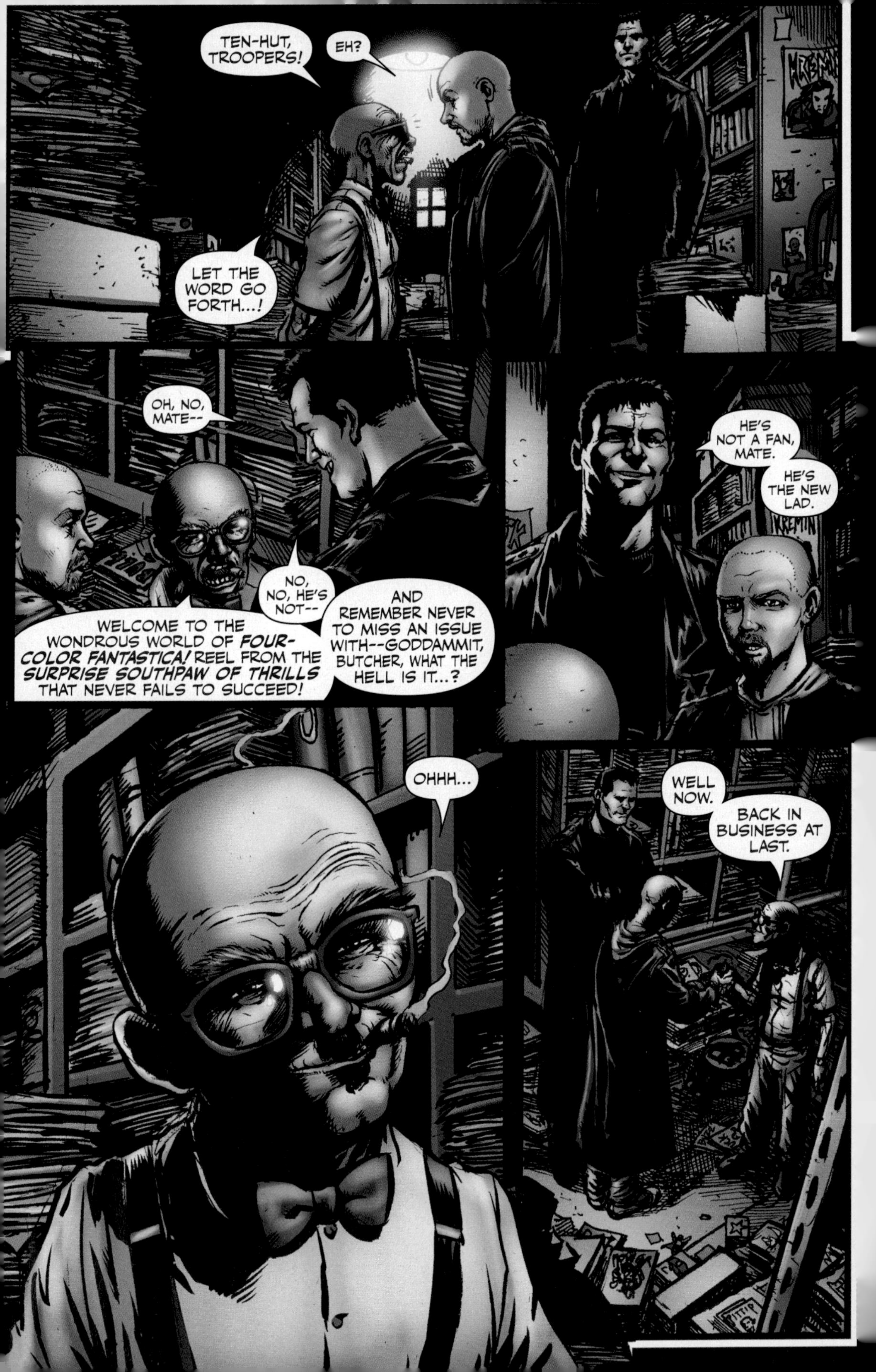

TEN-HUT, TROOPERS!
EH?
LET THE WORD GO FORTH...!
OH, NO, MATE--
NO, NO, HE'S NOT--
WELCOME TO THE WONDROUS WORLD OF *FOUR-COLOR FANTASTICA!* REEL FROM THE *SURPRISE SOUTHPAW OF THRILLS* THAT NEVER FAILS TO SUCCEED!
AND REMEMBER NEVER TO MISS AN ISSUE WITH--GODDAMMIT, BUTCHER, WHAT THE HELL IS IT...?
HE'S NOT A FAN, MATE.
HE'S THE NEW LAD.
OHHH...
WELL NOW.
BACK IN BUSINESS AT LAST.

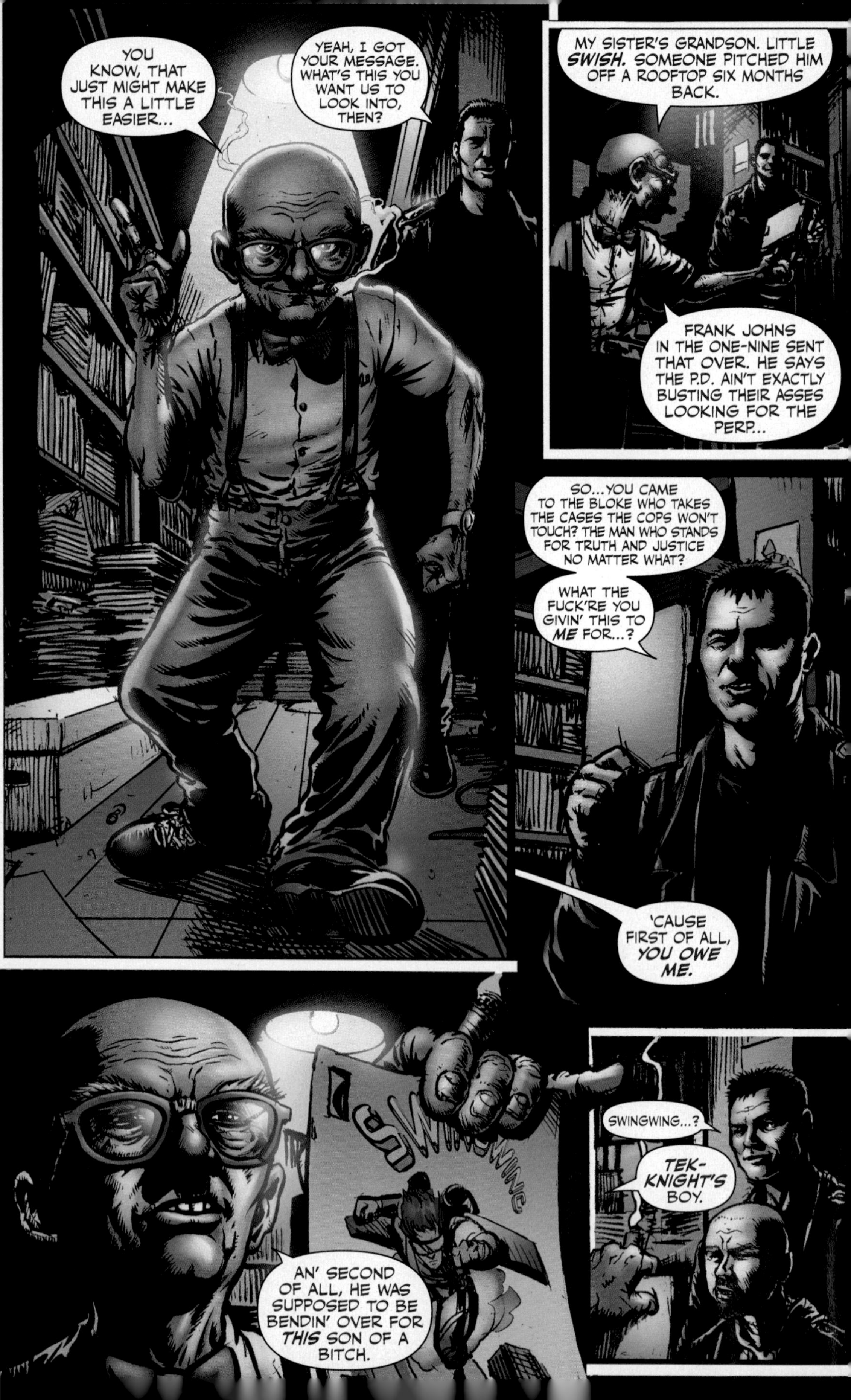
YEAH, I GOT YOUR MESSAGE. WHAT'S THIS YOU WANT US TO LOOK INTO, THEN?
YOU KNOW, THAT JUST MIGHT MAKE THIS A LITTLE EASIER...
MY SISTER'S GRANDSON. LITTLE SWISH. SOMEONE PITCHED HIM OFF A ROOFTOP SIX MONTHS BACK.
FRANK JOHNS IN THE ONE-NINE SENT THAT OVER. HE SAYS THE P.D. AIN'T EXACTLY BUSTING THEIR ASSES LOOKING FOR THE PERP...
SO...YOU CAME TO THE BLOKE WHO TAKES THE CASES THE COPS WON'T TOUCH? THE MAN WHO STANDS FOR TRUTH AND JUSTICE NO MATTER WHAT?
WHAT THE FUCK'RE YOU GIVIN' THIS TO ME FOR...?
'CAUSE FIRST OF ALL, YOU OWE ME.
SWINGWING
AN' SECOND OF ALL, HE WAS SUPPOSED TO BE BENDIN' OVER FOR THIS SON OF A BITCH.
SWINGWING...?
TEK-KNIGHT'S BOY.

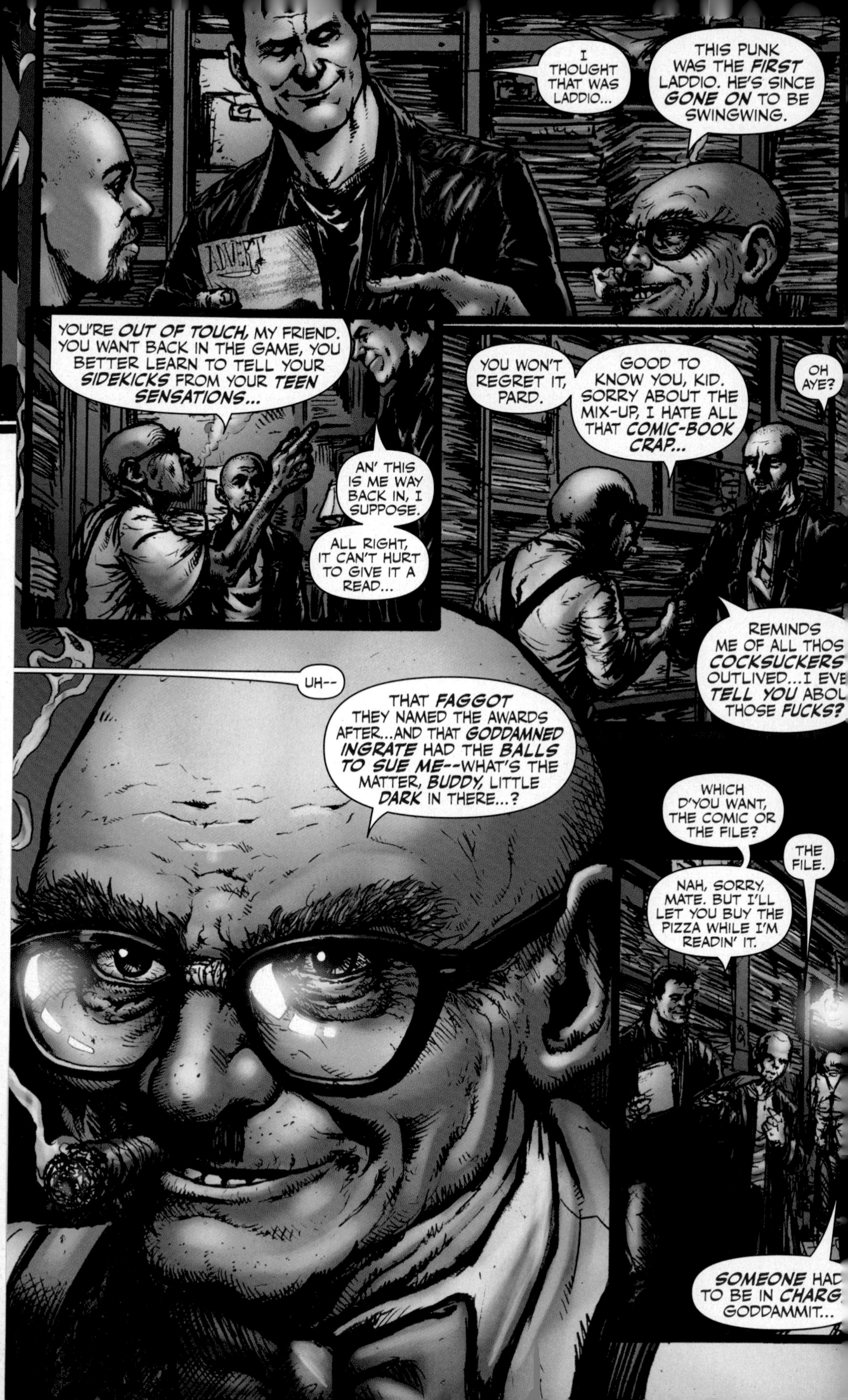
I THOUGHT THAT WAS LADDIO...
THIS PUNK WAS THE FIRST LADDIO. HE'S SINCE GONE ON TO BE SWINGWING.
YOU'RE OUT OF TOUCH, MY FRIEND. YOU WANT BACK IN THE GAME, YOU BETTER LEARN TO TELL YOUR SIDEKICKS FROM YOUR TEEN SENSATIONS...
AN' THIS IS ME WAY BACK IN, I SUPPOSE.
ALL RIGHT, IT CAN'T HURT TO GIVE IT A READ...
YOU WON'T REGRET IT, PARD.
GOOD TO KNOW YOU, KID. SORRY ABOUT THE MIX-UP, I HATE ALL THAT COMIC-BOOK CRAP...
OH AYE?
REMINDS ME OF ALL THOS COCKSUCKERS OUTLIVED...I EVE TELL YOU ABOU THOSE FUCKS?
UH--
THAT FAGGOT THEY NAMED THE AWARDS AFTER...AND THAT GODDAMNED INGRATE HAD THE BALLS TO SUE ME--WHAT'S THE MATTER, BUDDY, LITTLE DARK IN THERE...?
WHICH D'YOU WANT, THE COMIC OR THE FILE?
THE FILE.
NAH, SORRY, MATE. BUT I'LL LET YOU BUY THE PIZZA WHILE I'M READIN' IT.
SOMEONE HAD TO BE IN CHARG GODDAMMIT...

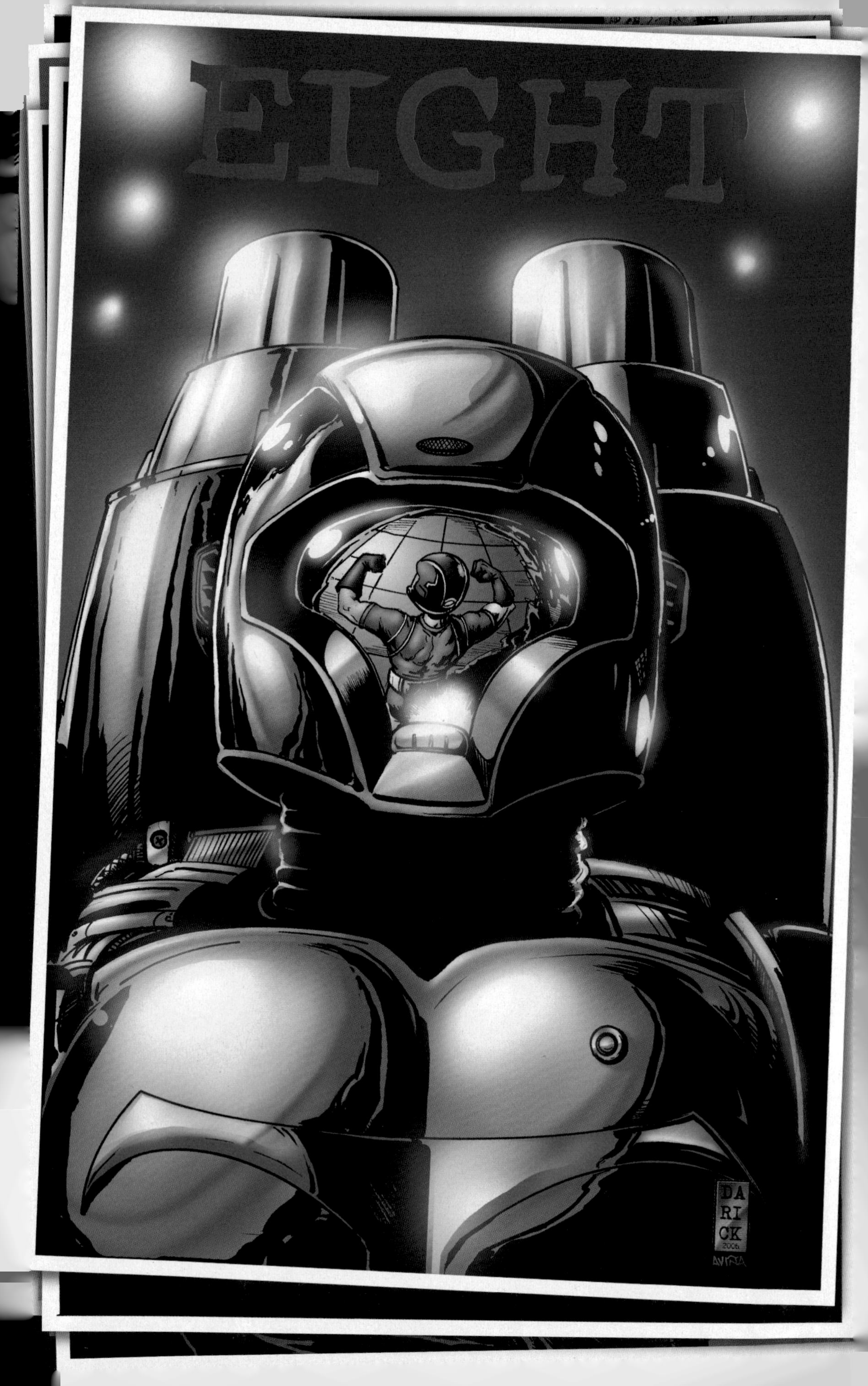
EIGHT
DA RI CK 2006

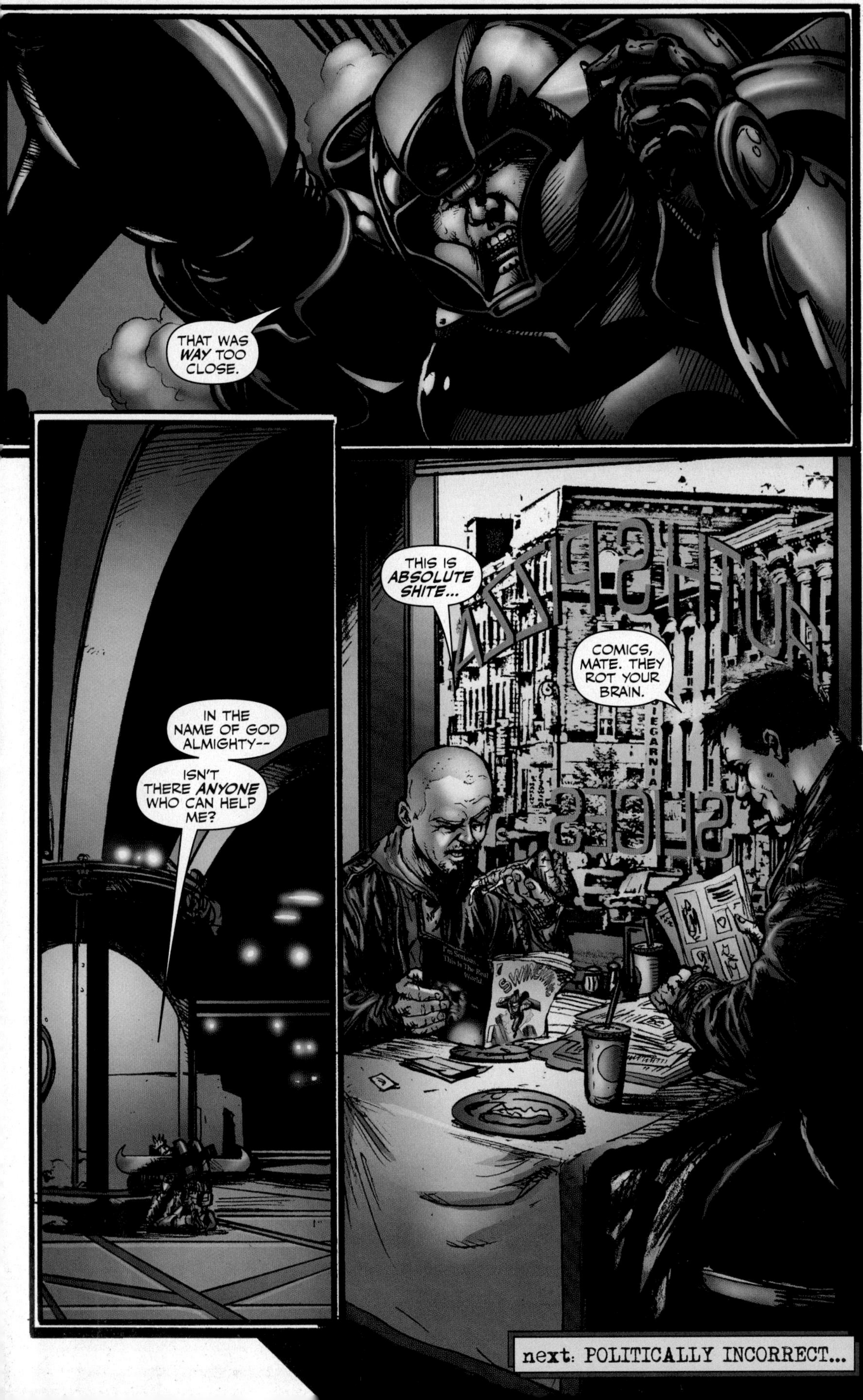
THAT WAS WAY TOO CLOSE.
IN THE NAME OF GOD ALMIGHTY--
ISN'T THERE ANYONE WHO CAN HELP ME?
THIS IS ABSOLUTE SHITE...
COMICS, MATE. THEY ROT YOUR BRAIN.
next: POLITICALLY INCORRECT...

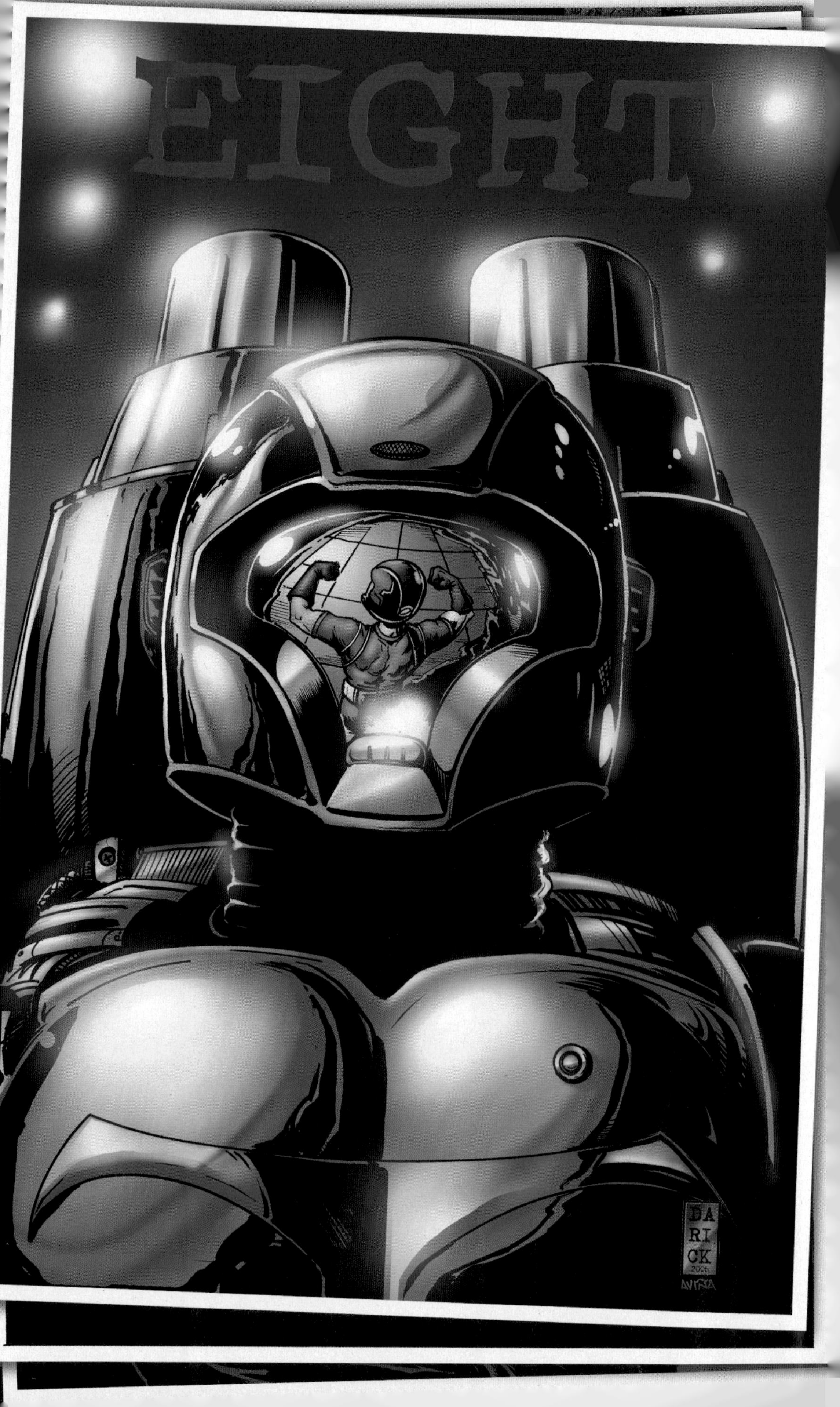
EIGHT
DA
RI
CK
2006

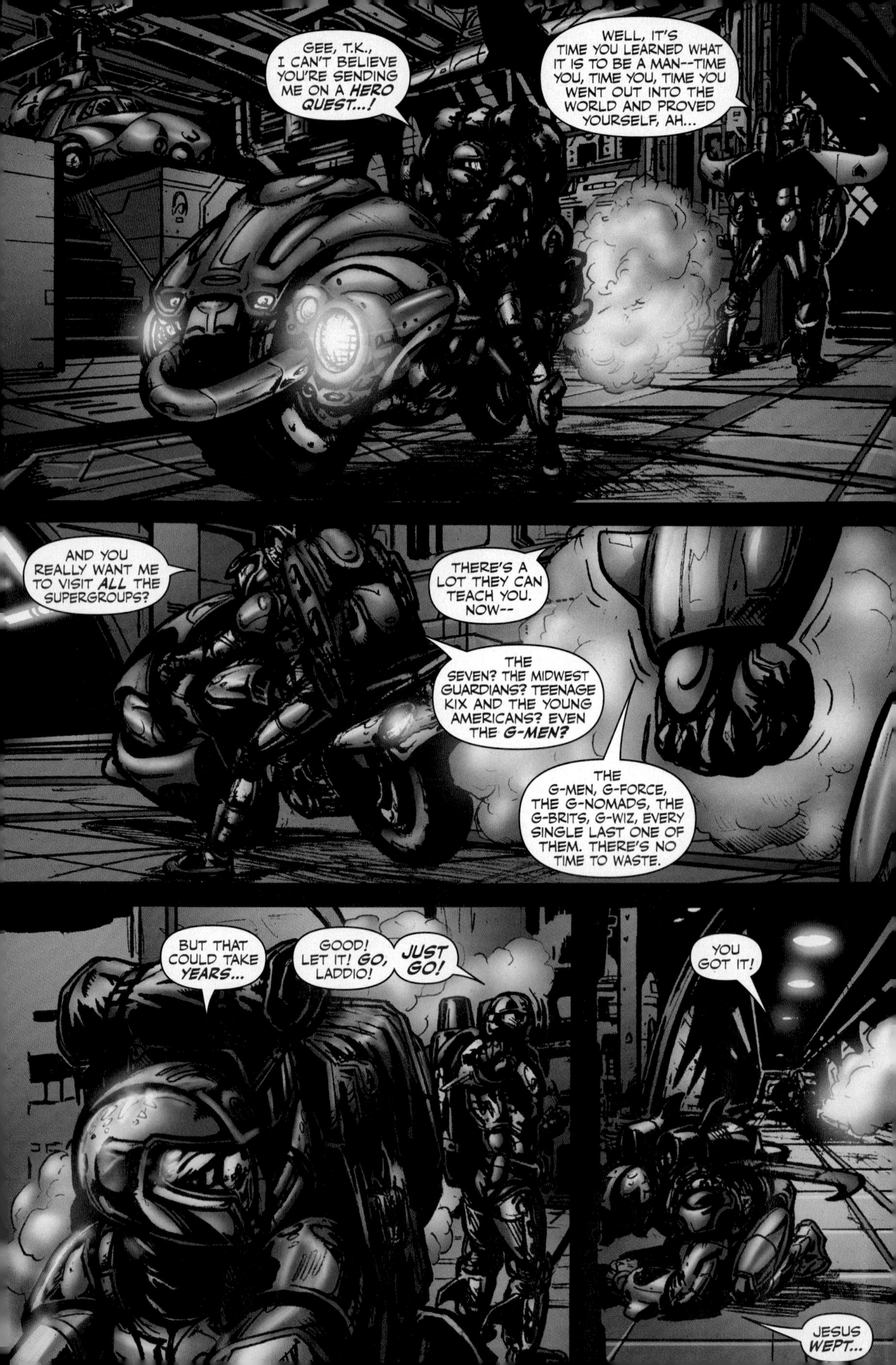
GEE, T.K., I CAN'T BELIEVE YOU'RE SENDING ME ON A *HERO QUEST...!*
WELL, IT'S TIME YOU LEARNED WHAT IT IS TO BE A MAN--TIME YOU, TIME YOU, TIME YOU WENT OUT INTO THE WORLD AND PROVED YOURSELF, AH...
AND YOU REALLY WANT ME TO VISIT *ALL* THE SUPERGROUPS?
THERE'S A LOT THEY CAN TEACH YOU. NOW--
THE SEVEN? THE MIDWEST GUARDIANS? TEENAGE KIX AND THE YOUNG AMERICANS? EVEN THE *G-MEN?*
THE G-MEN, G-FORCE, THE G-NOMADS, THE G-BRITS, G-WIZ, EVERY SINGLE LAST ONE OF THEM. THERE'S NO TIME TO WASTE.
BUT THAT COULD TAKE *YEARS...*
GOOD! LET IT! *GO,* LADDIO!
JUST GO!
YOU GOT IT!
JESUS *WEPT...*

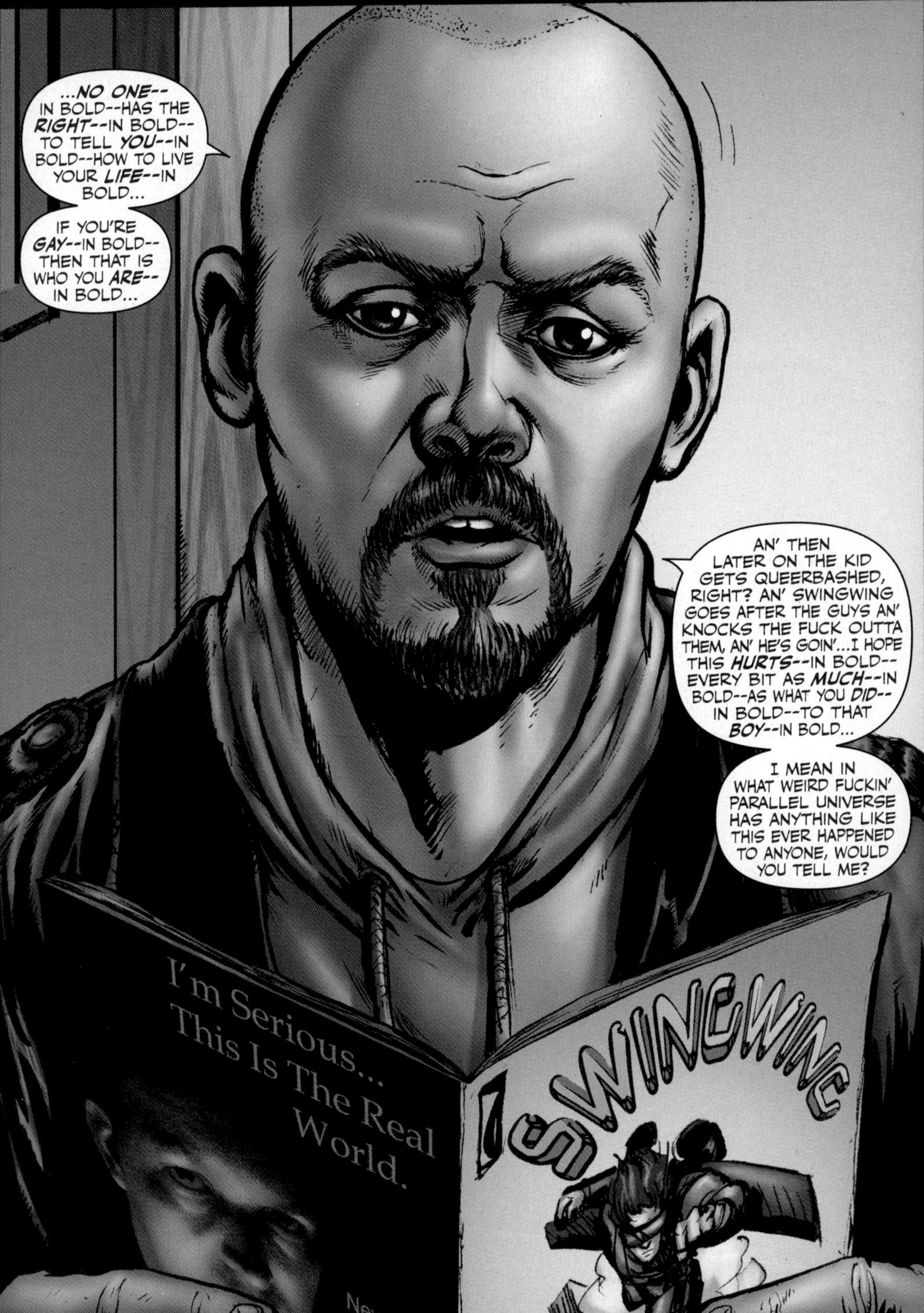
...NO ONE--IN BOLD--HAS THE RIGHT--IN BOLD--TO TELL YOU--IN BOLD--HOW TO LIVE YOUR LIFE--IN BOLD...
IF YOU'RE GAY--IN BOLD--THEN THAT IS WHO YOU ARE--IN BOLD...
AN' THEN LATER ON THE KID GETS QUEERBASHED, RIGHT? AN' SWINGWING GOES AFTER THE GUYS AN' KNOCKS THE FUCK OUTTA THEM, AN' HE'S GOIN'...I HOPE THIS HURTS--IN BOLD--EVERY BIT AS MUCH--IN BOLD--AS WHAT YOU DID--IN BOLD--TO THAT BOY--IN BOLD...
I MEAN IN WHAT WEIRD FUCKIN' PARALLEL UNIVERSE HAS ANYTHING LIKE THIS EVER HAPPENED TO ANYONE, WOULD YOU TELL ME?
I'm Serious... This Is The Real World.
SWINGWING

GET SOME

part two

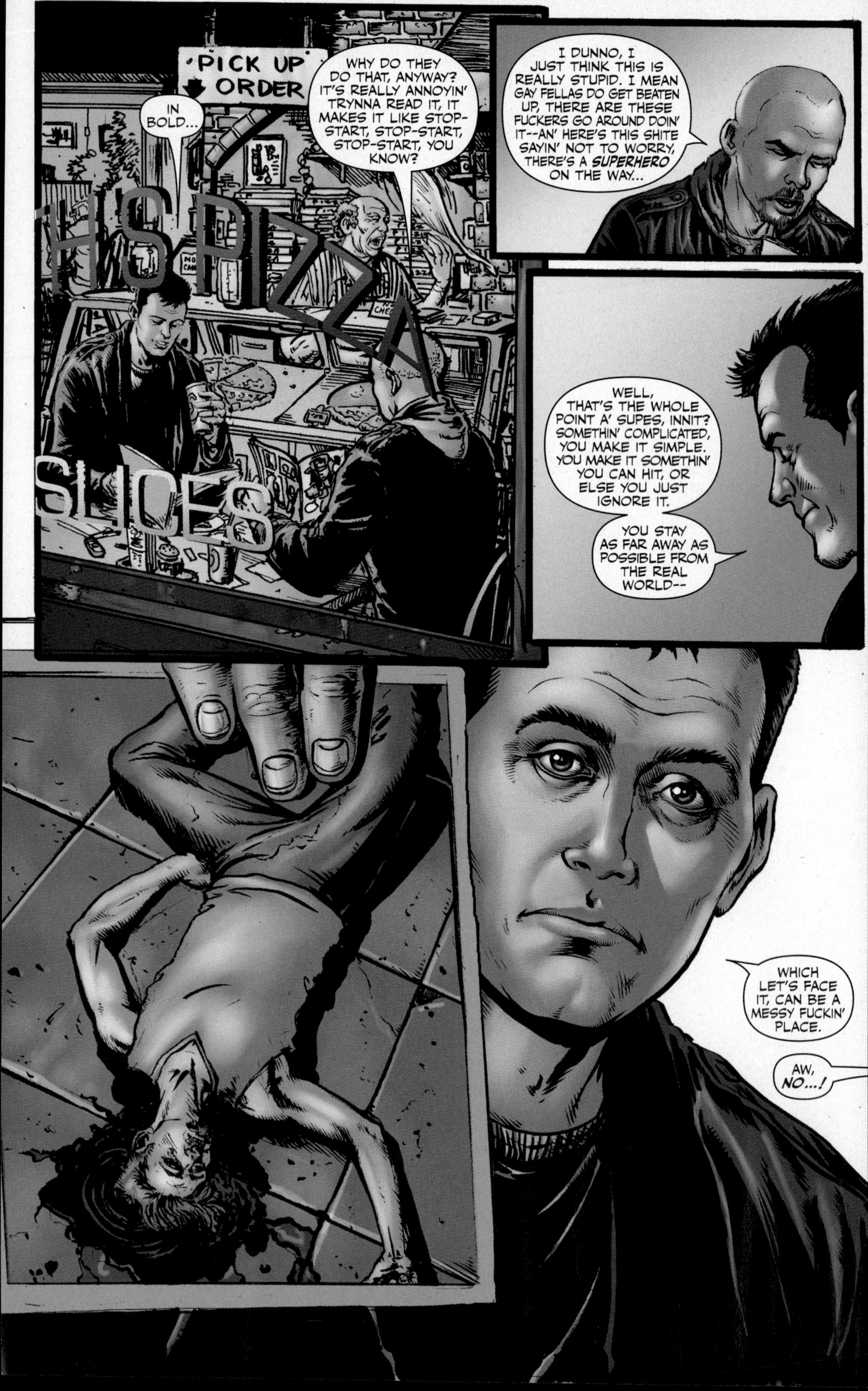
PICK UP ORDER
IN BOLD...
WHY DO THEY DO THAT, ANYWAY? IT'S REALLY ANNOYIN' TRYNNA READ IT, IT MAKES IT LIKE STOP-START, STOP-START, STOP-START, YOU KNOW?
THS PIZZA
SLICES
I DUNNO, I JUST THINK THIS IS REALLY STUPID. I MEAN GAY FELLAS DO GET BEATEN UP, THERE ARE THESE FUCKERS GO AROUND DOIN' IT--AN' HERE'S THIS SHITE SAYIN' NOT TO WORRY, THERE'S A *SUPERHERO* ON THE WAY...
WELL, THAT'S THE WHOLE POINT A' SUPES, INNIT? SOMETHIN' COMPLICATED, YOU MAKE IT SIMPLE. YOU MAKE IT SOMETHIN' YOU CAN HIT, OR ELSE YOU JUST IGNORE IT.
YOU STAY AS FAR AWAY AS POSSIBLE FROM THE REAL WORLD--
WHICH LET'S FACE IT, CAN BE A MESSY FUCKIN' PLACE.
AW, *NO...!*

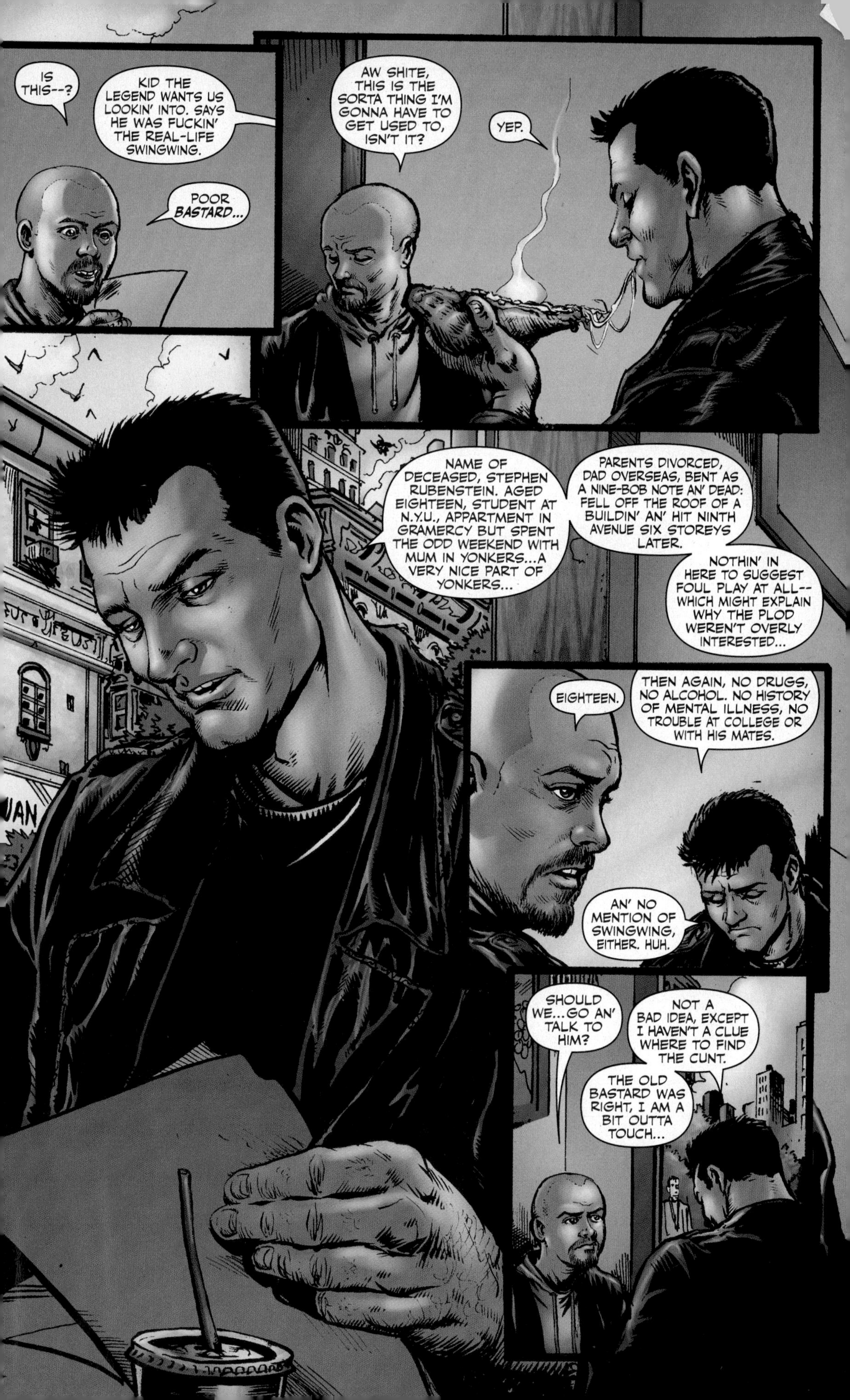
IS THIS--?
KID THE LEGEND WANTS US LOOKIN' INTO. SAYS HE WAS FUCKIN' THE REAL-LIFE SWINGWING.
POOR BASTARD...
AW SHITE, THIS IS THE SORTA THING I'M GONNA HAVE TO GET USED TO, ISN'T IT?
YEP.
NAME OF DECEASED, STEPHEN RUBENSTEIN. AGED EIGHTEEN, STUDENT AT N.Y.U., APPARTMENT IN GRAMERCY BUT SPENT THE ODD WEEKEND WITH MUM IN YONKERS...A VERY NICE PART OF YONKERS...
PARENTS DIVORCED, DAD OVERSEAS, BENT AS A NINE-BOB NOTE AN' DEAD: FELL OFF THE ROOF OF A BUILDIN' AN' HIT NINTH AVENUE SIX STOREYS LATER.
NOTHIN' IN HERE TO SUGGEST FOUL PLAY AT ALL--WHICH MIGHT EXPLAIN WHY THE PLOD WEREN'T OVERLY INTERESTED...
EIGHTEEN.
THEN AGAIN, NO DRUGS, NO ALCOHOL. NO HISTORY OF MENTAL ILLNESS, NO TROUBLE AT COLLEGE OR WITH HIS MATES.
AN' NO MENTION OF SWINGWING, EITHER. HUH.
SHOULD WE...GO AN' TALK TO HIM?
NOT A BAD IDEA, EXCEPT I HAVEN'T A CLUE WHERE TO FIND THE CUNT.
THE OLD BASTARD WAS RIGHT, I AM A BIT OUTTA TOUCH...

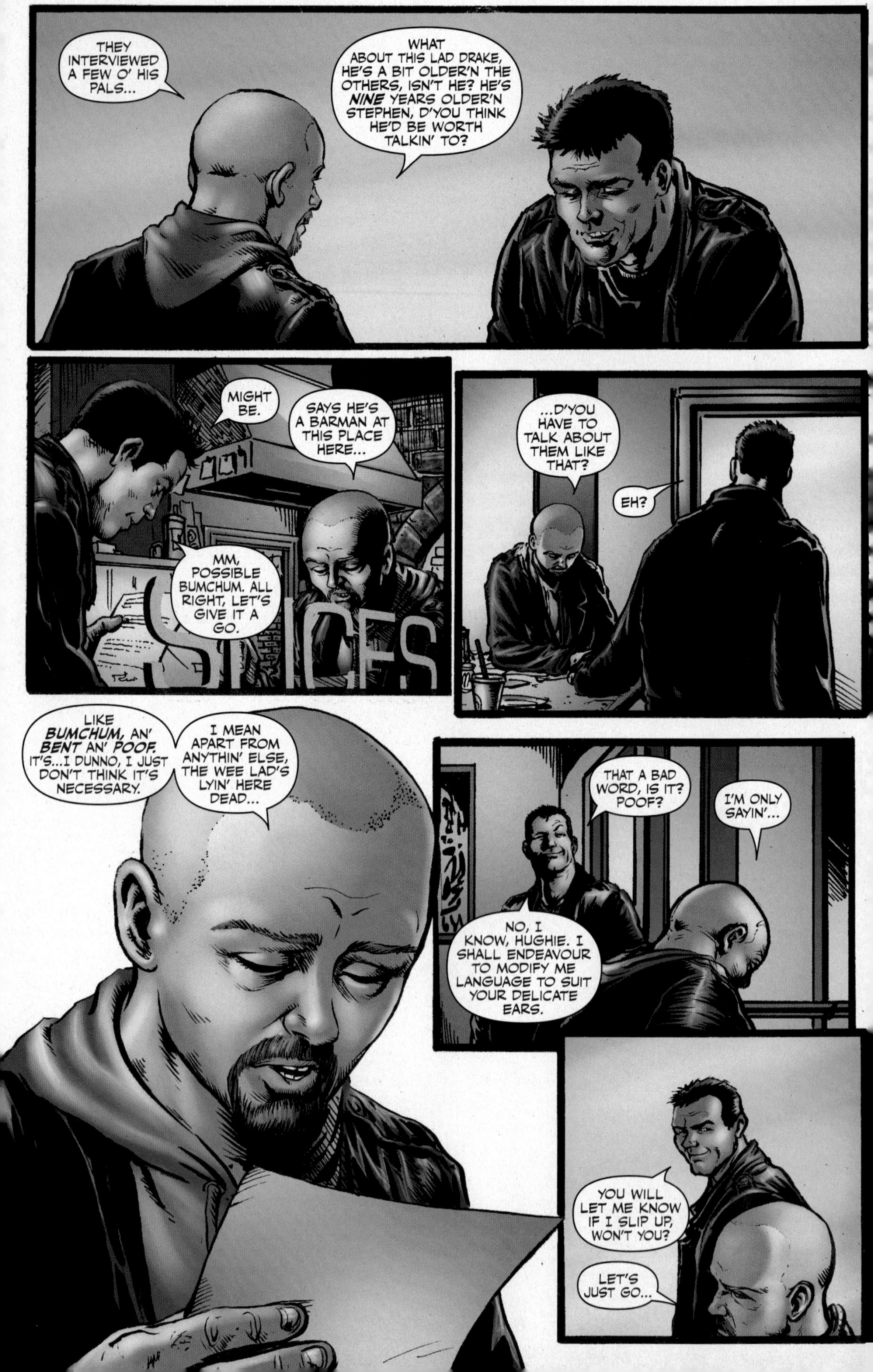
THEY INTERVIEWED A FEW O' HIS PALS...
WHAT ABOUT THIS LAD DRAKE, HE'S A BIT OLDER'N THE OTHERS, ISN'T HE? HE'S NINE YEARS OLDER'N STEPHEN, D'YOU THINK HE'D BE WORTH TALKIN' TO?
MIGHT BE.
SAYS HE'S A BARMAN AT THIS PLACE HERE...
MM, POSSIBLE BUMCHUM. ALL RIGHT, LET'S GIVE IT A GO.
SLICES
...D'YOU HAVE TO TALK ABOUT THEM LIKE THAT?
EH?
LIKE BUMCHUM, AN' BENT AN' POOF. IT'S...I DUNNO, I JUST DON'T THINK IT'S NECESSARY.
I MEAN APART FROM ANYTHIN' ELSE, THE WEE LAD'S LYIN' HERE DEAD...
THAT A BAD WORD, IS IT? POOF?
I'M ONLY SAYIN'...
NO, I KNOW, HUGHIE. I SHALL ENDEAVOUR TO MODIFY ME LANGUAGE TO SUIT YOUR DELICATE EARS.
YOU WILL LET ME KNOW IF I SLIP UP, WON'T YOU?
LET'S JUST GO...

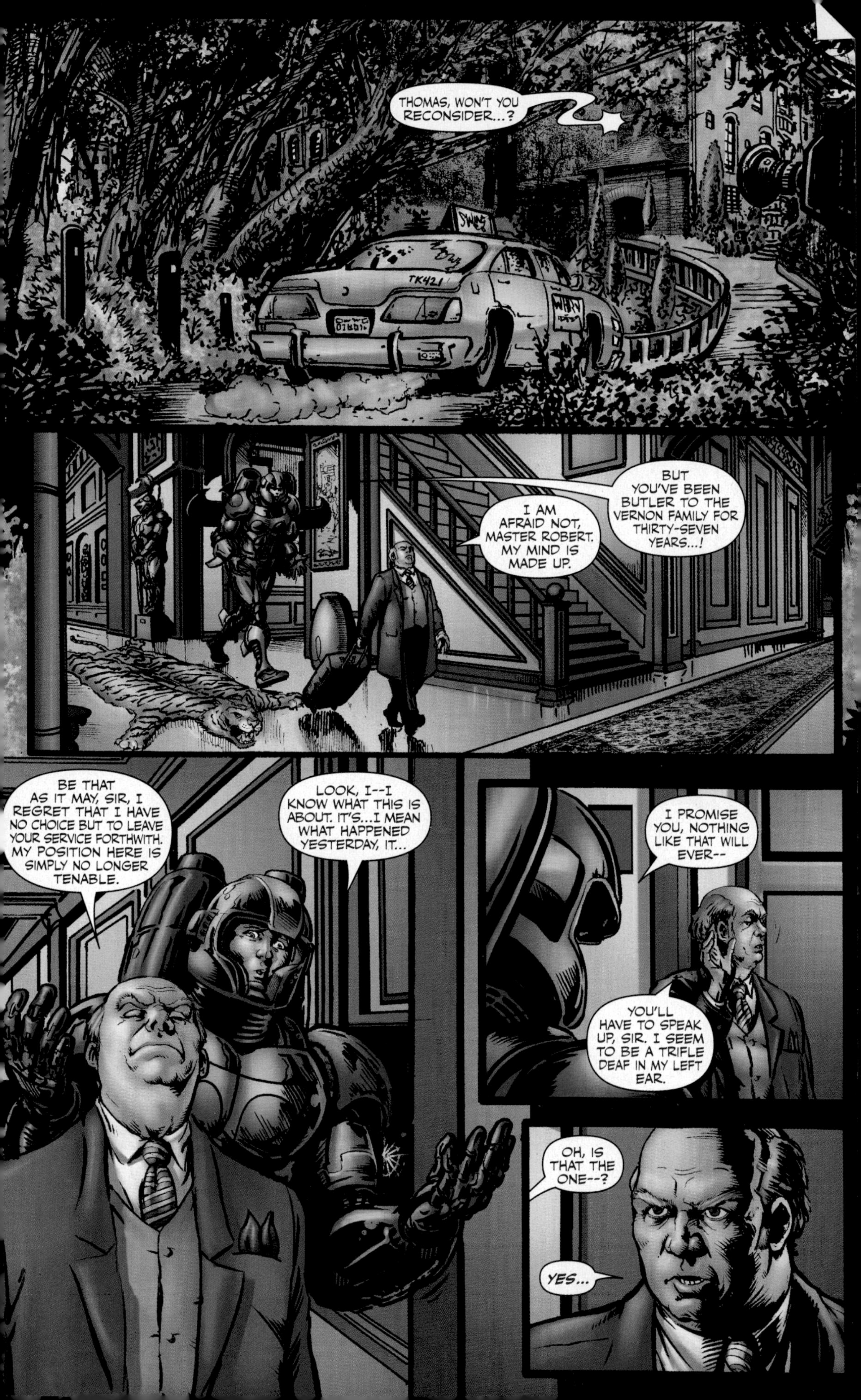
THOMAS, WON'T YOU RECONSIDER...?
TK421
BUT YOU'VE BEEN BUTLER TO THE VERNON FAMILY FOR THIRTY-SEVEN YEARS...!
I AM AFRAID NOT, MASTER ROBERT. MY MIND IS MADE UP.
BE THAT AS IT MAY, SIR, I REGRET THAT I HAVE NO CHOICE BUT TO LEAVE YOUR SERVICE FORTHWITH. MY POSITION HERE IS SIMPLY NO LONGER TENABLE.
LOOK, I--I KNOW WHAT THIS IS ABOUT. IT'S...I MEAN WHAT HAPPENED YESTERDAY, IT...
I PROMISE YOU, NOTHING LIKE THAT WILL EVER--
YOU'LL HAVE TO SPEAK UP, SIR. I SEEM TO BE A TRIFLE DEAF IN MY LEFT EAR.
OH, IS THAT THE ONE--?
YES...

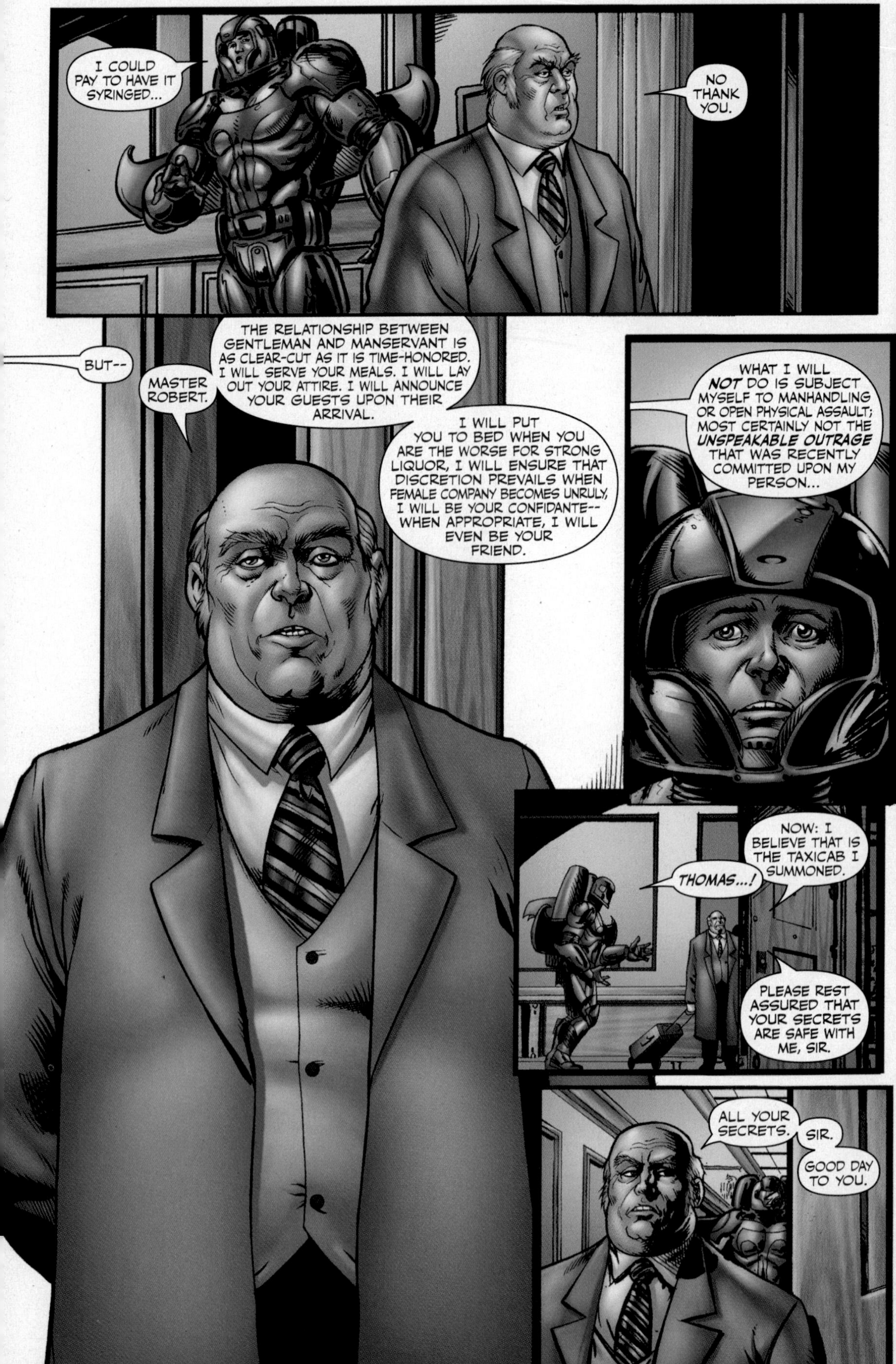

I COULD PAY TO HAVE IT SYRINGED...
NO THANK YOU.
BUT--
MASTER ROBERT.
THE RELATIONSHIP BETWEEN GENTLEMAN AND MANSERVANT IS AS CLEAR-CUT AS IT IS TIME-HONORED. I WILL SERVE YOUR MEALS. I WILL LAY OUT YOUR ATTIRE. I WILL ANNOUNCE YOUR GUESTS UPON THEIR ARRIVAL.
I WILL PUT YOU TO BED WHEN YOU ARE THE WORSE FOR STRONG LIQUOR, I WILL ENSURE THAT DISCRETION PREVAILS WHEN FEMALE COMPANY BECOMES UNRULY, I WILL BE YOUR CONFIDANTE-- WHEN APPROPRIATE, I WILL EVEN BE YOUR FRIEND.
WHAT I WILL NOT DO IS SUBJECT MYSELF TO MANHANDLING OR OPEN PHYSICAL ASSAULT; MOST CERTAINLY NOT THE UNSPEAKABLE OUTRAGE THAT WAS RECENTLY COMMITTED UPON MY PERSON...
NOW: I BELIEVE THAT IS THE TAXICAB I SUMMONED.
THOMAS...!
PLEASE REST ASSURED THAT YOUR SECRETS ARE SAFE WITH ME, SIR.
ALL YOUR SECRETS.
SIR.
GOOD DAY TO YOU.

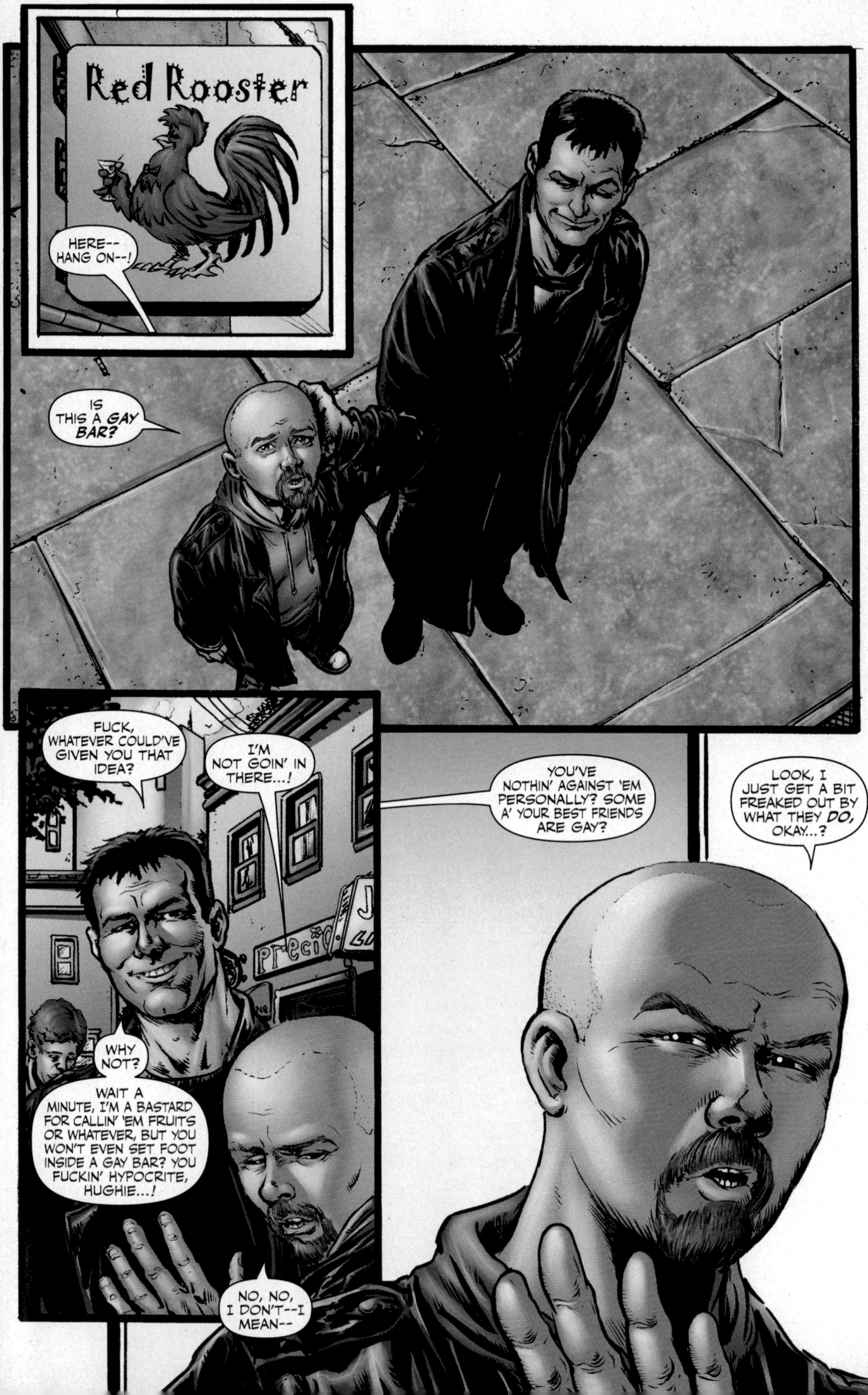
Red Rooster
HERE-- HANG ON--!
IS THIS A GAY BAR?
FUCK, WHATEVER COULD'VE GIVEN YOU THAT IDEA?
I'M NOT GOIN' IN THERE...!
YOU'VE NOTHIN' AGAINST 'EM PERSONALLY? SOME A' YOUR BEST FRIENDS ARE GAY?
LOOK, I JUST GET A BIT FREAKED OUT BY WHAT THEY DO, OKAY...?
WHY NOT?
WAIT A MINUTE, I'M A BASTARD FOR CALLIN' 'EM FRUITS OR WHATEVER, BUT YOU WON'T EVEN SET FOOT INSIDE A GAY BAR? YOU FUCKIN' HYPOCRITE, HUGHIE...!
NO, NO, I DON'T--I MEAN--

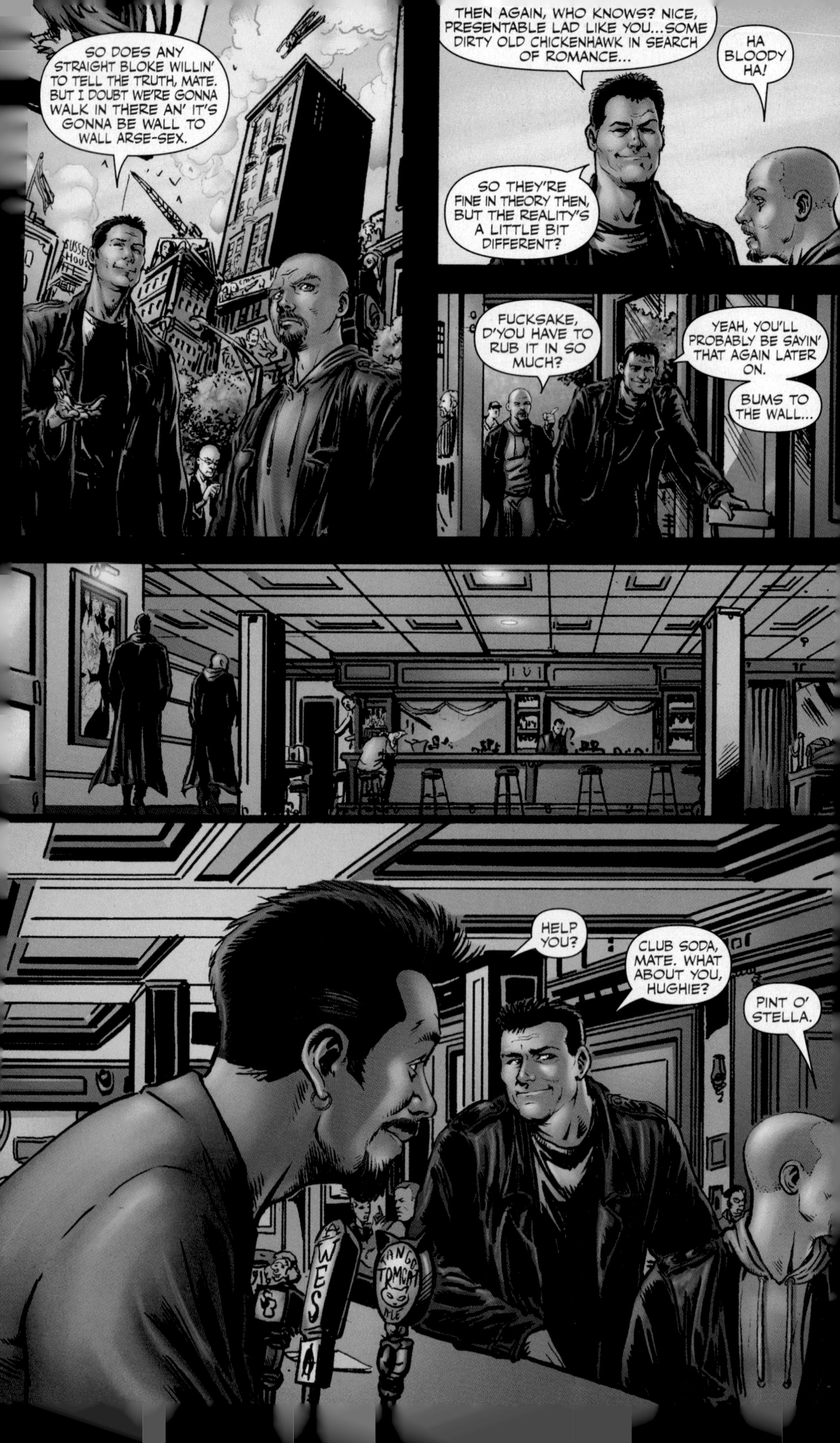
SO DOES ANY STRAIGHT BLOKE WILLIN' TO TELL THE TRUTH, MATE. BUT I DOUBT WE'RE GONNA WALK IN THERE AN' IT'S GONNA BE WALL TO WALL ARSE-SEX.
THEN AGAIN, WHO KNOWS? NICE, PRESENTABLE LAD LIKE YOU...SOME DIRTY OLD CHICKENHAWK IN SEARCH OF ROMANCE...
HA BLOODY HA!
SO THEY'RE FINE IN THEORY THEN, BUT THE REALITY'S A LITTLE BIT DIFFERENT?
FUCKSAKE, D'YOU HAVE TO RUB IT IN SO MUCH?
YEAH, YOU'LL PROBABLY BE SAYIN' THAT AGAIN LATER ON.
BUMS TO THE WALL...
HELP YOU?
CLUB SODA, MATE. WHAT ABOUT YOU, HUGHIE?
PINT O' STELLA.
WES
TOMCAT
ALE

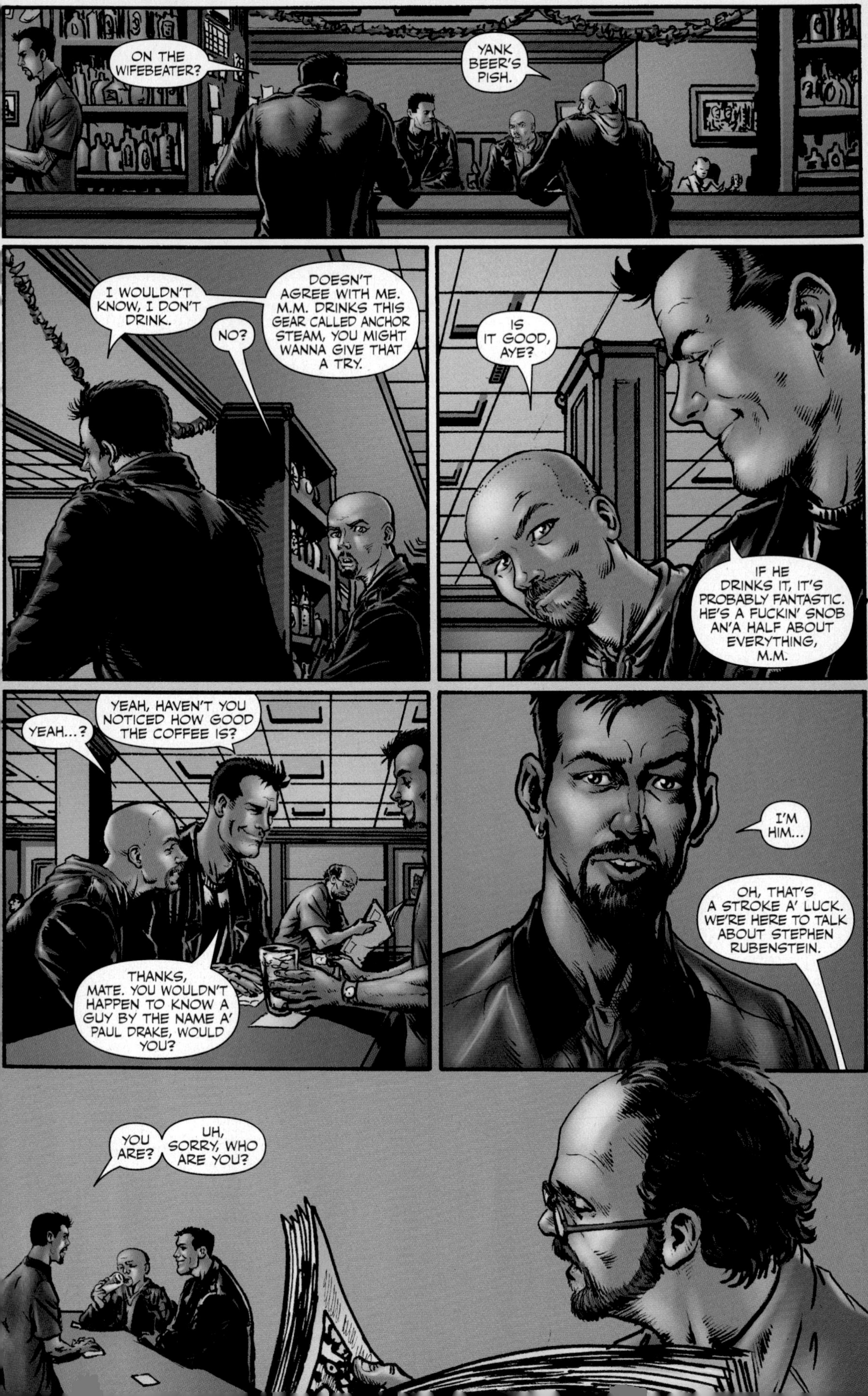
ON THE WIFEBEATER?
YANK BEER'S PISH.
I WOULDN'T KNOW, I DON'T DRINK.
DOESN'T AGREE WITH ME. M.M. DRINKS THIS GEAR CALLED ANCHOR STEAM, YOU MIGHT WANNA GIVE THAT A TRY.
NO?
IS IT GOOD, AYE?
IF HE DRINKS IT, IT'S PROBABLY FANTASTIC. HE'S A FUCKIN' SNOB AN'A HALF ABOUT EVERYTHING, M.M.
YEAH, HAVEN'T YOU NOTICED HOW GOOD THE COFFEE IS?
YEAH...?
THANKS, MATE. YOU WOULDN'T HAPPEN TO KNOW A GUY BY THE NAME A' PAUL DRAKE, WOULD YOU?
I'M HIM...
OH, THAT'S A STROKE A' LUCK. WE'RE HERE TO TALK ABOUT STEPHEN RUBENSTEIN.
UH, SORRY, WHO ARE YOU?
YOU ARE?

BECAUSE YOU'RE NOT THE POLICE, NOT TALKING LIKE THAT.

WELL SPOTTED. NO, WE'RE LONDON C.I.D., ON EXCHANGE WITH A COUPLE OF N.Y.P.D. DETECTIVES. WE GOT CHELSEA AN' THEY GOT TOOTING.

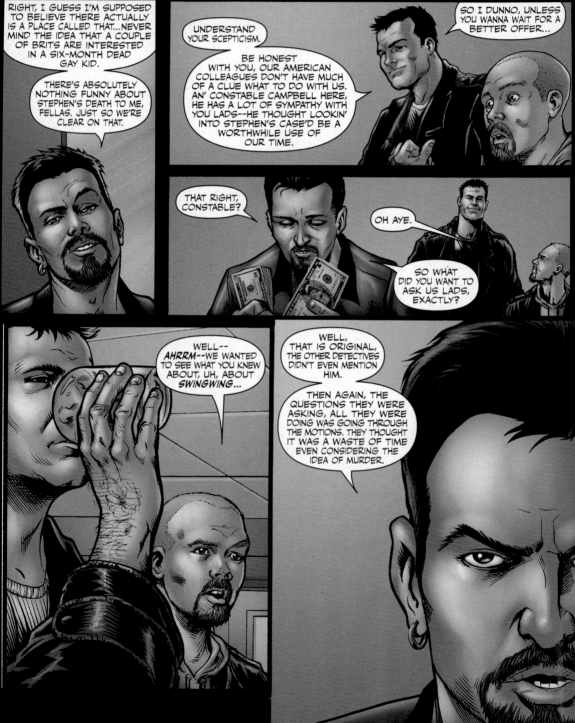

RIGHT, I GUESS I'M SUPPOSED TO BELIEVE THERE ACTUALLY IS A PLACE CALLED THAT...NEVER MIND THE IDEA THAT A COUPLE OF BRITS ARE INTERESTED IN A SIX-MONTH DEAD GAY KID.

THERE'S ABSOLUTELY NOTHING FUNNY ABOUT STEPHEN'S DEATH TO ME, FELLAS. JUST SO WE'RE CLEAR ON THAT.

UNDERSTAND YOUR SCEPTICISM.

BE HONEST WITH YOU, OUR AMERICAN COLLEAGUES DON'T HAVE MUCH OF A CLUE WHAT TO DO WITH US. AN' CONSTABLE CAMPBELL HERE, HE HAS A LOT OF SYMPATHY WITH YOU LADS--HE THOUGHT LOOKIN' INTO STEPHEN'S CASE'D BE A WORTHWHILE USE OF OUR TIME.

SO I DUNNO, UNLESS YOU WANNA WAIT FOR A BETTER OFFER...

THAT RIGHT, CONSTABLE?

OH AYE.

SO WHAT DID YOU WANT TO ASK US LADS, EXACTLY?

WELL-- AHRRM--WE WANTED TO SEE WHAT YOU KNEW ABOUT, UH, ABOUT SWINGWING...

WELL, THAT IS ORIGINAL, THE OTHER DETECTIVES DIDN'T EVEN MENTION HIM.

THEN AGAIN, THE QUESTIONS THEY WERE ASKING, ALL THEY WERE DOING WAS GOING THROUGH THE MOTIONS. THEY THOUGHT IT WAS A WASTE OF TIME EVEN CONSIDERING THE IDEA OF MURDER.

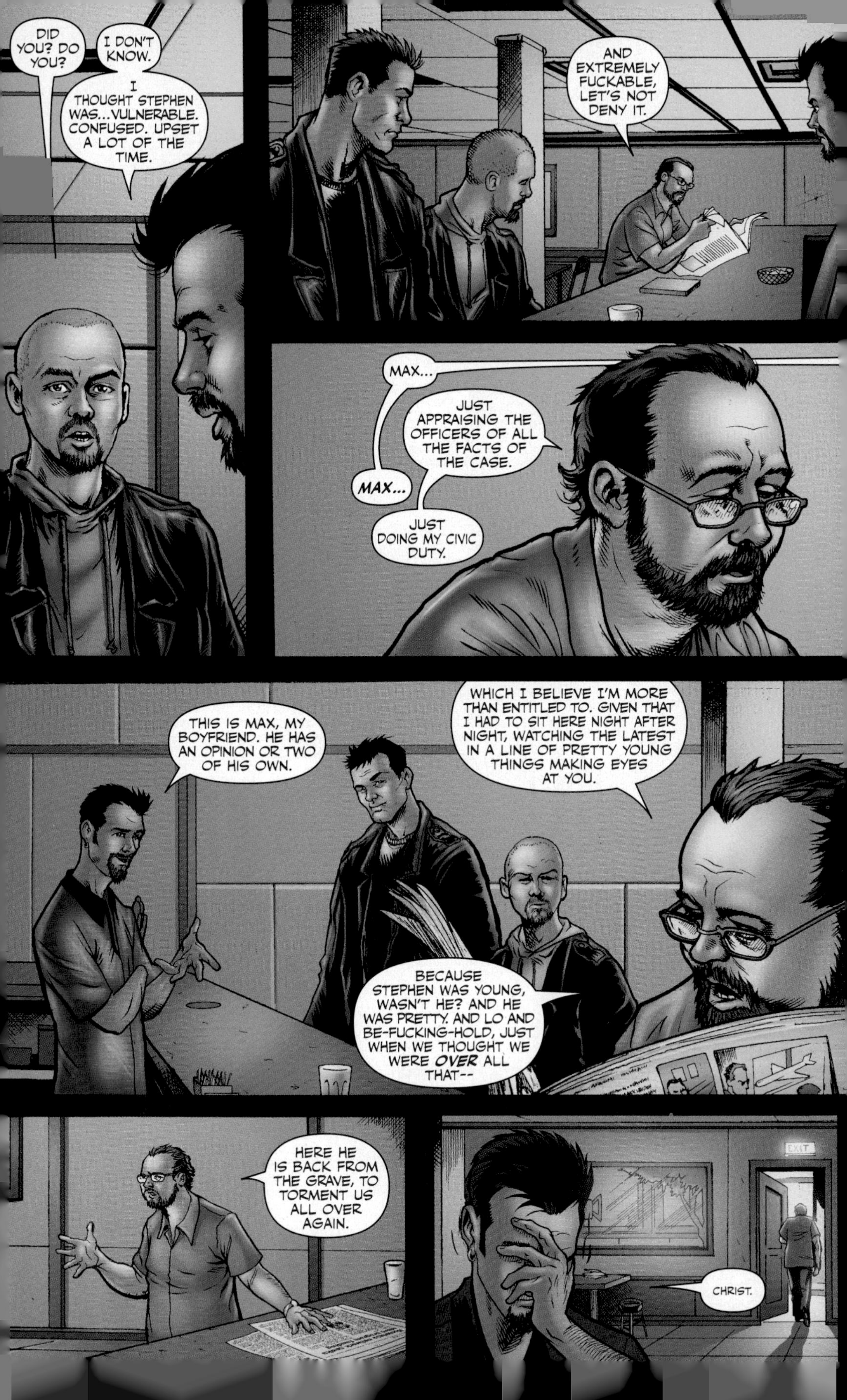
DID YOU? DO YOU?
I DON'T KNOW.
I THOUGHT STEPHEN WAS...VULNERABLE. CONFUSED. UPSET A LOT OF THE TIME.
AND EXTREMELY FUCKABLE, LET'S NOT DENY IT.
MAX...
JUST APPRAISING THE OFFICERS OF ALL THE FACTS OF THE CASE.
MAX...
JUST DOING MY CIVIC DUTY.
THIS IS MAX, MY BOYFRIEND. HE HAS AN OPINION OR TWO OF HIS OWN.
WHICH I BELIEVE I'M MORE THAN ENTITLED TO. GIVEN THAT I HAD TO SIT HERE NIGHT AFTER NIGHT, WATCHING THE LATEST IN A LINE OF PRETTY YOUNG THINGS MAKING EYES AT YOU.
BECAUSE STEPHEN WAS YOUNG, WASN'T HE? AND HE WAS PRETTY. AND LO AND BE-FUCKING-HOLD, JUST WHEN WE THOUGHT WE WERE OVER ALL THAT--
HERE HE IS BACK FROM THE GRAVE, TO TORMENT US ALL OVER AGAIN.
EXIT
CHRIST.

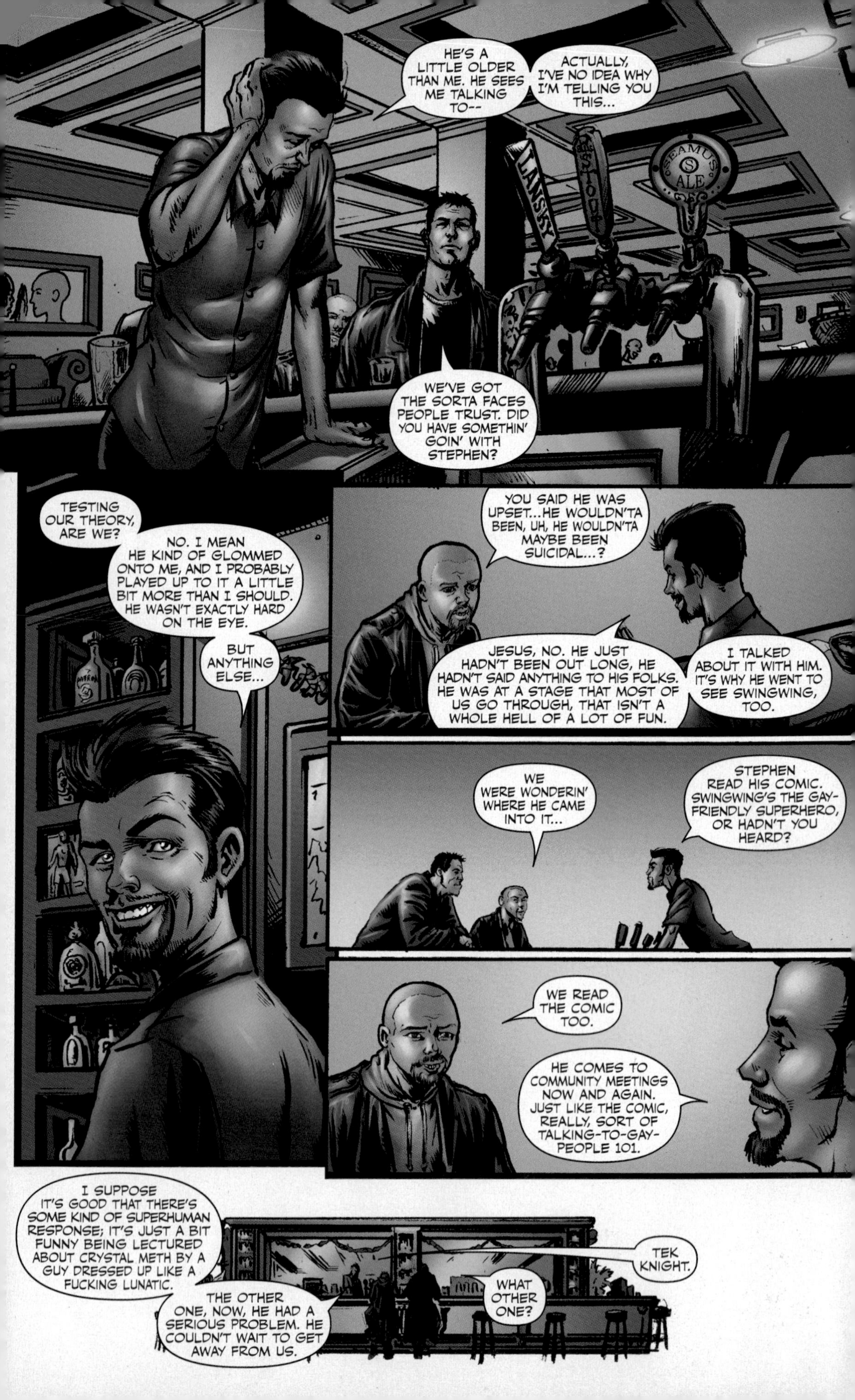
HE'S A LITTLE OLDER THAN ME. HE SEES ME TALKING TO--
ACTUALLY, I'VE NO IDEA WHY I'M TELLING YOU THIS...
LANSKY
STOUT
SEAMUS ALE
WE'VE GOT THE SORTA FACES PEOPLE TRUST. DID YOU HAVE SOMETHIN' GOIN' WITH STEPHEN?
TESTING OUR THEORY, ARE WE?
NO. I MEAN HE KIND OF GLOMMED ONTO ME, AND I PROBABLY PLAYED UP TO IT A LITTLE BIT MORE THAN I SHOULD. HE WASN'T EXACTLY HARD ON THE EYE.
BUT ANYTHING ELSE...
YOU SAID HE WAS UPSET...HE WOULDN'TA BEEN, UH, HE WOULDN'TA MAYBE BEEN SUICIDAL...?
JESUS, NO. HE JUST HADN'T BEEN OUT LONG, HE HADN'T SAID ANYTHING TO HIS FOLKS. HE WAS AT A STAGE THAT MOST OF US GO THROUGH, THAT ISN'T A WHOLE HELL OF A LOT OF FUN.
I TALKED ABOUT IT WITH HIM. IT'S WHY HE WENT TO SEE SWINGWING, TOO.
WE WERE WONDERIN' WHERE HE CAME INTO IT...
STEPHEN READ HIS COMIC. SWINGWING'S THE GAY-FRIENDLY SUPERHERO, OR HADN'T YOU HEARD?
WE READ THE COMIC TOO.
HE COMES TO COMMUNITY MEETINGS NOW AND AGAIN. JUST LIKE THE COMIC, REALLY, SORT OF TALKING-TO-GAY-PEOPLE 101.
I SUPPOSE IT'S GOOD THAT THERE'S SOME KIND OF SUPERHUMAN RESPONSE; IT'S JUST A BIT FUNNY BEING LECTURED ABOUT CRYSTAL METH BY A GUY DRESSED UP LIKE A FUCKING LUNATIC.
THE OTHER ONE, NOW, HE HAD A SERIOUS PROBLEM. HE COULDN'T WAIT TO GET AWAY FROM US.
WHAT OTHER ONE?
TEK KNIGHT.

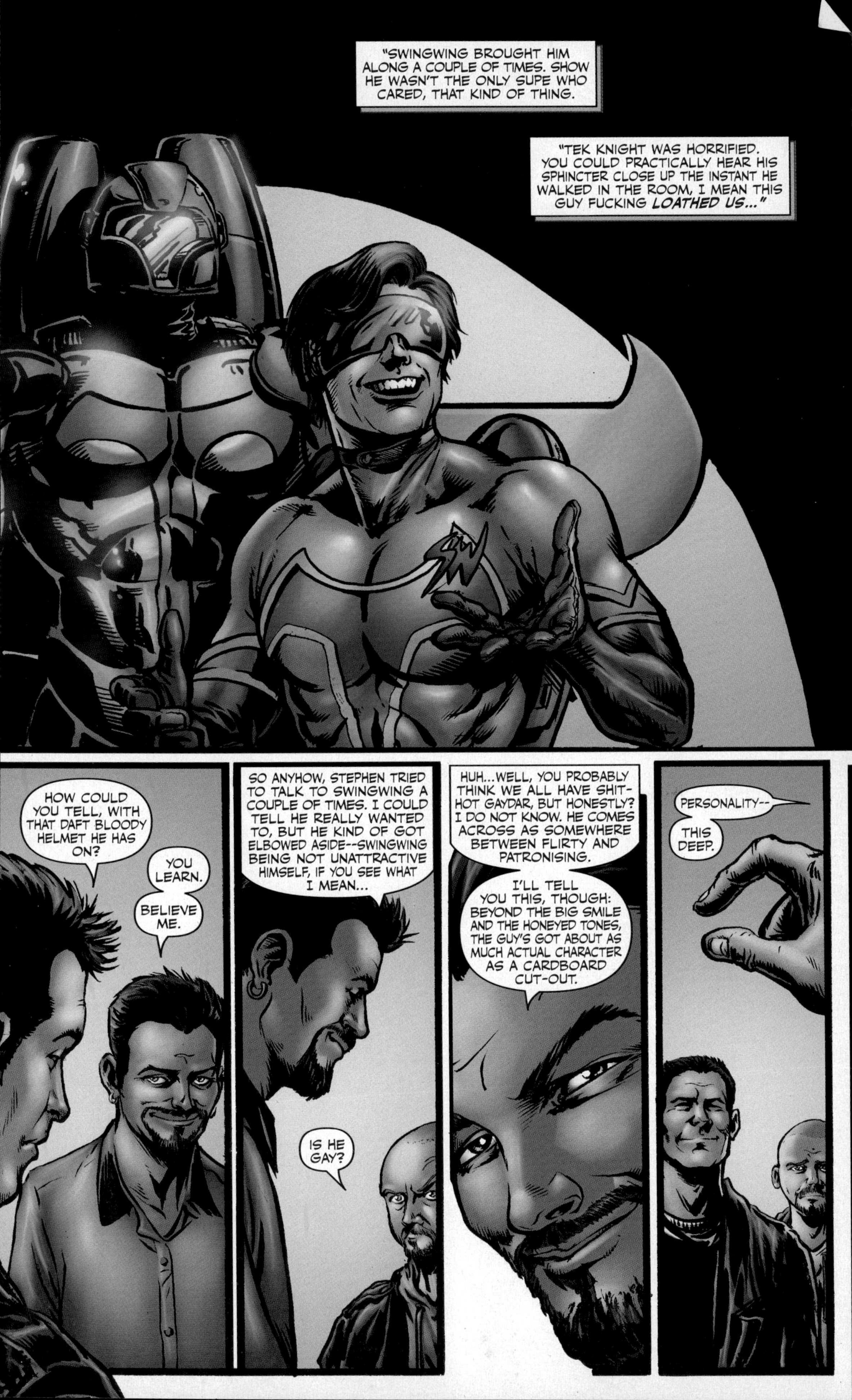
"SWINGWING BROUGHT HIM ALONG A COUPLE OF TIMES. SHOW HE WASN'T THE ONLY SUPE WHO CARED, THAT KIND OF THING.
"TEK KNIGHT WAS HORRIFIED. YOU COULD PRACTICALLY HEAR HIS SPHINCTER CLOSE UP THE INSTANT HE WALKED IN THE ROOM, I MEAN THIS GUY FUCKING *LOATHED US...*"
HOW COULD YOU TELL, WITH THAT DAFT BLOODY HELMET HE HAS ON?
YOU LEARN.
BELIEVE ME.
SO ANYHOW, STEPHEN TRIED TO TALK TO SWINGWING A COUPLE OF TIMES. I COULD TELL HE REALLY WANTED TO, BUT HE KIND OF GOT ELBOWED ASIDE--SWINGWING BEING NOT UNATTRACTIVE HIMSELF, IF YOU SEE WHAT I MEAN...
IS HE GAY?
HUH...WELL, YOU PROBABLY THINK WE ALL HAVE SHIT-HOT GAYDAR, BUT HONESTLY? I DO NOT KNOW. HE COMES ACROSS AS SOMEWHERE BETWEEN FLIRTY AND PATRONISING.
I'LL TELL YOU THIS, THOUGH: BEYOND THE BIG SMILE AND THE HONEYED TONES, THE GUY'S GOT ABOUT AS MUCH ACTUAL CHARACTER AS A CARDBOARD CUT-OUT.
PERSONALITY--
THIS DEEP.

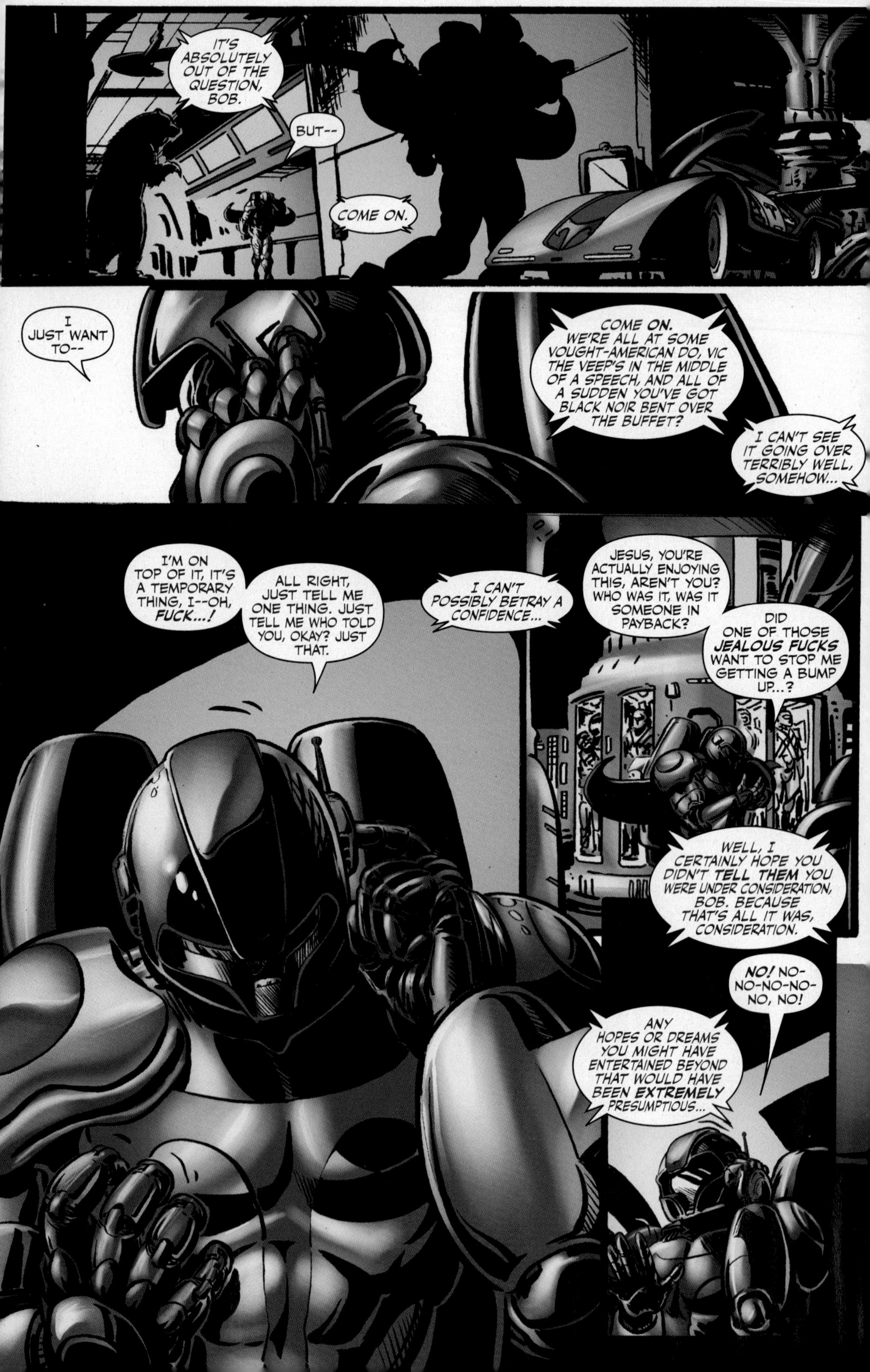
IT'S ABSOLUTELY OUT OF THE QUESTION, BOB.
BUT--
COME ON.
I JUST WANT TO--
COME ON. WE'RE ALL AT SOME VOUGHT-AMERICAN DO, VIC THE VEEP'S IN THE MIDDLE OF A SPEECH, AND ALL OF A SUDDEN YOU'VE GOT BLACK NOIR BENT OVER THE BUFFET?
I CAN'T SEE IT GOING OVER TERRIBLY WELL, SOMEHOW...
I'M ON TOP OF IT, IT'S A TEMPORARY THING, I--OH, FUCK...!
ALL RIGHT, JUST TELL ME ONE THING. JUST TELL ME WHO TOLD YOU, OKAY? JUST THAT.
I CAN'T POSSIBLY BETRAY A CONFIDENCE...
JESUS, YOU'RE ACTUALLY ENJOYING THIS, AREN'T YOU? WHO WAS IT, WAS IT SOMEONE IN PAYBACK?
DID ONE OF THOSE JEALOUS FUCKS WANT TO STOP ME GETTING A BUMP UP...?
WELL, I CERTAINLY HOPE YOU DIDN'T TELL THEM YOU WERE UNDER CONSIDERATION, BOB. BECAUSE THAT'S ALL IT WAS, CONSIDERATION.
NO! NO-NO-NO-NO-NO, NO!
ANY HOPES OR DREAMS YOU MIGHT HAVE ENTERTAINED BEYOND THAT WOULD HAVE BEEN EXTREMELY PRESUMPTIOUS...

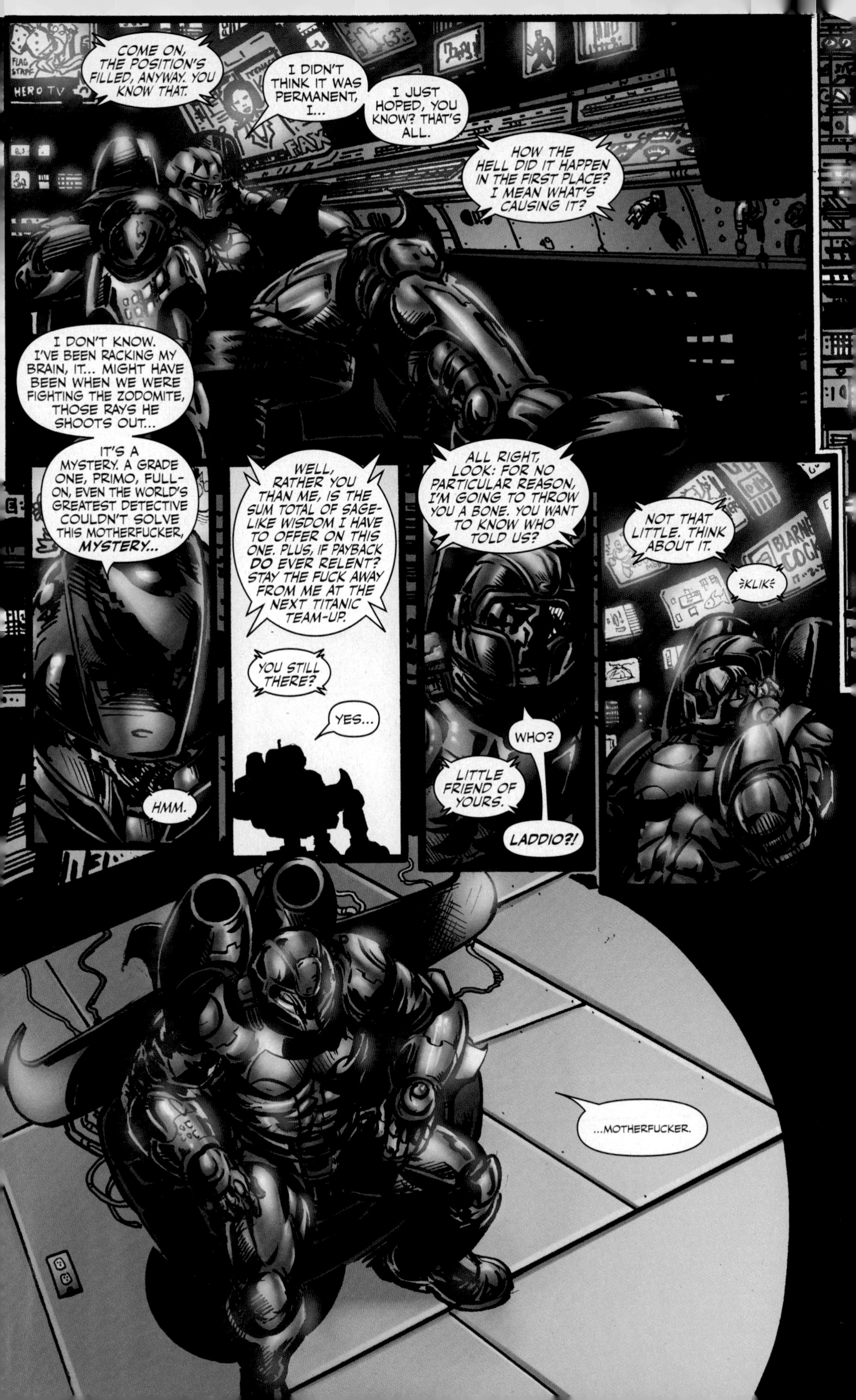
COME ON, THE POSITION'S FILLED, ANYWAY. YOU KNOW THAT.
I DIDN'T THINK IT WAS PERMANENT, I...
I JUST HOPED, YOU KNOW? THAT'S ALL.
HOW THE HELL DID IT HAPPEN IN THE FIRST PLACE? I MEAN WHAT'S CAUSING IT?
I DON'T KNOW. I'VE BEEN RACKING MY BRAIN, IT... MIGHT HAVE BEEN WHEN WE WERE FIGHTING THE ZODOMITE, THOSE RAYS HE SHOOTS OUT...
IT'S A MYSTERY. A GRADE ONE, PRIMO, FULL-ON, EVEN THE WORLD'S GREATEST DETECTIVE COULDN'T SOLVE THIS MOTHERFUCKER, MYSTERY...
HMM.
WELL, RATHER YOU THAN ME, IS THE SUM TOTAL OF SAGE-LIKE WISDOM I HAVE TO OFFER ON THIS ONE. PLUS, IF PAYBACK DO EVER RELENT? STAY THE FUCK AWAY FROM ME AT THE NEXT TITANIC TEAM-UP.
YOU STILL THERE?
YES...
ALL RIGHT, LOOK: FOR NO PARTICULAR REASON, I'M GOING TO THROW YOU A BONE. YOU WANT TO KNOW WHO TOLD US?
WHO?
LITTLE FRIEND OF YOURS.
LADDIO?!
NOT THAT LITTLE. THINK ABOUT IT.
KLIK
...MOTHERFUCKER.

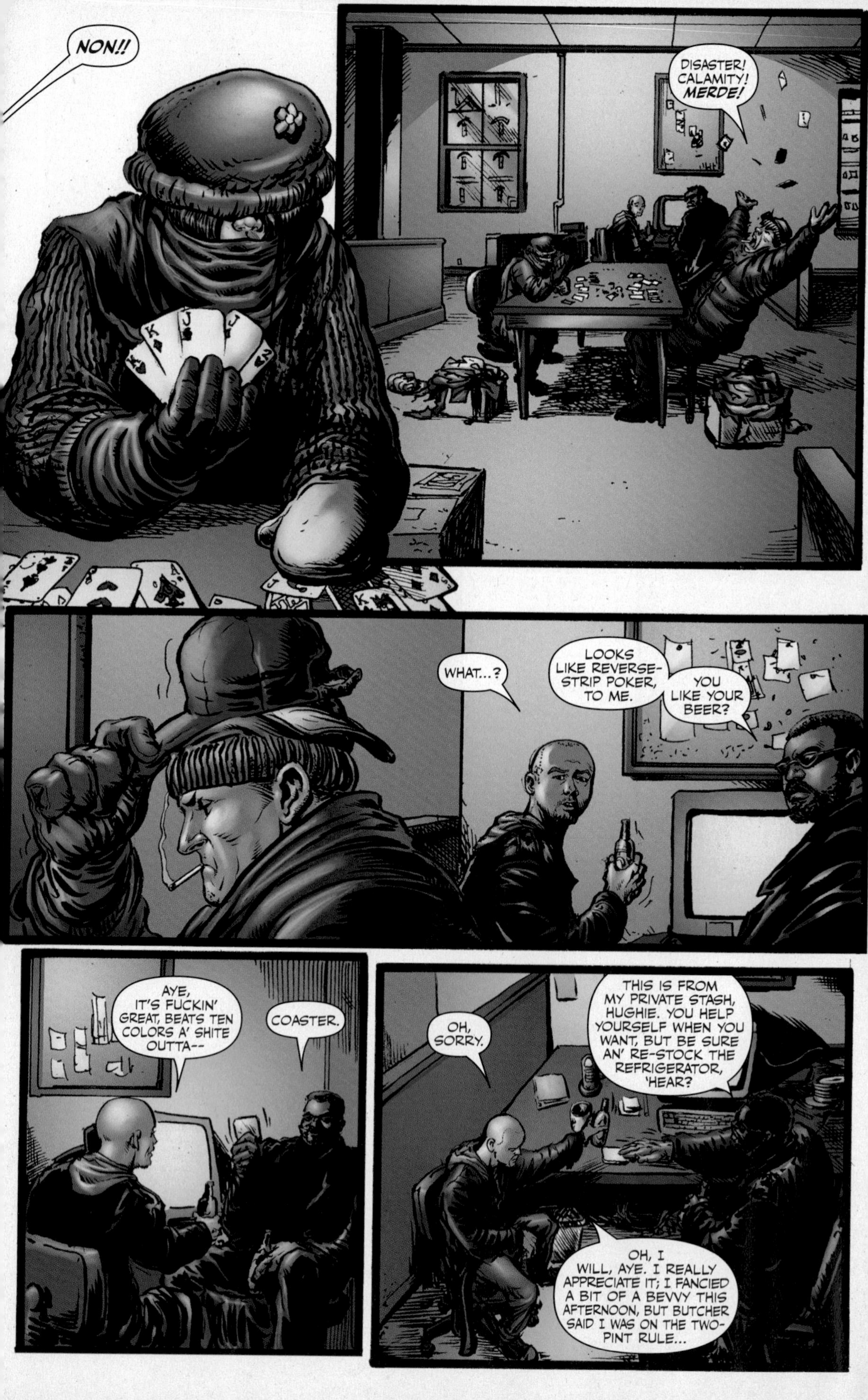
NON!!
DISASTER! CALAMITY! MERDE!
WHAT...?
LOOKS LIKE REVERSE-STRIP POKER, TO ME.
YOU LIKE YOUR BEER?
AYE, IT'S FUCKIN' GREAT, BEATS TEN COLORS A' SHITE OUTTA--
COASTER.
OH, SORRY.
THIS IS FROM MY PRIVATE STASH, HUGHIE. YOU HELP YOURSELF WHEN YOU WANT, BUT BE SURE AN' RE-STOCK THE REFRIGERATOR, 'HEAR?
OH, I WILL, AYE. I REALLY APPRECIATE IT; I FANCIED A BIT OF A BEVVY THIS AFTERNOON, BUT BUTCHER SAID I WAS ON THE TWO-PINT RULE...

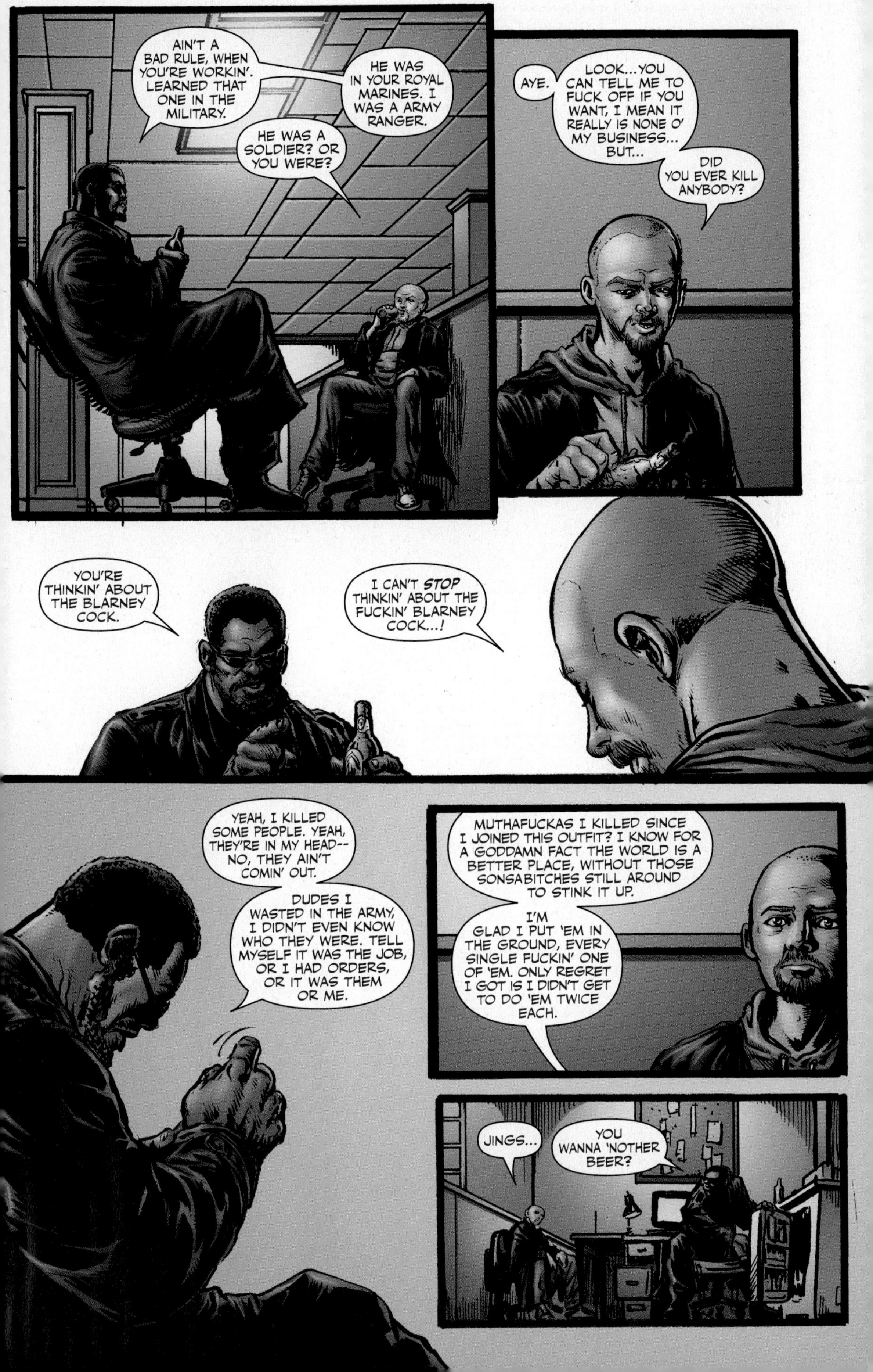

AIN'T A BAD RULE, WHEN YOU'RE WORKIN'. LEARNED THAT ONE IN THE MILITARY.
HE WAS A SOLDIER? OR YOU WERE?
HE WAS IN YOUR ROYAL MARINES. I WAS A ARMY RANGER.
AYE.
LOOK...YOU CAN TELL ME TO FUCK OFF IF YOU WANT, I MEAN IT REALLY IS NONE O' MY BUSINESS... BUT...
DID YOU EVER KILL ANYBODY?
YOU'RE THINKIN' ABOUT THE BLARNEY COCK.
I CAN'T STOP THINKIN' ABOUT THE FUCKIN' BLARNEY COCK...!
YEAH, I KILLED SOME PEOPLE. YEAH, THEY'RE IN MY HEAD-- NO, THEY AIN'T COMIN' OUT.
DUDES I WASTED IN THE ARMY, I DIDN'T EVEN KNOW WHO THEY WERE. TELL MYSELF IT WAS THE JOB, OR I HAD ORDERS, OR IT WAS THEM OR ME.
MUTHAFUCKAS I KILLED SINCE I JOINED THIS OUTFIT? I KNOW FOR A GODDAMN FACT THE WORLD IS A BETTER PLACE, WITHOUT THOSE SONSABITCHES STILL AROUND TO STINK IT UP.
I'M GLAD I PUT 'EM IN THE GROUND, EVERY SINGLE FUCKIN' ONE OF 'EM. ONLY REGRET I GOT IS I DIDN'T GET TO DO 'EM TWICE EACH.
JINGS...
YOU WANNA 'NOTHER BEER?

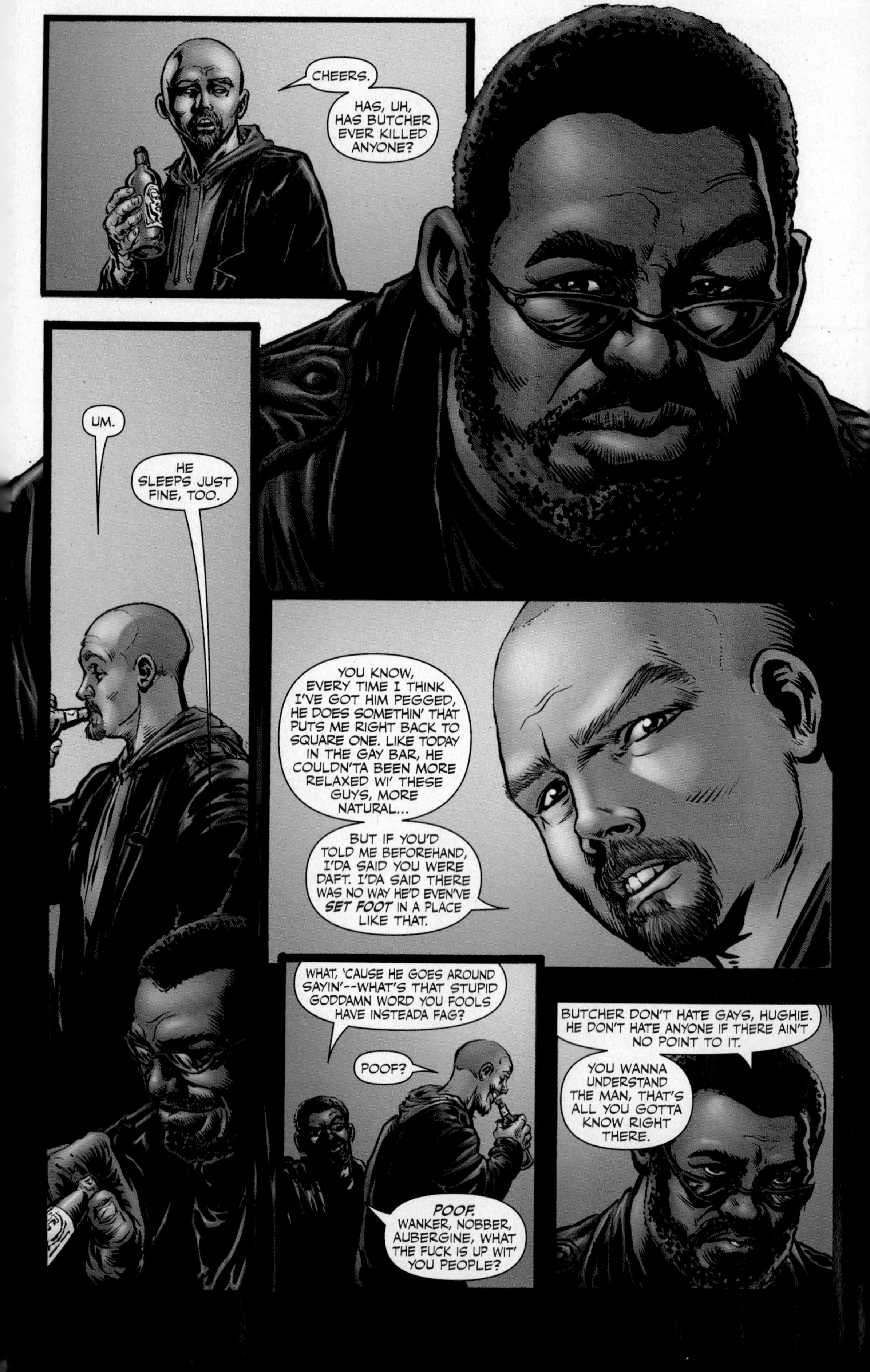
CHEERS.
HAS, UH, HAS BUTCHER EVER KILLED ANYONE?
UM.
HE SLEEPS JUST FINE, TOO.
YOU KNOW, EVERY TIME I THINK I'VE GOT HIM PEGGED, HE DOES SOMETHIN' THAT PUTS ME RIGHT BACK TO SQUARE ONE. LIKE TODAY IN THE GAY BAR, HE COULDN'TA BEEN MORE RELAXED WI' THESE GUYS, MORE NATURAL...
BUT IF YOU'D TOLD ME BEFOREHAND, I'DA SAID YOU WERE DAFT. I'DA SAID THERE WAS NO WAY HE'D EVEN'VE *SET FOOT* IN A PLACE LIKE THAT.
WHAT, 'CAUSE HE GOES AROUND SAYIN'--WHAT'S THAT STUPID GODDAMN WORD YOU FOOLS HAVE INSTEADA FAG?
POOF?
POOF. WANKER, NOBBER, AUBERGINE, WHAT THE FUCK IS UP WIT' YOU PEOPLE?
BUTCHER DON'T HATE GAYS, HUGHIE. HE DON'T HATE ANYONE IF THERE AIN'T NO POINT TO IT.
YOU WANNA UNDERSTAND THE MAN, THAT'S ALL YOU GOTTA KNOW RIGHT THERE.

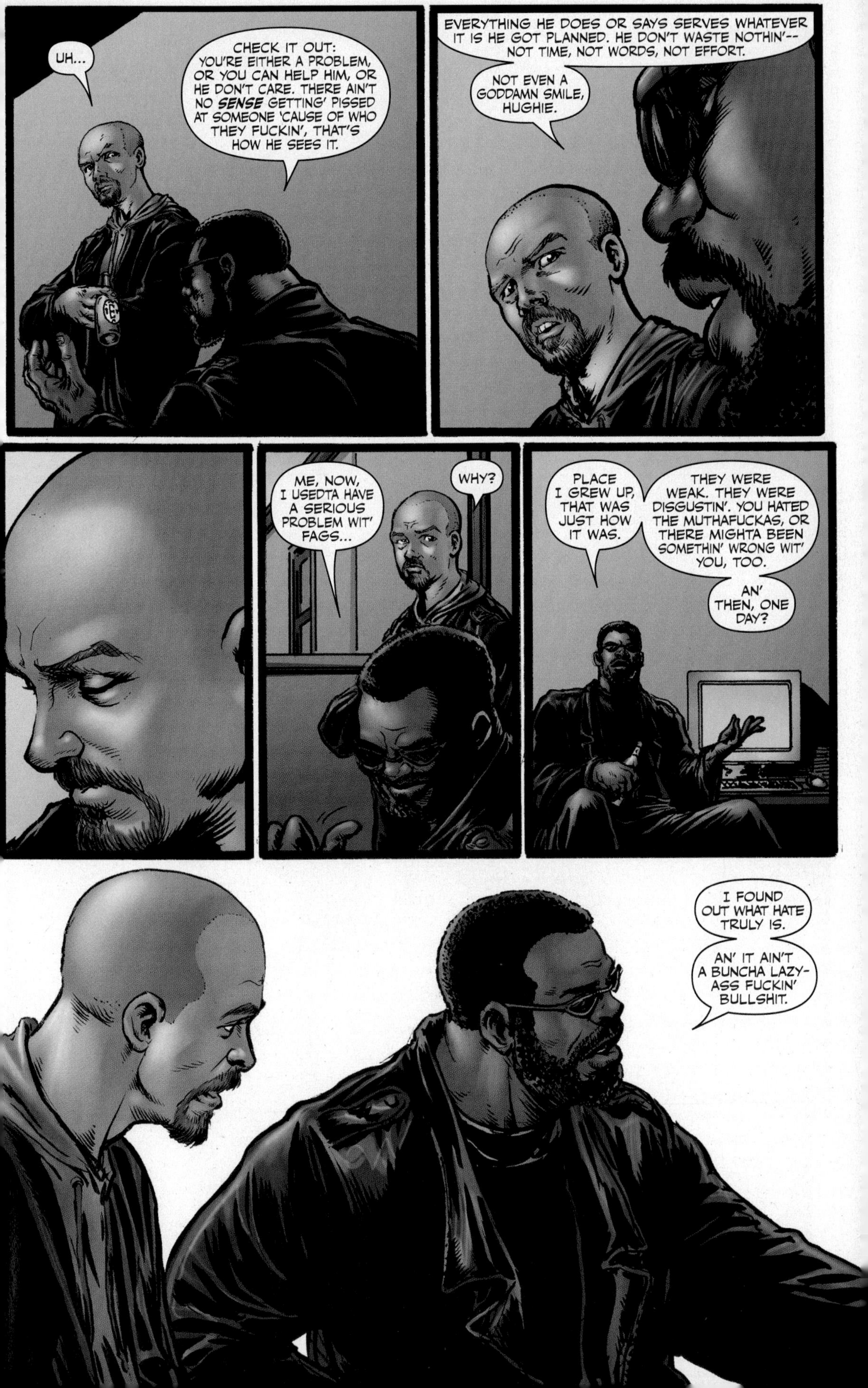
UH...
CHECK IT OUT: YOU'RE EITHER A PROBLEM, OR YOU CAN HELP HIM, OR HE DON'T CARE. THERE AIN'T NO SENSE GETTING' PISSED AT SOMEONE 'CAUSE OF WHO THEY FUCKIN', THAT'S HOW HE SEES IT.
EVERYTHING HE DOES OR SAYS SERVES WHATEVER IT IS HE GOT PLANNED. HE DON'T WASTE NOTHIN'-- NOT TIME, NOT WORDS, NOT EFFORT.
NOT EVEN A GODDAMN SMILE, HUGHIE.
ME, NOW, I USEDTA HAVE A SERIOUS PROBLEM WIT' FAGS...
WHY?
PLACE I GREW UP, THAT WAS JUST HOW IT WAS.
THEY WERE WEAK. THEY WERE DISGUSTIN'. YOU HATED THE MUTHAFUCKAS, OR THERE MIGHTA BEEN SOMETHIN' WRONG WIT' YOU, TOO.
AN' THEN, ONE DAY?
I FOUND OUT WHAT HATE TRULY IS.
AN' IT AIN'T A BUNCHA LAZY-ASS FUCKIN' BULLSHIT.

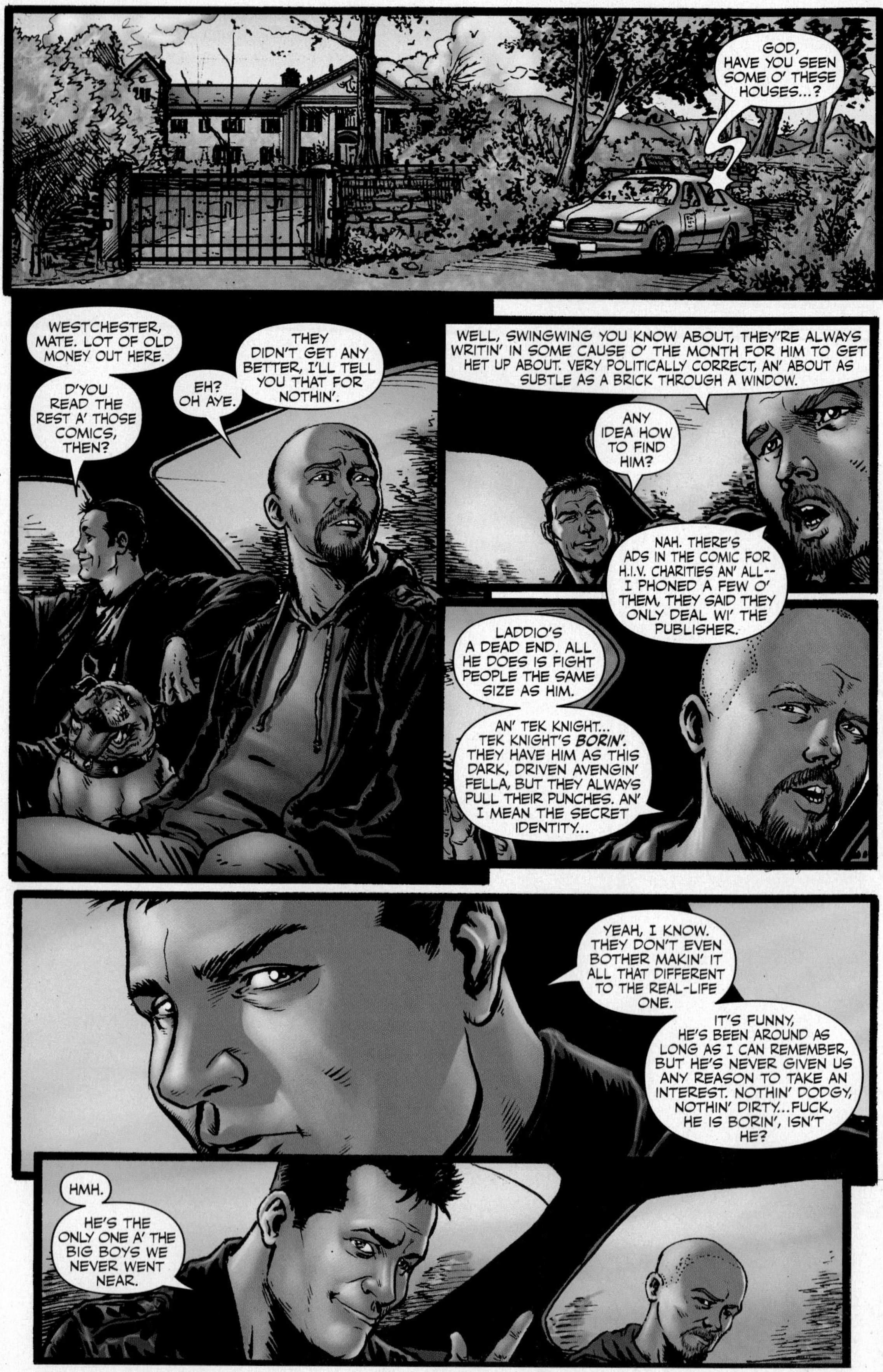
GOD, HAVE YOU SEEN SOME O' THESE HOUSES...?
WESTCHESTER, MATE. LOT OF OLD MONEY OUT HERE.
D'YOU READ THE REST A' THOSE COMICS, THEN?
EH? OH AYE.
THEY DIDN'T GET ANY BETTER, I'LL TELL YOU THAT FOR NOTHIN'.
WELL, SWINGWING YOU KNOW ABOUT, THEY'RE ALWAYS WRITIN' IN SOME CAUSE O' THE MONTH FOR HIM TO GET HET UP ABOUT. VERY POLITICALLY CORRECT, AN' ABOUT AS SUBTLE AS A BRICK THROUGH A WINDOW.
ANY IDEA HOW TO FIND HIM?
NAH. THERE'S ADS IN THE COMIC FOR H.I.V. CHARITIES AN' ALL-- I PHONED A FEW O' THEM, THEY SAID THEY ONLY DEAL WI' THE PUBLISHER.
LADDIO'S A DEAD END. ALL HE DOES IS FIGHT PEOPLE THE SAME SIZE AS HIM.
AN' TEK KNIGHT... TEK KNIGHT'S *BORIN'*. THEY HAVE HIM AS THIS DARK, DRIVEN AVENGIN' FELLA, BUT THEY ALWAYS PULL THEIR PUNCHES. AN' I MEAN THE SECRET IDENTITY...
YEAH, I KNOW. THEY DON'T EVEN BOTHER MAKIN' IT ALL THAT DIFFERENT TO THE REAL-LIFE ONE.
IT'S FUNNY, HE'S BEEN AROUND AS LONG AS I CAN REMEMBER, BUT HE'S NEVER GIVEN US ANY REASON TO TAKE AN INTEREST. NOTHIN' DODGY, NOTHIN' DIRTY...FUCK, HE IS BORIN', ISN'T HE?
HMH.
HE'S THE ONLY ONE A' THE BIG BOYS WE NEVER WENT NEAR.

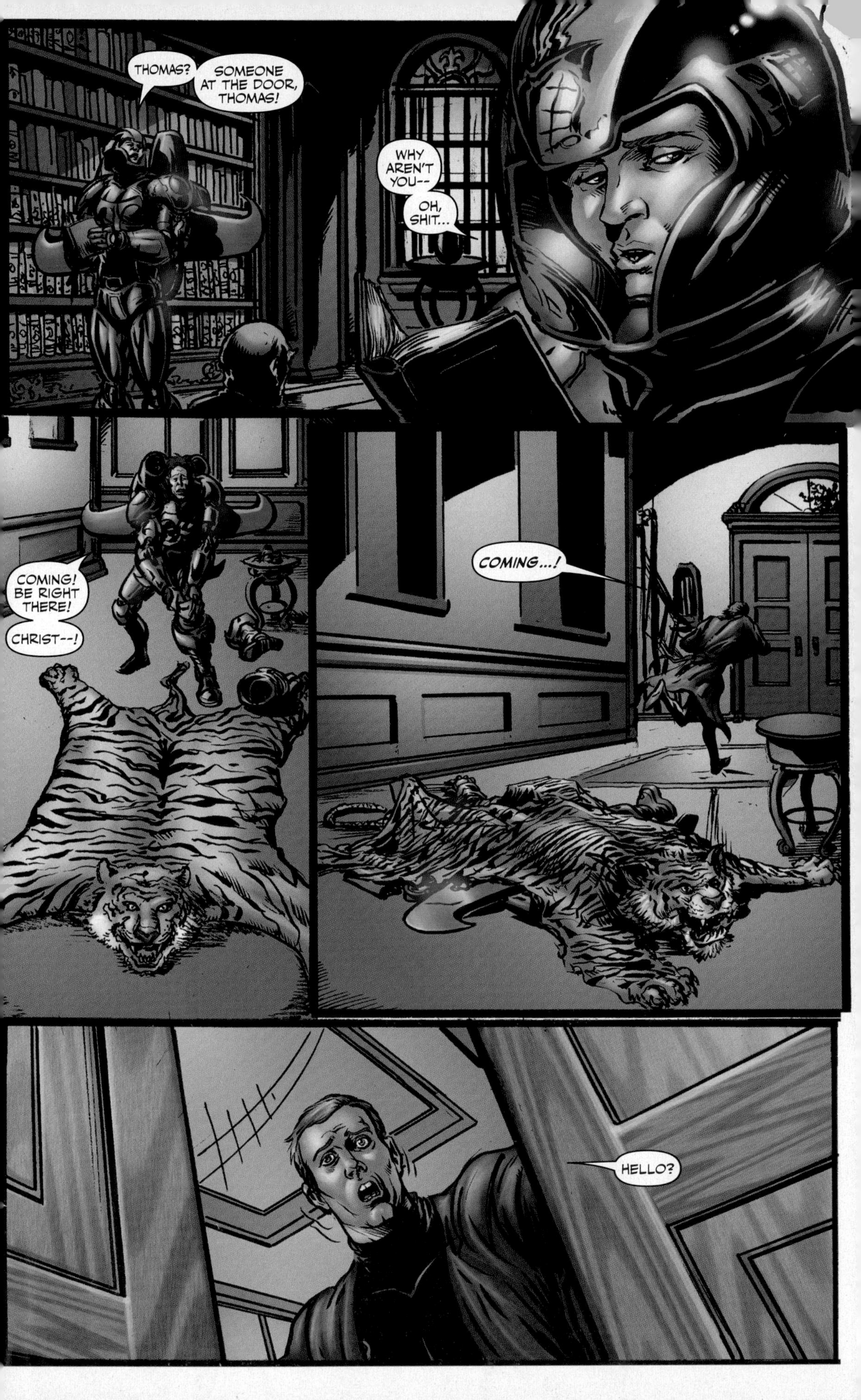
THOMAS?
SOMEONE AT THE DOOR, THOMAS!
WHY AREN'T YOU--
OH, SHIT...
COMING! BE RIGHT THERE!
CHRIST--!
COMING...!
HELLO?

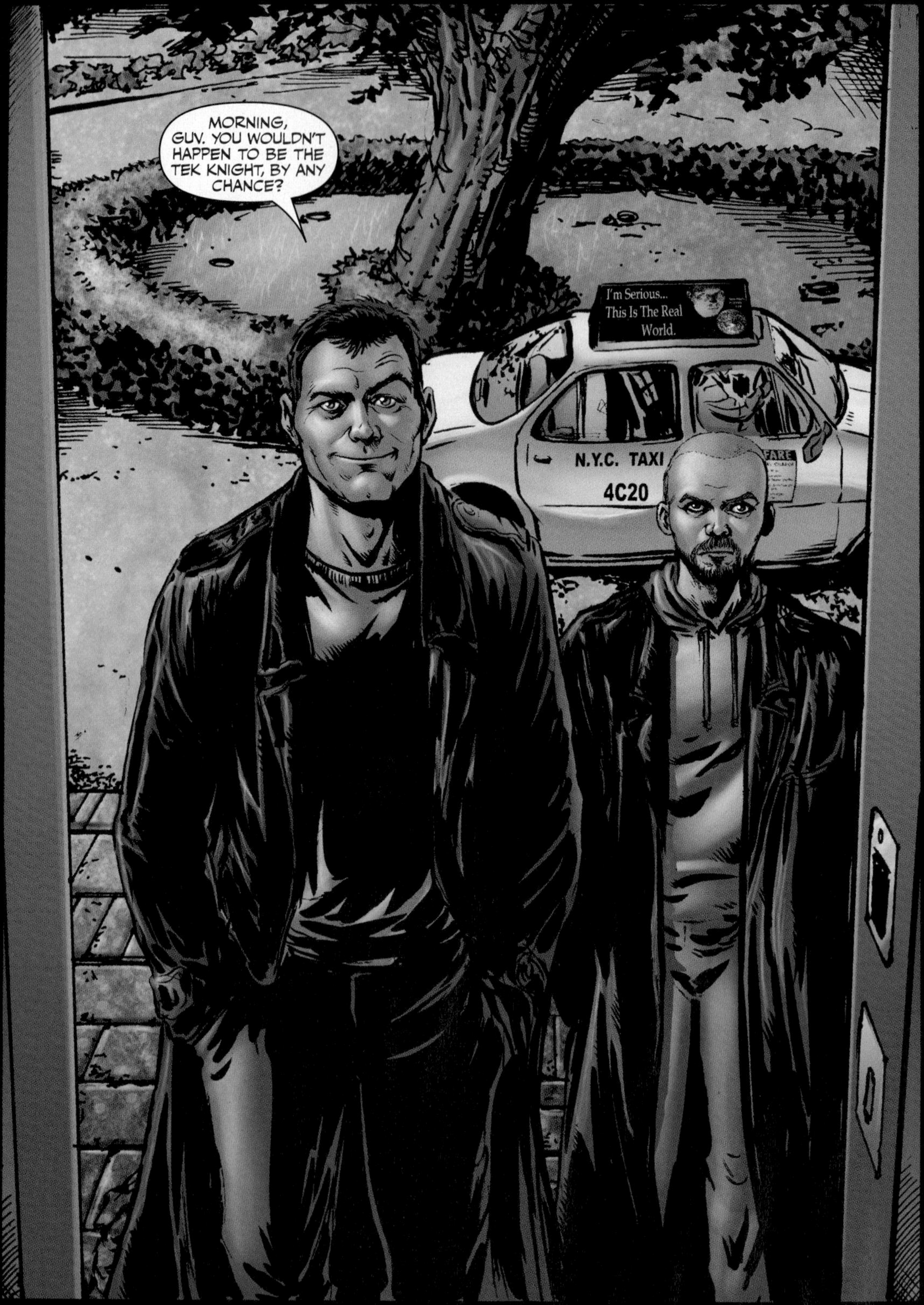
MORNING, GUV. YOU WOULDN'T HAPPEN TO BE THE TEK KNIGHT, BY ANY CHANCE?
I'm Serious... This Is The Real World.
N.Y.C. TAXI
4C20
FARE

next: DIRTY BUSINESS IN THE TEK CAVE

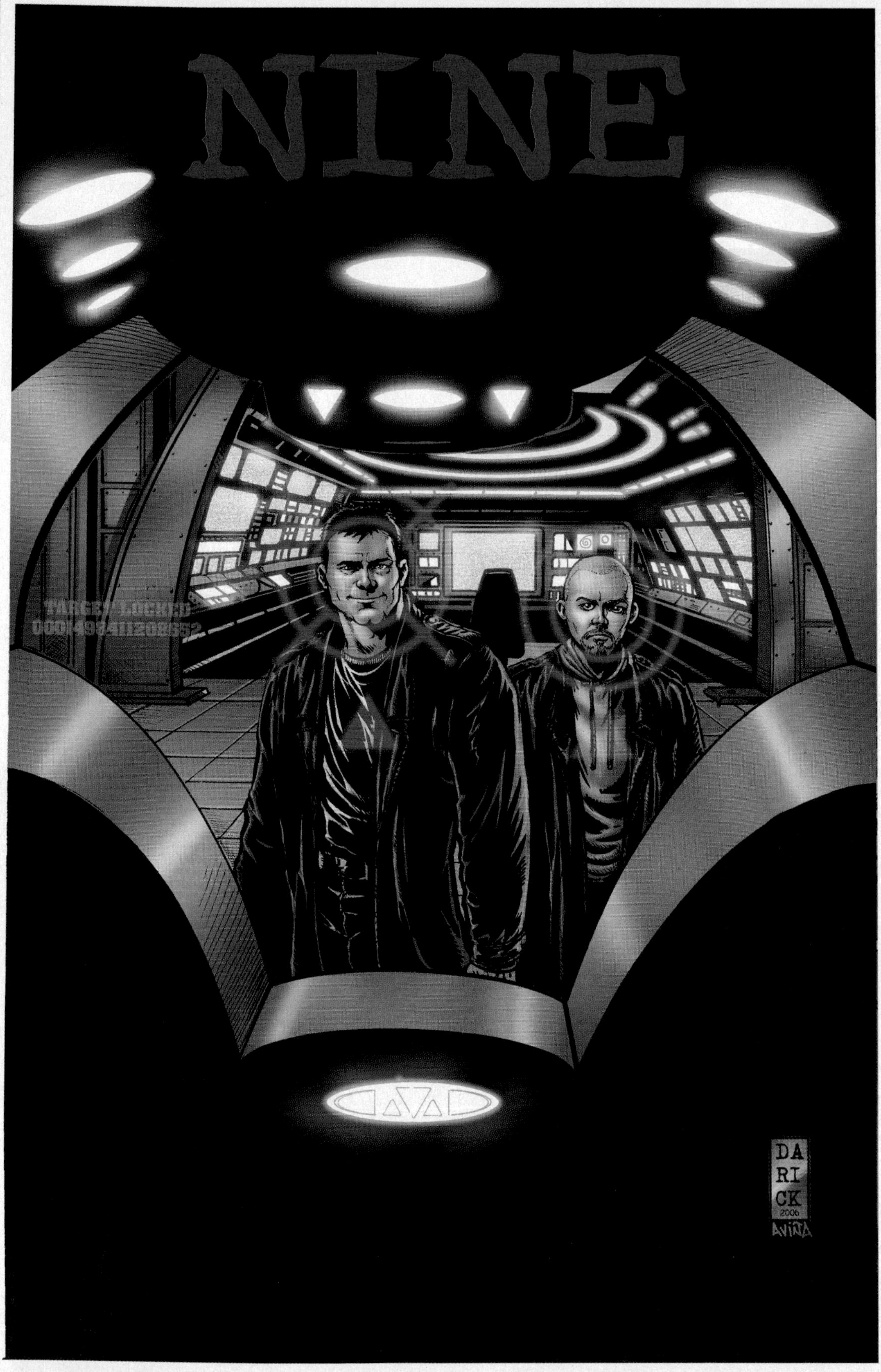
NINE
TARGET LOCKED
DA
RI
CK
2006
AVIÑA

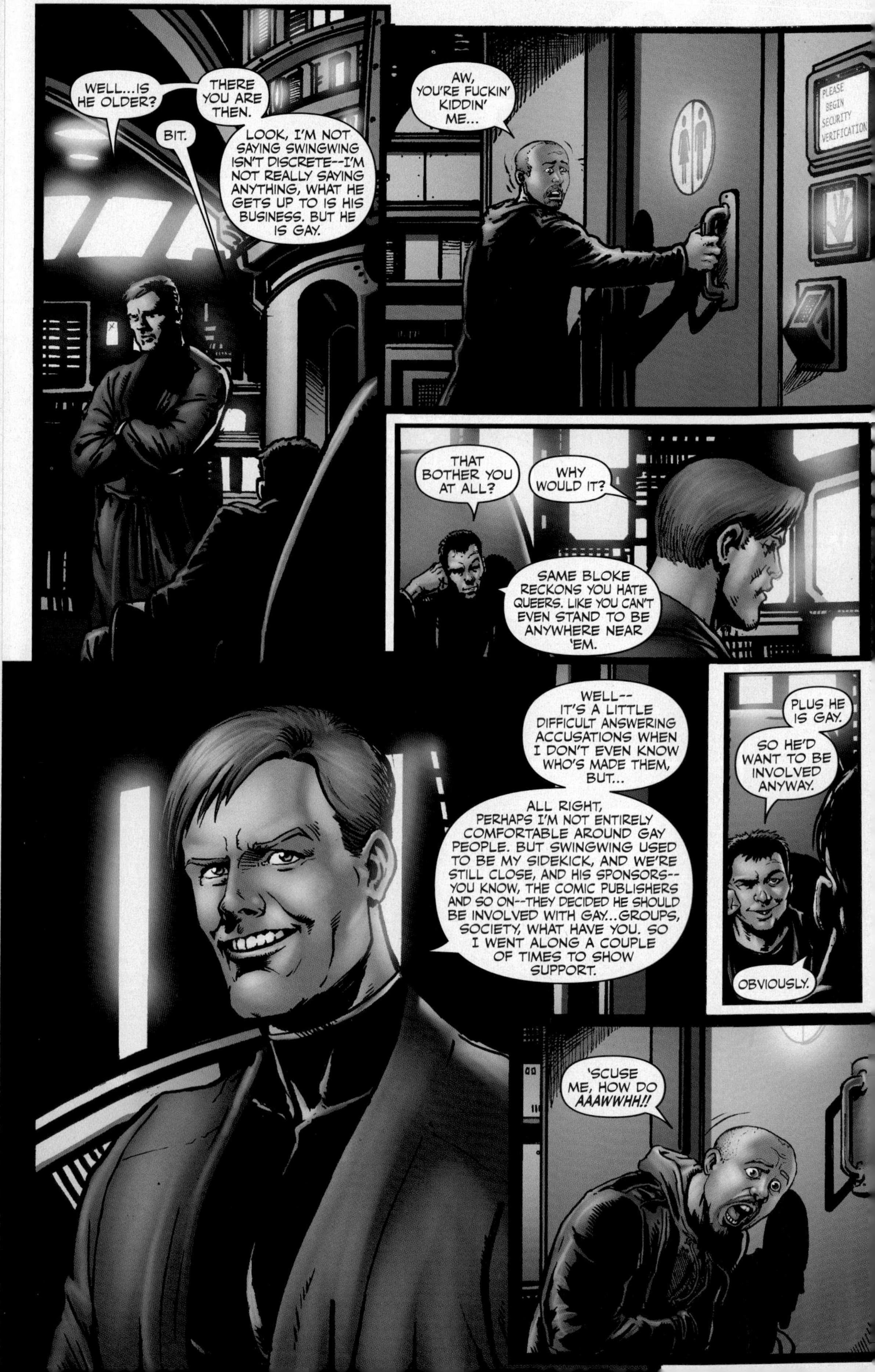
WELL...IS HE OLDER?
THERE YOU ARE THEN.
BIT.
LOOK, I'M NOT SAYING SWINGWING ISN'T DISCRETE--I'M NOT REALLY SAYING ANYTHING, WHAT HE GETS UP TO IS HIS BUSINESS. BUT HE IS GAY.
AW, YOU'RE FUCKIN' KIDDIN' ME...
PLEASE BEGIN SECURITY VERIFICATION
THAT BOTHER YOU AT ALL?
WHY WOULD IT?
SAME BLOKE RECKONS YOU HATE QUEERS. LIKE YOU CAN'T EVEN STAND TO BE ANYWHERE NEAR 'EM.
WELL-- IT'S A LITTLE DIFFICULT ANSWERING ACCUSATIONS WHEN I DON'T EVEN KNOW WHO'S MADE THEM, BUT...
ALL RIGHT, PERHAPS I'M NOT ENTIRELY COMFORTABLE AROUND GAY PEOPLE. BUT SWINGWING USED TO BE MY SIDEKICK, AND WE'RE STILL CLOSE, AND HIS SPONSORS-- YOU KNOW, THE COMIC PUBLISHERS AND SO ON--THEY DECIDED HE SHOULD BE INVOLVED WITH GAY...GROUPS, SOCIETY, WHAT HAVE YOU. SO I WENT ALONG A COUPLE OF TIMES TO SHOW SUPPORT.
PLUS HE IS GAY.
SO HE'D WANT TO BE INVOLVED ANYWAY.
OBVIOUSLY.
'SCUSE ME, HOW DO AAAWWHH!!

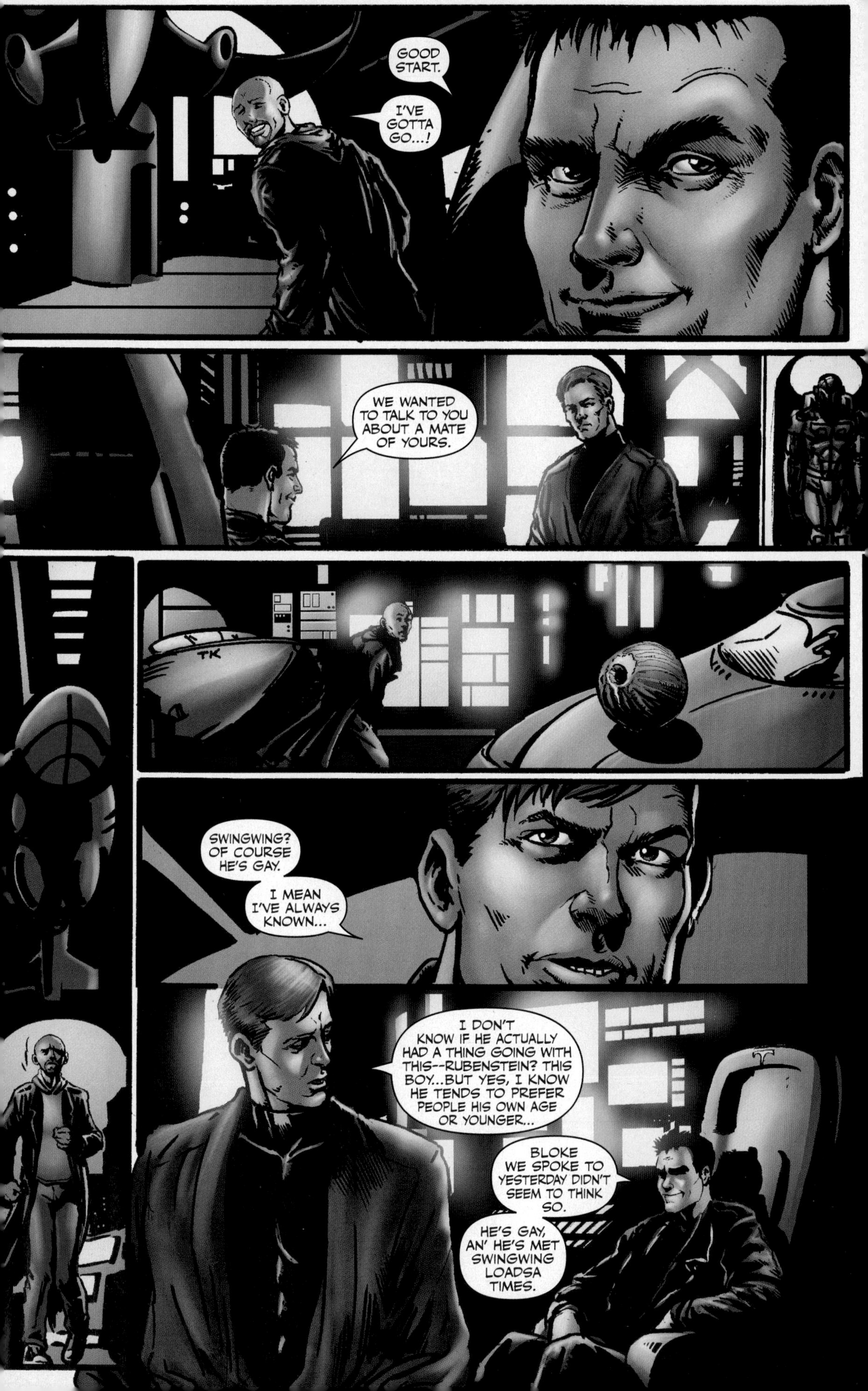
GOOD START.
I'VE GOTTA GO...!
WE WANTED TO TALK TO YOU ABOUT A MATE OF YOURS.
TK
SWINGWING? OF COURSE HE'S GAY.
I MEAN I'VE ALWAYS KNOWN...
I DON'T KNOW IF HE ACTUALLY HAD A THING GOING WITH THIS--RUBENSTEIN? THIS BOY...BUT YES, I KNOW HE TENDS TO PREFER PEOPLE HIS OWN AGE OR YOUNGER...
BLOKE WE SPOKE TO YESTERDAY DIDN'T SEEM TO THINK SO.
HE'S GAY, AN' HE'S MET SWINGWING LOADSA TIMES.

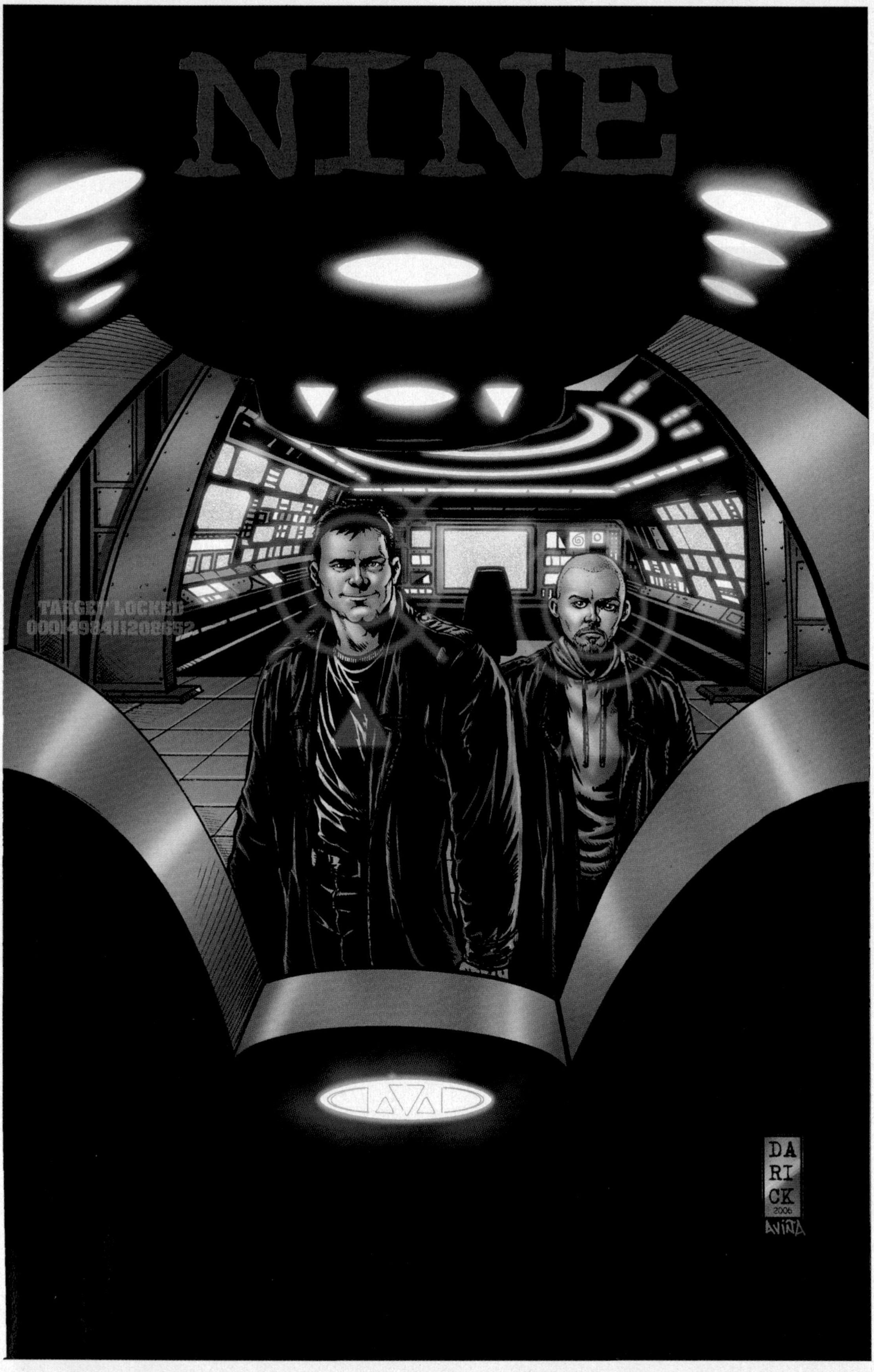
NINE
TARGET LOCKED
DARICK 2006

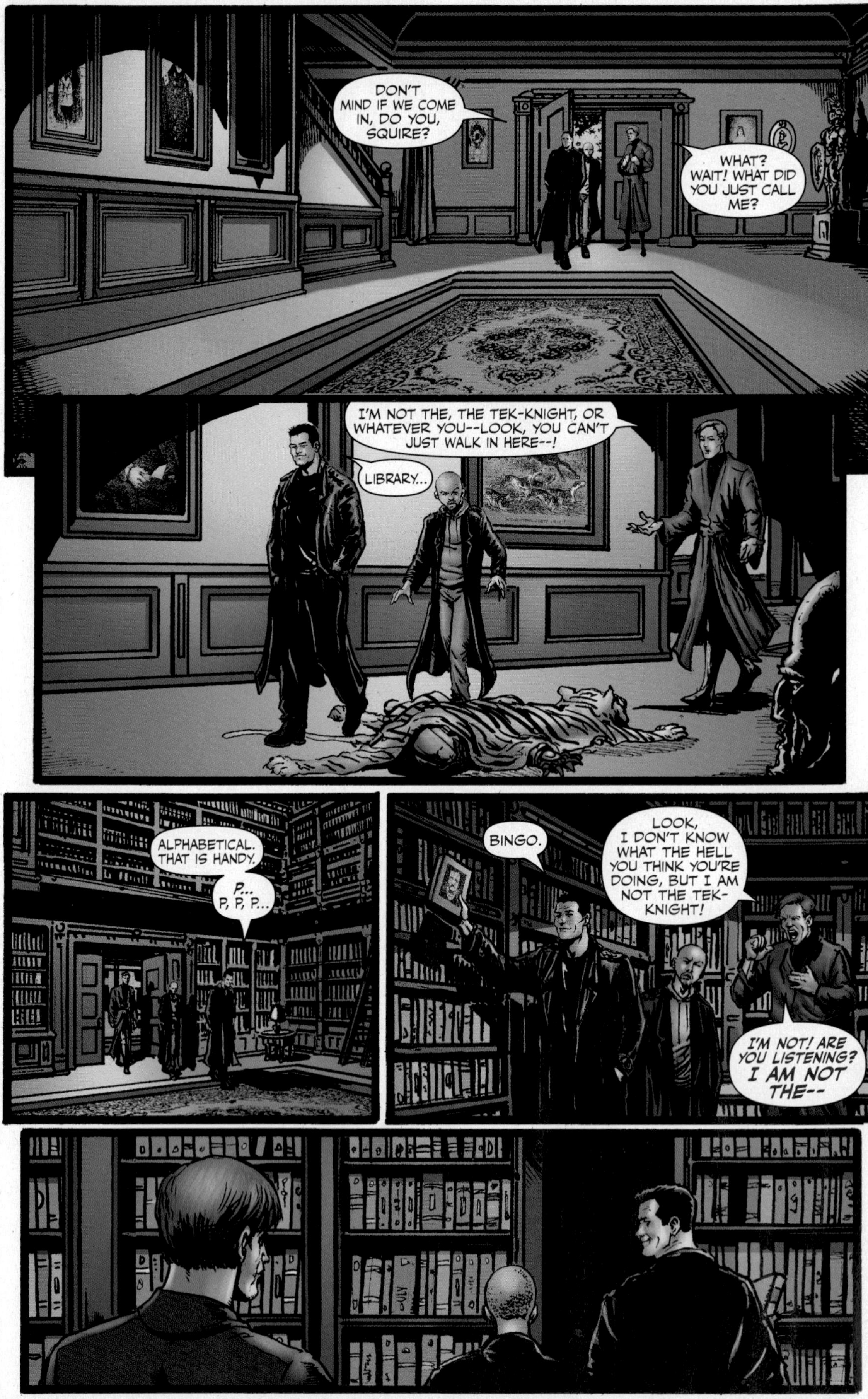
DON'T MIND IF WE COME IN, DO YOU, SQUIRE?
WHAT? WAIT! WHAT DID YOU JUST CALL ME?
I'M NOT THE, THE TEK-KNIGHT, OR WHATEVER YOU--LOOK, YOU CAN'T JUST WALK IN HERE--!
LIBRARY...
ALPHABETICAL. THAT IS HANDY.
P... P, P, P...
BINGO.
LOOK, I DON'T KNOW WHAT THE HELL YOU THINK YOU'RE DOING, BUT I AM NOT THE TEK-KNIGHT!
I'M NOT! ARE YOU LISTENING? I AM NOT THE--

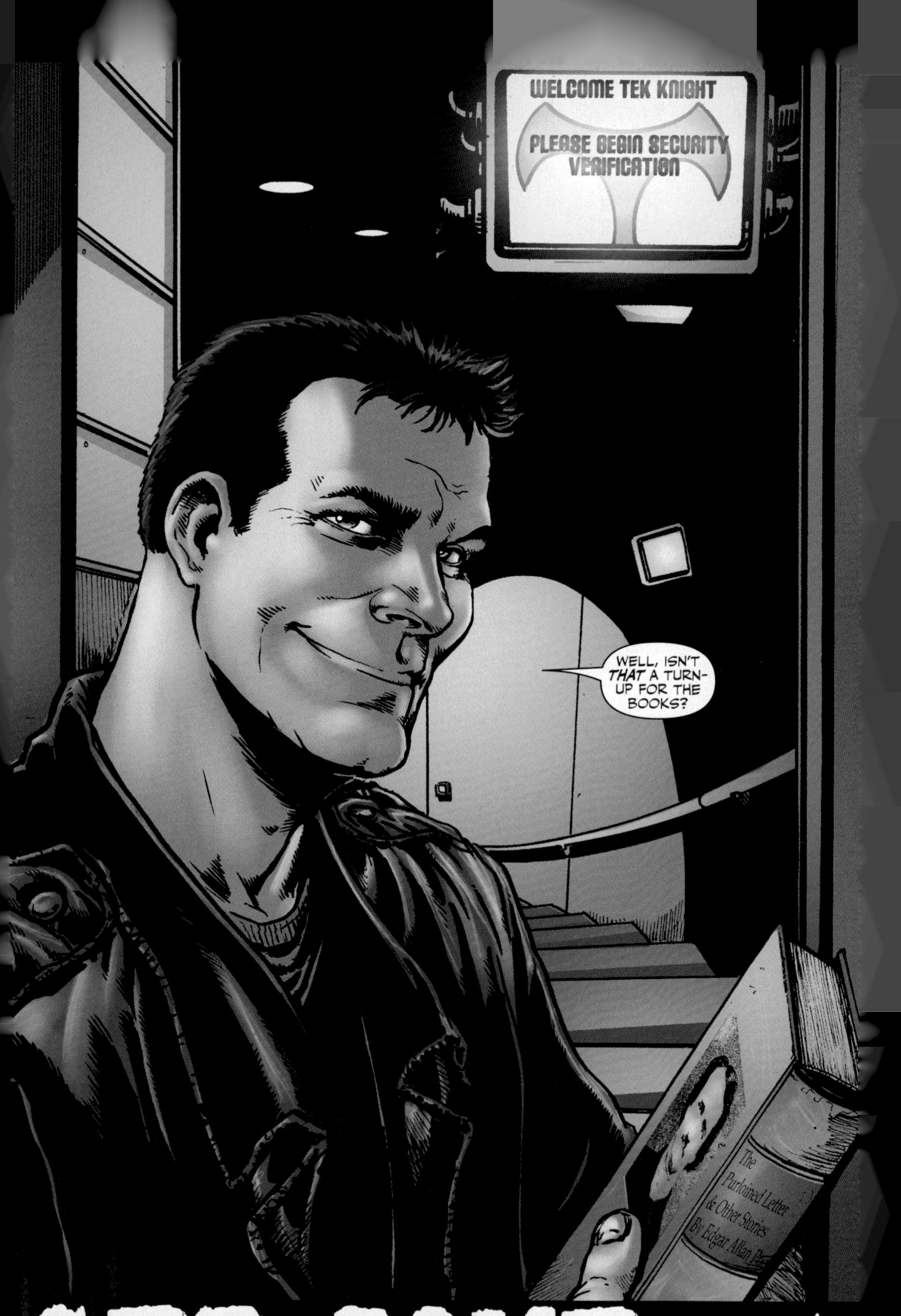
WELCOME TEK KNIGHT
PLEASE BEGIN SECURITY VERIFICATION
WELL, ISN'T *THAT* A TURN-UP FOR THE BOOKS?
The Purloined Letter & Other Stories By Edgar Allan

GET SOME part three

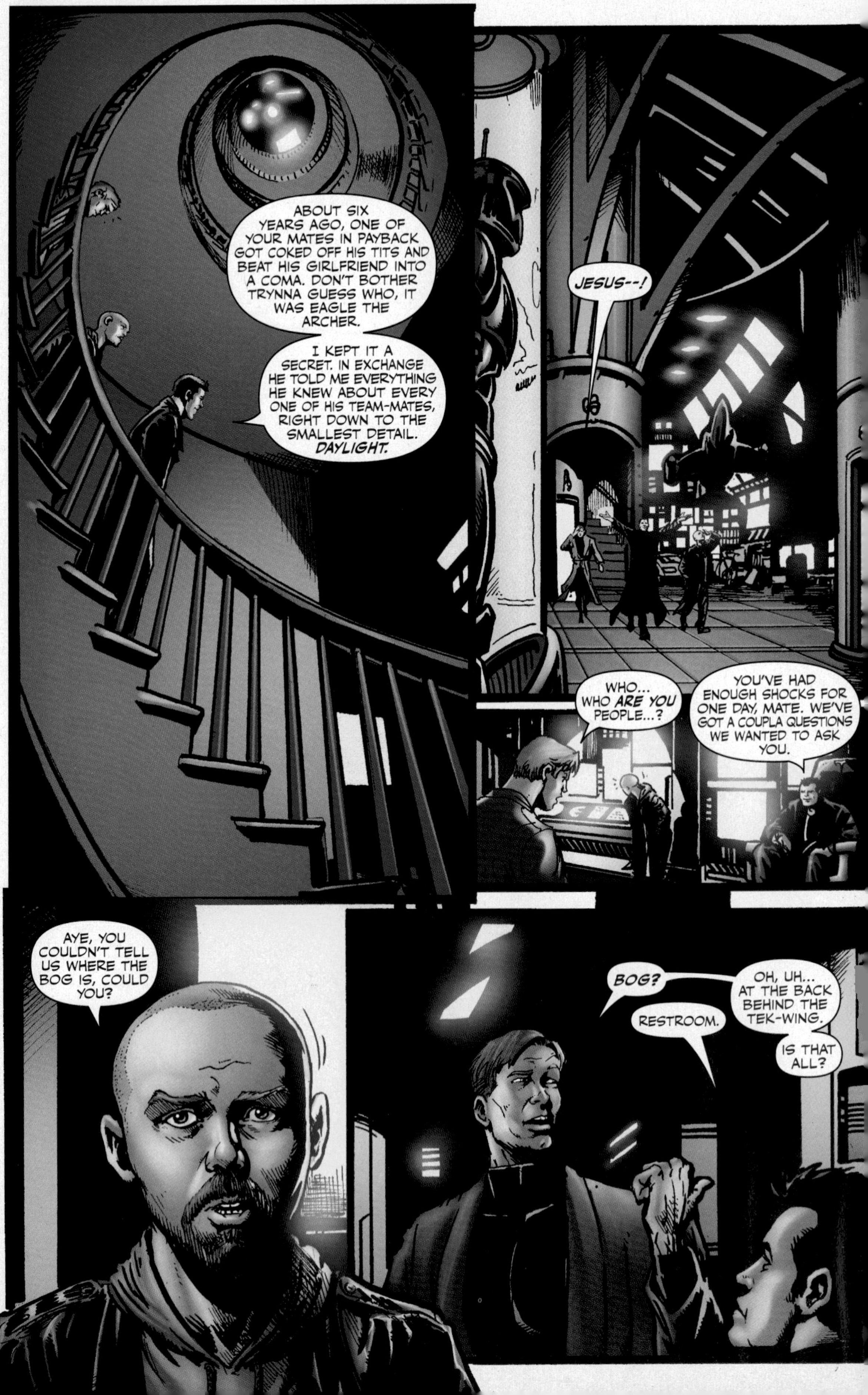
ABOUT SIX YEARS AGO, ONE OF YOUR MATES IN PAYBACK GOT COKED OFF HIS TITS AND BEAT HIS GIRLFRIEND INTO A COMA. DON'T BOTHER TRYNNA GUESS WHO, IT WAS EAGLE THE ARCHER.
I KEPT IT A SECRET. IN EXCHANGE HE TOLD ME EVERYTHING HE KNEW ABOUT EVERY ONE OF HIS TEAM-MATES, RIGHT DOWN TO THE SMALLEST DETAIL. DAYLIGHT.
JESUS--!
WHO... WHO ARE YOU PEOPLE...?
YOU'VE HAD ENOUGH SHOCKS FOR ONE DAY, MATE. WE'VE GOT A COUPLA QUESTIONS WE WANTED TO ASK YOU.
AYE, YOU COULDN'T TELL US WHERE THE BOG IS, COULD YOU?
BOG?
RESTROOM.
OH, UH... AT THE BACK BEHIND THE TEK-WING.
IS THAT ALL?

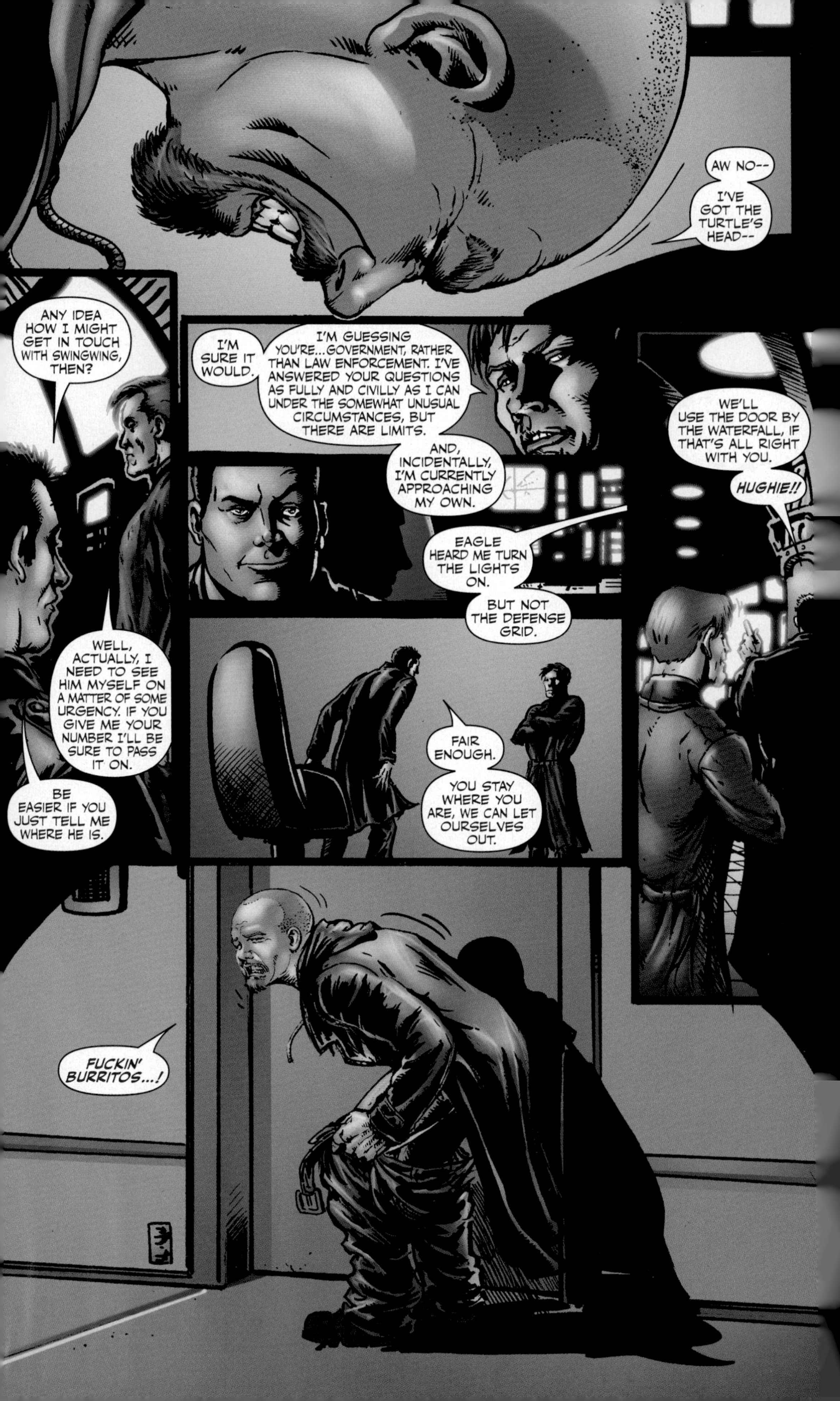
AW NO--
I'VE GOT THE TURTLE'S HEAD--
ANY IDEA HOW I MIGHT GET IN TOUCH WITH SWINGWING, THEN?
I'M SURE IT WOULD.
I'M GUESSING YOU'RE...GOVERNMENT, RATHER THAN LAW ENFORCEMENT. I'VE ANSWERED YOUR QUESTIONS AS FULLY AND CIVILLY AS I CAN UNDER THE SOMEWHAT UNUSUAL CIRCUMSTANCES, BUT THERE ARE LIMITS.
AND, INCIDENTALLY, I'M CURRENTLY APPROACHING MY OWN.
EAGLE HEARD ME TURN THE LIGHTS ON.
BUT NOT THE DEFENSE GRID.
WELL, ACTUALLY, I NEED TO SEE HIM MYSELF ON A MATTER OF SOME URGENCY. IF YOU GIVE ME YOUR NUMBER I'LL BE SURE TO PASS IT ON.
BE EASIER IF YOU JUST TELL ME WHERE HE IS.
FAIR ENOUGH.
YOU STAY WHERE YOU ARE, WE CAN LET OURSELVES OUT.
WE'LL USE THE DOOR BY THE WATERFALL, IF THAT'S ALL RIGHT WITH YOU.
HUGHIE!!
FUCKIN' BURRITOS...!

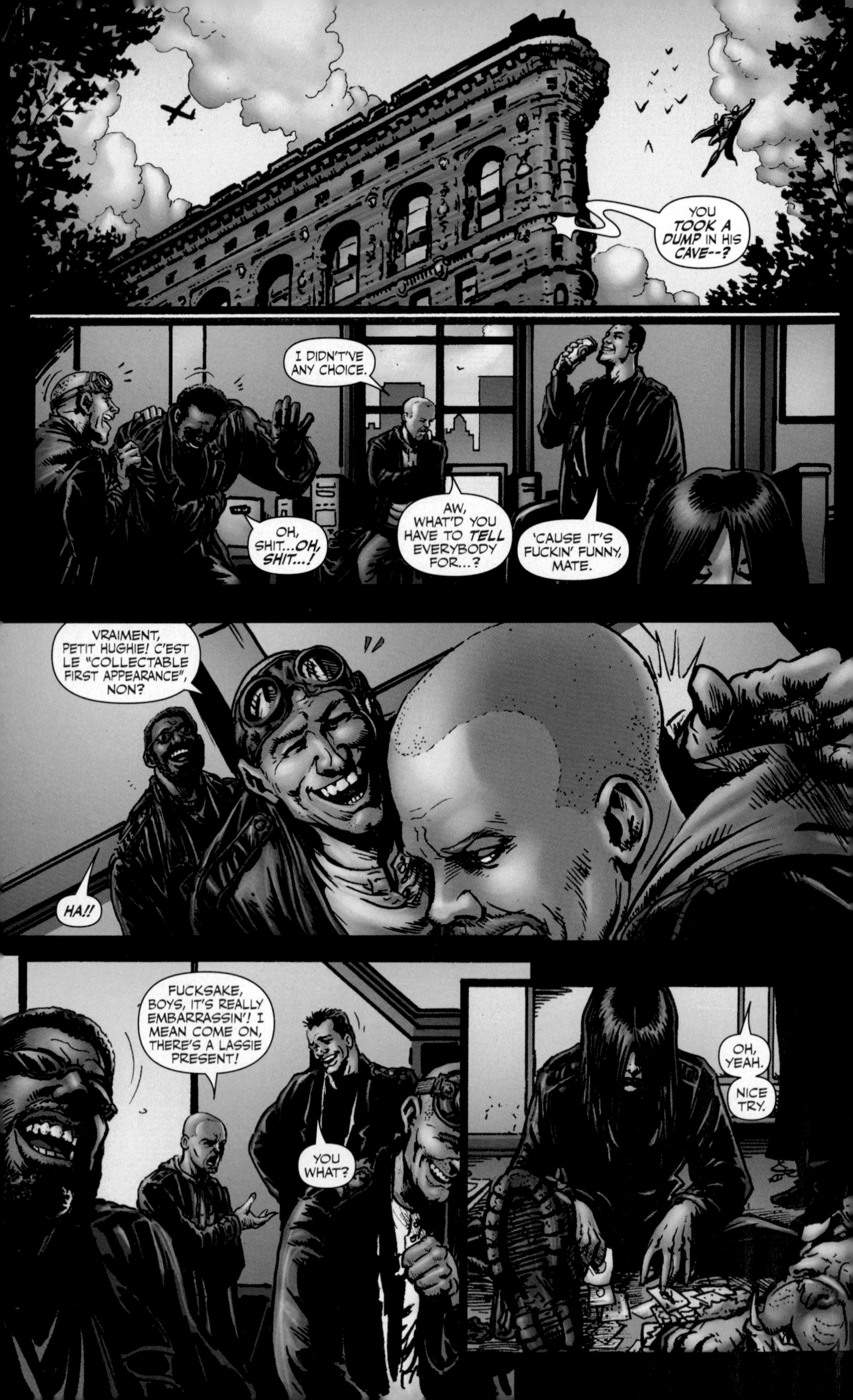
YOU TOOK A DUMP IN HIS CAVE--?
I DIDN'T'VE ANY CHOICE.
OH, SHIT...OH, SHIT...!
AW, WHAT'D YOU HAVE TO TELL EVERYBODY FOR...?
'CAUSE IT'S FUCKIN' FUNNY, MATE.
VRAIMENT, PETIT HUGHIE! C'EST LE "COLLECTABLE FIRST APPEARANCE", NON?
HA!!
FUCKSAKE, BOYS, IT'S REALLY EMBARRASSIN'! I MEAN COME ON, THERE'S A LASSIE PRESENT!
YOU WHAT?
OH, YEAH.
NICE TRY.

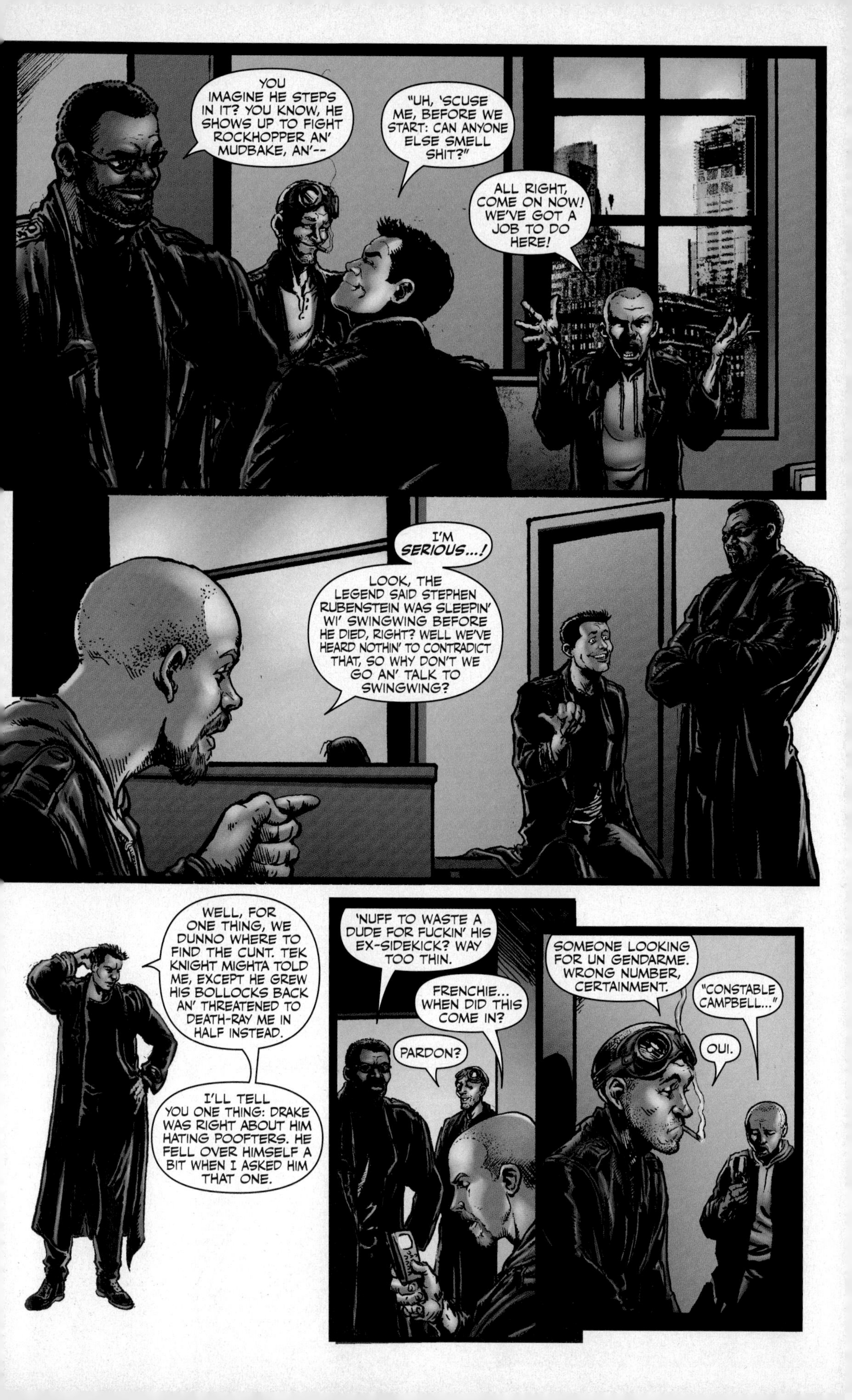
YOU IMAGINE HE STEPS IN IT? YOU KNOW, HE SHOWS UP TO FIGHT ROCKHOPPER AN' MUDBAKE, AN'--
"UH, 'SCUSE ME, BEFORE WE START: CAN ANYONE ELSE SMELL SHIT?"
ALL RIGHT, COME ON NOW! WE'VE GOT A JOB TO DO HERE!
I'M SERIOUS...!
LOOK, THE LEGEND SAID STEPHEN RUBENSTEIN WAS SLEEPIN' WI' SWINGWING BEFORE HE DIED, RIGHT? WELL WE'VE HEARD NOTHIN' TO CONTRADICT THAT, SO WHY DON'T WE GO AN' TALK TO SWINGWING?
WELL, FOR ONE THING, WE DUNNO WHERE TO FIND THE CUNT. TEK KNIGHT MIGHTA TOLD ME, EXCEPT HE GREW HIS BOLLOCKS BACK AN' THREATENED TO DEATH-RAY ME IN HALF INSTEAD.
I'LL TELL YOU ONE THING: DRAKE WAS RIGHT ABOUT HIM HATING POOFTERS. HE FELL OVER HIMSELF A BIT WHEN I ASKED HIM THAT ONE.
'NUFF TO WASTE A DUDE FOR FUCKIN' HIS EX-SIDEKICK? WAY TOO THIN.
FRENCHIE... WHEN DID THIS COME IN?
PARDON?
SOMEONE LOOKING FOR UN GENDARME. WRONG NUMBER, CERTAINMENT.
"CONSTABLE CAMPBELL..."
OUI.

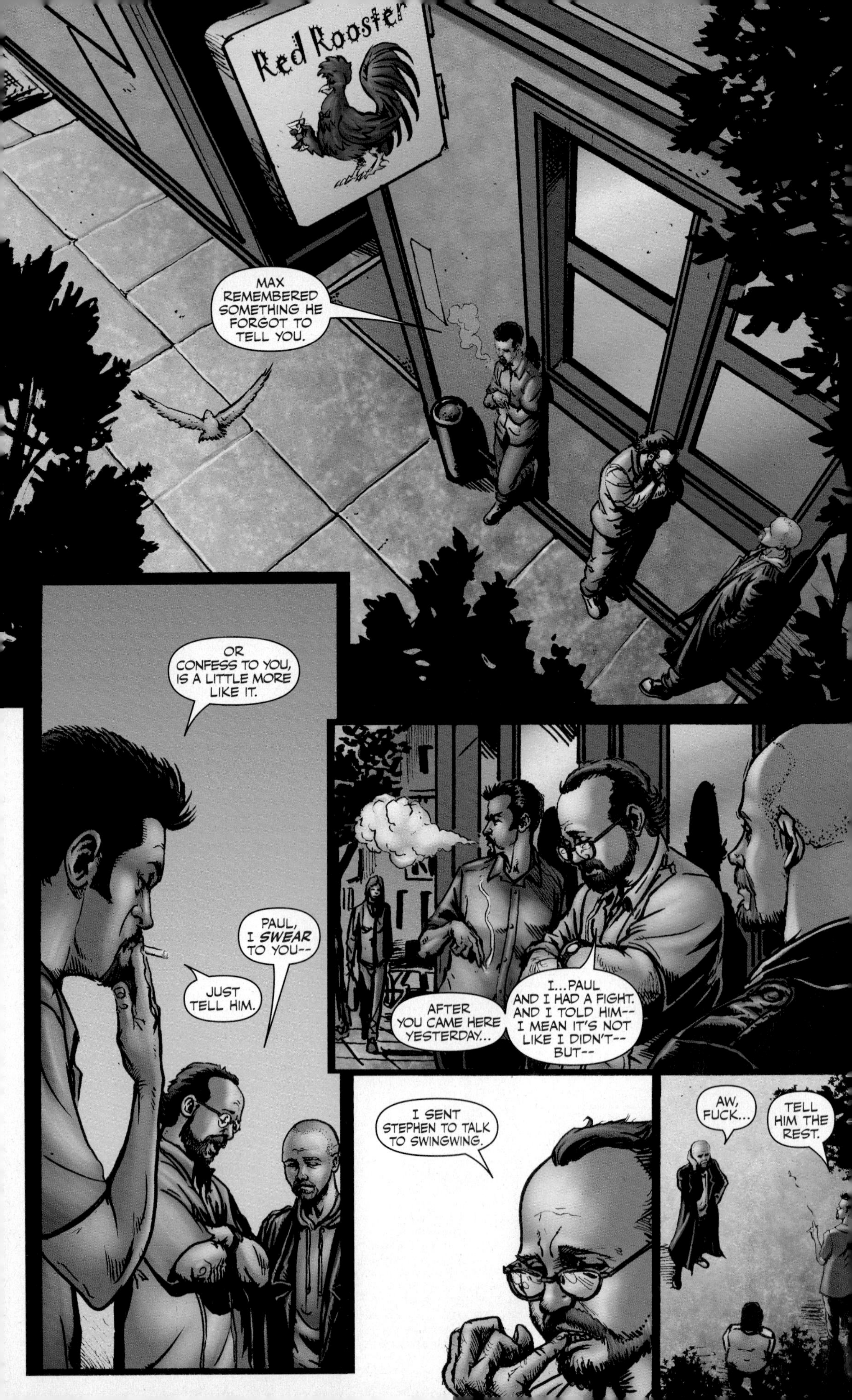
Red Rooster
MAX REMEMBERED SOMETHING HE FORGOT TO TELL YOU.
OR CONFESS TO YOU, IS A LITTLE MORE LIKE IT.
PAUL, I SWEAR TO YOU--
JUST TELL HIM.
AFTER YOU CAME HERE YESTERDAY...
I...PAUL AND I HAD A FIGHT. AND I TOLD HIM-- I MEAN IT'S NOT LIKE I DIDN'T-- BUT--
I SENT STEPHEN TO TALK TO SWINGWING.
AW, FUCK...
TELL HIM THE REST.

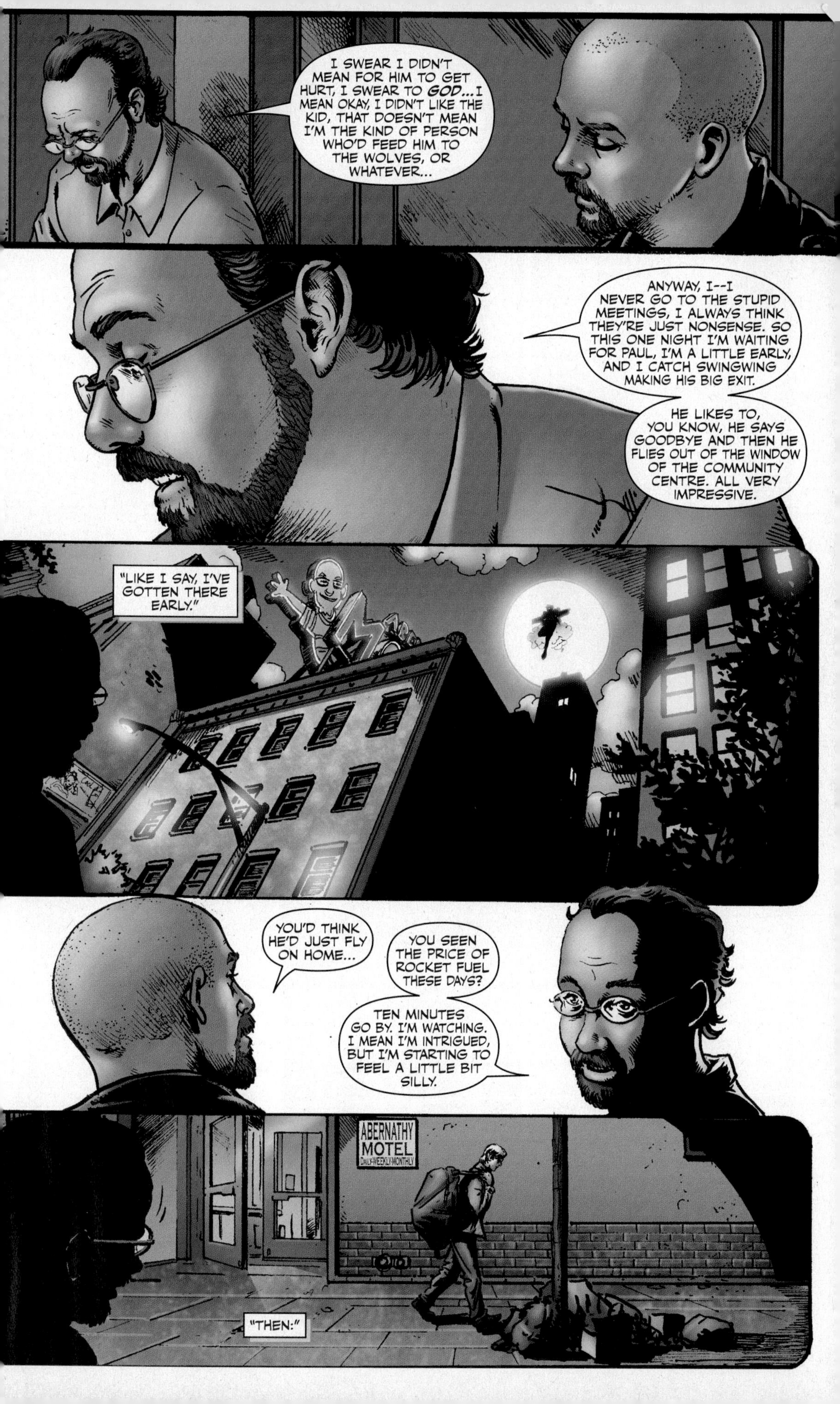
I SWEAR I DIDN'T MEAN FOR HIM TO GET HURT, I SWEAR TO *GOD*... I MEAN OKAY, I DIDN'T LIKE THE KID, THAT DOESN'T MEAN I'M THE KIND OF PERSON WHO'D FEED HIM TO THE WOLVES, OR WHATEVER...
ANYWAY, I--I NEVER GO TO THE STUPID MEETINGS, I ALWAYS THINK THEY'RE JUST NONSENSE. SO THIS ONE NIGHT I'M WAITING FOR PAUL, I'M A LITTLE EARLY, AND I CATCH SWINGWING MAKING HIS BIG EXIT.
HE LIKES TO, YOU KNOW, HE SAYS GOODBYE AND THEN HE FLIES OUT OF THE WINDOW OF THE COMMUNITY CENTRE. ALL VERY IMPRESSIVE.
"LIKE I SAY, I'VE GOTTEN THERE EARLY."
YOU'D THINK HE'D JUST FLY ON HOME...
YOU SEEN THE PRICE OF ROCKET FUEL THESE DAYS?
TEN MINUTES GO BY. I'M WATCHING. I MEAN I'M INTRIGUED, BUT I'M STARTING TO FEEL A LITTLE BIT SILLY.
ABERNATHY MOTEL
DAILY-WEEKLY-MONTHLY
"THEN:"

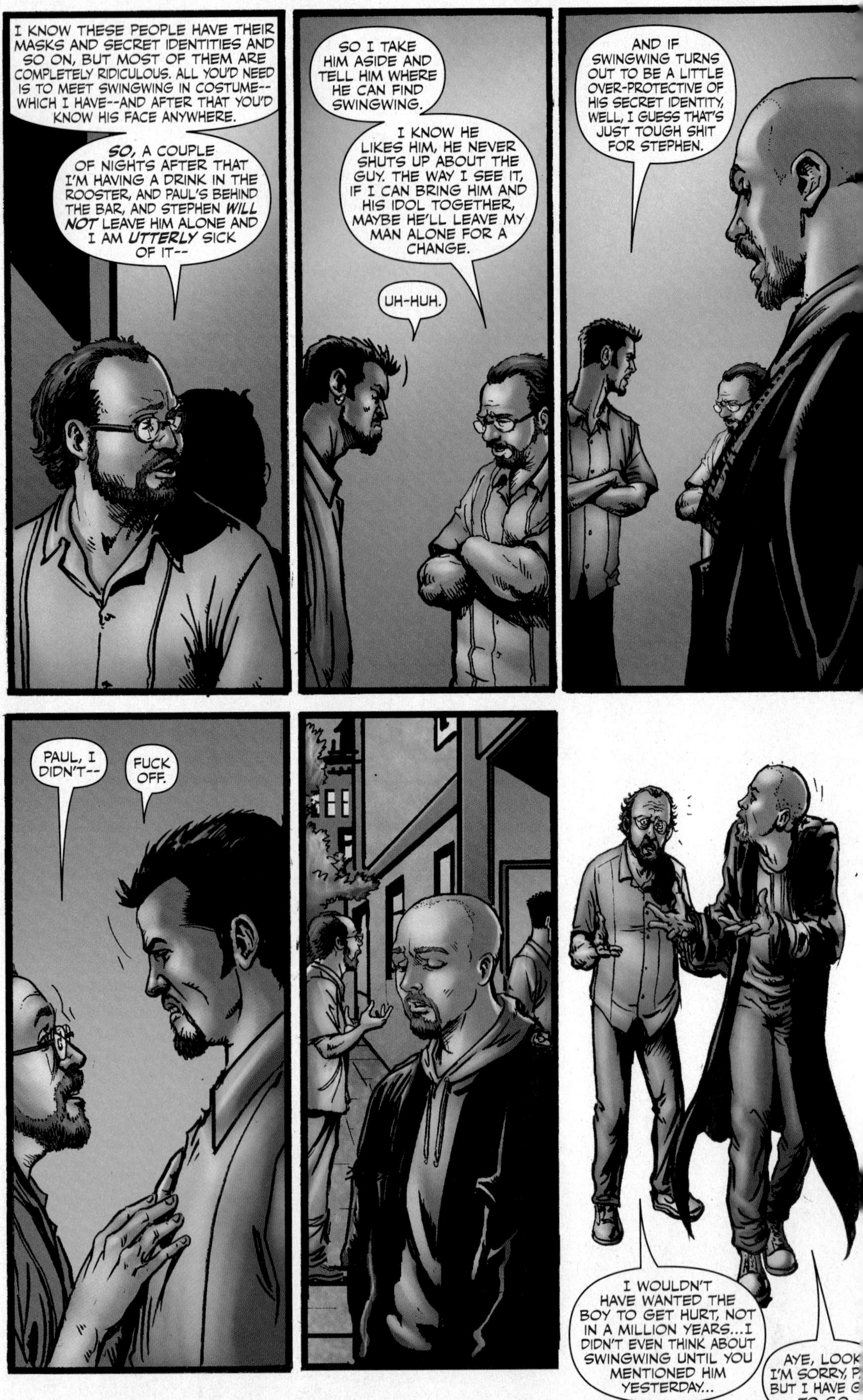

I KNOW THESE PEOPLE HAVE THEIR MASKS AND SECRET IDENTITIES AND SO ON, BUT MOST OF THEM ARE COMPLETELY RIDICULOUS. ALL YOU'D NEED IS TO MEET SWINGWING IN COSTUME--WHICH I HAVE--AND AFTER THAT YOU'D KNOW HIS FACE ANYWHERE.
SO, A COUPLE OF NIGHTS AFTER THAT I'M HAVING A DRINK IN THE ROOSTER, AND PAUL'S BEHIND THE BAR, AND STEPHEN WILL NOT LEAVE HIM ALONE AND I AM UTTERLY SICK OF IT--
SO I TAKE HIM ASIDE AND TELL HIM WHERE HE CAN FIND SWINGWING.
I KNOW HE LIKES HIM, HE NEVER SHUTS UP ABOUT THE GUY. THE WAY I SEE IT, IF I CAN BRING HIM AND HIS IDOL TOGETHER, MAYBE HE'LL LEAVE MY MAN ALONE FOR A CHANGE.
UH-HUH.
AND IF SWINGWING TURNS OUT TO BE A LITTLE OVER-PROTECTIVE OF HIS SECRET IDENTITY, WELL, I GUESS THAT'S JUST TOUGH SHIT FOR STEPHEN.
PAUL, I DIDN'T--
FUCK OFF.
I WOULDN'T HAVE WANTED THE BOY TO GET HURT, NOT IN A MILLION YEARS...I DIDN'T EVEN THINK ABOUT SWINGWING UNTIL YOU MENTIONED HIM YESTERDAY...
AYE, LOOK I'M SORRY, BUT I HAVE TO GO.

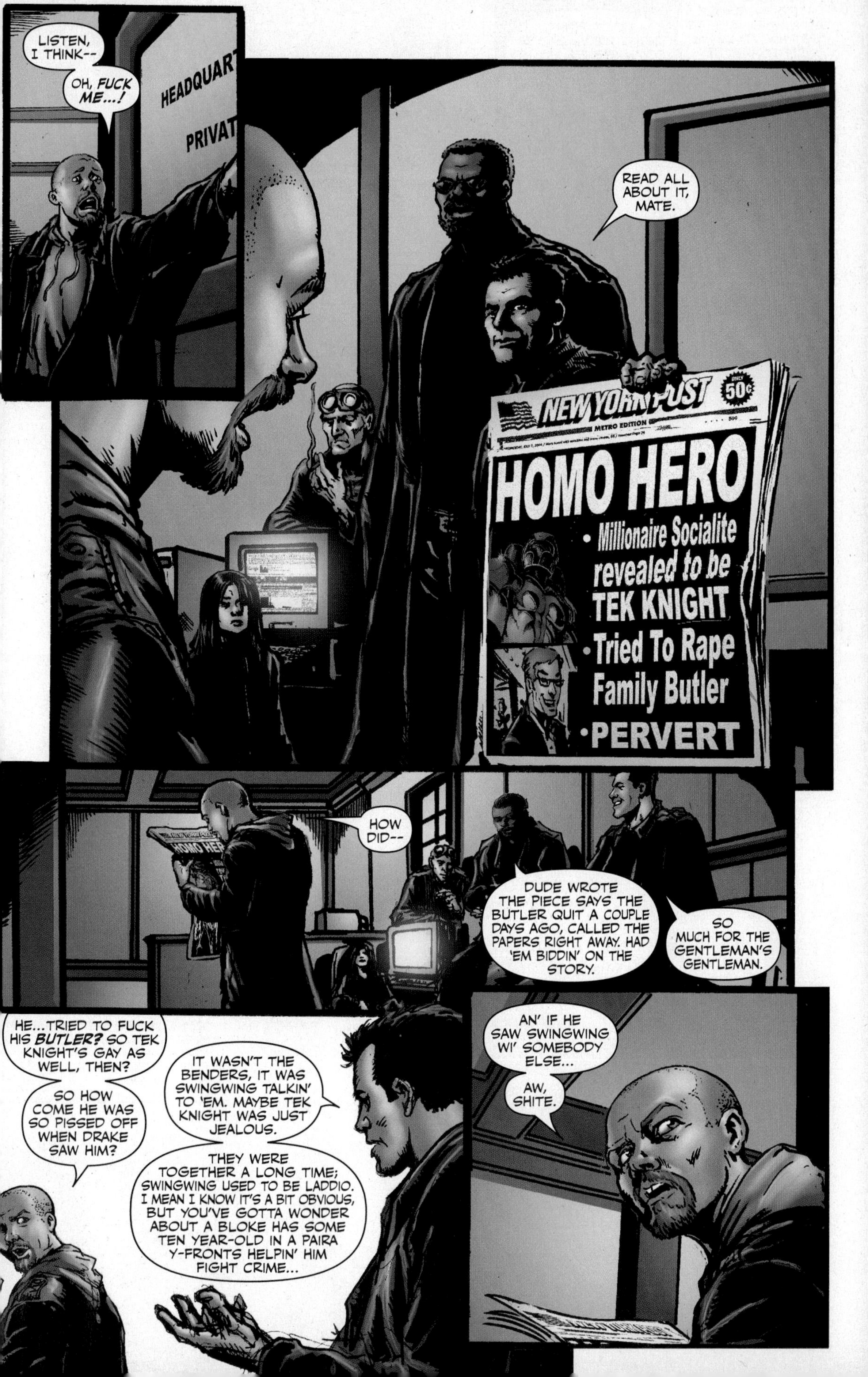

LISTEN, I THINK--
OH, FUCK ME...!
HEADQUART
PRIVAT
READ ALL ABOUT IT, MATE.
NEW YORK POST
ONLY 50¢
METRO EDITION
HOMO HERO
• Millionaire Socialite revealed to be TEK KNIGHT
• Tried To Rape Family Butler
• PERVERT
HOW DID--
DUDE WROTE THE PIECE SAYS THE BUTLER QUIT A COUPLE DAYS AGO, CALLED THE PAPERS RIGHT AWAY. HAD 'EM BIDDIN' ON THE STORY.
SO MUCH FOR THE GENTLEMAN'S GENTLEMAN.
HE...TRIED TO FUCK HIS BUTLER? SO TEK KNIGHT'S GAY AS WELL, THEN?
SO HOW COME HE WAS SO PISSED OFF WHEN DRAKE SAW HIM?
IT WASN'T THE BENDERS, IT WAS SWINGWING TALKIN' TO 'EM. MAYBE TEK KNIGHT WAS JUST JEALOUS.
THEY WERE TOGETHER A LONG TIME; SWINGWING USED TO BE LADDIO. I MEAN I KNOW IT'S A BIT OBVIOUS, BUT YOU'VE GOTTA WONDER ABOUT A BLOKE HAS SOME TEN YEAR-OLD IN A PAIRA Y-FRONTS HELPIN' HIM FIGHT CRIME...
AN' IF HE SAW SWINGWING WI' SOMEBODY ELSE...
AW, SHITE.

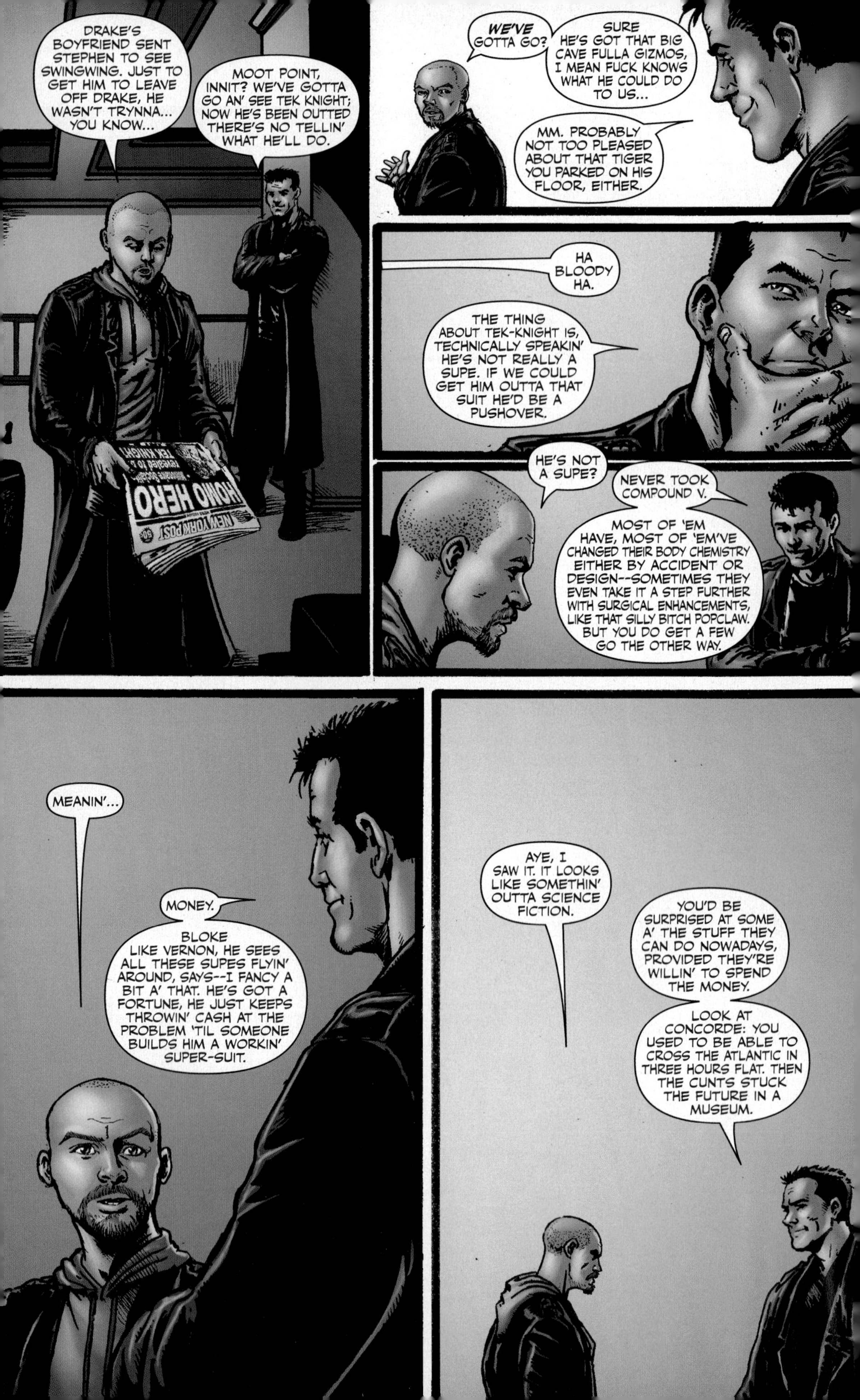
DRAKE'S BOYFRIEND SENT STEPHEN TO SEE SWINGWING. JUST TO GET HIM TO LEAVE OFF DRAKE, HE WASN'T TRYNNA... YOU KNOW...
MOOT POINT, INNIT? WE'VE GOTTA GO AN' SEE TEK KNIGHT; NOW HE'S BEEN OUTTED THERE'S NO TELLIN' WHAT HE'LL DO.
NEW YORK POST
HOMO HERO!
TEK KNIGHT
WE'VE GOTTA GO?
SURE HE'S GOT THAT BIG CAVE FULLA GIZMOS, I MEAN FUCK KNOWS WHAT HE COULD DO TO US...
MM. PROBABLY NOT TOO PLEASED ABOUT THAT TIGER YOU PARKED ON HIS FLOOR, EITHER.
HA BLOODY HA.
THE THING ABOUT TEK-KNIGHT IS, TECHNICALLY SPEAKIN' HE'S NOT REALLY A SUPE. IF WE COULD GET HIM OUTTA THAT SUIT HE'D BE A PUSHOVER.
HE'S NOT A SUPE?
NEVER TOOK COMPOUND V.
MOST OF 'EM HAVE, MOST OF 'EM'VE CHANGED THEIR BODY CHEMISTRY EITHER BY ACCIDENT OR DESIGN--SOMETIMES THEY EVEN TAKE IT A STEP FURTHER WITH SURGICAL ENHANCEMENTS, LIKE THAT SILLY BITCH POPCLAW. BUT YOU DO GET A FEW GO THE OTHER WAY.
MEANIN'...
MONEY.
BLOKE LIKE VERNON, HE SEES ALL THESE SUPES FLYIN' AROUND, SAYS--I FANCY A BIT A' THAT. HE'S GOT A FORTUNE, HE JUST KEEPS THROWIN' CASH AT THE PROBLEM 'TIL SOMEONE BUILDS HIM A WORKIN' SUPER-SUIT.
AYE, I SAW IT. IT LOOKS LIKE SOMETHIN' OUTTA SCIENCE FICTION.
YOU'D BE SURPRISED AT SOME A' THE STUFF THEY CAN DO NOWADAYS, PROVIDED THEY'RE WILLIN' TO SPEND THE MONEY.
LOOK AT CONCORDE: YOU USED TO BE ABLE TO CROSS THE ATLANTIC IN THREE HOURS FLAT. THEN THE CUNTS STUCK THE FUTURE IN A MUSEUM.

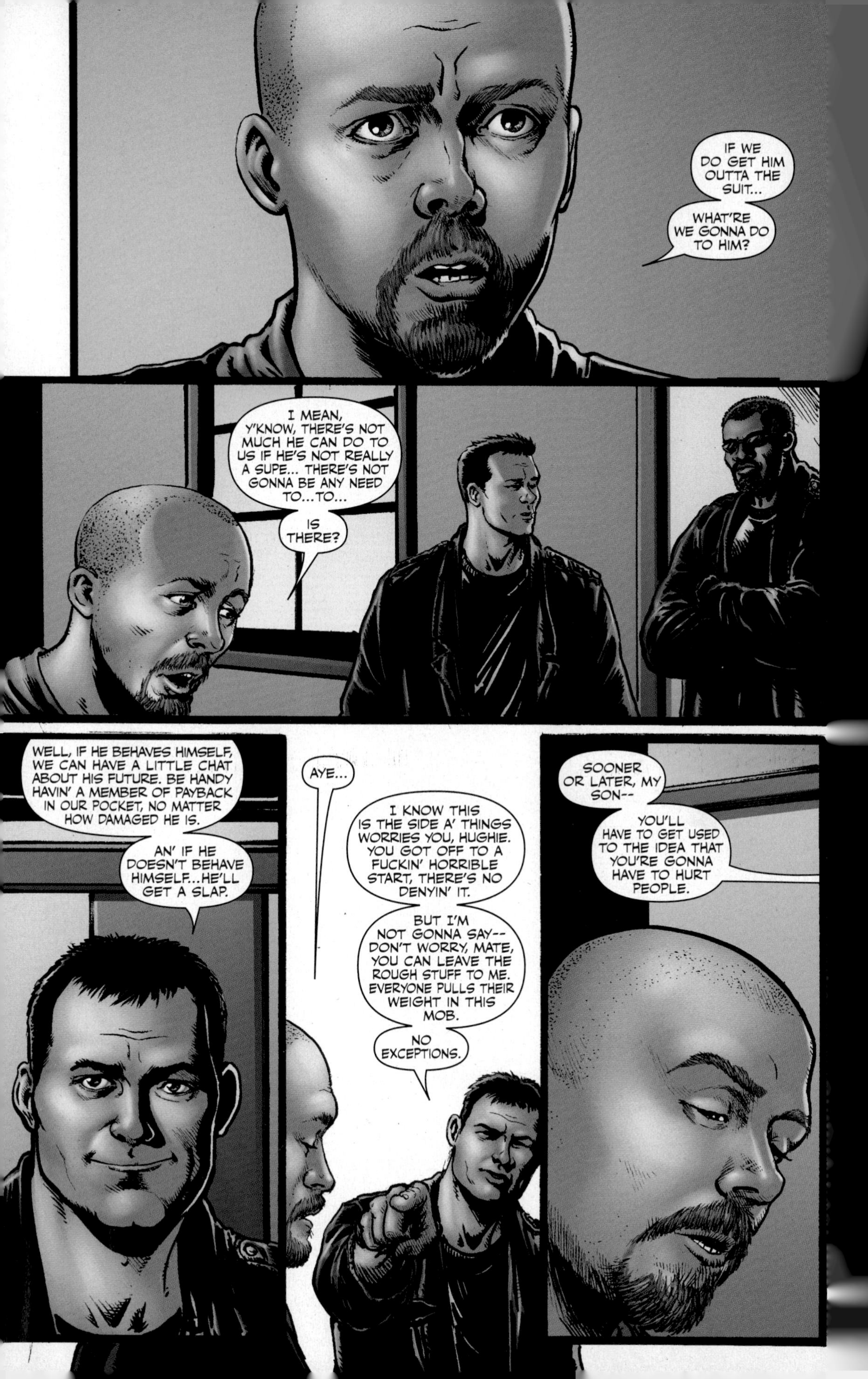
IF WE DO GET HIM OUTTA THE SUIT...
WHAT'RE WE GONNA DO TO HIM?
I MEAN, Y'KNOW, THERE'S NOT MUCH HE CAN DO TO US IF HE'S NOT REALLY A SUPE... THERE'S NOT GONNA BE ANY NEED TO...TO...
IS THERE?
WELL, IF HE BEHAVES HIMSELF, WE CAN HAVE A LITTLE CHAT ABOUT HIS FUTURE. BE HANDY HAVIN' A MEMBER OF PAYBACK IN OUR POCKET, NO MATTER HOW DAMAGED HE IS.
AN' IF HE DOESN'T BEHAVE HIMSELF...HE'LL GET A SLAP.
AYE...
I KNOW THIS IS THE SIDE A' THINGS WORRIES YOU, HUGHIE. YOU GOT OFF TO A FUCKIN' HORRIBLE START, THERE'S NO DENYIN' IT.
BUT I'M NOT GONNA SAY-- DON'T WORRY, MATE, YOU CAN LEAVE THE ROUGH STUFF TO ME. EVERYONE PULLS THEIR WEIGHT IN THIS MOB.
NO EXCEPTIONS.
SOONER OR LATER, MY SON--
YOU'LL HAVE TO GET USED TO THE IDEA THAT YOU'RE GONNA HAVE TO HURT PEOPLE.

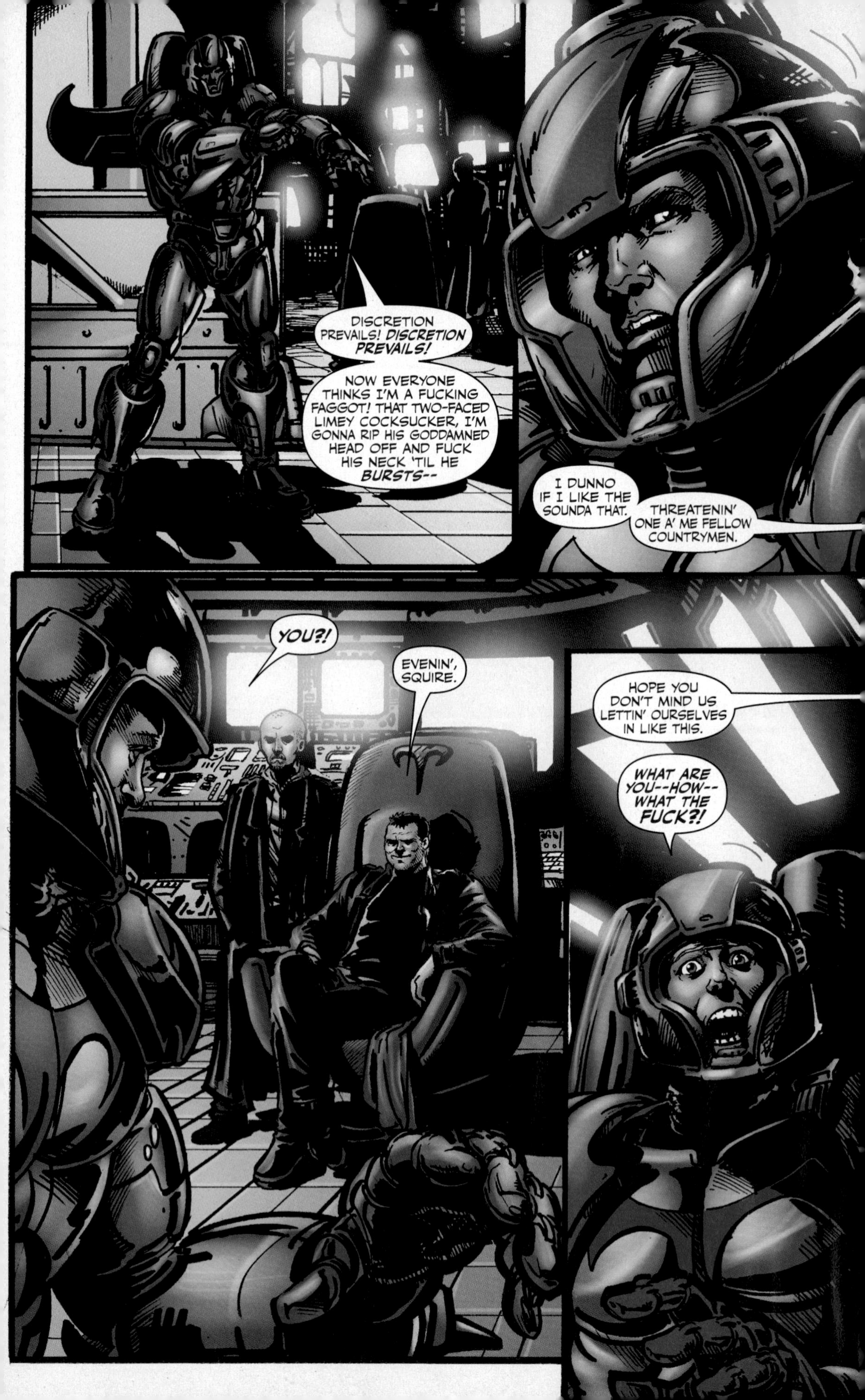
DISCRETION PREVAILS! DISCRETION PREVAILS!
NOW EVERYONE THINKS I'M A FUCKING FAGGOT! THAT TWO-FACED LIMEY COCKSUCKER, I'M GONNA RIP HIS GODDAMNED HEAD OFF AND FUCK HIS NECK 'TIL HE BURSTS--
I DUNNO IF I LIKE THE SOUNDA THAT.
THREATENIN' ONE A' ME FELLOW COUNTRYMEN.
YOU?!
EVENIN', SQUIRE.
HOPE YOU DON'T MIND US LETTIN' OURSELVES IN LIKE THIS.
WHAT ARE YOU--HOW--WHAT THE FUCK?!

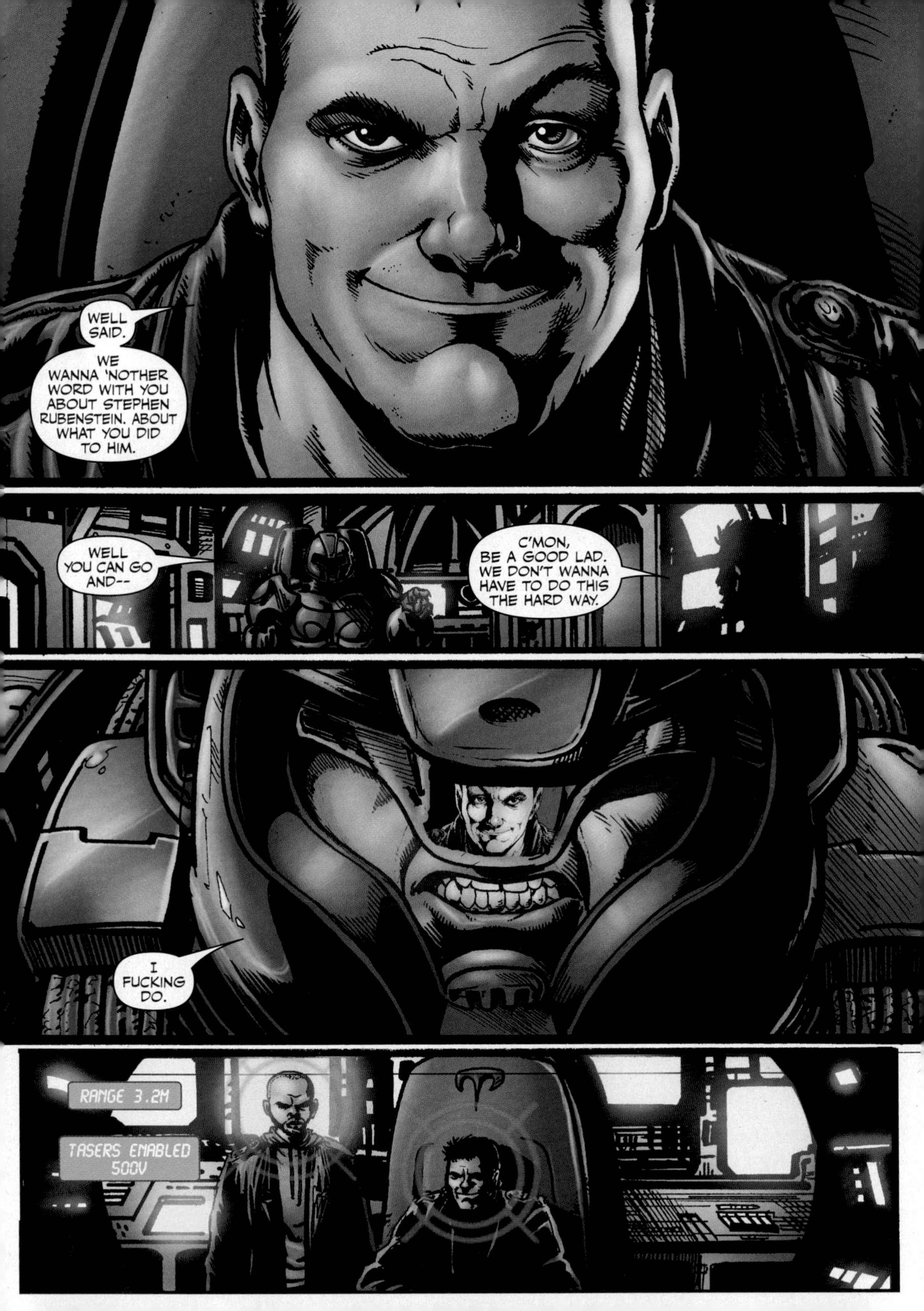
WELL SAID.
WE WANNA 'NOTHER WORD WITH YOU ABOUT STEPHEN RUBENSTEIN. ABOUT WHAT YOU DID TO HIM.
WELL YOU CAN GO AND--
C'MON, BE A GOOD LAD. WE DON'T WANNA HAVE TO DO THIS THE HARD WAY.
I FUCKING DO.
RANGE 3.2M
TASERS ENABLED 500V

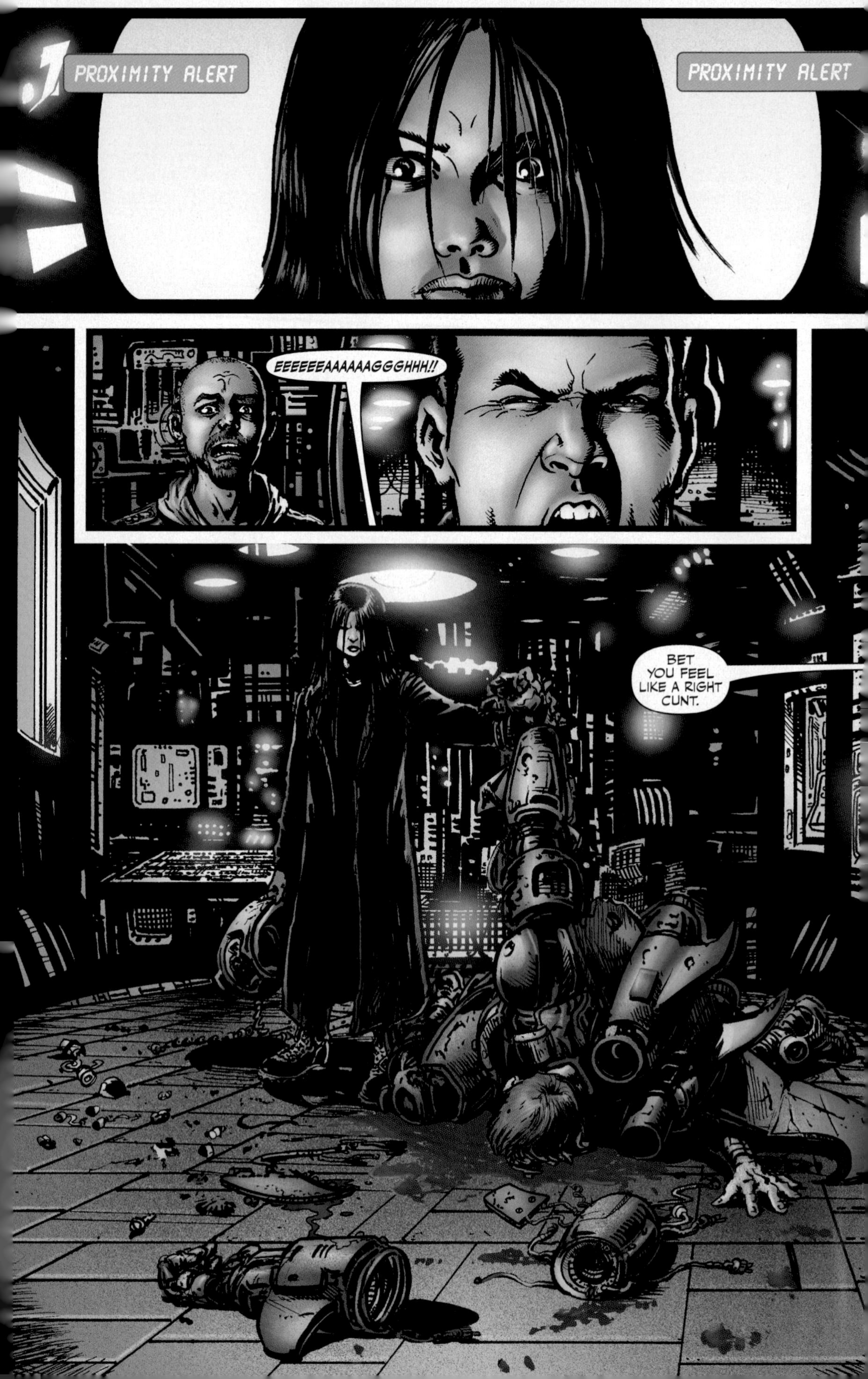
PROXIMITY ALERT
PROXIMITY ALERT
EEEEEEAAAAAAGGGHHH!!
BET YOU FEEL LIKE A RIGHT CUNT.

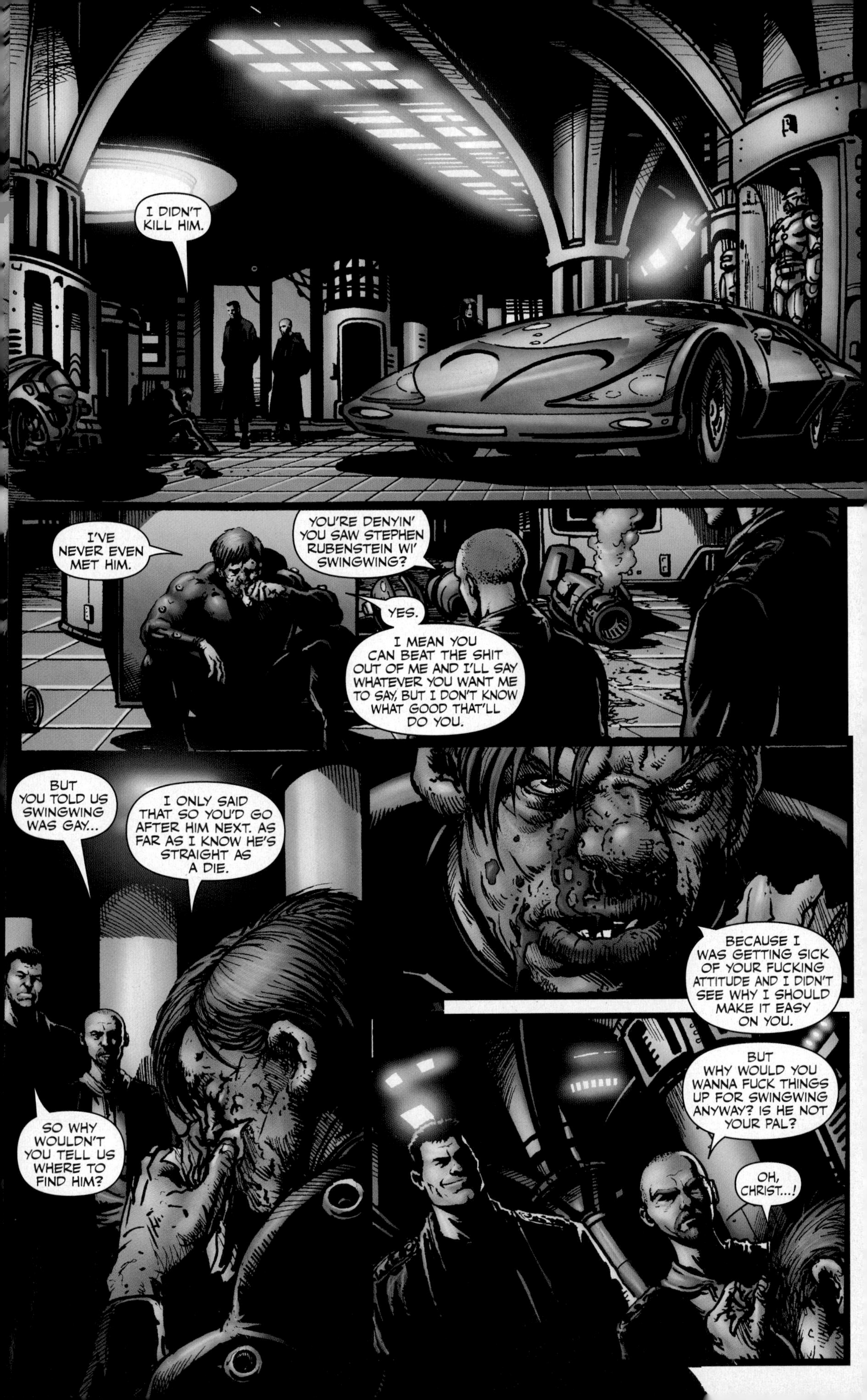
I DIDN'T KILL HIM.
I'VE NEVER EVEN MET HIM.
YOU'RE DENYIN' YOU SAW STEPHEN RUBENSTEIN WI' SWINGWING?
YES.
I MEAN YOU CAN BEAT THE SHIT OUT OF ME AND I'LL SAY WHATEVER YOU WANT ME TO SAY, BUT I DON'T KNOW WHAT GOOD THAT'LL DO YOU.
BUT YOU TOLD US SWINGWING WAS GAY...
I ONLY SAID THAT SO YOU'D GO AFTER HIM NEXT. AS FAR AS I KNOW HE'S STRAIGHT AS A DIE.
SO WHY WOULDN'T YOU TELL US WHERE TO FIND HIM?
BECAUSE I WAS GETTING SICK OF YOUR FUCKING ATTITUDE AND I DIDN'T SEE WHY I SHOULD MAKE IT EASY ON YOU.
BUT WHY WOULD YOU WANNA FUCK THINGS UP FOR SWINGWING ANYWAY? IS HE NOT YOUR PAL?
OH, CHRIST...!

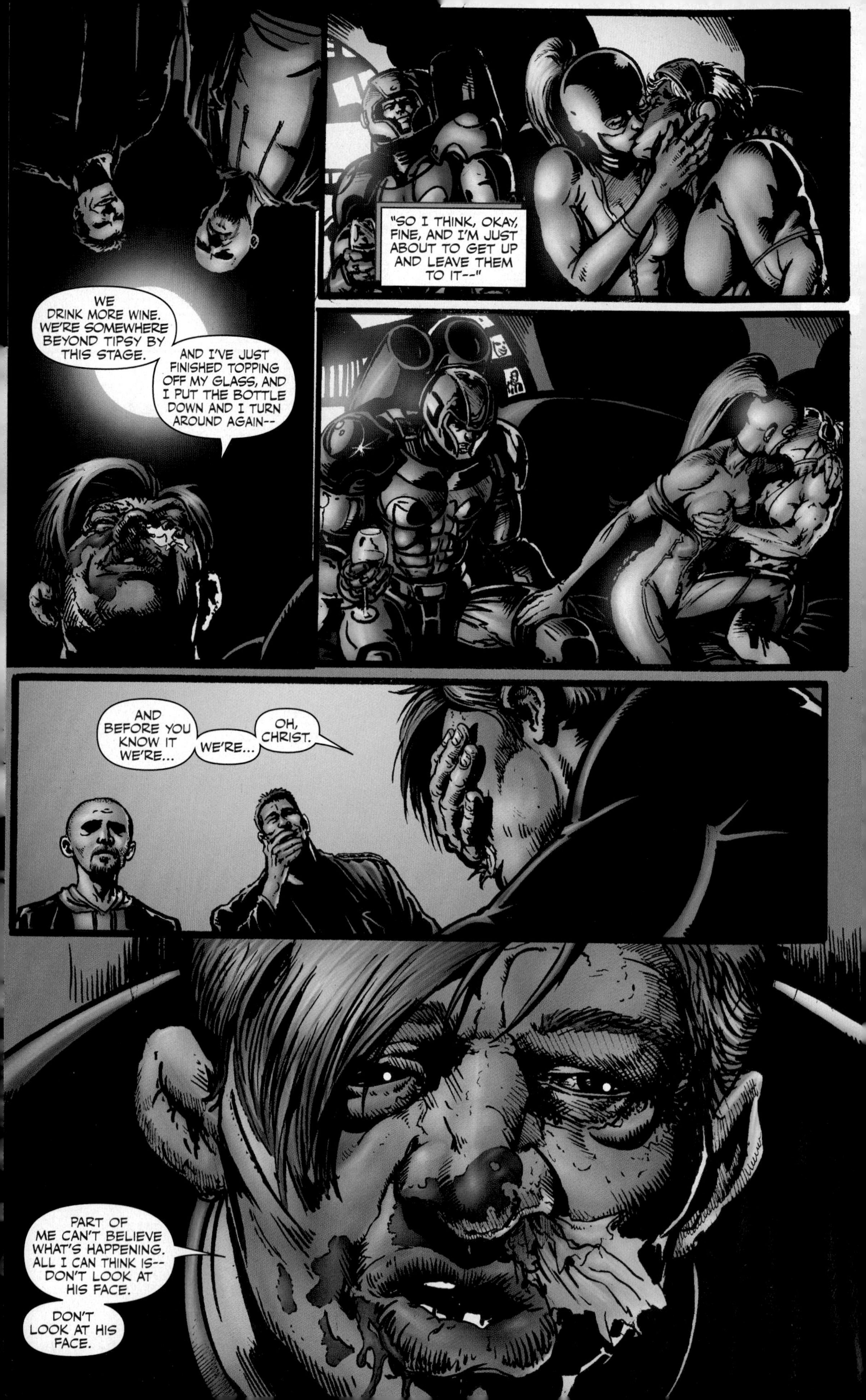
"SO I THINK, OKAY, FINE, AND I'M JUST ABOUT TO GET UP AND LEAVE THEM TO IT--"
WE DRINK MORE WINE. WE'RE SOMEWHERE BEYOND TIPSY BY THIS STAGE.
AND I'VE JUST FINISHED TOPPING OFF MY GLASS, AND I PUT THE BOTTLE DOWN AND I TURN AROUND AGAIN--
AND BEFORE YOU KNOW IT WE'RE...
WE'RE...
OH, CHRIST.
PART OF ME CAN'T BELIEVE WHAT'S HAPPENING. ALL I CAN THINK IS-- DON'T LOOK AT HIS FACE.
DON'T LOOK AT HIS FACE.

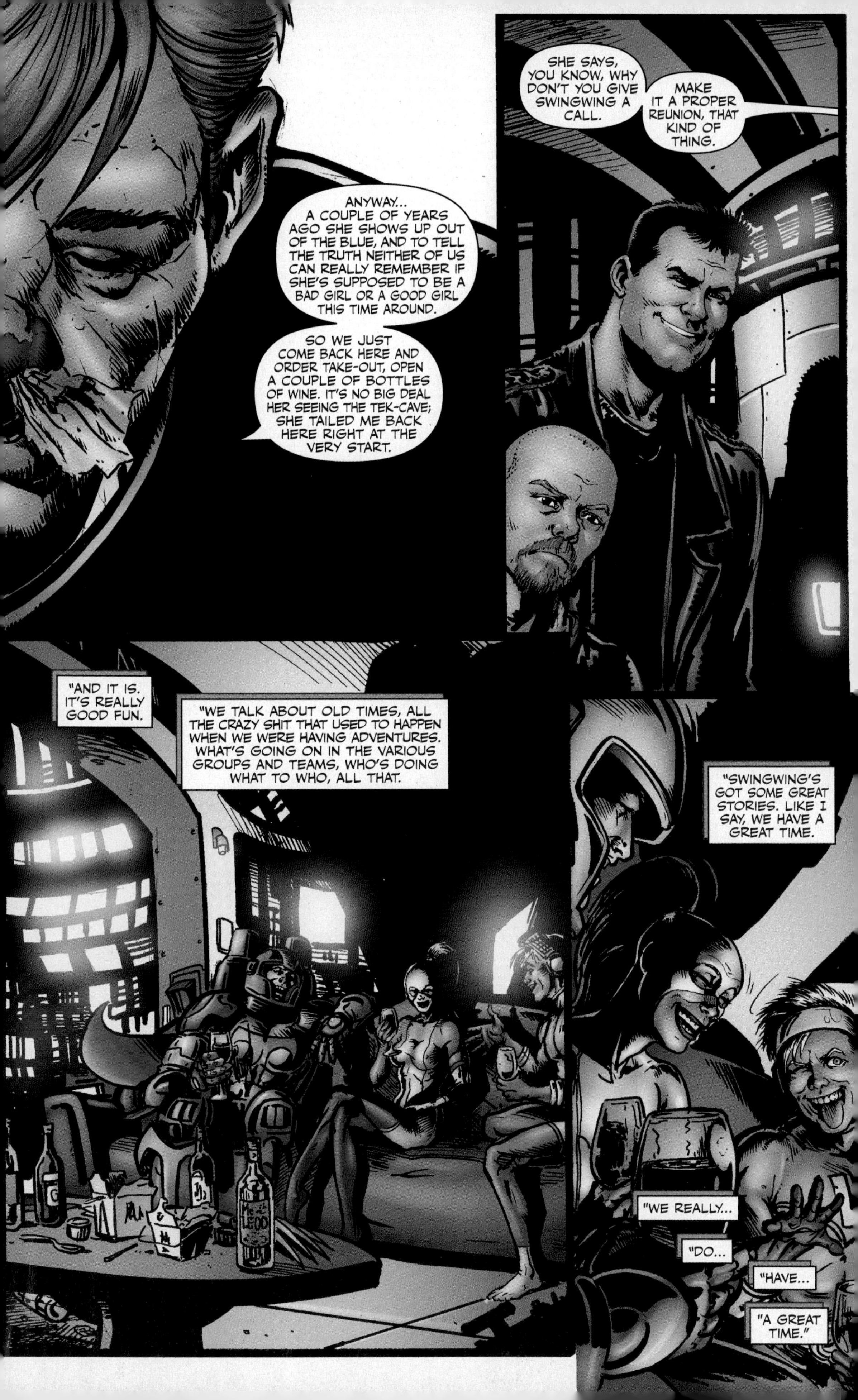
ANYWAY... A COUPLE OF YEARS AGO SHE SHOWS UP OUT OF THE BLUE, AND TO TELL THE TRUTH NEITHER OF US CAN REALLY REMEMBER IF SHE'S SUPPOSED TO BE A BAD GIRL OR A GOOD GIRL THIS TIME AROUND.
SO WE JUST COME BACK HERE AND ORDER TAKE-OUT, OPEN A COUPLE OF BOTTLES OF WINE. IT'S NO BIG DEAL HER SEEING THE TEK-CAVE; SHE TAILED ME BACK HERE RIGHT AT THE VERY START.
SHE SAYS, YOU KNOW, WHY DON'T YOU GIVE SWINGWING A CALL.
MAKE IT A PROPER REUNION, THAT KIND OF THING.
"AND IT IS. IT'S REALLY GOOD FUN.
"WE TALK ABOUT OLD TIMES, ALL THE CRAZY SHIT THAT USED TO HAPPEN WHEN WE WERE HAVING ADVENTURES. WHAT'S GOING ON IN THE VARIOUS GROUPS AND TEAMS, WHO'S DOING WHAT TO WHO, ALL THAT.
"SWINGWING'S GOT SOME GREAT STORIES. LIKE I SAY, WE HAVE A GREAT TIME.
"WE REALLY...
"DO...
"HAVE...
"A GREAT TIME."

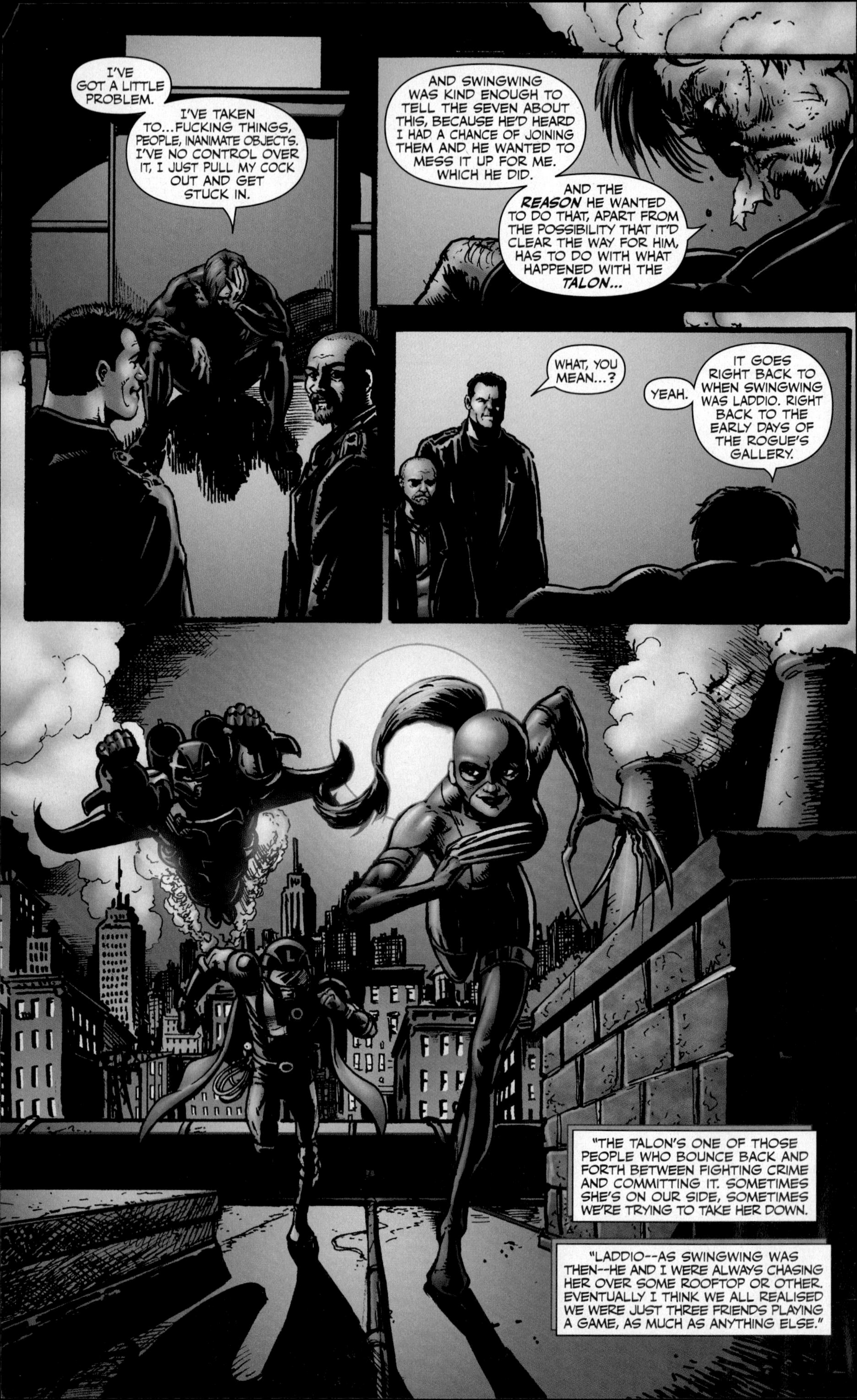
I'VE GOT A LITTLE PROBLEM.
I'VE TAKEN TO...FUCKING THINGS, PEOPLE, INANIMATE OBJECTS. I'VE NO CONTROL OVER IT, I JUST PULL MY COCK OUT AND GET STUCK IN.
AND SWINGWING WAS KIND ENOUGH TO TELL THE SEVEN ABOUT THIS, BECAUSE HE'D HEARD I HAD A CHANCE OF JOINING THEM AND HE WANTED TO MESS IT UP FOR ME. WHICH HE DID.
AND THE REASON HE WANTED TO DO THAT, APART FROM THE POSSIBILITY THAT IT'D CLEAR THE WAY FOR HIM, HAS TO DO WITH WHAT HAPPENED WITH THE TALON...
WHAT, YOU MEAN...?
YEAH.
IT GOES RIGHT BACK TO WHEN SWINGWING WAS LADDIO. RIGHT BACK TO THE EARLY DAYS OF THE ROGUE'S GALLERY.
"THE TALON'S ONE OF THOSE PEOPLE WHO BOUNCE BACK AND FORTH BETWEEN FIGHTING CRIME AND COMMITTING IT. SOMETIMES SHE'S ON OUR SIDE, SOMETIMES WE'RE TRYING TO TAKE HER DOWN.
"LADDIO--AS SWINGWING WAS THEN--HE AND I WERE ALWAYS CHASING HER OVER SOME ROOFTOP OR OTHER. EVENTUALLY I THINK WE ALL REALISED WE WERE JUST THREE FRIENDS PLAYING A GAME, AS MUCH AS ANYTHING ELSE."

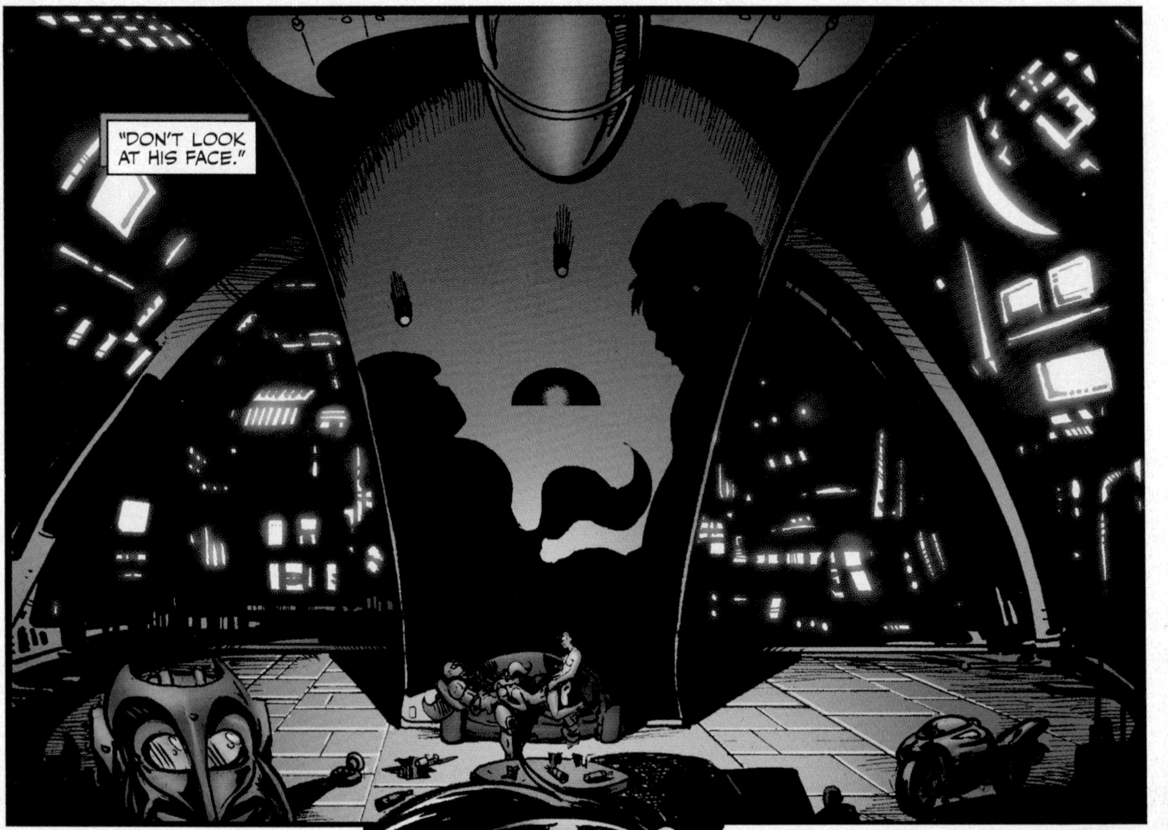
"DON'T LOOK AT HIS FACE."

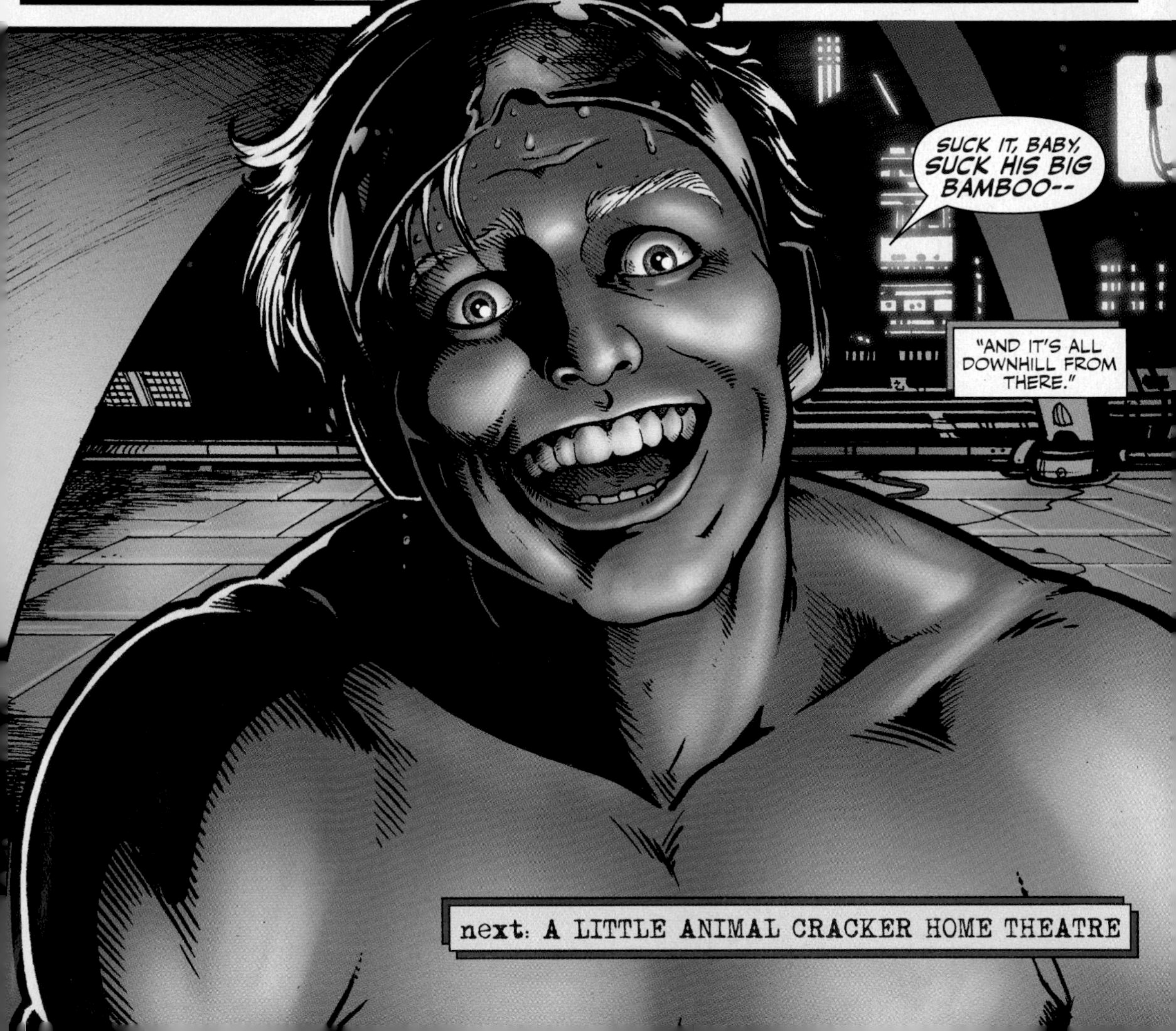
SUCK IT, BABY, SUCK HIS BIG BAMBOO--
"AND IT'S ALL DOWNHILL FROM THERE."
next: A LITTLE ANIMAL CRACKER HOME THEATRE

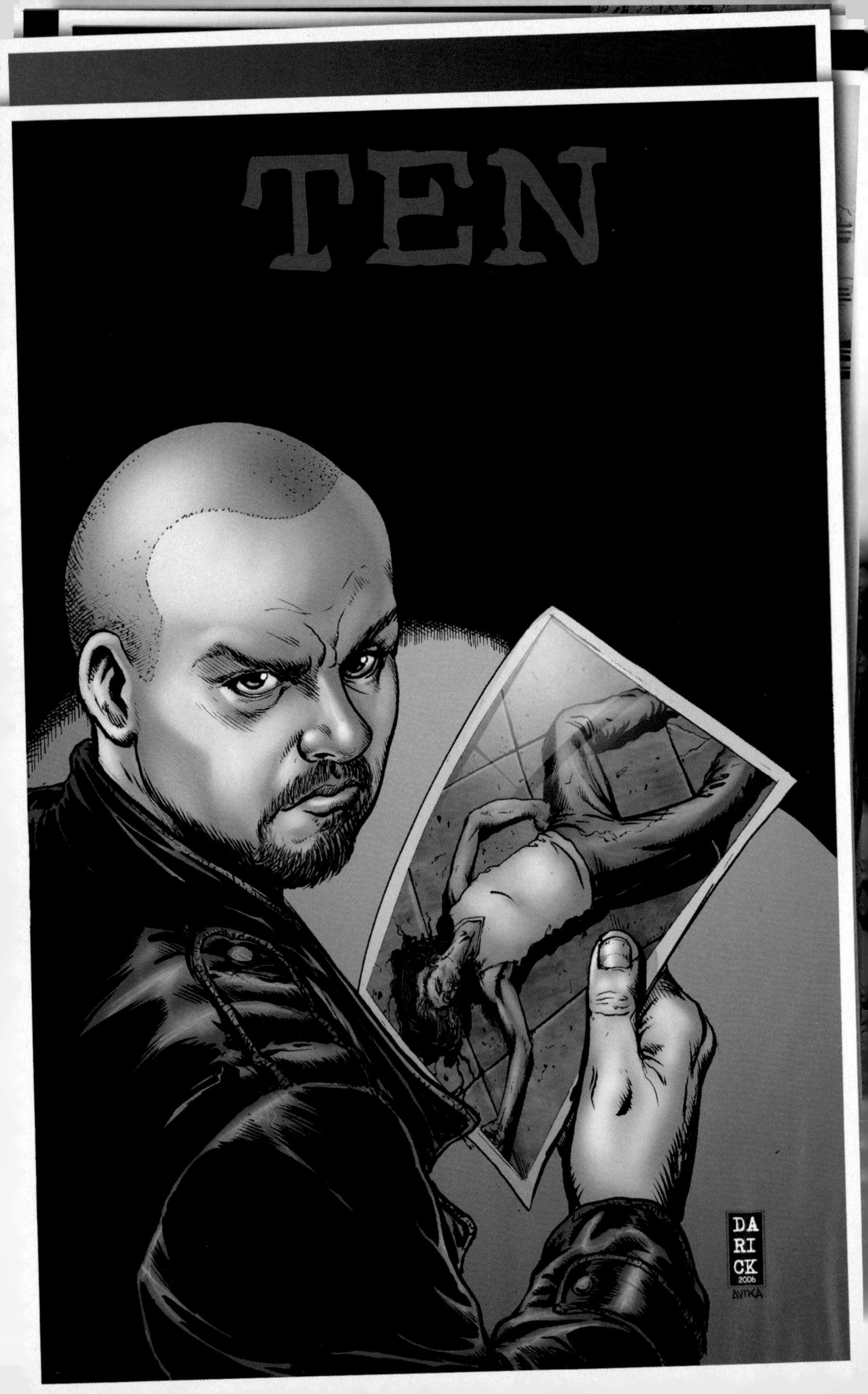
TEN
DA
RI
CK
2006
AVIKA

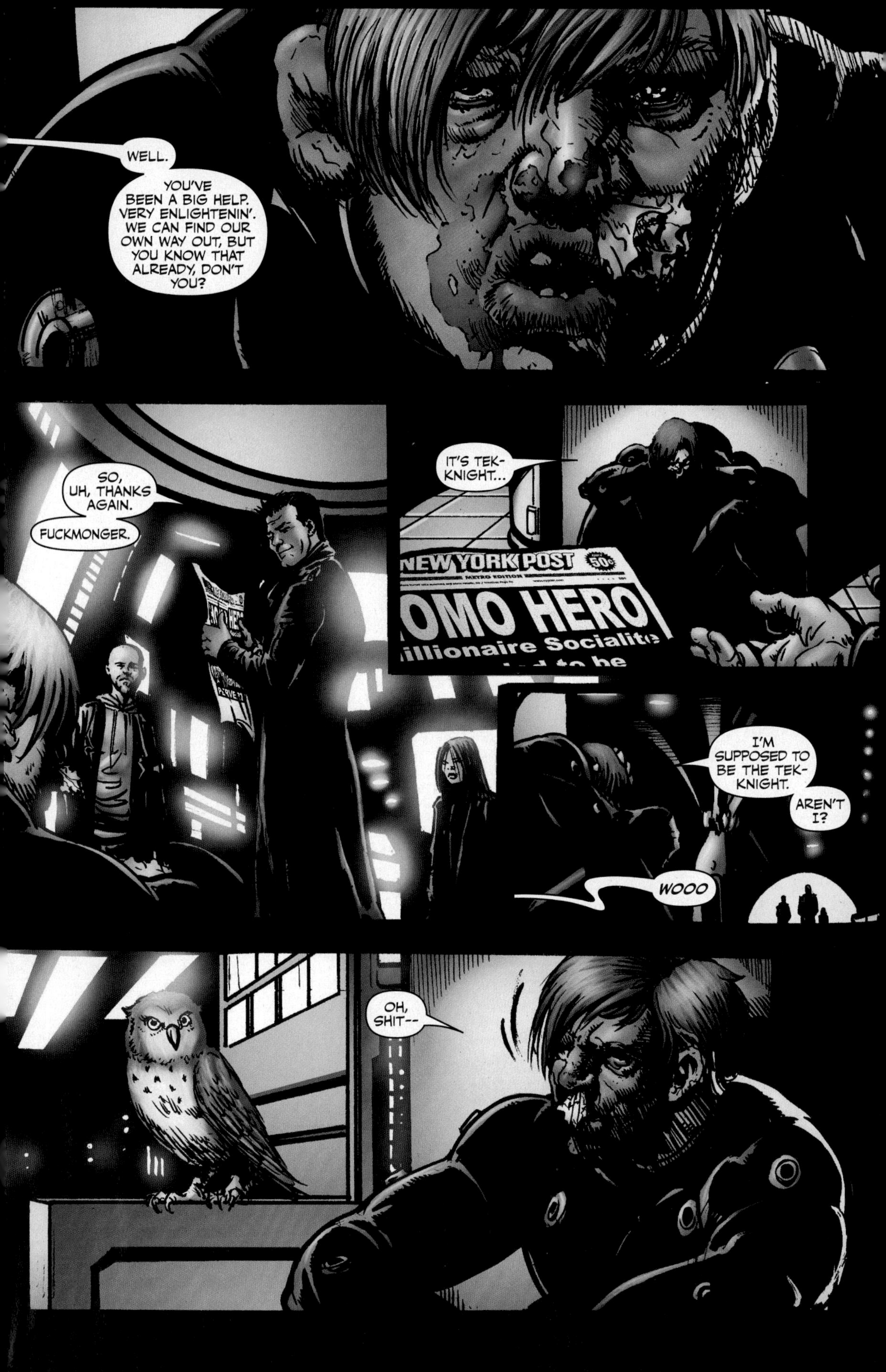
WELL.
YOU'VE BEEN A BIG HELP. VERY ENLIGHTENIN'. WE CAN FIND OUR OWN WAY OUT, BUT YOU KNOW THAT ALREADY, DON'T YOU?
SO, UH, THANKS AGAIN.
FUCKMONGER.
IT'S TEK-KNIGHT...
NEW YORK POST
50¢
OMO HERO
illionaire Socialite
I'M SUPPOSED TO BE THE TEK-KNIGHT.
AREN'T I?
WOOO
OH, SHIT--

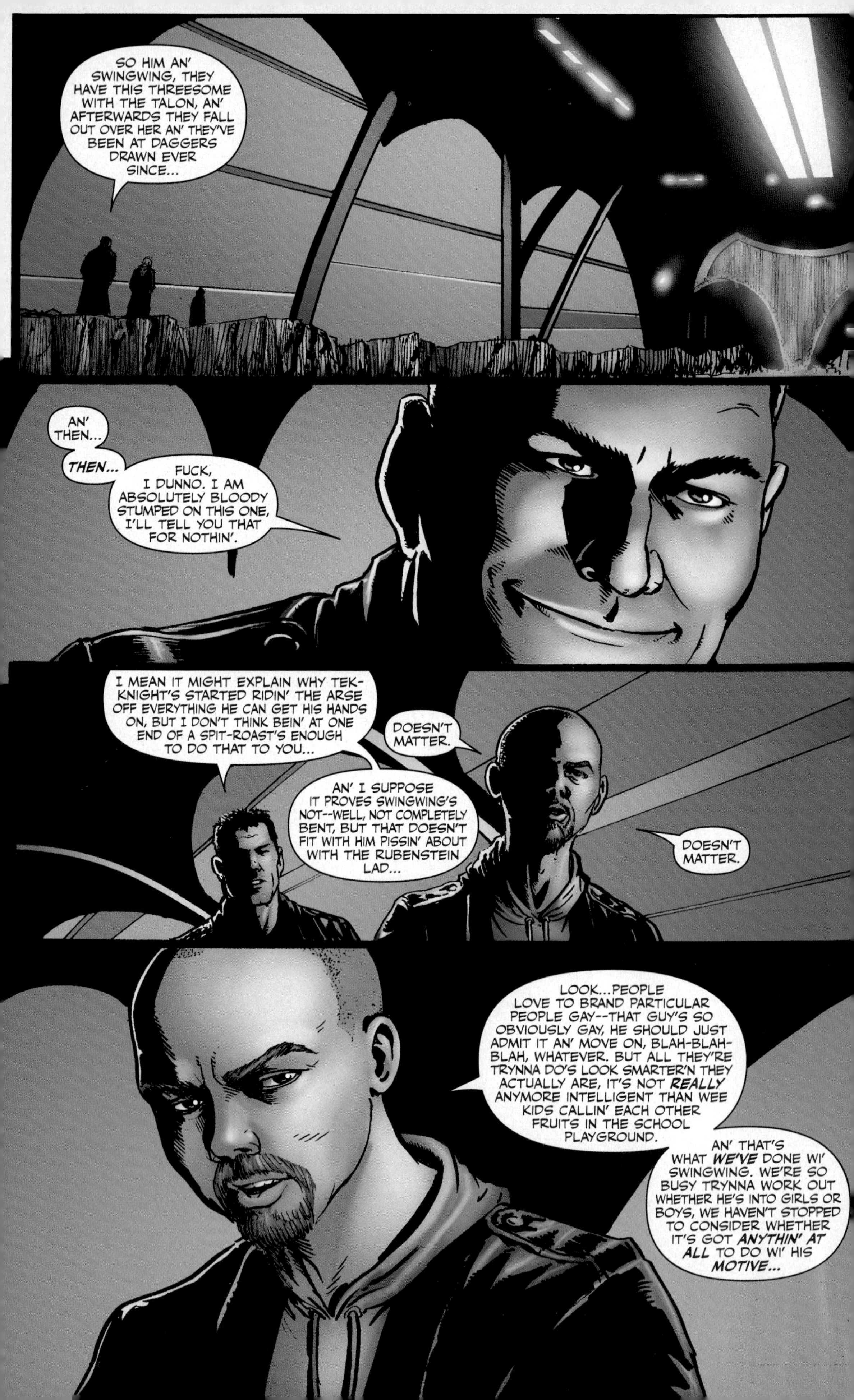
SO HIM AN' SWINGWING, THEY HAVE THIS THREESOME WITH THE TALON, AN' AFTERWARDS THEY FALL OUT OVER HER AN' THEY'VE BEEN AT DAGGERS DRAWN EVER SINCE...
AN' THEN...
THEN...
FUCK, I DUNNO. I AM ABSOLUTELY BLOODY STUMPED ON THIS ONE, I'LL TELL YOU THAT FOR NOTHIN'.
I MEAN IT MIGHT EXPLAIN WHY TEK-KNIGHT'S STARTED RIDIN' THE ARSE OFF EVERYTHING HE CAN GET HIS HANDS ON, BUT I DON'T THINK BEIN' AT ONE END OF A SPIT-ROAST'S ENOUGH TO DO THAT TO YOU...
DOESN'T MATTER.
AN' I SUPPOSE IT PROVES SWINGWING'S NOT--WELL, NOT COMPLETELY BENT, BUT THAT DOESN'T FIT WITH HIM PISSIN' ABOUT WITH THE RUBENSTEIN LAD...
DOESN'T MATTER.
LOOK...PEOPLE LOVE TO BRAND PARTICULAR PEOPLE GAY--THAT GUY'S SO OBVIOUSLY GAY, HE SHOULD JUST ADMIT IT AN' MOVE ON, BLAH-BLAH-BLAH, WHATEVER. BUT ALL THEY'RE TRYNNA DO'S LOOK SMARTER'N THEY ACTUALLY ARE, IT'S NOT *REALLY* ANYMORE INTELLIGENT THAN WEE KIDS CALLIN' EACH OTHER FRUITS IN THE SCHOOL PLAYGROUND.
AN' THAT'S WHAT *WE'VE* DONE WI' SWINGWING. WE'RE SO BUSY TRYNNA WORK OUT WHETHER HE'S INTO GIRLS OR BOYS, WE HAVEN'T STOPPED TO CONSIDER WHETHER IT'S GOT *ANYTHIN' AT ALL* TO DO WI' HIS *MOTIVE...*

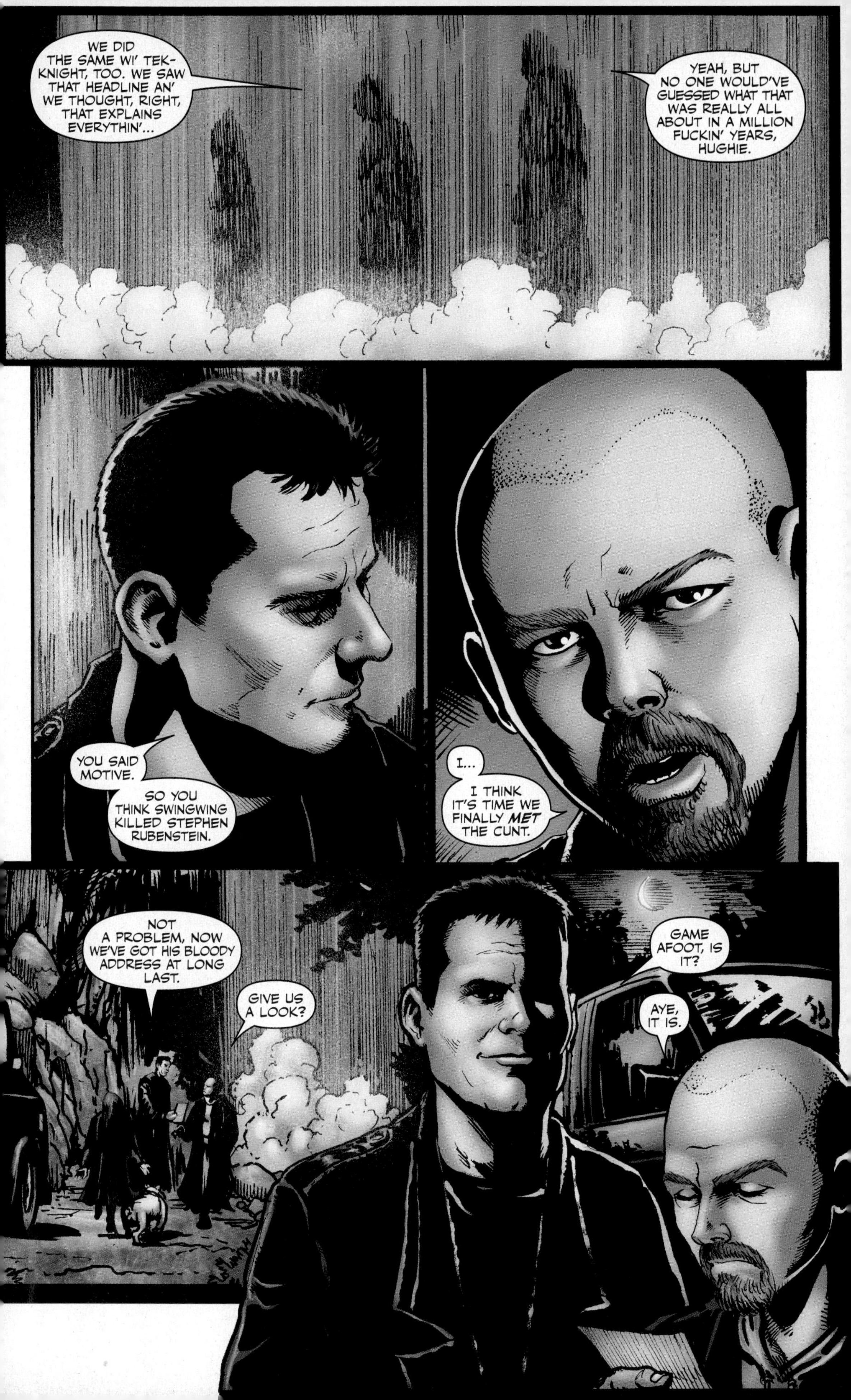
WE DID THE SAME WI' TEK-KNIGHT, TOO. WE SAW THAT HEADLINE AN' WE THOUGHT, RIGHT, THAT EXPLAINS EVERYTHIN'...
YEAH, BUT NO ONE WOULD'VE GUESSED WHAT THAT WAS REALLY ALL ABOUT IN A MILLION FUCKIN' YEARS, HUGHIE.
YOU SAID MOTIVE.
SO YOU THINK SWINGWING KILLED STEPHEN RUBENSTEIN.
I...
I THINK IT'S TIME WE FINALLY *MET* THE CUNT.
NOT A PROBLEM, NOW WE'VE GOT HIS BLOODY ADDRESS AT LONG LAST.
GIVE US A LOOK?
GAME AFOOT, IS IT?
AYE, IT IS.

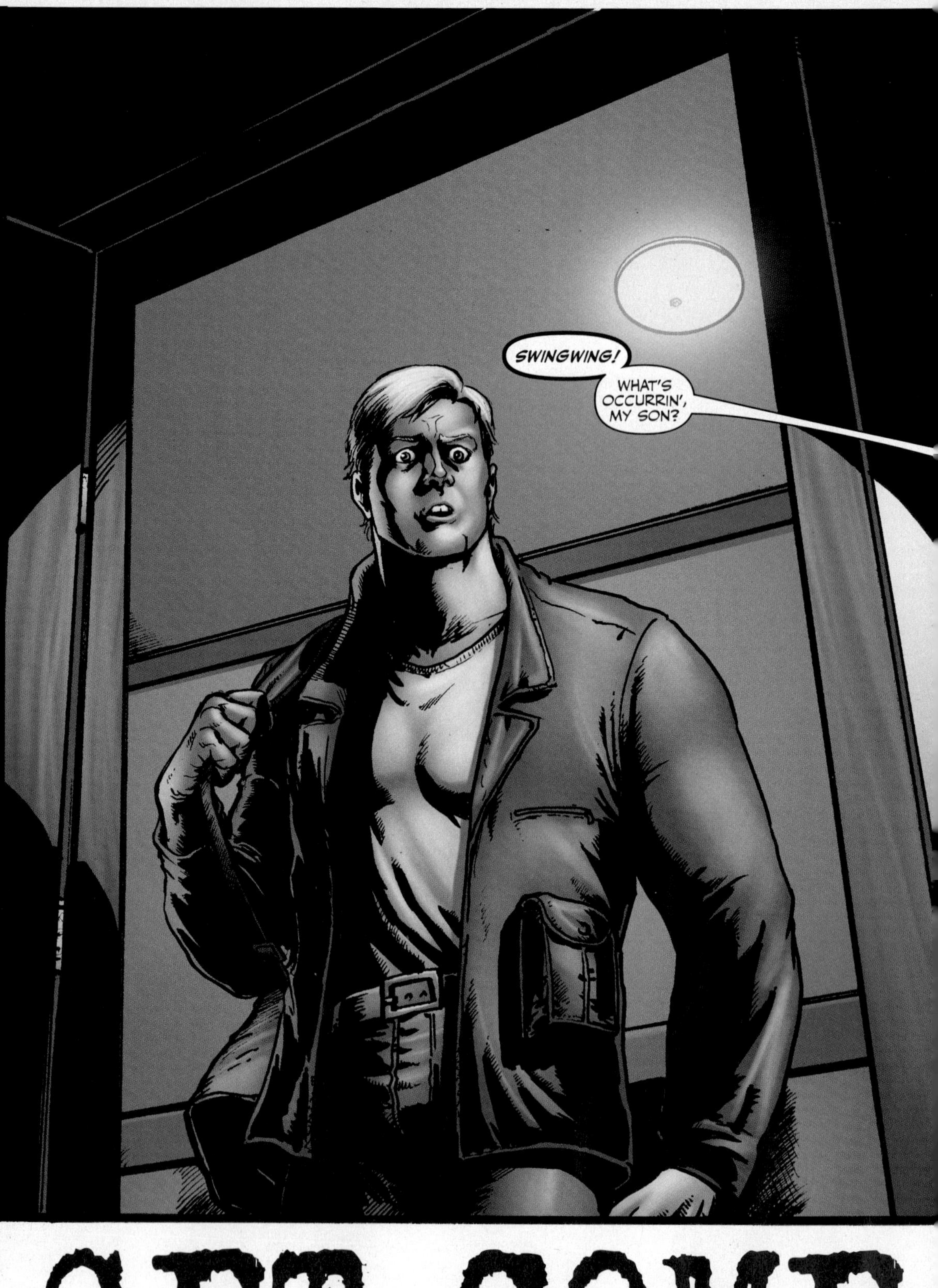
SWINGWING!
WHAT'S OCCURRIN', MY SON?

GET SOME
conclusion

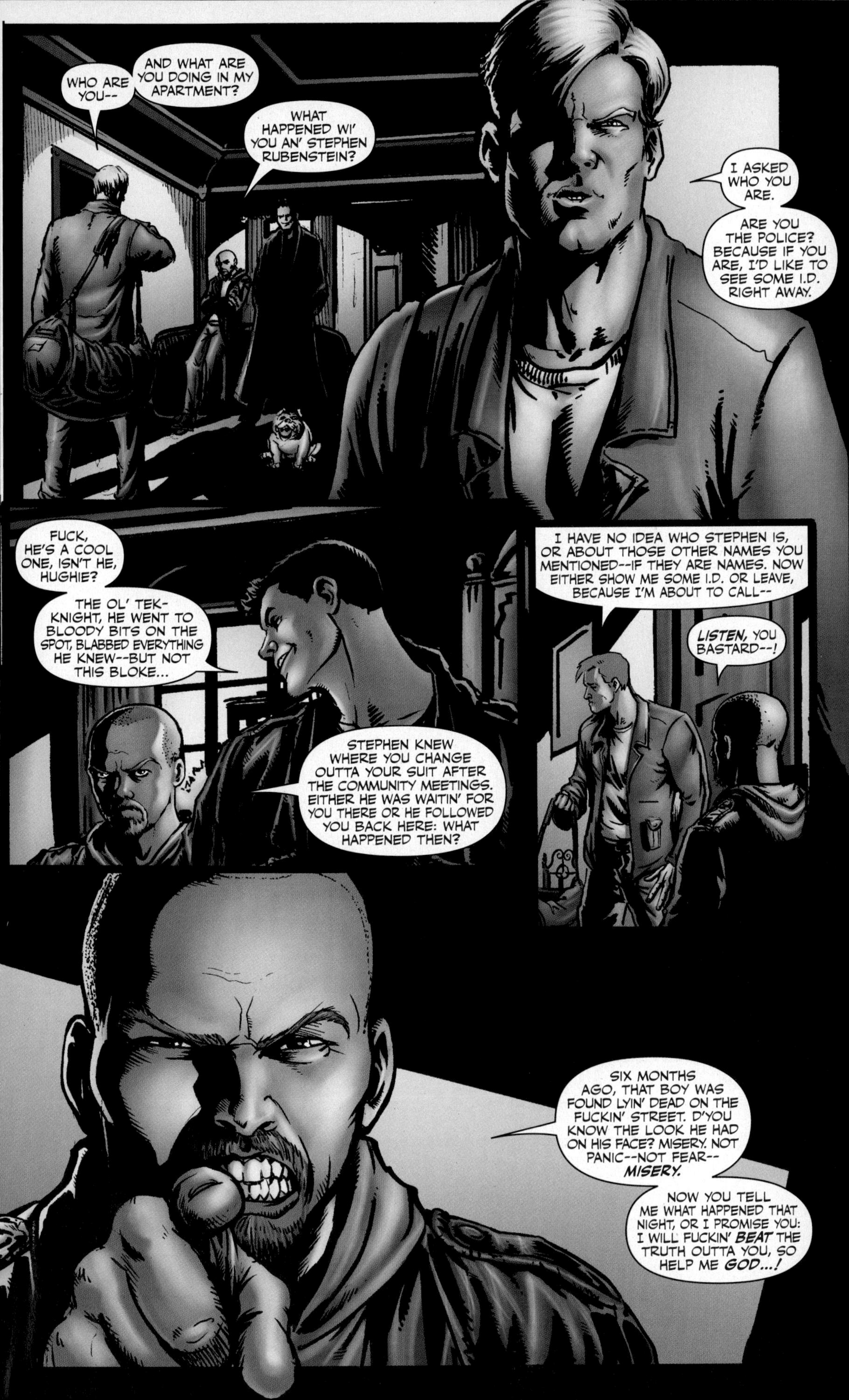
WHO ARE YOU--
AND WHAT ARE YOU DOING IN MY APARTMENT?
WHAT HAPPENED WI' YOU AN' STEPHEN RUBENSTEIN?
I ASKED WHO YOU ARE.
ARE YOU THE POLICE? BECAUSE IF YOU ARE, I'D LIKE TO SEE SOME I.D. RIGHT AWAY.
FUCK, HE'S A COOL ONE, ISN'T HE, HUGHIE?
THE OL' TEK-KNIGHT, HE WENT TO BLOODY BITS ON THE SPOT, BLABBED EVERYTHING HE KNEW--BUT NOT THIS BLOKE...
STEPHEN KNEW WHERE YOU CHANGE OUTTA YOUR SUIT AFTER THE COMMUNITY MEETINGS. EITHER HE WAS WAITIN' FOR YOU THERE OR HE FOLLOWED YOU BACK HERE: WHAT HAPPENED THEN?
I HAVE NO IDEA WHO STEPHEN IS, OR ABOUT THOSE OTHER NAMES YOU MENTIONED--IF THEY ARE NAMES. NOW EITHER SHOW ME SOME I.D. OR LEAVE, BECAUSE I'M ABOUT TO CALL--
LISTEN, YOU BASTARD--!
SIX MONTHS AGO, THAT BOY WAS FOUND LYIN' DEAD ON THE FUCKIN' STREET. D'YOU KNOW THE LOOK HE HAD ON HIS FACE? MISERY. NOT PANIC--NOT FEAR--*MISERY.*
NOW YOU TELL ME WHAT HAPPENED THAT NIGHT, OR I PROMISE YOU: I WILL FUCKIN' *BEAT* THE TRUTH OUTTA YOU, SO HELP ME *GOD...!*

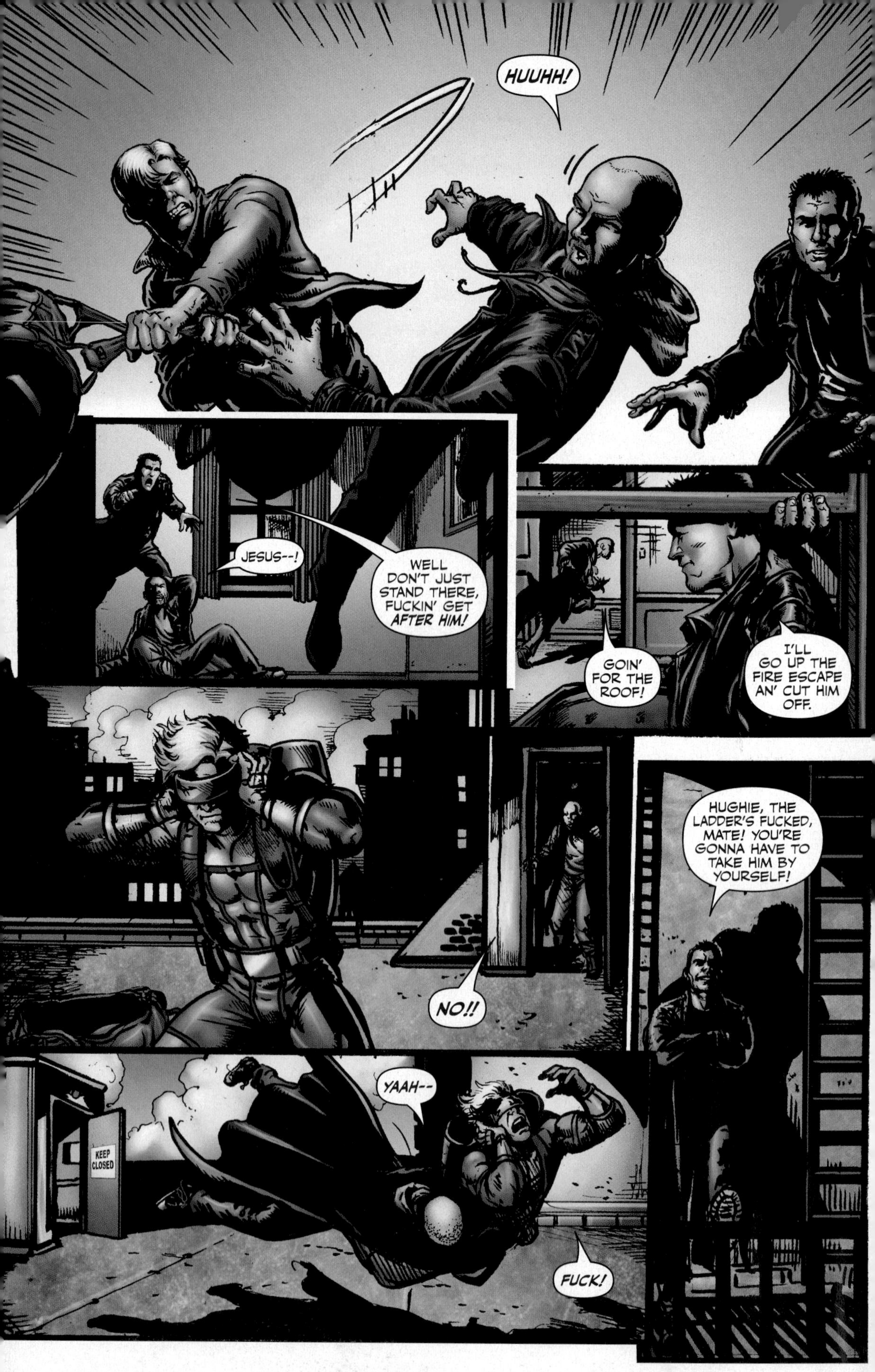
HUUHH!
JESUS--!
WELL DON'T JUST STAND THERE, FUCKIN' GET AFTER HIM!
GOIN' FOR THE ROOF!
I'LL GO UP THE FIRE ESCAPE AN' CUT HIM OFF.
NO!!
HUGHIE, THE LADDER'S FUCKED, MATE! YOU'RE GONNA HAVE TO TAKE HIM BY YOURSELF!
YAAH--
KEEP CLOSED
FUCK!

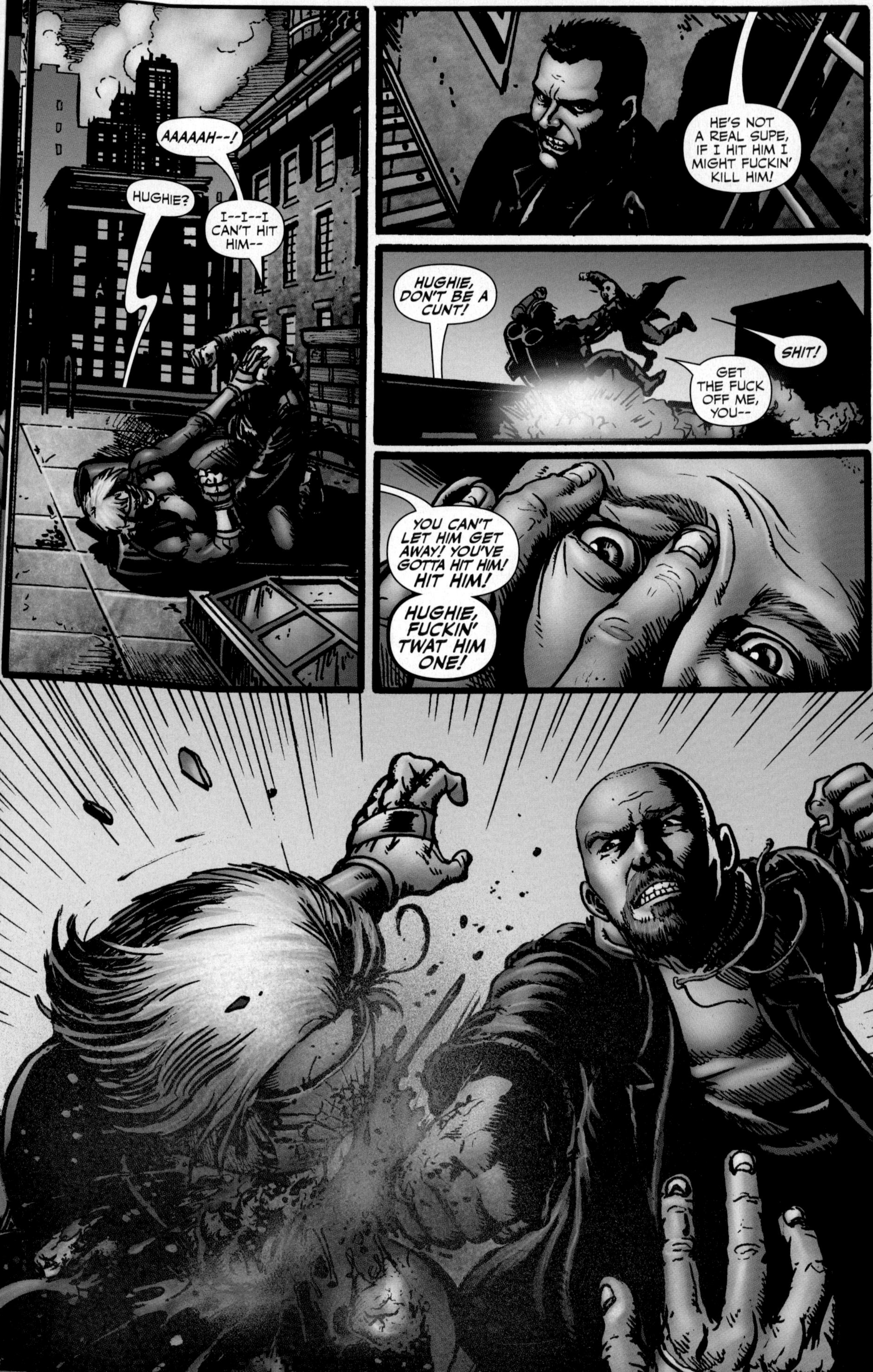
AAAAAH--!
HUGHIE?
I--I--I CAN'T HIT HIM--
HE'S NOT A REAL SUPE, IF I HIT HIM I MIGHT FUCKIN' KILL HIM!
HUGHIE, DON'T BE A CUNT!
SHIT!
GET THE FUCK OFF ME, YOU--
YOU CAN'T LET HIM GET AWAY! YOU'VE GOTTA HIT HIM! HIT HIM!
HUGHIE, FUCKIN' TWAT HIM ONE!

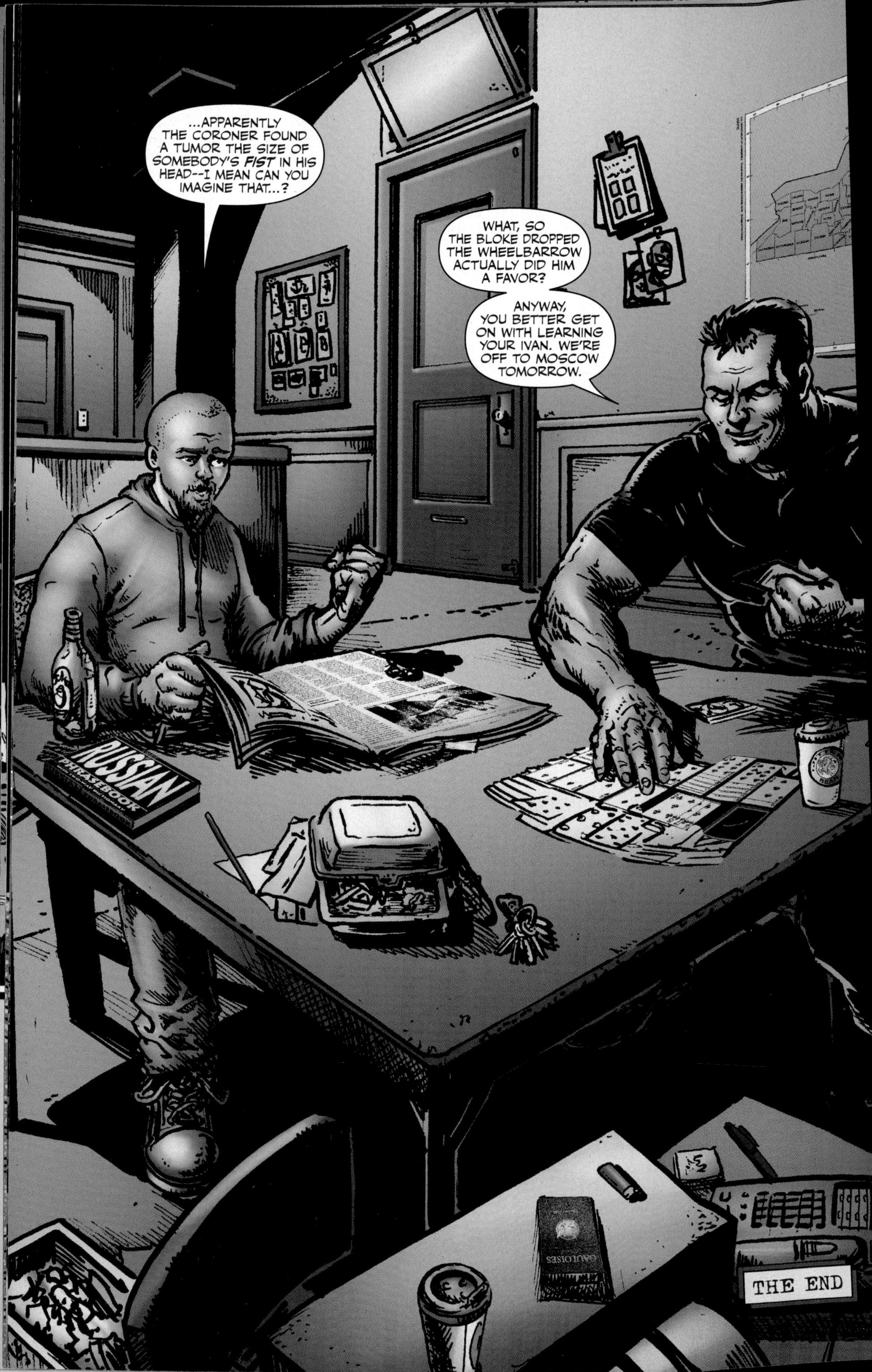
...APPARENTLY THE CORONER FOUND A TUMOR THE SIZE OF SOMEBODY'S *FIST* IN HIS HEAD--I MEAN CAN YOU IMAGINE THAT...?
WHAT, SO THE BLOKE DROPPED THE WHEELBARROW ACTUALLY DID HIM A FAVOR?
ANYWAY, YOU BETTER GET ON WITH LEARNING YOUR IVAN. WE'RE OFF TO MOSCOW TOMORROW.
RUSSIAN PHRASEBOOK
GAULOISES
THE END

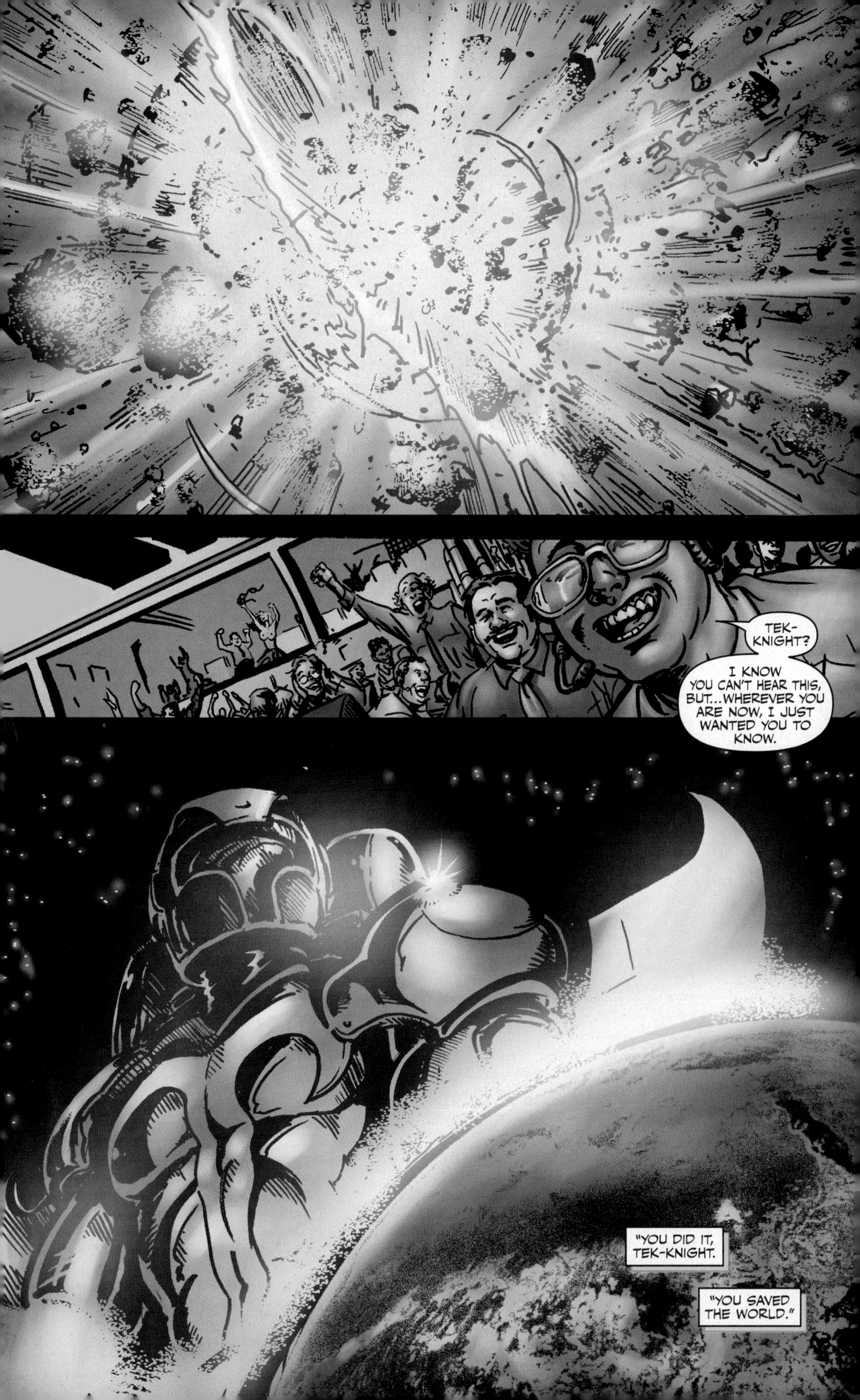
TEK-KNIGHT?
I KNOW YOU CAN'T HEAR THIS, BUT...WHEREVER YOU ARE NOW, I JUST WANTED YOU TO KNOW.
"YOU DID IT, TEK-KNIGHT.
"YOU SAVED THE WORLD."

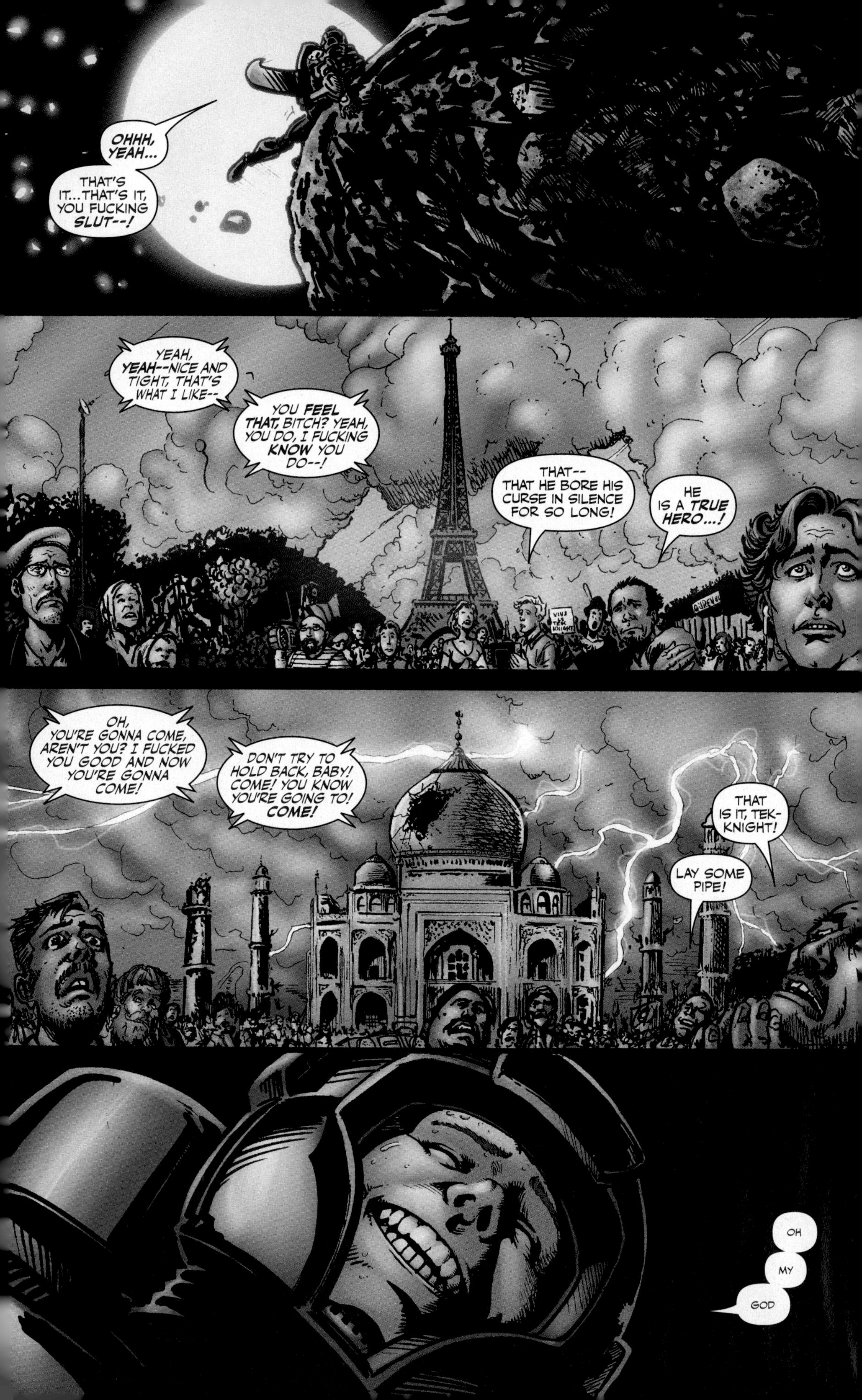
OHHH, YEAH...
THAT'S IT...THAT'S IT, YOU FUCKING SLUT--!
YEAH, YEAH--NICE AND TIGHT, THAT'S WHAT I LIKE--
YOU FEEL THAT, BITCH? YEAH, YOU DO, I FUCKING KNOW YOU DO--!
THAT-- THAT HE BORE HIS CURSE IN SILENCE FOR SO LONG!
HE IS A TRUE HERO...!
OH, YOU'RE GONNA COME, AREN'T YOU? I FUCKED YOU GOOD AND NOW YOU'RE GONNA COME!
DON'T TRY TO HOLD BACK, BABY! COME! YOU KNOW YOU'RE GOING TO! COME!
THAT IS IT, TEK-KNIGHT!
LAY SOME PIPE!
OH
MY
GOD

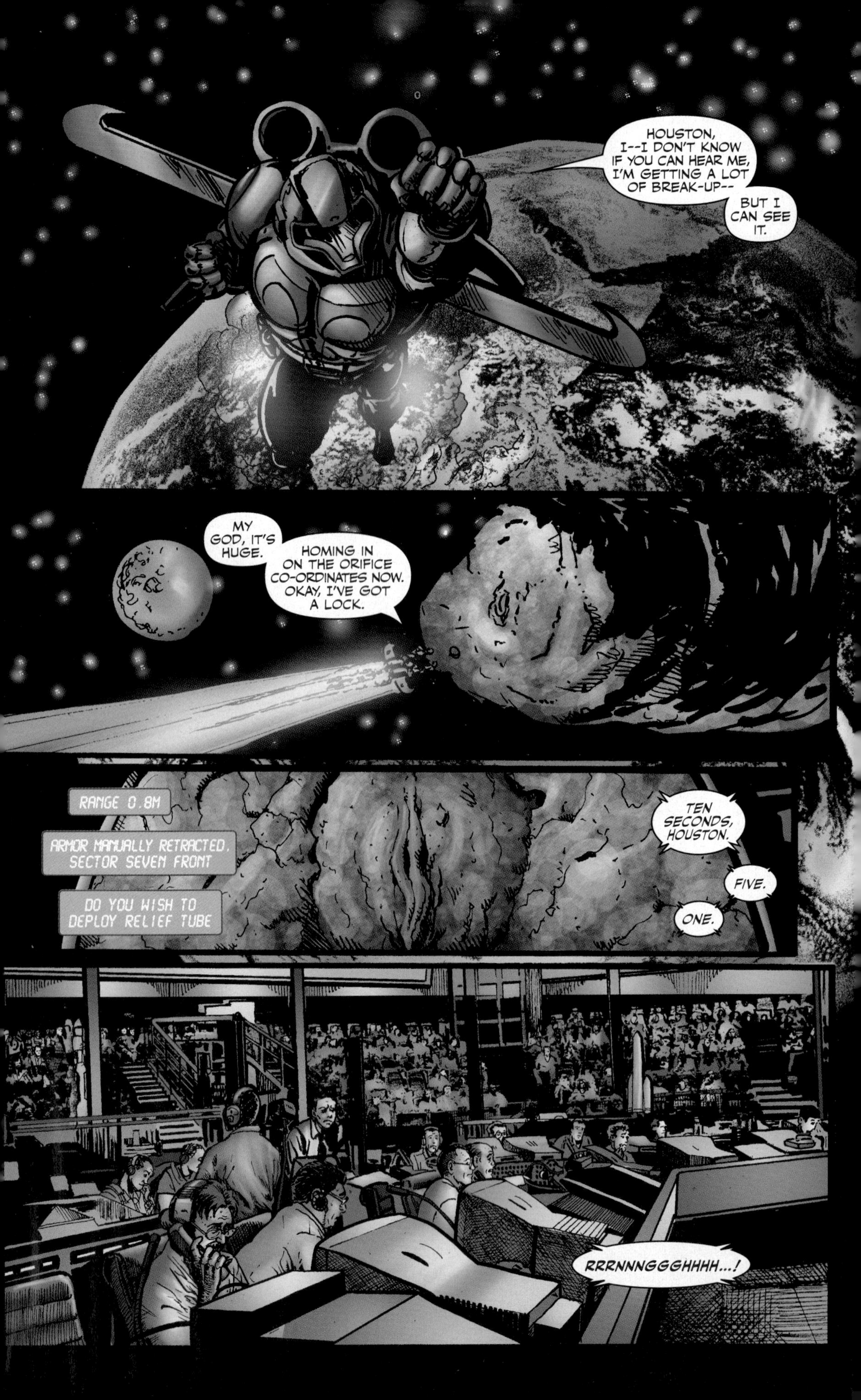
HOUSTON, I--I DON'T KNOW IF YOU CAN HEAR ME, I'M GETTING A LOT OF BREAK-UP--
BUT I CAN SEE IT.
MY GOD, IT'S HUGE.
HOMING IN ON THE ORIFICE CO-ORDINATES NOW. OKAY, I'VE GOT A LOCK.
RANGE 0.8M
ARMOR MANUALLY RETRACTED. SECTOR SEVEN FRONT
DO YOU WISH TO DEPLOY RELIEF TUBE
TEN SECONDS, HOUSTON.
FIVE.
ONE.
RRRNNNGGGHHHH...!

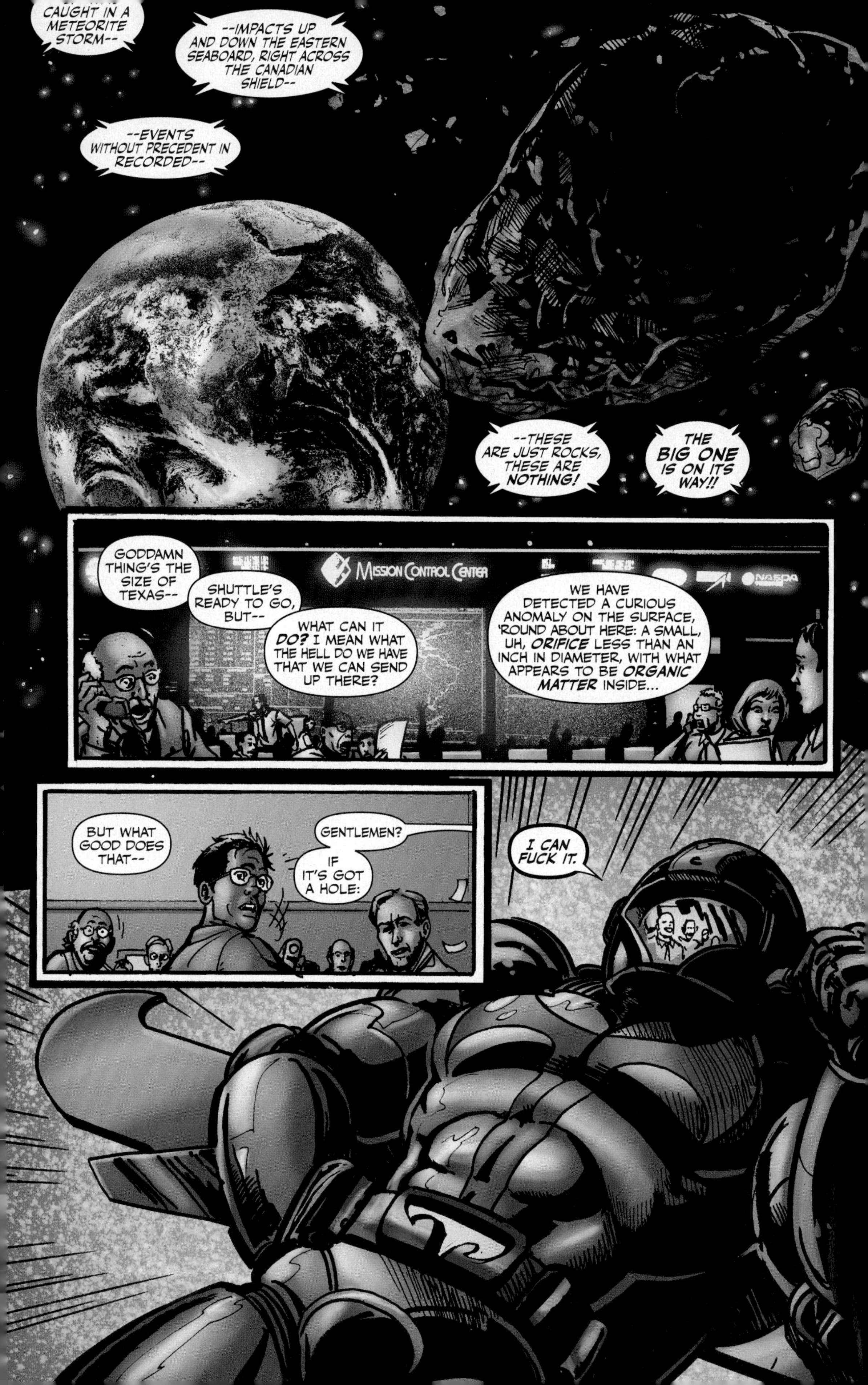
CAUGHT IN A METEORITE STORM--
--IMPACTS UP AND DOWN THE EASTERN SEABOARD, RIGHT ACROSS THE CANADIAN SHIELD--
--EVENTS WITHOUT PRECEDENT IN RECORDED--
--THESE ARE JUST ROCKS, THESE ARE NOTHING!
THE BIG ONE IS ON ITS WAY!!
MISSION CONTROL CENTER
GODDAMN THING'S THE SIZE OF TEXAS--
SHUTTLE'S READY TO GO, BUT--
WHAT CAN IT DO? I MEAN WHAT THE HELL DO WE HAVE THAT WE CAN SEND UP THERE?
WE HAVE DETECTED A CURIOUS ANOMALY ON THE SURFACE, 'ROUND ABOUT HERE: A SMALL, UH, ORIFICE LESS THAN AN INCH IN DIAMETER, WITH WHAT APPEARS TO BE ORGANIC MATTER INSIDE...
BUT WHAT GOOD DOES THAT--
GENTLEMEN?
IF IT'S GOT A HOLE:
I CAN FUCK IT.

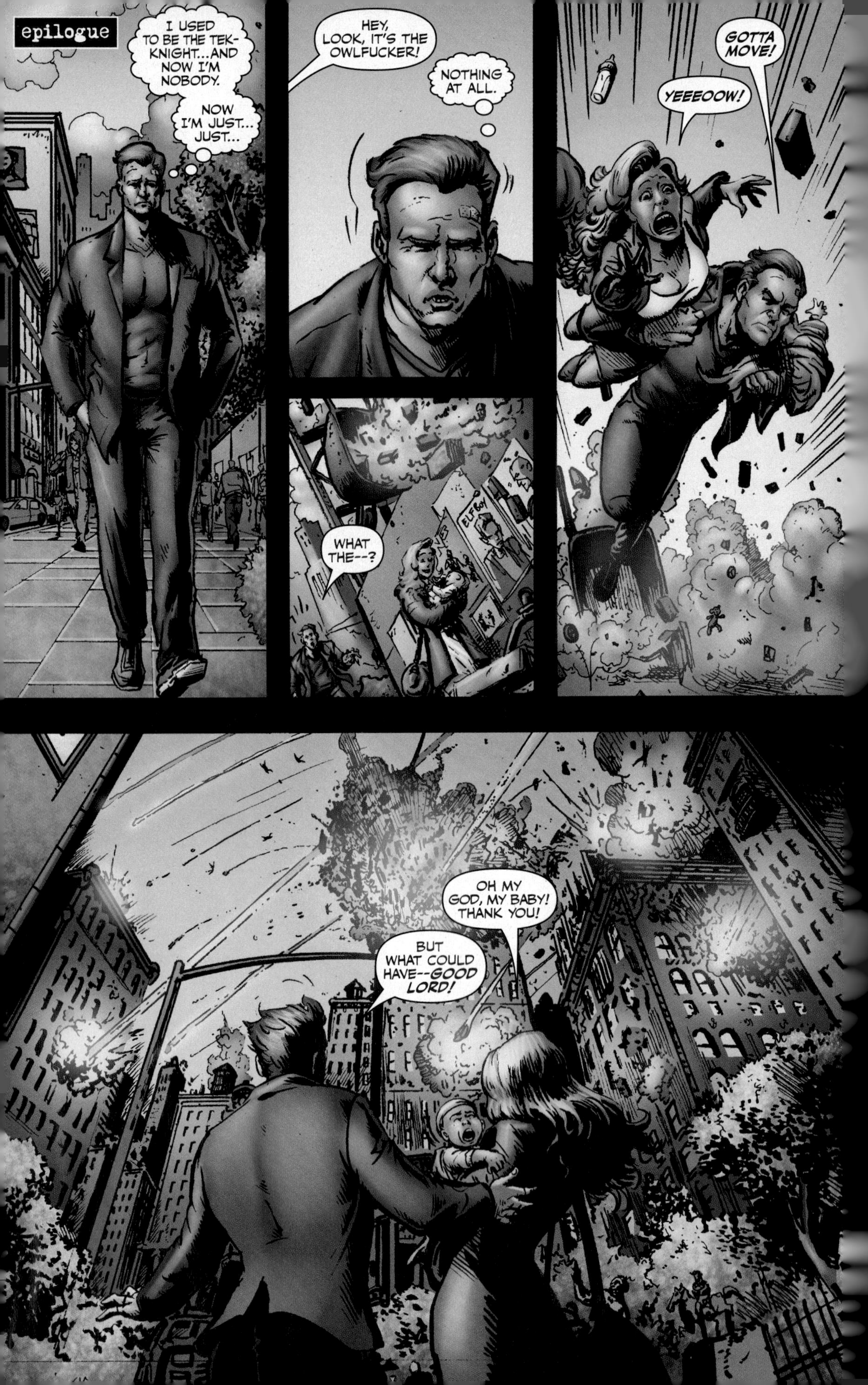
epilogue
I USED TO BE THE TEK-KNIGHT...AND NOW I'M NOBODY.
NOW I'M JUST... JUST...
HEY, LOOK, IT'S THE OWLFUCKER!
NOTHING AT ALL.
WHAT THE--?
GOTTA MOVE!
YEEEOOW!
ELFBOY
OH MY GOD, MY BABY! THANK YOU!
BUT WHAT COULD HAVE--GOOD LORD!

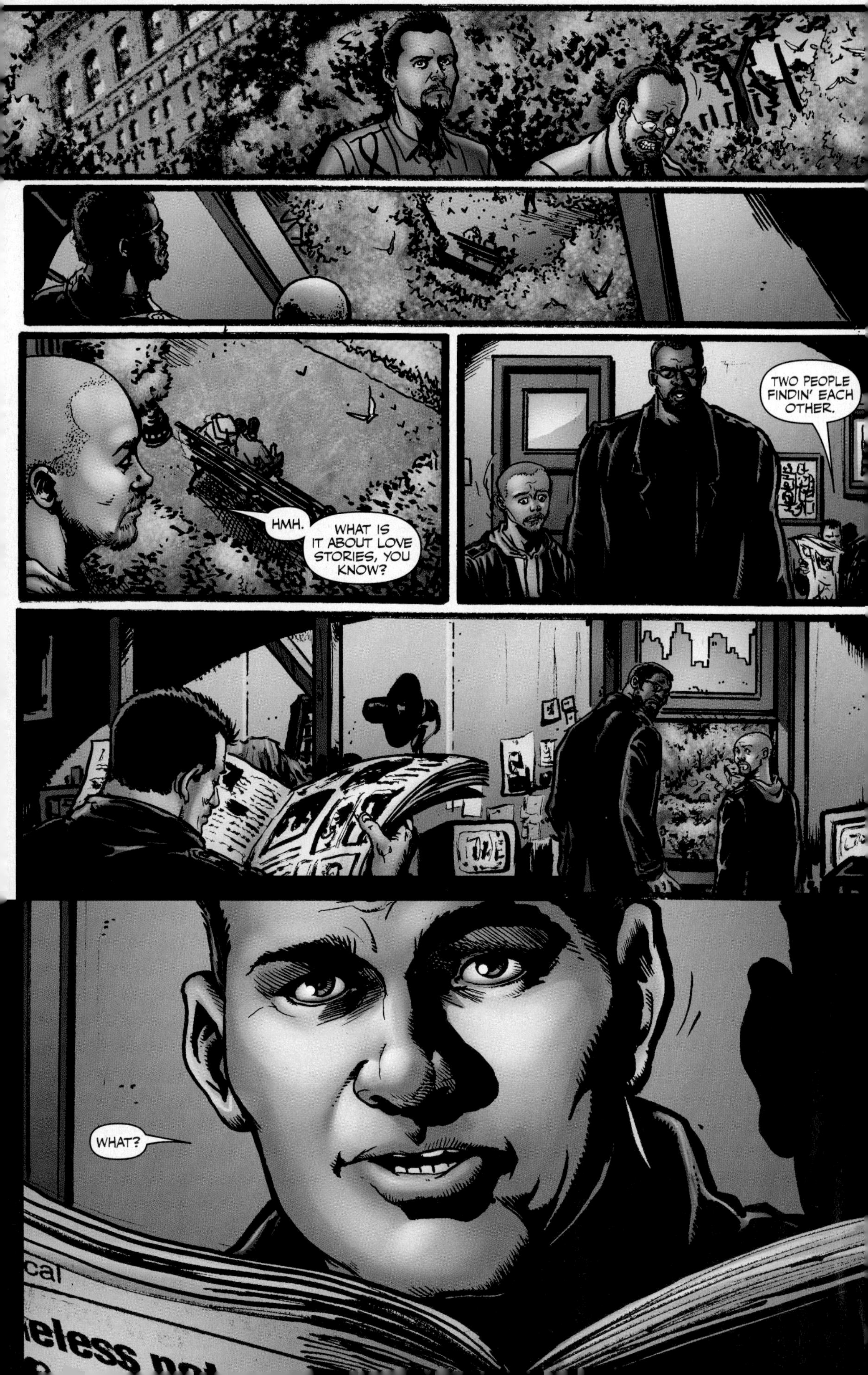
HMH.
WHAT IS IT ABOUT LOVE STORIES, YOU KNOW?
TWO PEOPLE FINDIN' EACH OTHER.
WHAT?

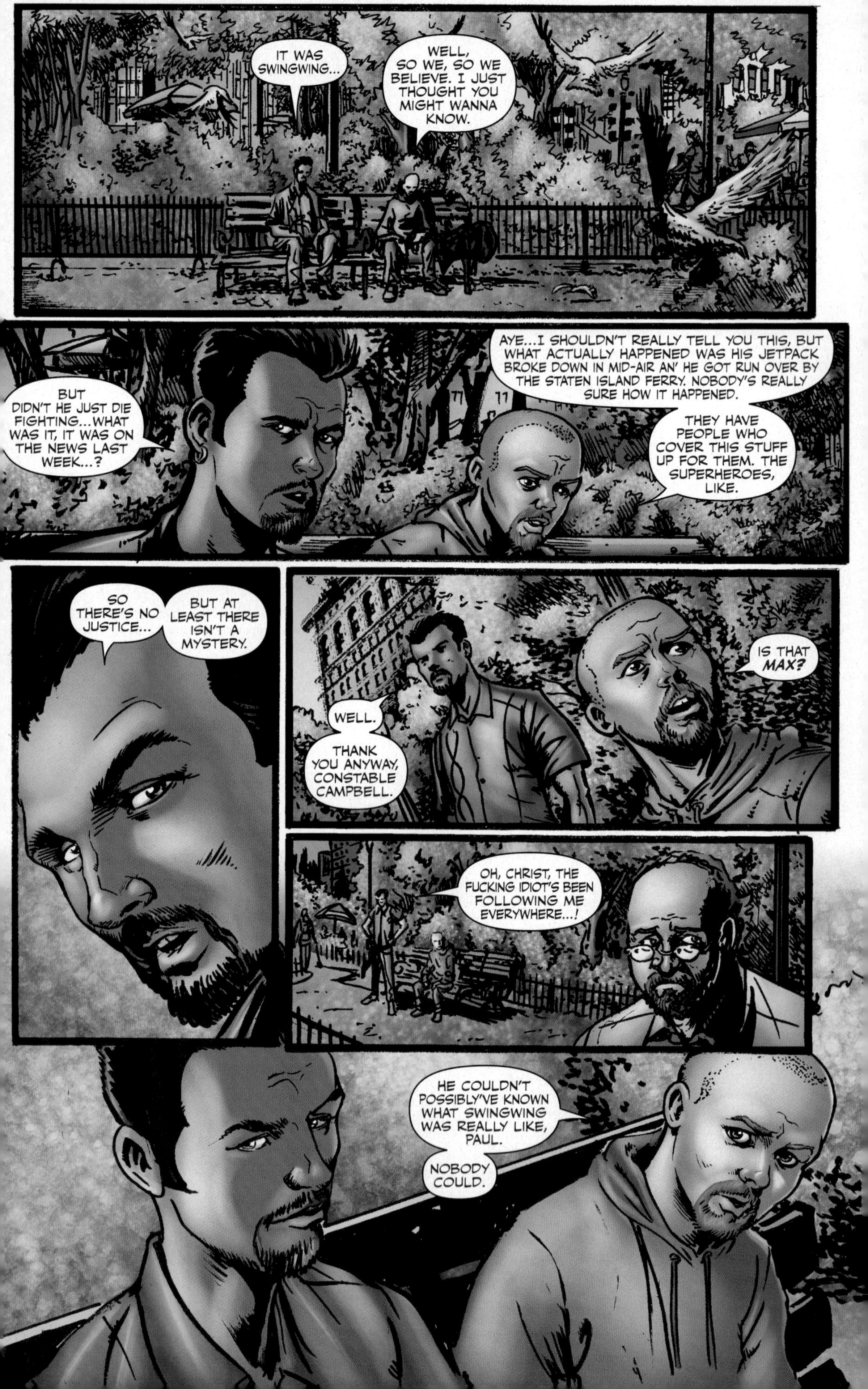
IT WAS SWINGWING...
WELL, SO WE, SO WE BELIEVE. I JUST THOUGHT YOU MIGHT WANNA KNOW.
BUT DIDN'T HE JUST DIE FIGHTING...WHAT WAS IT, IT WAS ON THE NEWS LAST WEEK...?
AYE...I SHOULDN'T REALLY TELL YOU THIS, BUT WHAT ACTUALLY HAPPENED WAS HIS JETPACK BROKE DOWN IN MID-AIR AN' HE GOT RUN OVER BY THE STATEN ISLAND FERRY. NOBODY'S REALLY SURE HOW IT HAPPENED.
THEY HAVE PEOPLE WHO COVER THIS STUFF UP FOR THEM. THE SUPERHEROES, LIKE.
SO THERE'S NO JUSTICE...
BUT AT LEAST THERE ISN'T A MYSTERY.
WELL.
THANK YOU ANYWAY, CONSTABLE CAMPBELL.
IS THAT *MAX?*
OH, CHRIST, THE FUCKING IDIOT'S BEEN FOLLOWING ME EVERYWHERE...!
HE COULDN'T POSSIBLY'VE KNOWN WHAT SWINGWING WAS REALLY LIKE, PAUL.
NOBODY COULD.

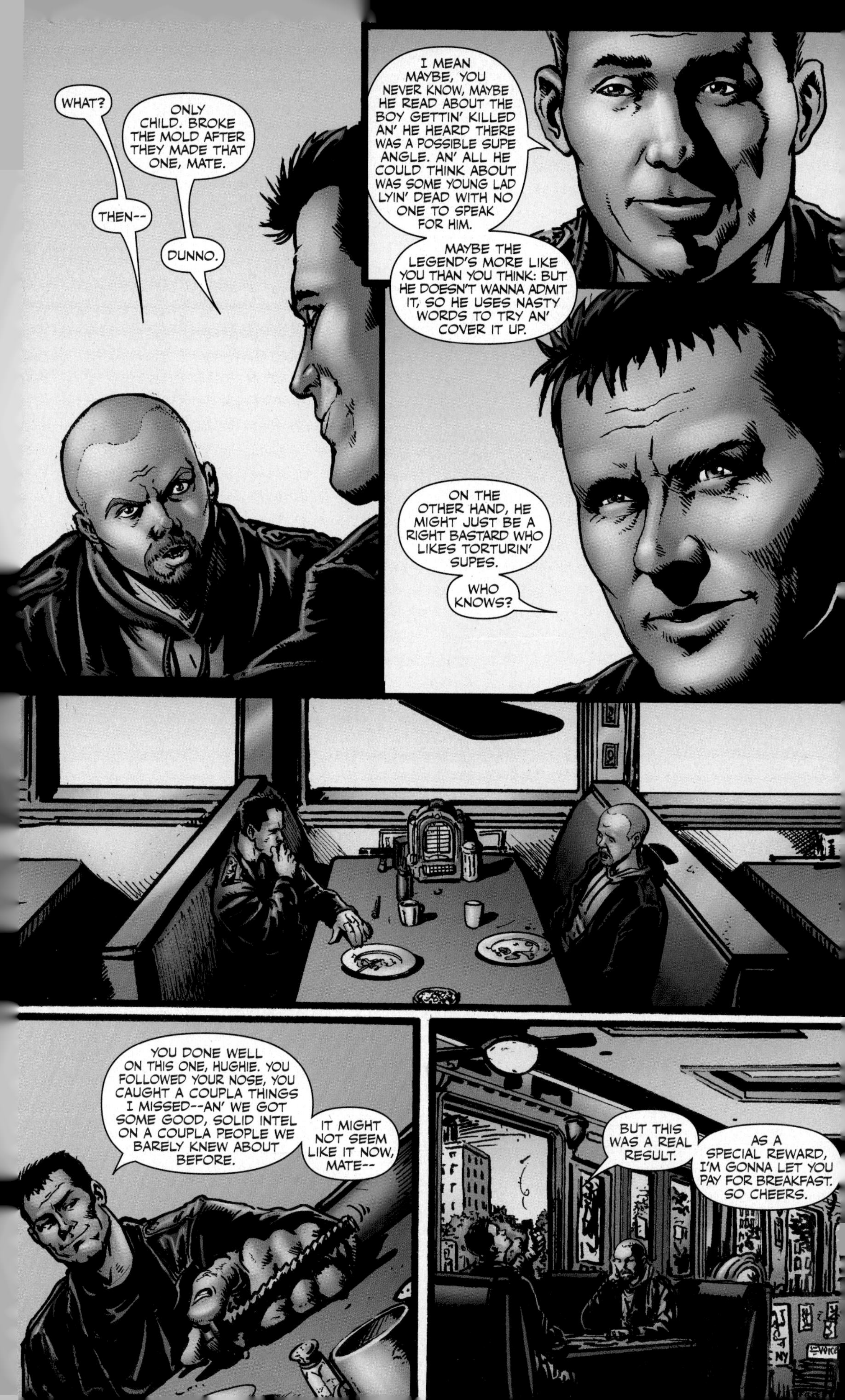
WHAT?
ONLY CHILD. BROKE THE MOLD AFTER THEY MADE THAT ONE, MATE.
THEN--
DUNNO.
I MEAN MAYBE, YOU NEVER KNOW, MAYBE HE READ ABOUT THE BOY GETTIN' KILLED AN' HE HEARD THERE WAS A POSSIBLE SUPE ANGLE. AN' ALL HE COULD THINK ABOUT WAS SOME YOUNG LAD LYIN' DEAD WITH NO ONE TO SPEAK FOR HIM.
MAYBE THE LEGEND'S MORE LIKE YOU THAN YOU THINK: BUT HE DOESN'T WANNA ADMIT IT, SO HE USES NASTY WORDS TO TRY AN' COVER IT UP.
ON THE OTHER HAND, HE MIGHT JUST BE A RIGHT BASTARD WHO LIKES TORTURIN' SUPES.
WHO KNOWS?
YOU DONE WELL ON THIS ONE, HUGHIE. YOU FOLLOWED YOUR NOSE, YOU CAUGHT A COUPLA THINGS I MISSED--AN' WE GOT SOME GOOD, SOLID INTEL ON A COUPLA PEOPLE WE BARELY KNEW ABOUT BEFORE.
IT MIGHT NOT SEEM LIKE IT NOW, MATE--
BUT THIS WAS A REAL RESULT.
AS A SPECIAL REWARD, I'M GONNA LET YOU PAY FOR BREAKFAST. SO CHEERS.

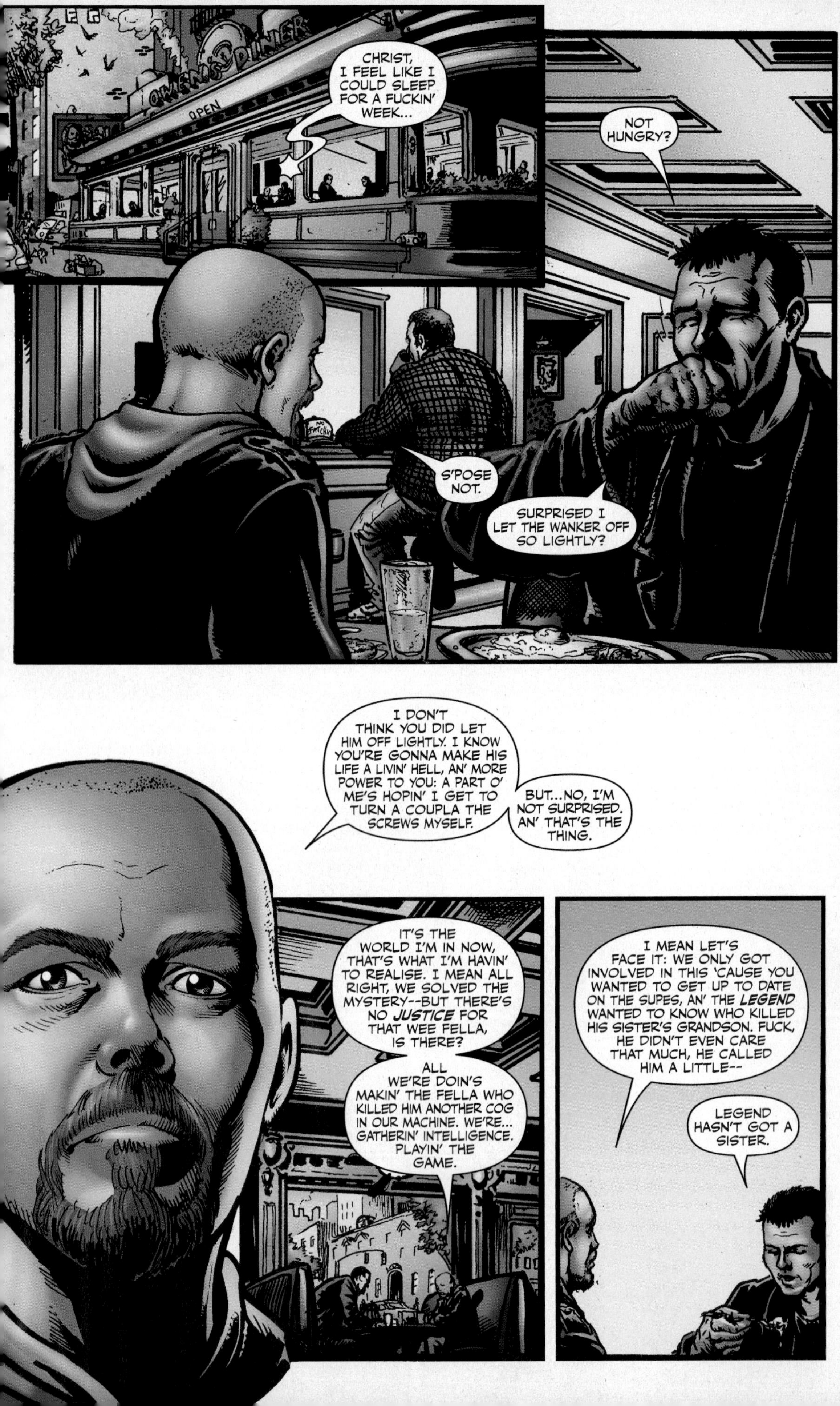
CHRIST, I FEEL LIKE I COULD SLEEP FOR A FUCKIN' WEEK...
NOT HUNGRY?
S'POSE NOT.
SURPRISED I LET THE WANKER OFF SO LIGHTLY?
I DON'T THINK YOU DID LET HIM OFF LIGHTLY. I KNOW YOU'RE GONNA MAKE HIS LIFE A LIVIN' HELL, AN' MORE POWER TO YOU: A PART O' ME'S HOPIN' I GET TO TURN A COUPLA THE SCREWS MYSELF.
BUT...NO, I'M NOT SURPRISED. AN' THAT'S THE THING.
IT'S THE WORLD I'M IN NOW, THAT'S WHAT I'M HAVIN' TO REALISE. I MEAN ALL RIGHT, WE SOLVED THE MYSTERY--BUT THERE'S NO JUSTICE FOR THAT WEE FELLA, IS THERE?
ALL WE'RE DOIN'S MAKIN' THE FELLA WHO KILLED HIM ANOTHER COG IN OUR MACHINE. WE'RE... GATHERIN' INTELLIGENCE. PLAYIN' THE GAME.
I MEAN LET'S FACE IT: WE ONLY GOT INVOLVED IN THIS 'CAUSE YOU WANTED TO GET UP TO DATE ON THE SUPES, AN' THE LEGEND WANTED TO KNOW WHO KILLED HIS SISTER'S GRANDSON. FUCK, HE DIDN'T EVEN CARE THAT MUCH, HE CALLED HIM A LITTLE--
LEGEND HASN'T GOT A SISTER.

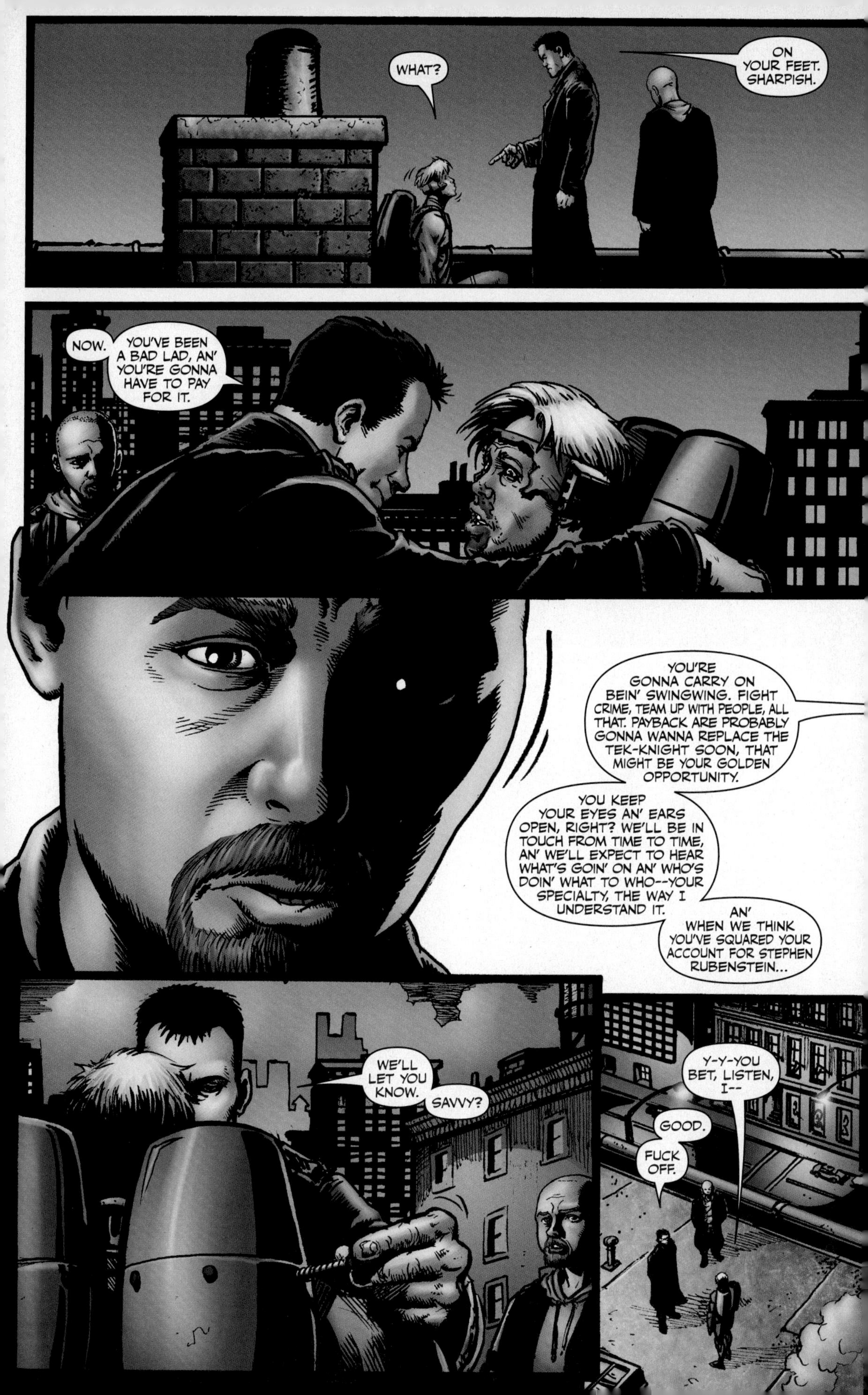
WHAT?
ON YOUR FEET. SHARPISH.
NOW.
YOU'VE BEEN A BAD LAD, AN' YOU'RE GONNA HAVE TO PAY FOR IT.
YOU'RE GONNA CARRY ON BEIN' SWINGWING. FIGHT CRIME, TEAM UP WITH PEOPLE, ALL THAT. PAYBACK ARE PROBABLY GONNA WANNA REPLACE THE TEK-KNIGHT SOON, THAT MIGHT BE YOUR GOLDEN OPPORTUNITY.
YOU KEEP YOUR EYES AN' EARS OPEN, RIGHT? WE'LL BE IN TOUCH FROM TIME TO TIME, AN' WE'LL EXPECT TO HEAR WHAT'S GOIN' ON AN' WHO'S DOIN' WHAT TO WHO--YOUR SPECIALTY, THE WAY I UNDERSTAND IT.
AN' WHEN WE THINK YOU'VE SQUARED YOUR ACCOUNT FOR STEPHEN RUBENSTEIN...
WE'LL LET YOU KNOW.
SAVVY?
Y-Y-YOU BET, LISTEN, I--
GOOD.
FUCK OFF.

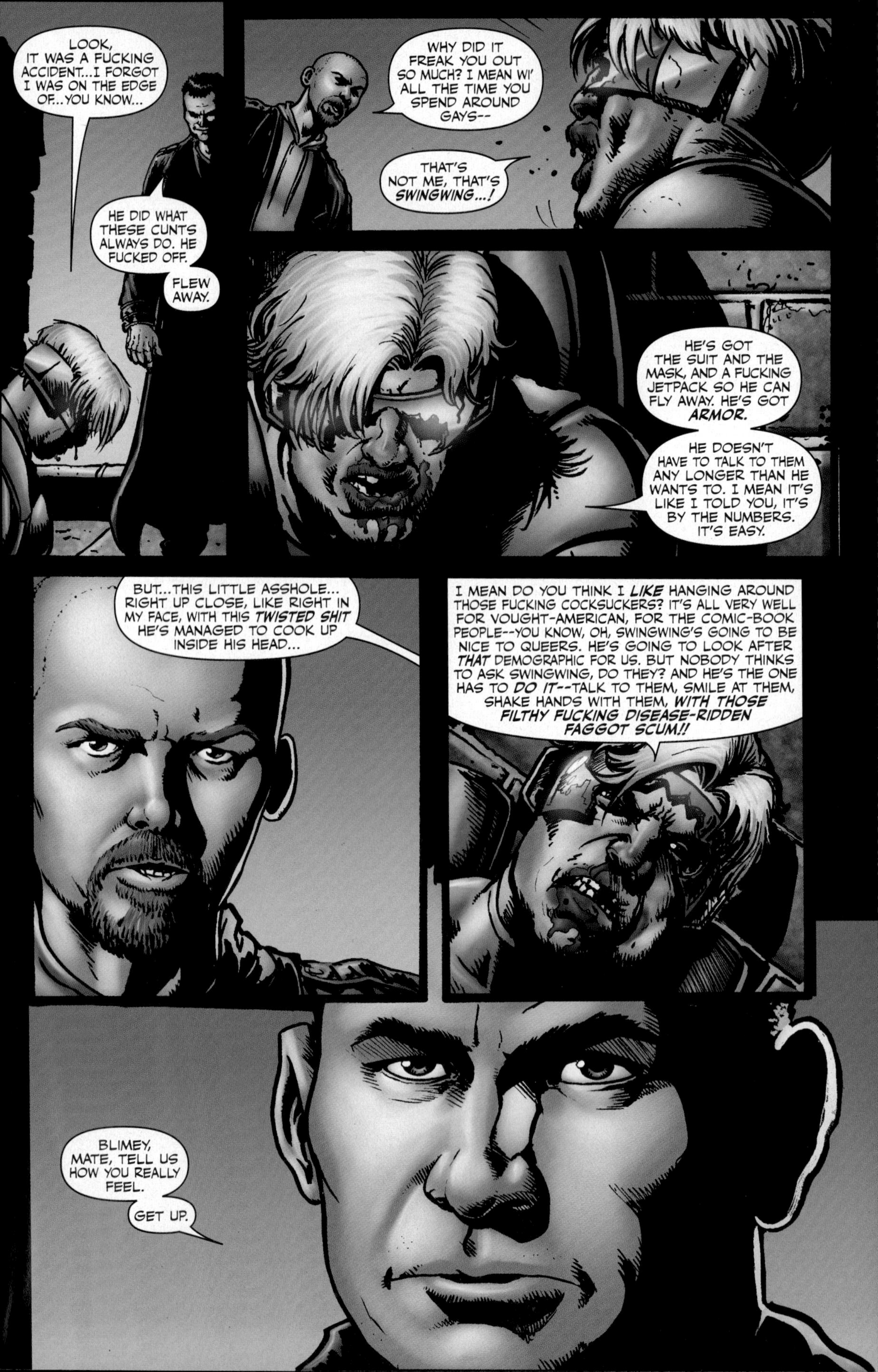

LOOK, IT WAS A FUCKING ACCIDENT...I FORGOT I WAS ON THE EDGE OF...YOU KNOW...
WHY DID IT FREAK YOU OUT SO MUCH? I MEAN WI' ALL THE TIME YOU SPEND AROUND GAYS--
THAT'S NOT ME, THAT'S SWINGWING...!
HE DID WHAT THESE CUNTS ALWAYS DO. HE FUCKED OFF.
FLEW AWAY.
HE'S GOT THE SUIT AND THE MASK, AND A FUCKING JETPACK SO HE CAN FLY AWAY. HE'S GOT ARMOR.
HE DOESN'T HAVE TO TALK TO THEM ANY LONGER THAN HE WANTS TO. I MEAN IT'S LIKE I TOLD YOU, IT'S BY THE NUMBERS. IT'S EASY.
BUT...THIS LITTLE ASSHOLE... RIGHT UP CLOSE, LIKE RIGHT IN MY FACE, WITH THIS TWISTED SHIT HE'S MANAGED TO COOK UP INSIDE HIS HEAD...
I MEAN DO YOU THINK I LIKE HANGING AROUND THOSE FUCKING COCKSUCKERS? IT'S ALL VERY WELL FOR VOUGHT-AMERICAN, FOR THE COMIC-BOOK PEOPLE--YOU KNOW, OH, SWINGWING'S GOING TO BE NICE TO QUEERS. HE'S GOING TO LOOK AFTER THAT DEMOGRAPHIC FOR US. BUT NOBODY THINKS TO ASK SWINGWING, DO THEY? AND HE'S THE ONE HAS TO DO IT--TALK TO THEM, SMILE AT THEM, SHAKE HANDS WITH THEM, WITH THOSE FILTHY FUCKING DISEASE-RIDDEN FAGGOT SCUM!!
BLIMEY, MATE, TELL US HOW YOU REALLY FEEL.
GET UP.

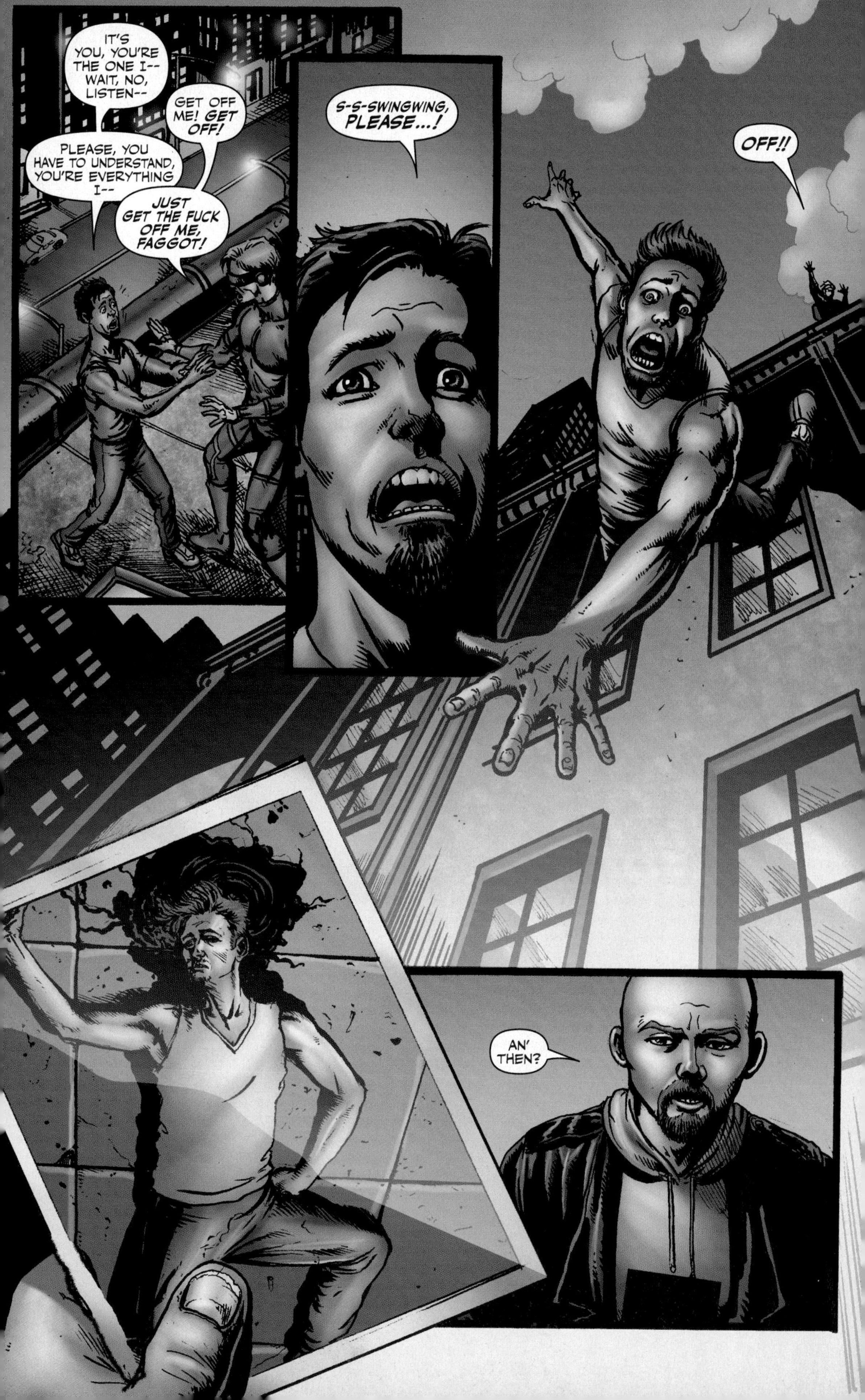
IT'S YOU, YOU'RE THE ONE I-- WAIT, NO, LISTEN--
GET OFF ME! GET OFF!
PLEASE, YOU HAVE TO UNDERSTAND, YOU'RE EVERYTHING I--
JUST GET THE FUCK OFF ME, FAGGOT!
S-S-SWINGWING, PLEASE...!
OFF!!
AN' THEN?

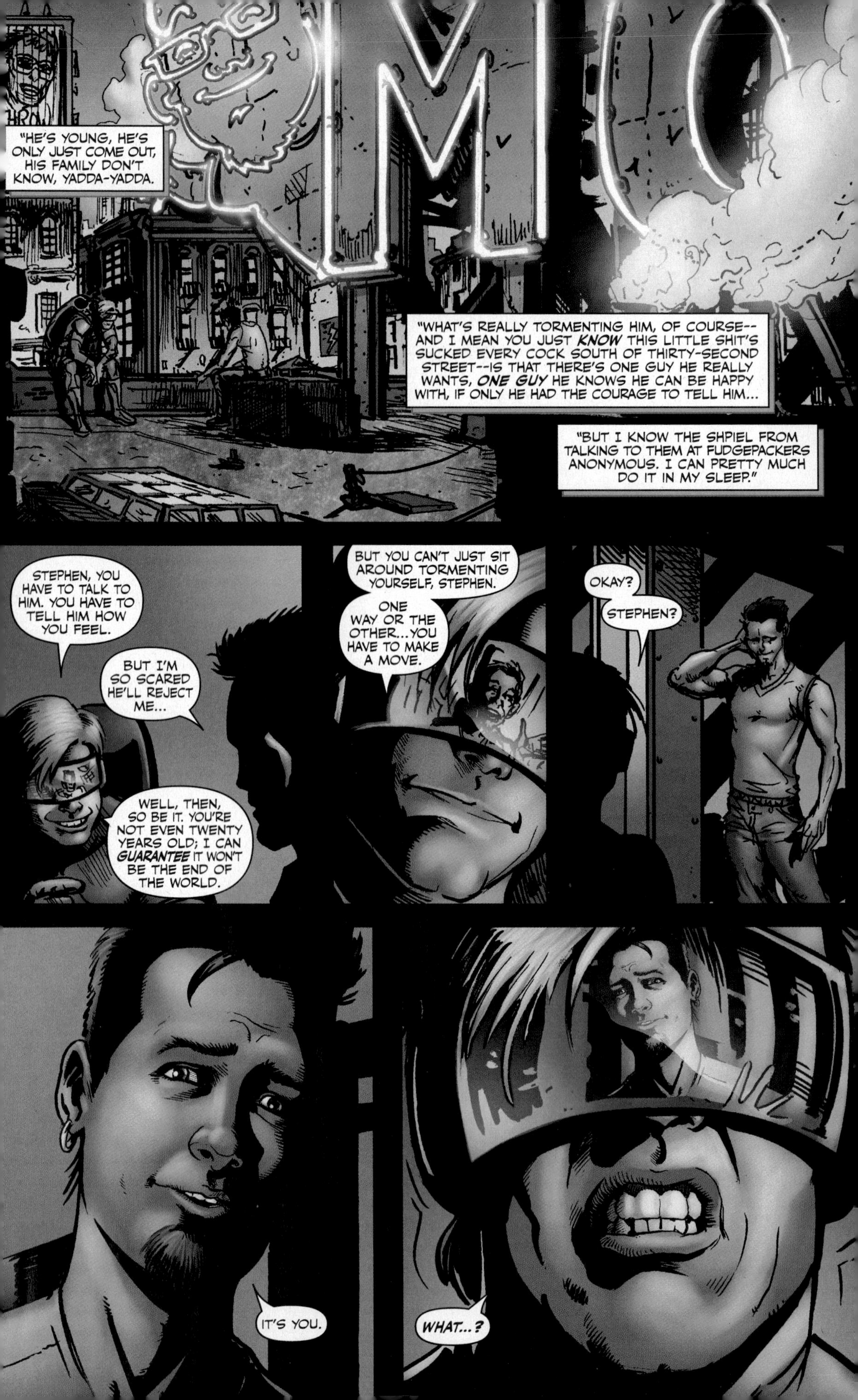

"HE'S YOUNG, HE'S ONLY JUST COME OUT, HIS FAMILY DON'T KNOW, YADDA-YADDA.
"WHAT'S REALLY TORMENTING HIM, OF COURSE-- AND I MEAN YOU JUST KNOW THIS LITTLE SHIT'S SUCKED EVERY COCK SOUTH OF THIRTY-SECOND STREET--IS THAT THERE'S ONE GUY HE REALLY WANTS, ONE GUY HE KNOWS HE CAN BE HAPPY WITH, IF ONLY HE HAD THE COURAGE TO TELL HIM...
"BUT I KNOW THE SHPIEL FROM TALKING TO THEM AT FUDGEPACKERS ANONYMOUS. I CAN PRETTY MUCH DO IT IN MY SLEEP."
STEPHEN, YOU HAVE TO TALK TO HIM. YOU HAVE TO TELL HIM HOW YOU FEEL.
BUT I'M SO SCARED HE'LL REJECT ME...
WELL, THEN, SO BE IT. YOU'RE NOT EVEN TWENTY YEARS OLD; I CAN GUARANTEE IT WON'T BE THE END OF THE WORLD.
BUT YOU CAN'T JUST SIT AROUND TORMENTING YOURSELF, STEPHEN.
ONE WAY OR THE OTHER...YOU HAVE TO MAKE A MOVE.
OKAY?
STEPHEN?
IT'S YOU.
WHAT...?

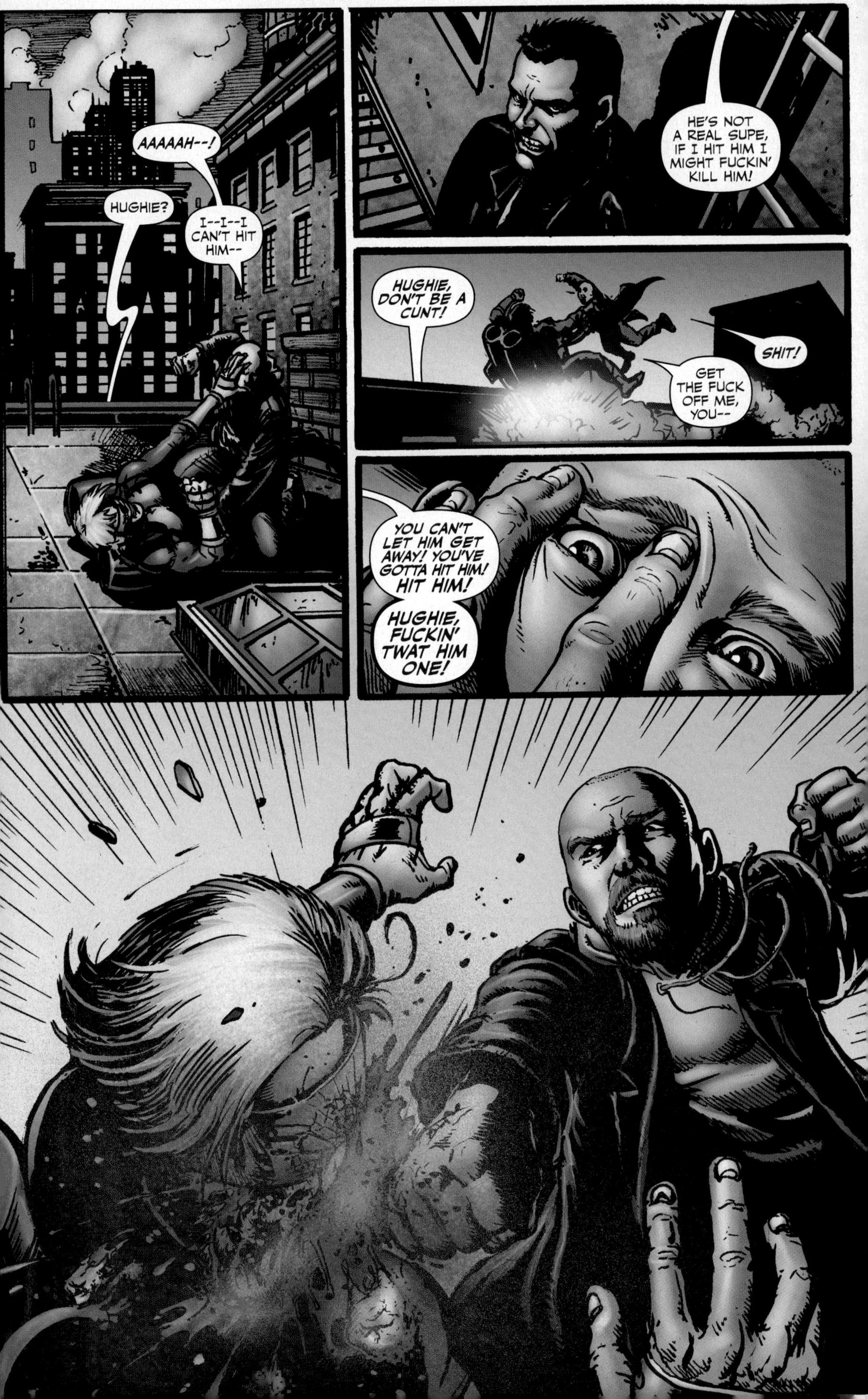
AAAAAH--!
HUGHIE?
I--I--I CAN'T HIT HIM--
HE'S NOT A REAL SUPE, IF I HIT HIM I MIGHT FUCKIN' KILL HIM!
HUGHIE, DON'T BE A CUNT!
SHIT!
GET THE FUCK OFF ME, YOU--
YOU CAN'T LET HIM GET AWAY! YOU'VE GOTTA HIT HIM! HIT HIM!
HUGHIE, FUCKIN' TWAT HIM ONE!

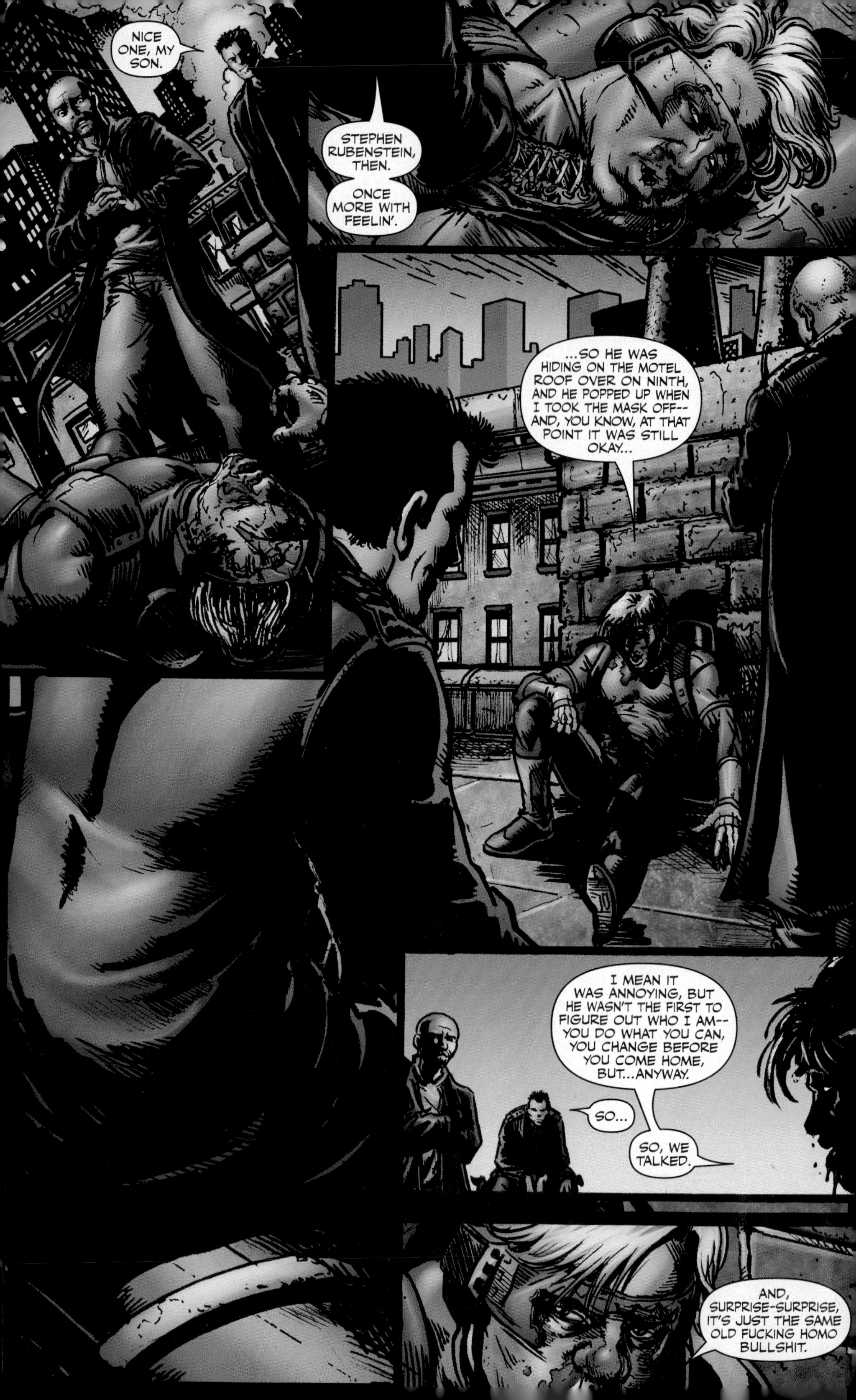
NICE ONE, MY SON.
STEPHEN RUBENSTEIN, THEN.
ONCE MORE WITH FEELIN'.
...SO HE WAS HIDING ON THE MOTEL ROOF OVER ON NINTH, AND HE POPPED UP WHEN I TOOK THE MASK OFF-- AND, YOU KNOW, AT THAT POINT IT WAS STILL OKAY...
I MEAN IT WAS ANNOYING, BUT HE WASN'T THE FIRST TO FIGURE OUT WHO I AM-- YOU DO WHAT YOU CAN, YOU CHANGE BEFORE YOU COME HOME, BUT...ANYWAY.
SO...
SO, WE TALKED.
AND, SURPRISE-SURPRISE, IT'S JUST THE SAME OLD FUCKING HOMO BULLSHIT.

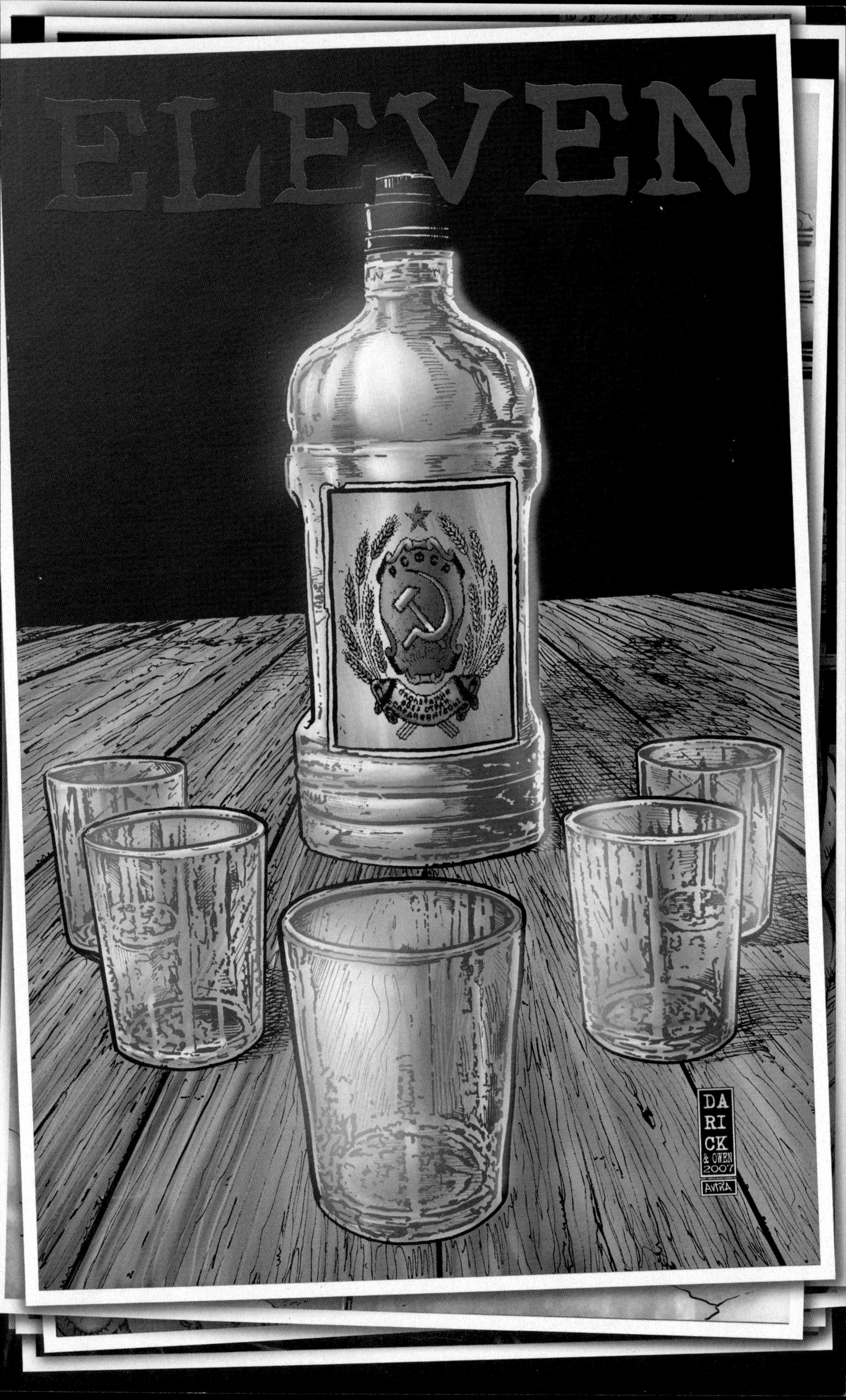
ELEVEN
DA
RI
CK
& OWEN
2007

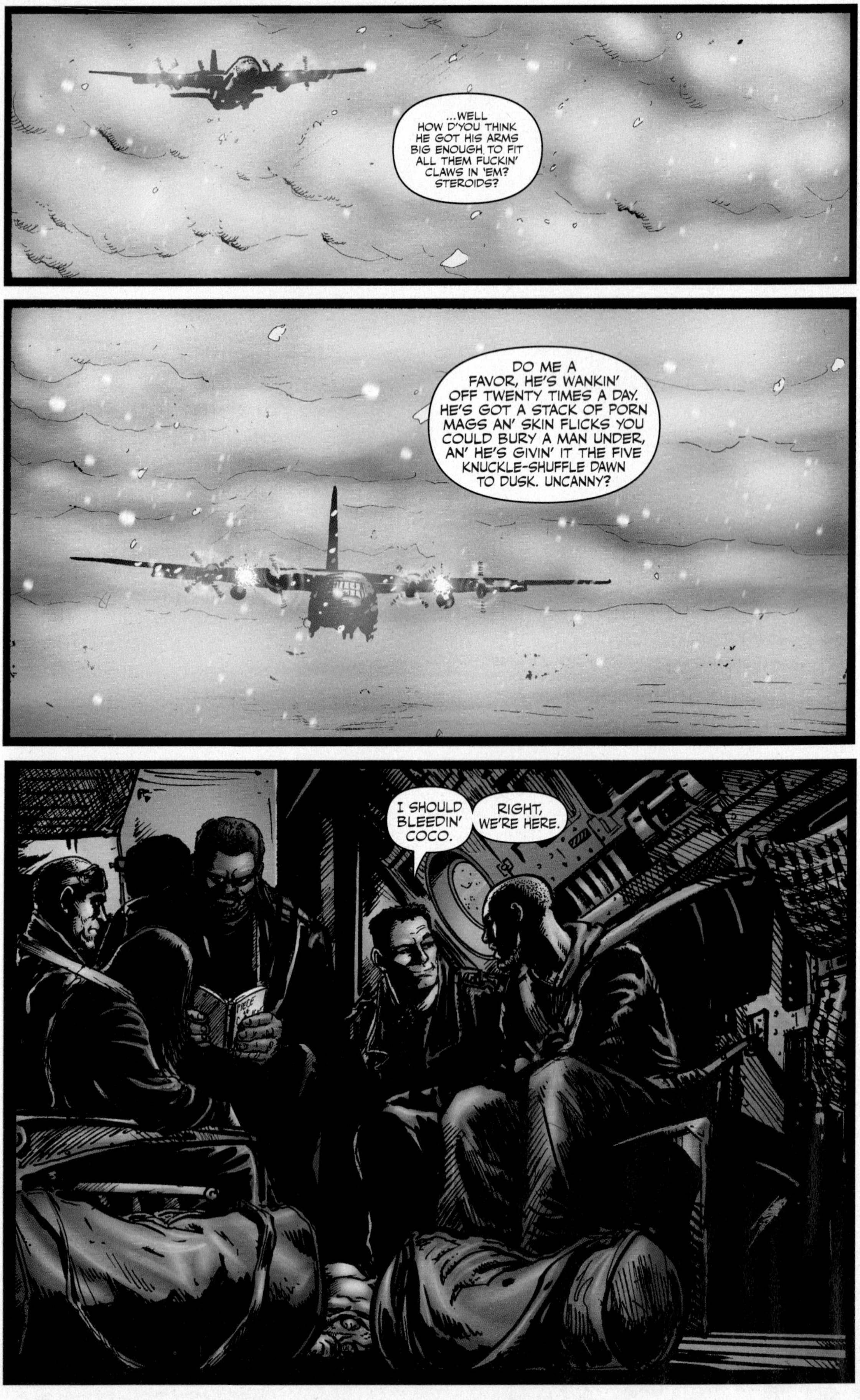
...WELL HOW D'YOU THINK HE GOT HIS ARMS BIG ENOUGH TO FIT ALL THEM FUCKIN' CLAWS IN 'EM? STEROIDS?
DO ME A FAVOR, HE'S WANKIN' OFF TWENTY TIMES A DAY. HE'S GOT A STACK OF PORN MAGS AN' SKIN FLICKS YOU COULD BURY A MAN UNDER, AN' HE'S GIVIN' IT THE FIVE KNUCKLE-SHUFFLE DAWN TO DUSK. UNCANNY?
I SHOULD BLEEDIN' COCO.
RIGHT, WE'RE HERE.

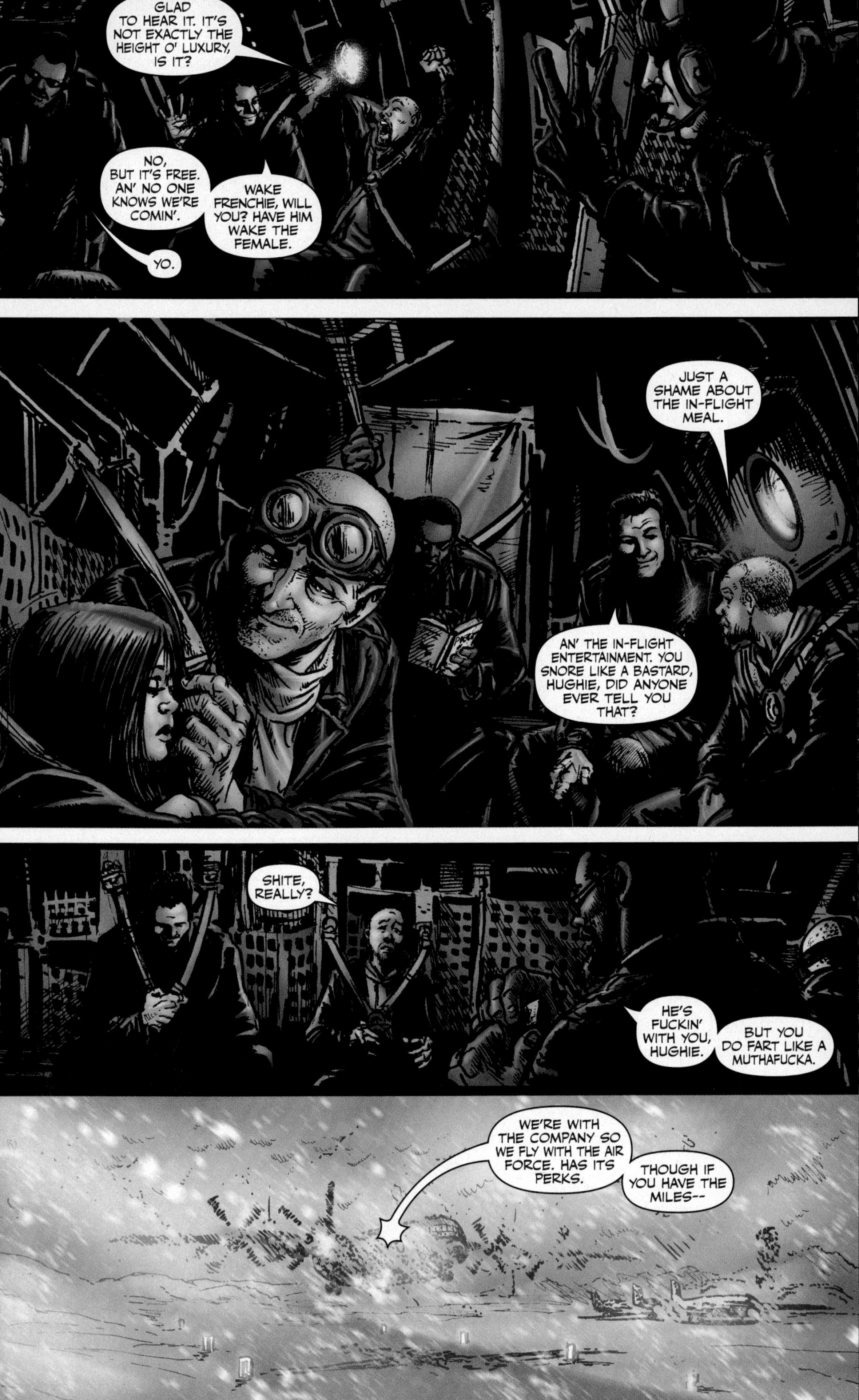
GLAD TO HEAR IT. IT'S NOT EXACTLY THE HEIGHT O' LUXURY, IS IT?
NO, BUT IT'S FREE. AN' NO ONE KNOWS WE'RE COMIN'.
WAKE FRENCHIE, WILL YOU? HAVE HIM WAKE THE FEMALE.
YO.
JUST A SHAME ABOUT THE IN-FLIGHT MEAL.
AN' THE IN-FLIGHT ENTERTAINMENT. YOU SNORE LIKE A BASTARD, HUGHIE, DID ANYONE EVER TELL YOU THAT?
SHITE, REALLY?
HE'S FUCKIN' WITH YOU, HUGHIE.
BUT YOU DO FART LIKE A MUTHAFUCKA.
WE'RE WITH THE COMPANY SO WE FLY WITH THE AIR FORCE. HAS ITS PERKS.
THOUGH IF YOU HAVE THE MILES--

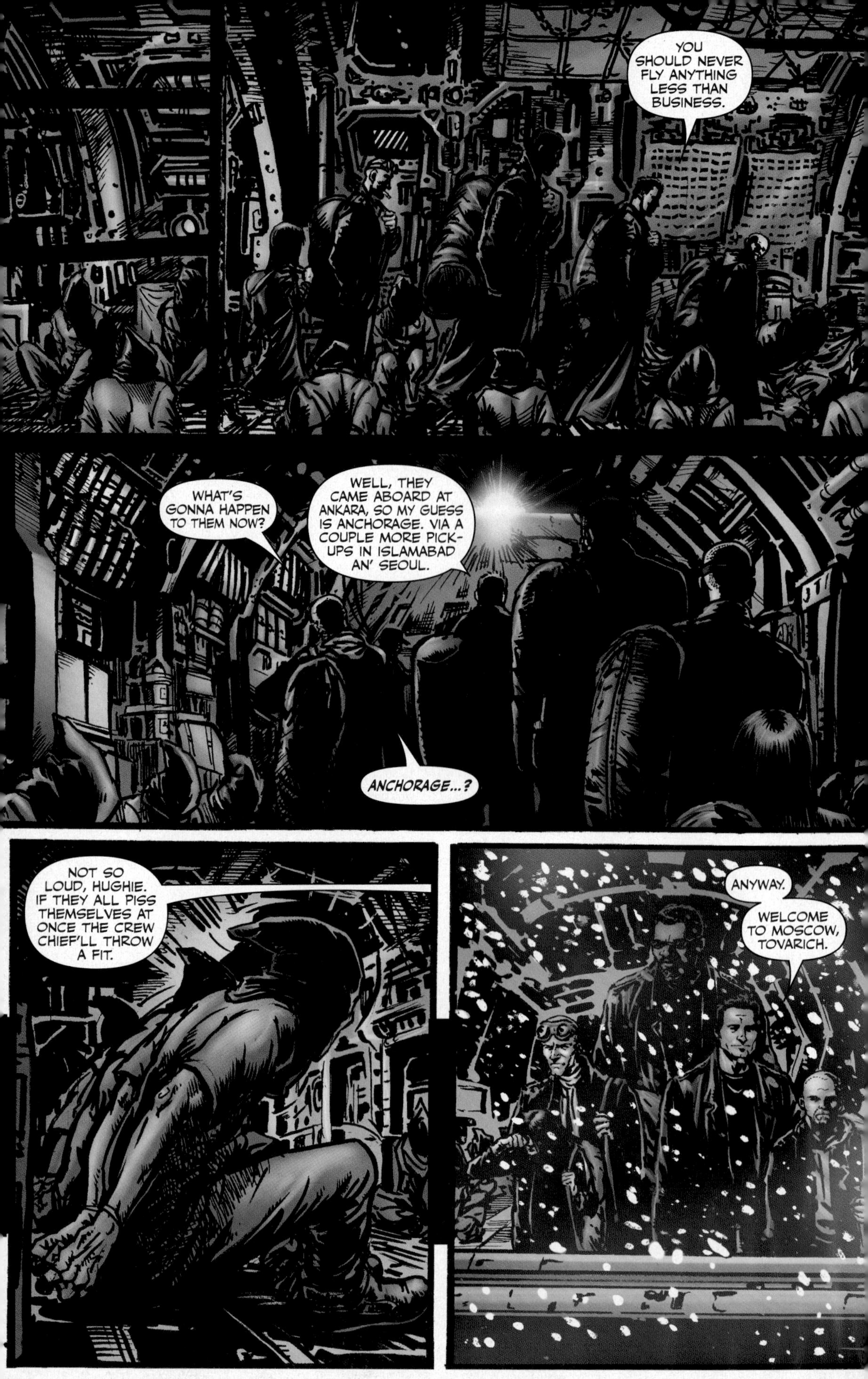
YOU SHOULD NEVER FLY ANYTHING LESS THAN BUSINESS.
WHAT'S GONNA HAPPEN TO THEM NOW?
WELL, THEY CAME ABOARD AT ANKARA, SO MY GUESS IS ANCHORAGE. VIA A COUPLE MORE PICK-UPS IN ISLAMABAD AN' SEOUL.
ANCHORAGE...?
NOT SO LOUD, HUGHIE. IF THEY ALL PISS THEMSELVES AT ONCE THE CREW CHIEF'LL THROW A FIT.
ANYWAY.
WELCOME TO MOSCOW, TOVARICH.

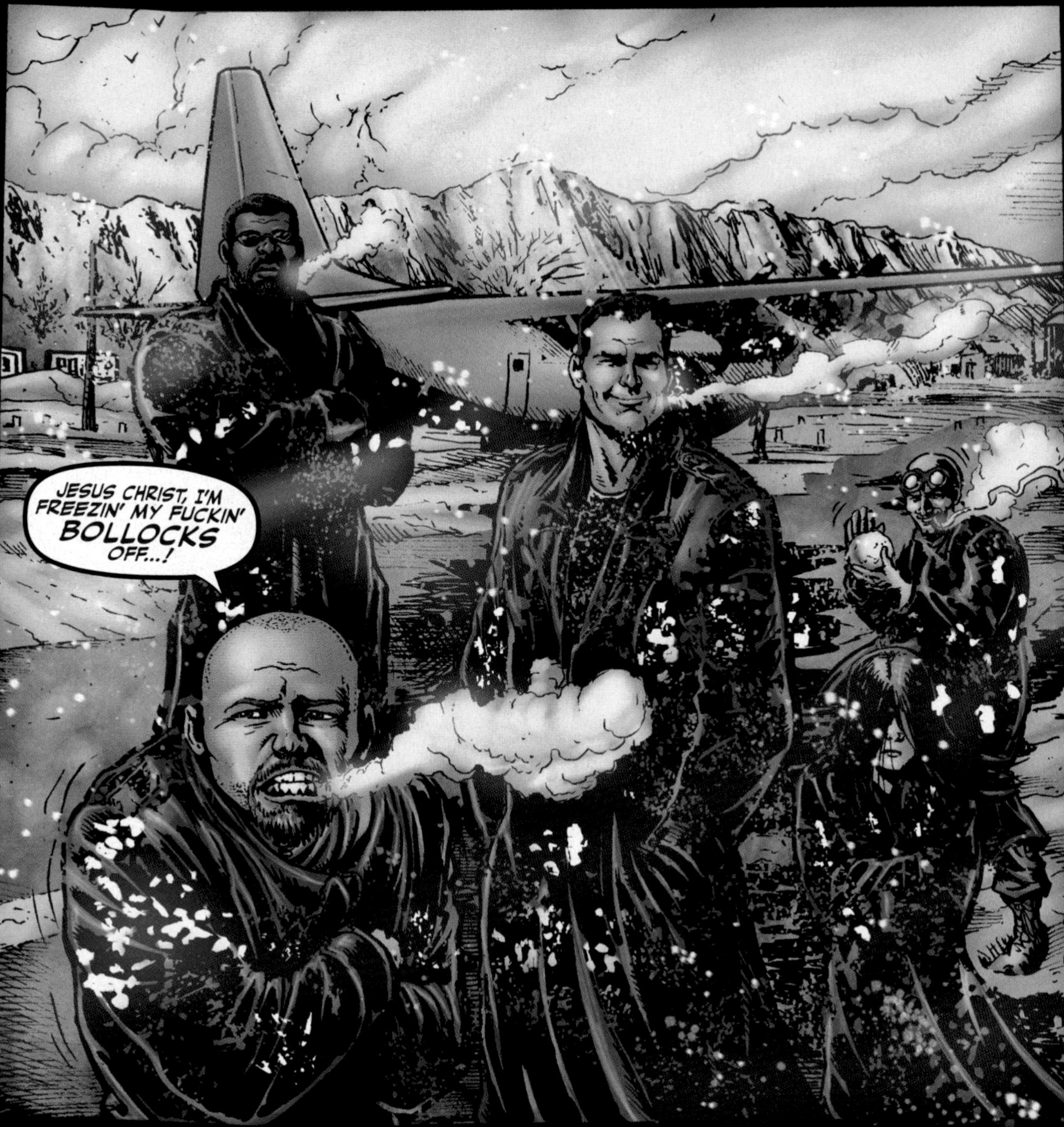
JESUS CHRIST, I'M FREEZIN' MY FUCKIN' BOLLOCKS OFF...!

GLORIOUS FIVE YEAR PLAN

part one

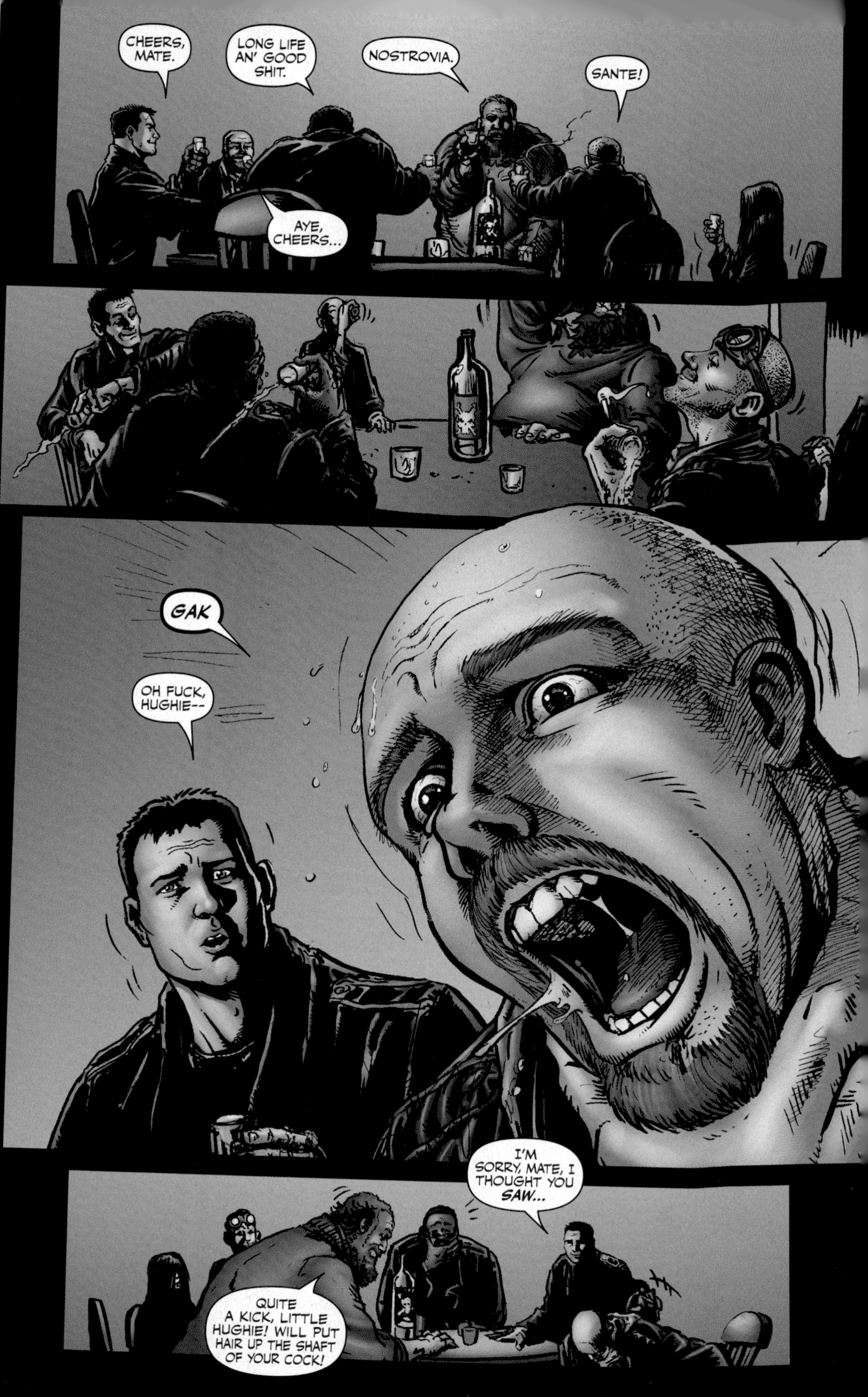
CHEERS, MATE.
LONG LIFE AN' GOOD SHIT.
NOSTROVIA.
SANTE!
AYE, CHEERS...
GAK
OH FUCK, HUGHIE--
I'M SORRY, MATE, I THOUGHT YOU SAW...
QUITE A KICK, LITTLE HUGHIE! WILL PUT HAIR UP THE SHAFT OF YOUR COCK!

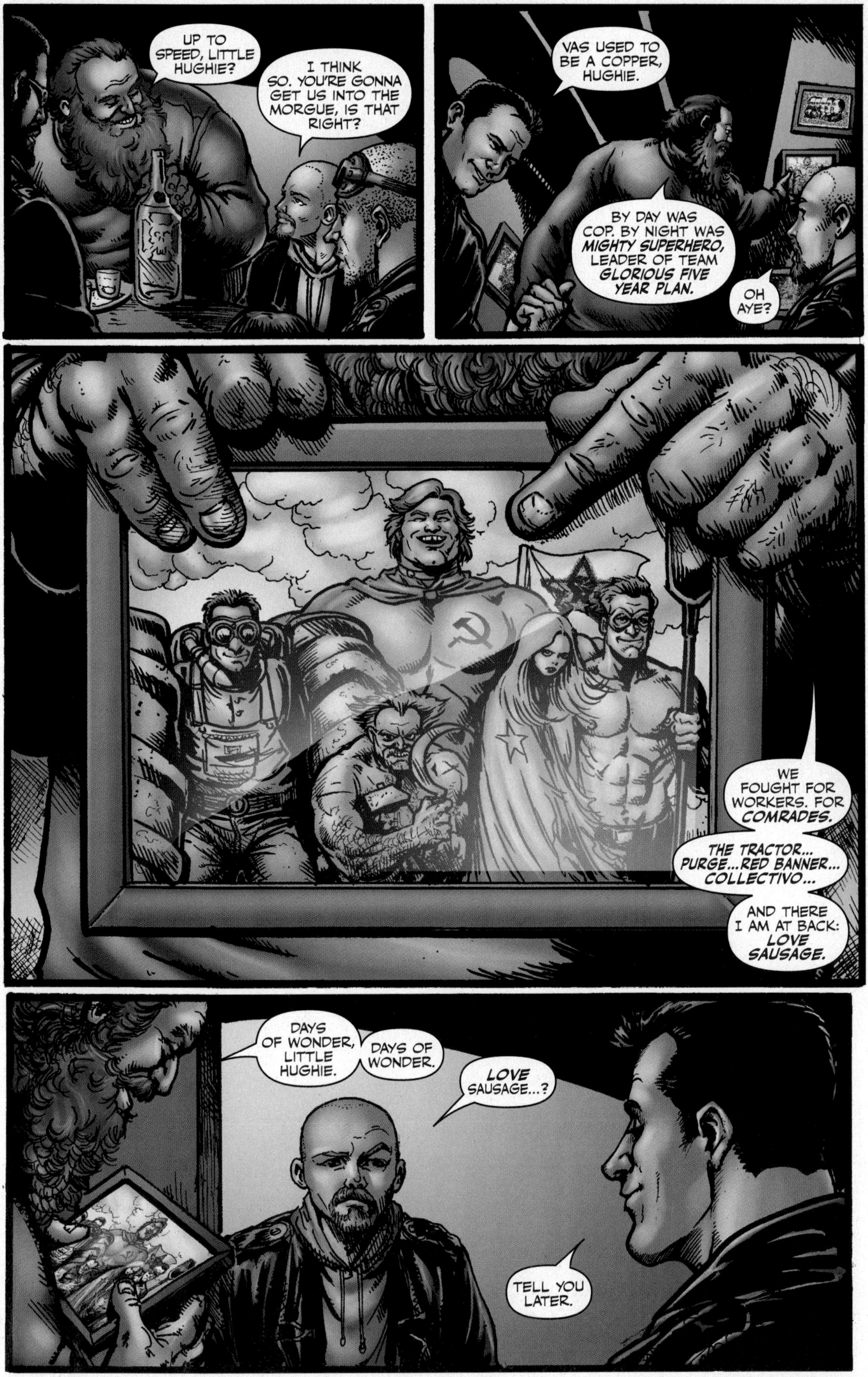
UP TO SPEED, LITTLE HUGHIE?
I THINK SO. YOU'RE GONNA GET US INTO THE MORGUE, IS THAT RIGHT?
VAS USED TO BE A COPPER, HUGHIE.
BY DAY WAS COP. BY NIGHT WAS MIGHTY SUPERHERO, LEADER OF TEAM GLORIOUS FIVE YEAR PLAN.
OH AYE?
WE FOUGHT FOR WORKERS. FOR COMRADES.
THE TRACTOR... PURGE...RED BANNER... COLLECTIVO...
AND THERE I AM AT BACK: LOVE SAUSAGE.
DAYS OF WONDER, LITTLE HUGHIE.
DAYS OF WONDER.
LOVE SAUSAGE...?
TELL YOU LATER.

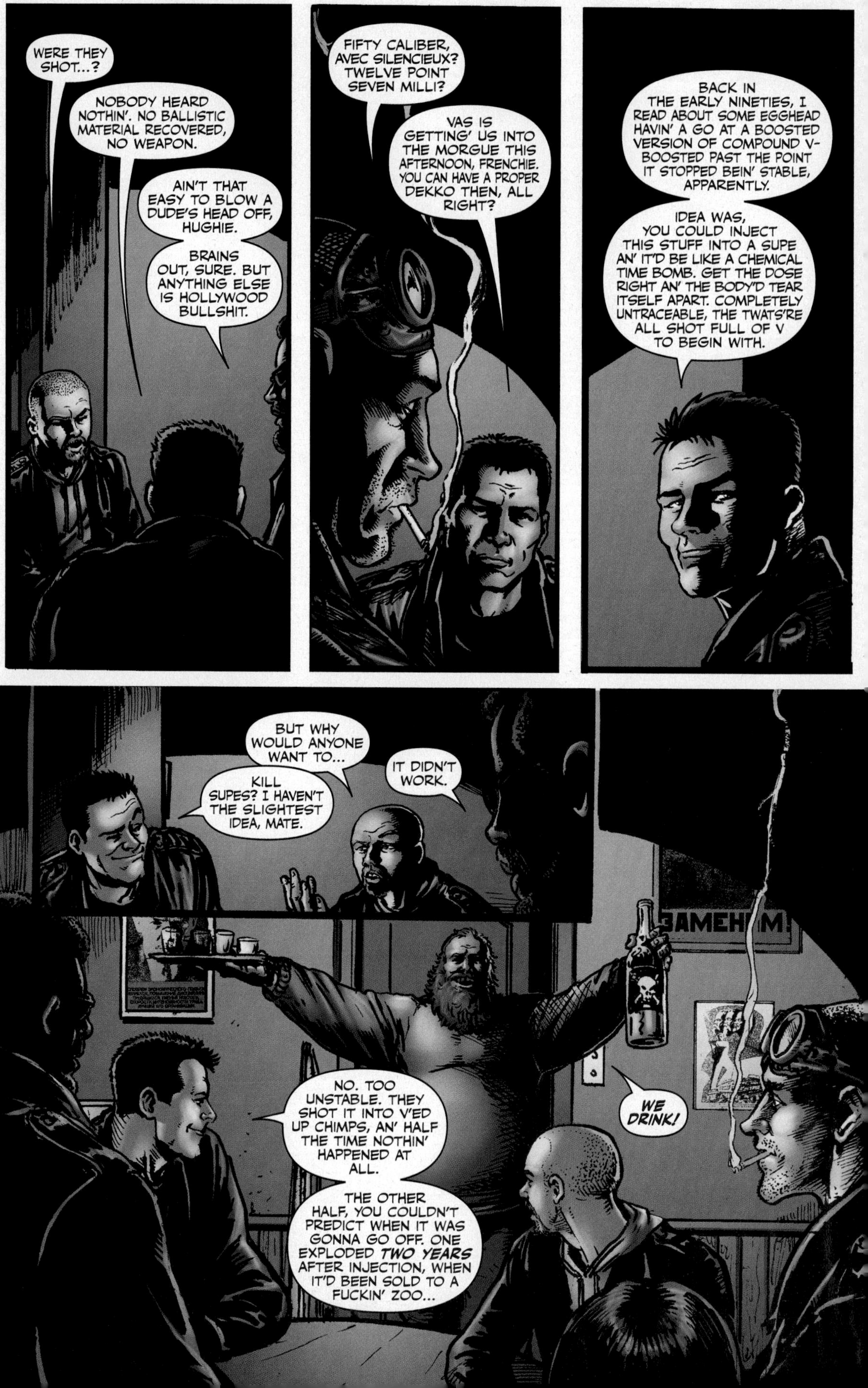
WERE THEY SHOT...?
NOBODY HEARD NOTHIN'. NO BALLISTIC MATERIAL RECOVERED, NO WEAPON.
AIN'T THAT EASY TO BLOW A DUDE'S HEAD OFF, HUGHIE.
BRAINS OUT, SURE. BUT ANYTHING ELSE IS HOLLYWOOD BULLSHIT.
FIFTY CALIBER, AVEC SILENCIEUX? TWELVE POINT SEVEN MILLI?
VAS IS GETTING' US INTO THE MORGUE THIS AFTERNOON, FRENCHIE. YOU CAN HAVE A PROPER DEKKO THEN, ALL RIGHT?
BACK IN THE EARLY NINETIES, I READ ABOUT SOME EGGHEAD HAVIN' A GO AT A BOOSTED VERSION OF COMPOUND V-BOOSTED PAST THE POINT IT STOPPED BEIN' STABLE, APPARENTLY.
IDEA WAS, YOU COULD INJECT THIS STUFF INTO A SUPE AN' IT'D BE LIKE A CHEMICAL TIME BOMB. GET THE DOSE RIGHT AN' THE BODY'D TEAR ITSELF APART. COMPLETELY UNTRACEABLE, THE TWATS'RE ALL SHOT FULL OF V TO BEGIN WITH.
BUT WHY WOULD ANYONE WANT TO...
KILL SUPES? I HAVEN'T THE SLIGHTEST IDEA, MATE.
IT DIDN'T WORK.
NO. TOO UNSTABLE. THEY SHOT IT INTO V'ED UP CHIMPS, AN' HALF THE TIME NOTHIN' HAPPENED AT ALL.
THE OTHER HALF, YOU COULDN'T PREDICT WHEN IT WAS GONNA GO OFF. ONE EXPLODED *TWO YEARS* AFTER INJECTION, WHEN IT'D BEEN SOLD TO A FUCKIN' ZOO...
WE DRINK!

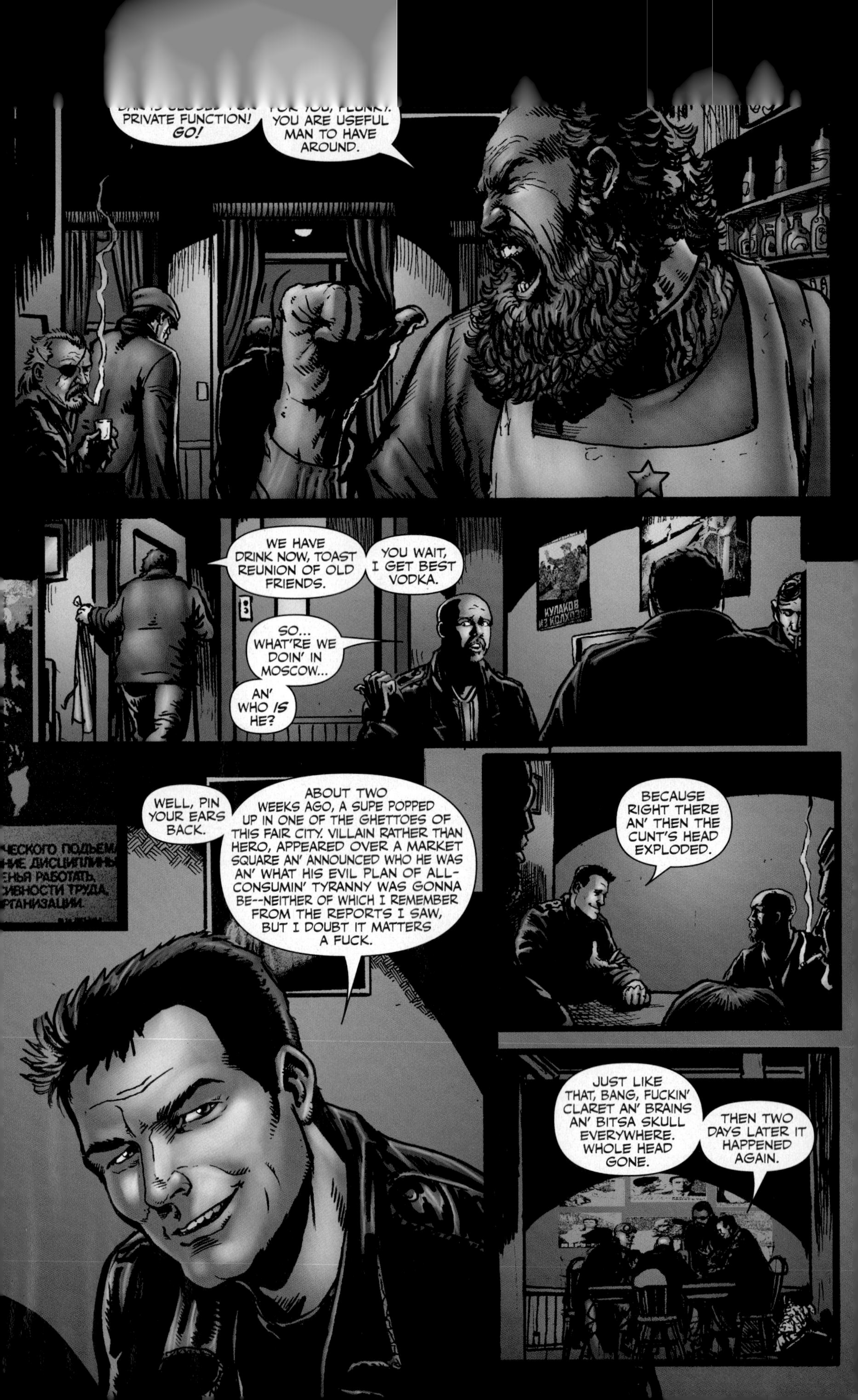
PRIVATE FUNCTION! GO!
YOU ARE USEFUL MAN TO HAVE AROUND.
WE HAVE DRINK NOW, TOAST REUNION OF OLD FRIENDS.
YOU WAIT, I GET BEST VODKA.
КУЛАКОВ
SO... WHAT'RE WE DOIN' IN MOSCOW...
AN' WHO IS HE?
WELL, PIN YOUR EARS BACK.
ABOUT TWO WEEKS AGO, A SUPE POPPED UP IN ONE OF THE GHETTOES OF THIS FAIR CITY. VILLAIN RATHER THAN HERO, APPEARED OVER A MARKET SQUARE AN' ANNOUNCED WHO HE WAS AN' WHAT HIS EVIL PLAN OF ALL-CONSUMIN' TYRANNY WAS GONNA BE--NEITHER OF WHICH I REMEMBER FROM THE REPORTS I SAW, BUT I DOUBT IT MATTERS A FUCK.
BECAUSE RIGHT THERE AN' THEN THE CUNT'S HEAD EXPLODED.
JUST LIKE THAT, BANG, FUCKIN' CLARET AN' BRAINS AN' BITSA SKULL EVERYWHERE. WHOLE HEAD GONE.
THEN TWO DAYS LATER IT HAPPENED AGAIN.

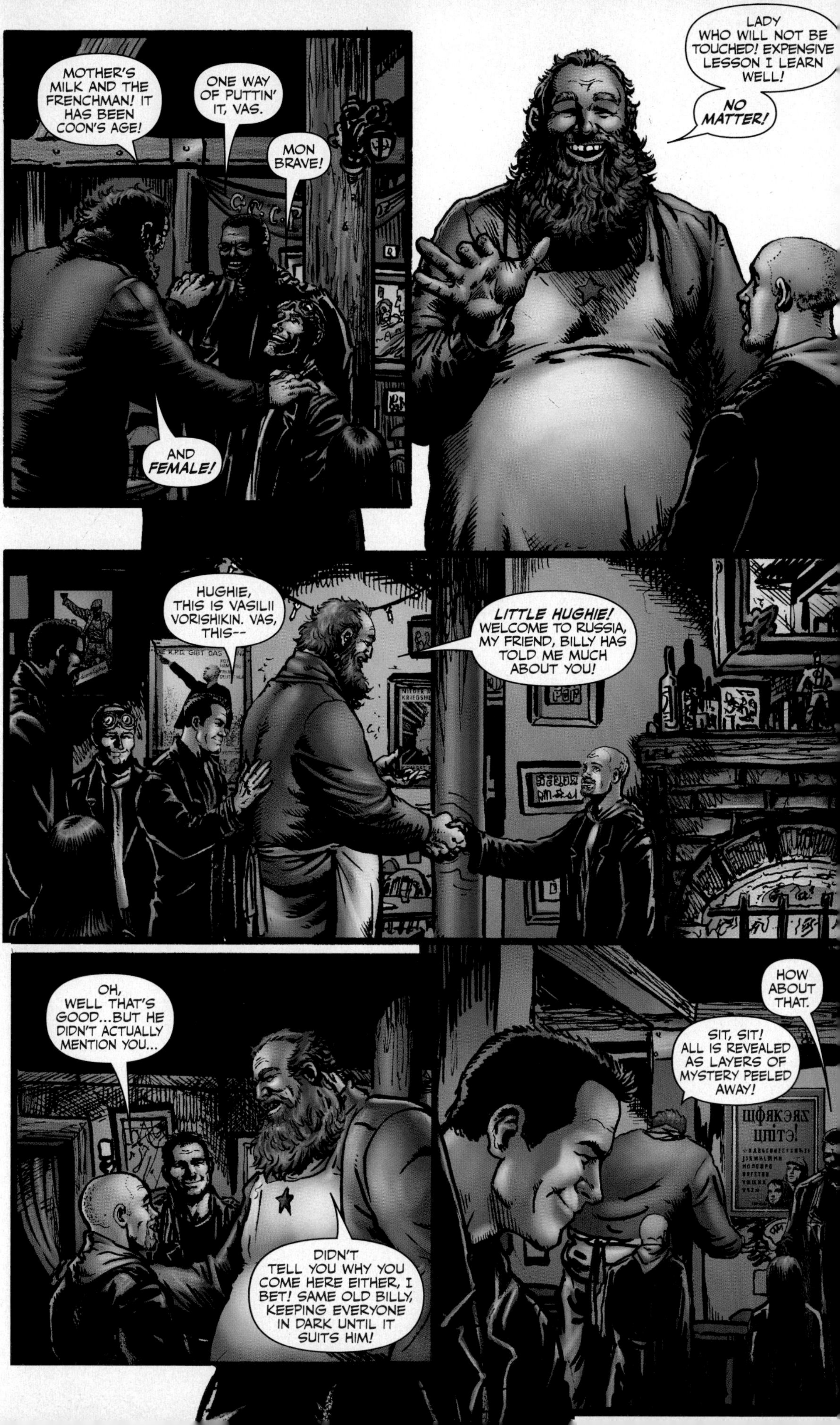
MOTHER'S MILK AND THE FRENCHMAN! IT HAS BEEN COON'S AGE!
ONE WAY OF PUTTIN' IT, VAS.
MON BRAVE!
AND FEMALE!
LADY WHO WILL NOT BE TOUCHED! EXPENSIVE LESSON I LEARN WELL!
NO MATTER!
HUGHIE, THIS IS VASILII VORISHIKIN. VAS, THIS--
LITTLE HUGHIE! WELCOME TO RUSSIA, MY FRIEND, BILLY HAS TOLD ME MUCH ABOUT YOU!
OH, WELL THAT'S GOOD...BUT HE DIDN'T ACTUALLY MENTION YOU...
DIDN'T TELL YOU WHY YOU COME HERE EITHER, I BET! SAME OLD BILLY, KEEPING EVERYONE IN DARK UNTIL IT SUITS HIM!
HOW ABOUT THAT.
SIT, SIT! ALL IS REVEALED AS LAYERS OF MYSTERY PEELED AWAY!

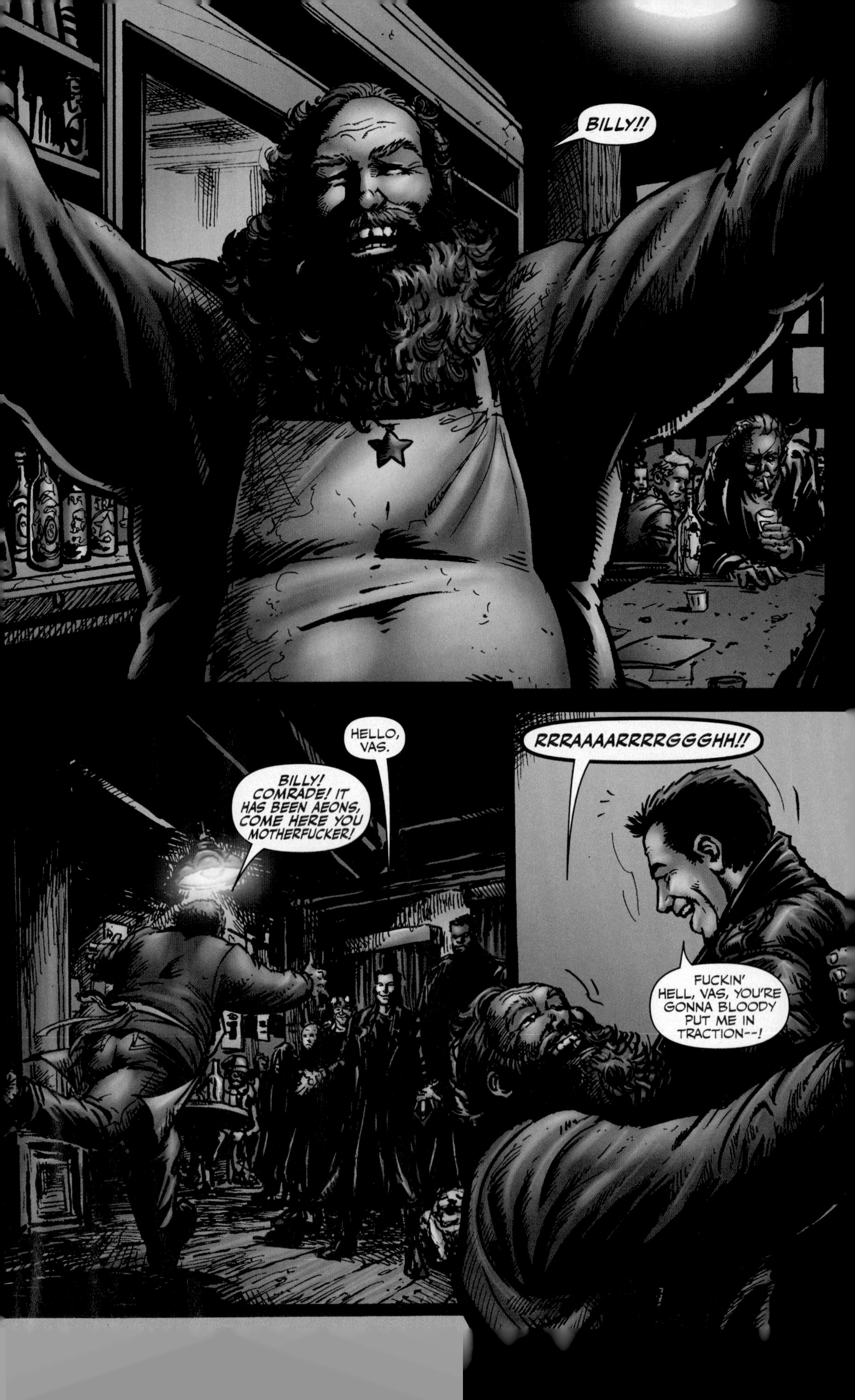
BILLY!!
HELLO, VAS.
BILLY! COMRADE! IT HAS BEEN AEONS, COME HERE YOU MOTHERFUCKER!
RRRAAAARRRRGGGHH!!
FUCKIN' HELL, VAS, YOU'RE GONNA BLOODY PUT ME IN TRACTION--!

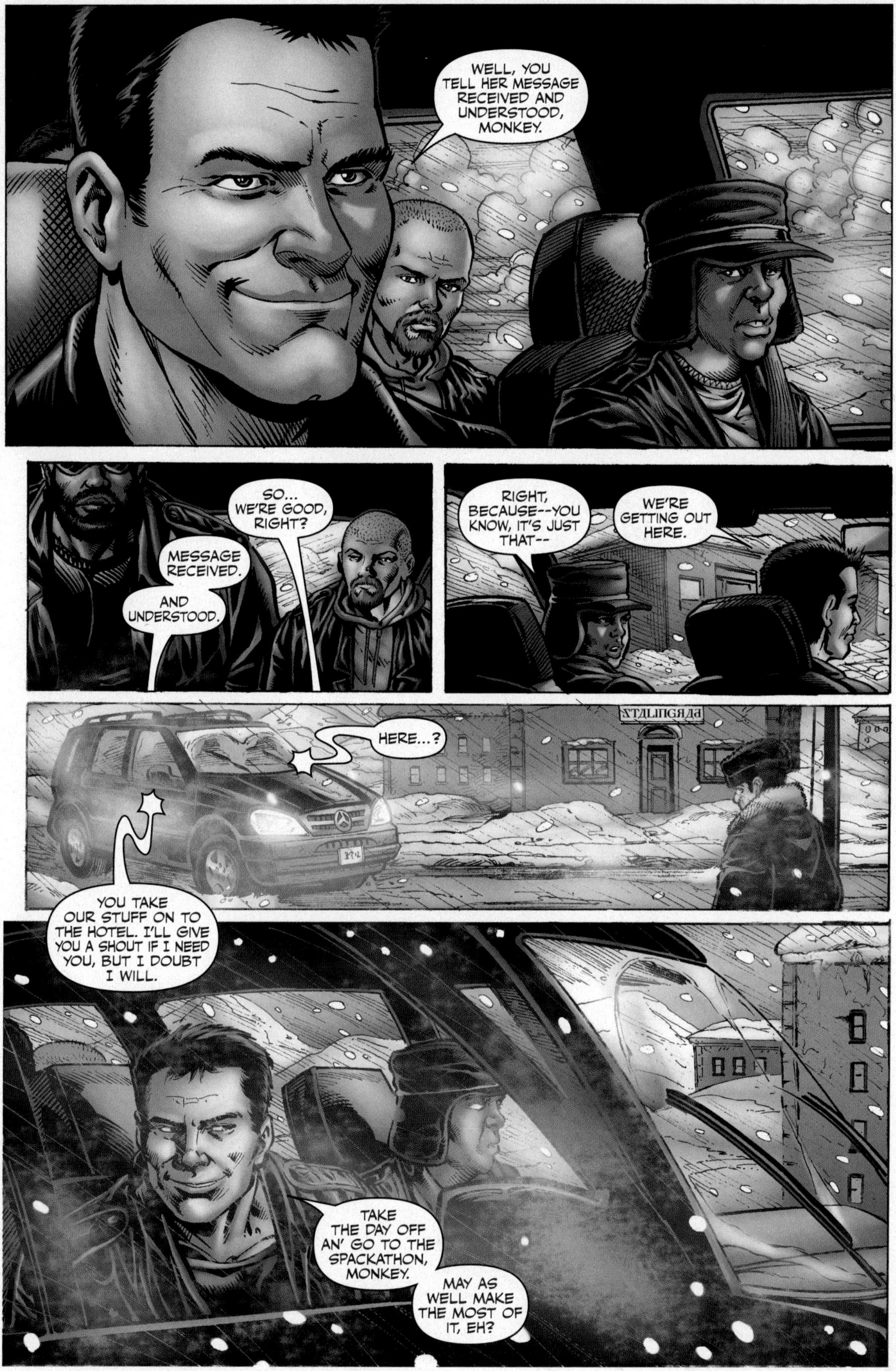
WELL, YOU TELL HER MESSAGE RECEIVED AND UNDERSTOOD, MONKEY.
SO... WE'RE GOOD, RIGHT?
MESSAGE RECEIVED.
AND UNDERSTOOD.
RIGHT, BECAUSE--YOU KNOW, IT'S JUST THAT--
WE'RE GETTING OUT HERE.
STALINGRAD
HERE...?
YOU TAKE OUR STUFF ON TO THE HOTEL. I'LL GIVE YOU A SHOUT IF I NEED YOU, BUT I DOUBT I WILL.
TAKE THE DAY OFF AN' GO TO THE SPACKATHON, MONKEY.
MAY AS WELL MAKE THE MOST OF IT, EH?

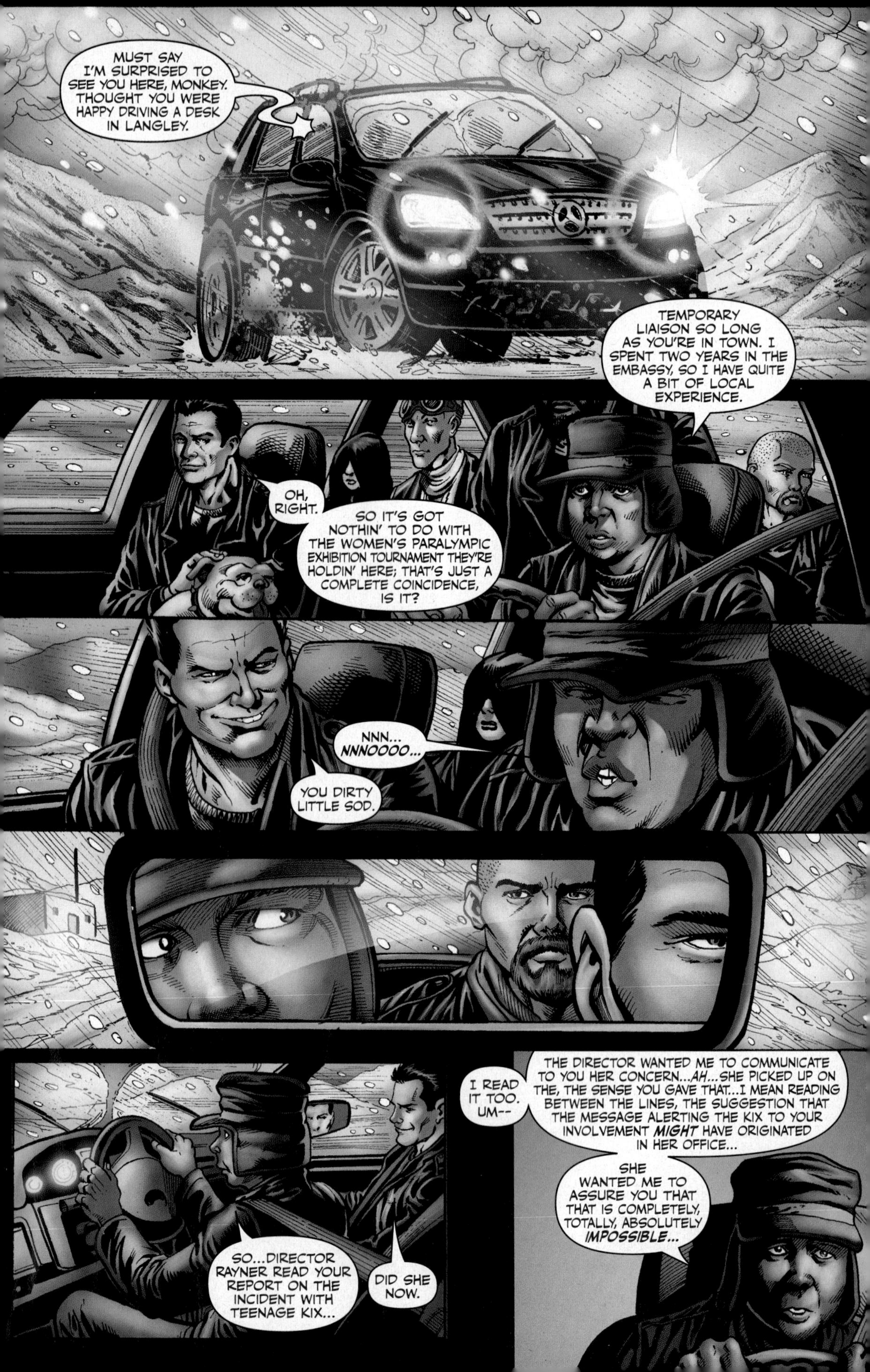
MUST SAY I'M SURPRISED TO SEE YOU HERE, MONKEY. THOUGHT YOU WERE HAPPY DRIVING A DESK IN LANGLEY.
TEMPORARY LIAISON SO LONG AS YOU'RE IN TOWN. I SPENT TWO YEARS IN THE EMBASSY, SO I HAVE QUITE A BIT OF LOCAL EXPERIENCE.
OH, RIGHT.
SO IT'S GOT NOTHIN' TO DO WITH THE WOMEN'S PARALYMPIC EXHIBITION TOURNAMENT THEY'RE HOLDIN' HERE; THAT'S JUST A COMPLETE COINCIDENCE, IS IT?
NNN... NNNOOOO...
YOU DIRTY LITTLE SOD.
SO...DIRECTOR RAYNER READ YOUR REPORT ON THE INCIDENT WITH TEENAGE KIX...
DID SHE NOW.
I READ IT TOO. UM--
THE DIRECTOR WANTED ME TO COMMUNICATE TO YOU HER CONCERN...AH...SHE PICKED UP ON THE, THE SENSE YOU GAVE THAT...I MEAN READING BETWEEN THE LINES, THE SUGGESTION THAT THE MESSAGE ALERTING THE KIX TO YOUR INVOLVEMENT MIGHT HAVE ORIGINATED IN HER OFFICE...
SHE WANTED ME TO ASSURE YOU THAT THAT IS COMPLETELY, TOTALLY, ABSOLUTELY IMPOSSIBLE...

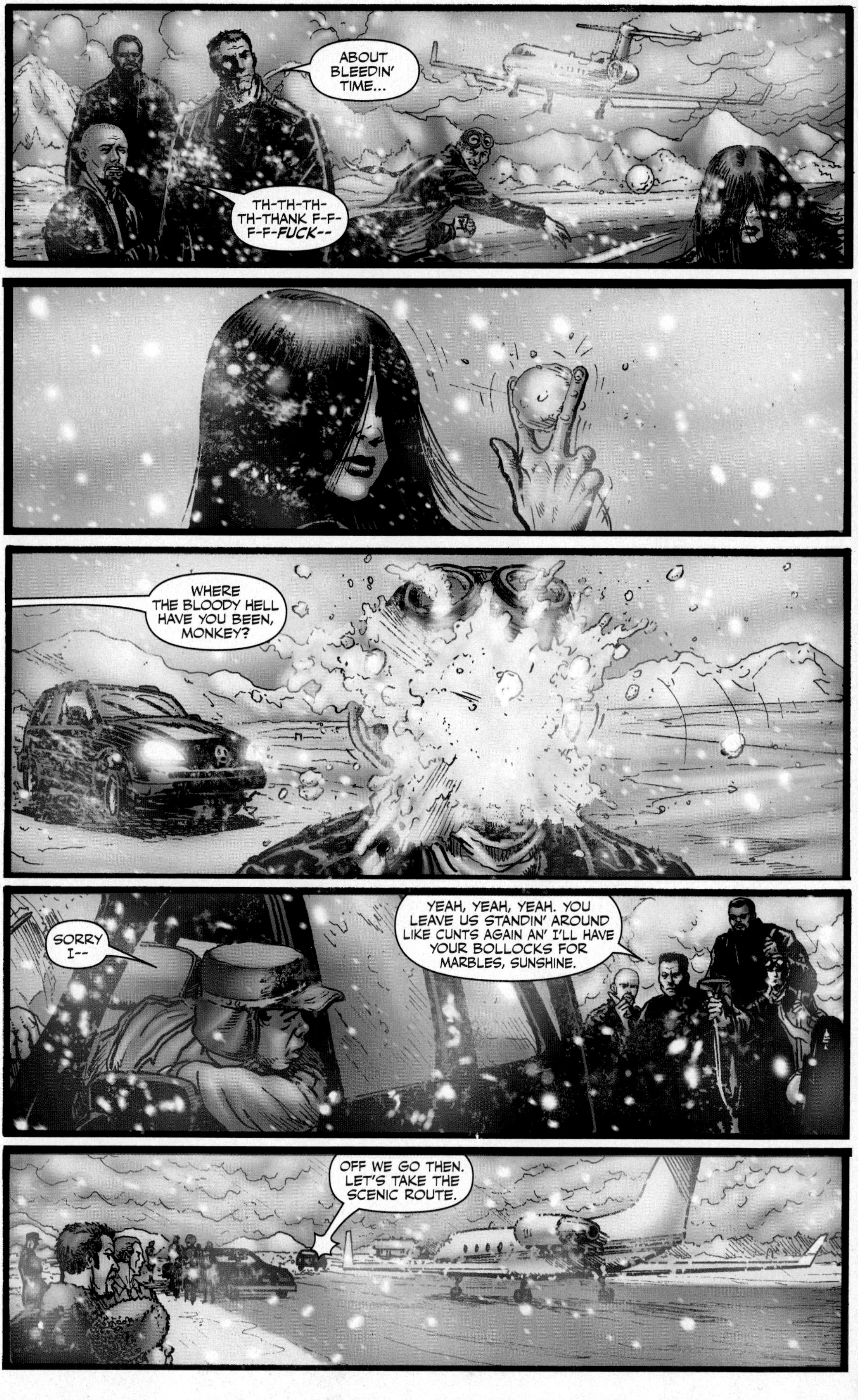
ABOUT BLEEDIN' TIME...
TH-TH-TH-TH-THANK F-F-F-F-FUCK--
WHERE THE BLOODY HELL HAVE YOU BEEN, MONKEY?
SORRY I--
YEAH, YEAH, YEAH. YOU LEAVE US STANDIN' AROUND LIKE CUNTS AGAIN AN' I'LL HAVE YOUR BOLLOCKS FOR MARBLES, SUNSHINE.
OFF WE GO THEN. LET'S TAKE THE SCENIC ROUTE.

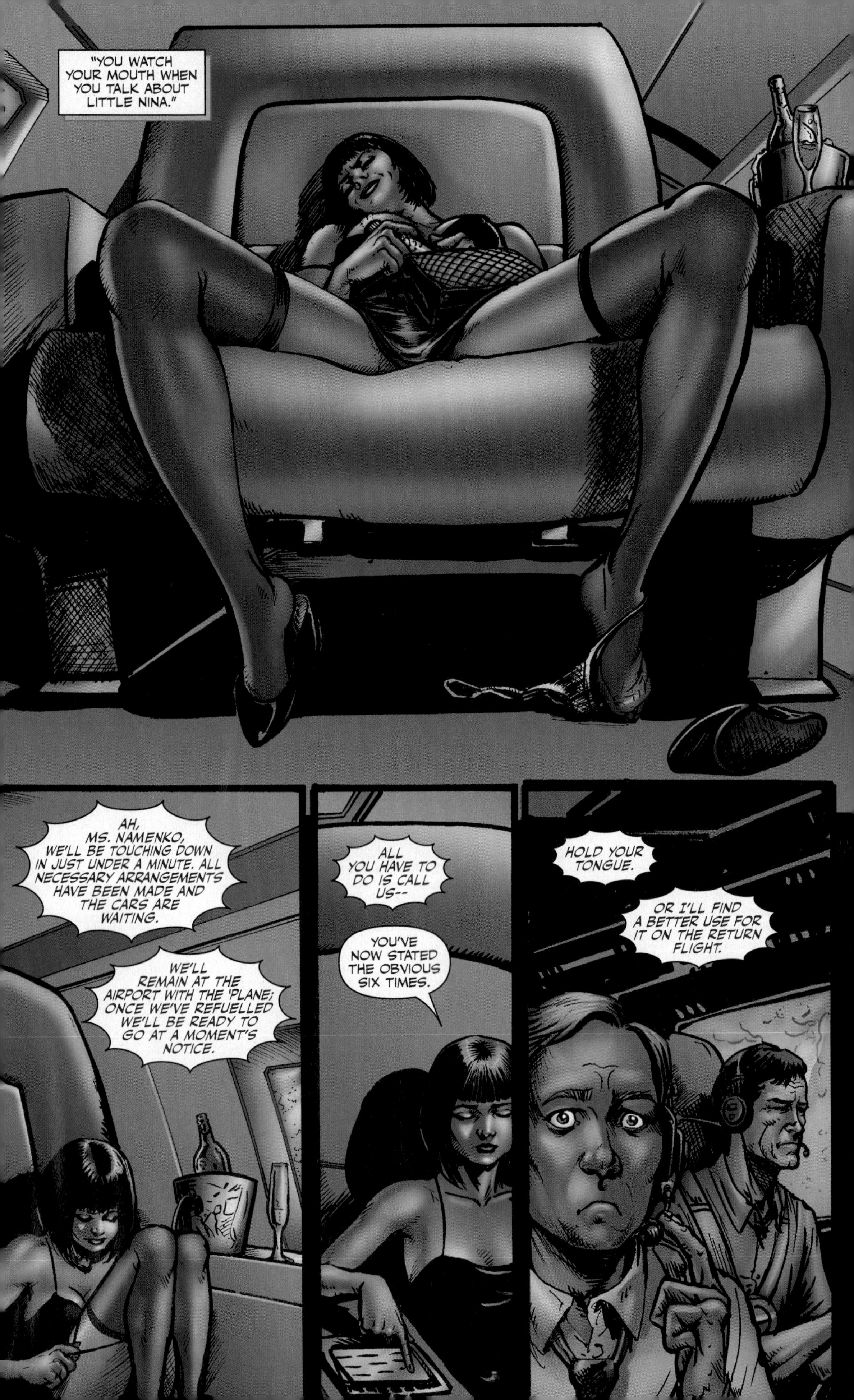
"YOU WATCH YOUR MOUTH WHEN YOU TALK ABOUT LITTLE NINA."
AH, MS. NAMENKO, WE'LL BE TOUCHING DOWN IN JUST UNDER A MINUTE. ALL NECESSARY ARRANGEMENTS HAVE BEEN MADE AND THE CARS ARE WAITING.
WE'LL REMAIN AT THE AIRPORT WITH THE 'PLANE; ONCE WE'VE REFUELLED WE'LL BE READY TO GO AT A MOMENT'S NOTICE.
ALL YOU HAVE TO DO IS CALL US--
YOU'VE NOW STATED THE OBVIOUS SIX TIMES.
HOLD YOUR TONGUE.
OR I'LL FIND A BETTER USE FOR IT ON THE RETURN FLIGHT.

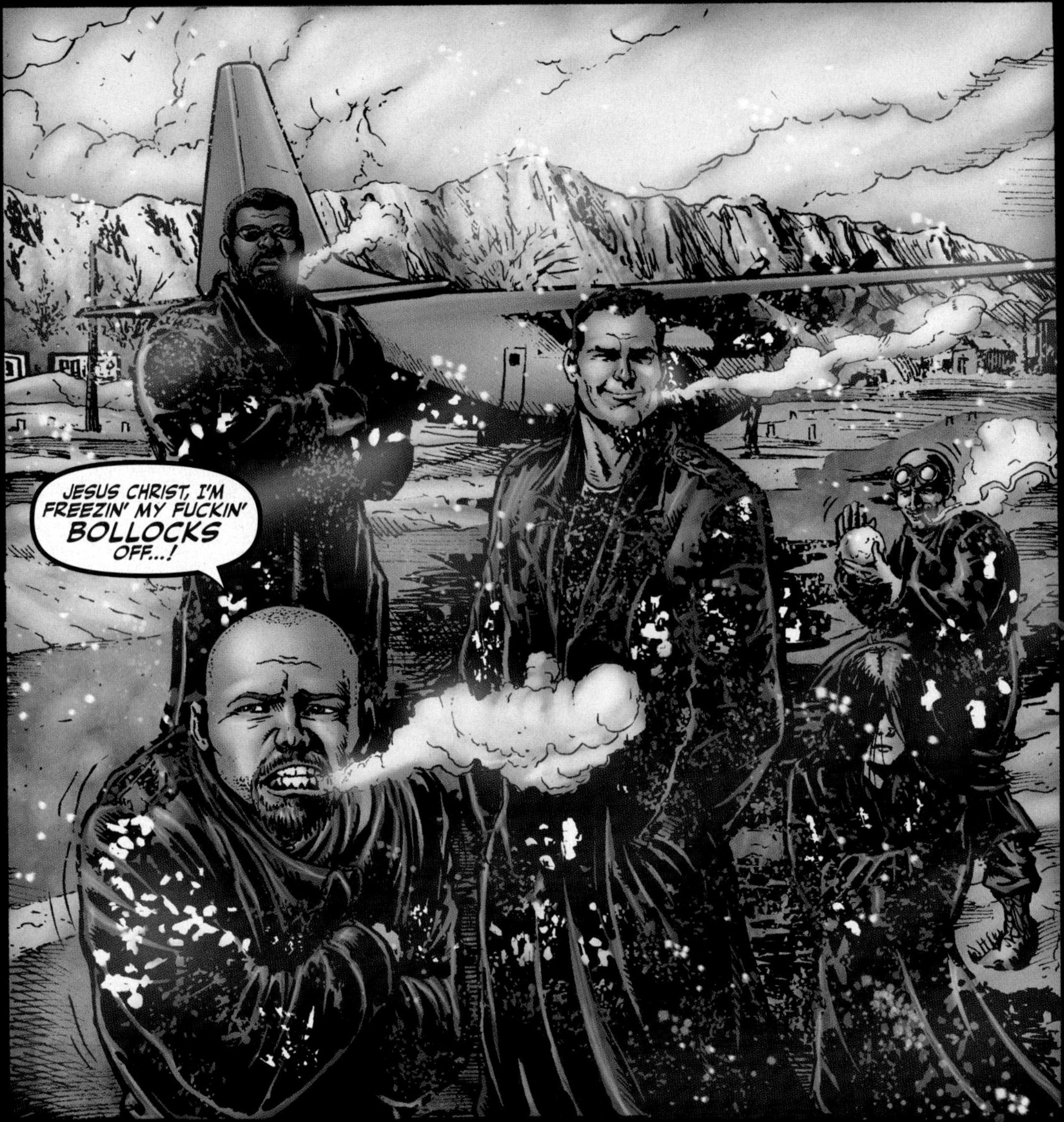
JESUS CHRIST, I'M FREEZIN' MY FUCKIN' BOLLOCKS OFF...!

GLORIOUS FIVE YEAR PLAN

part one

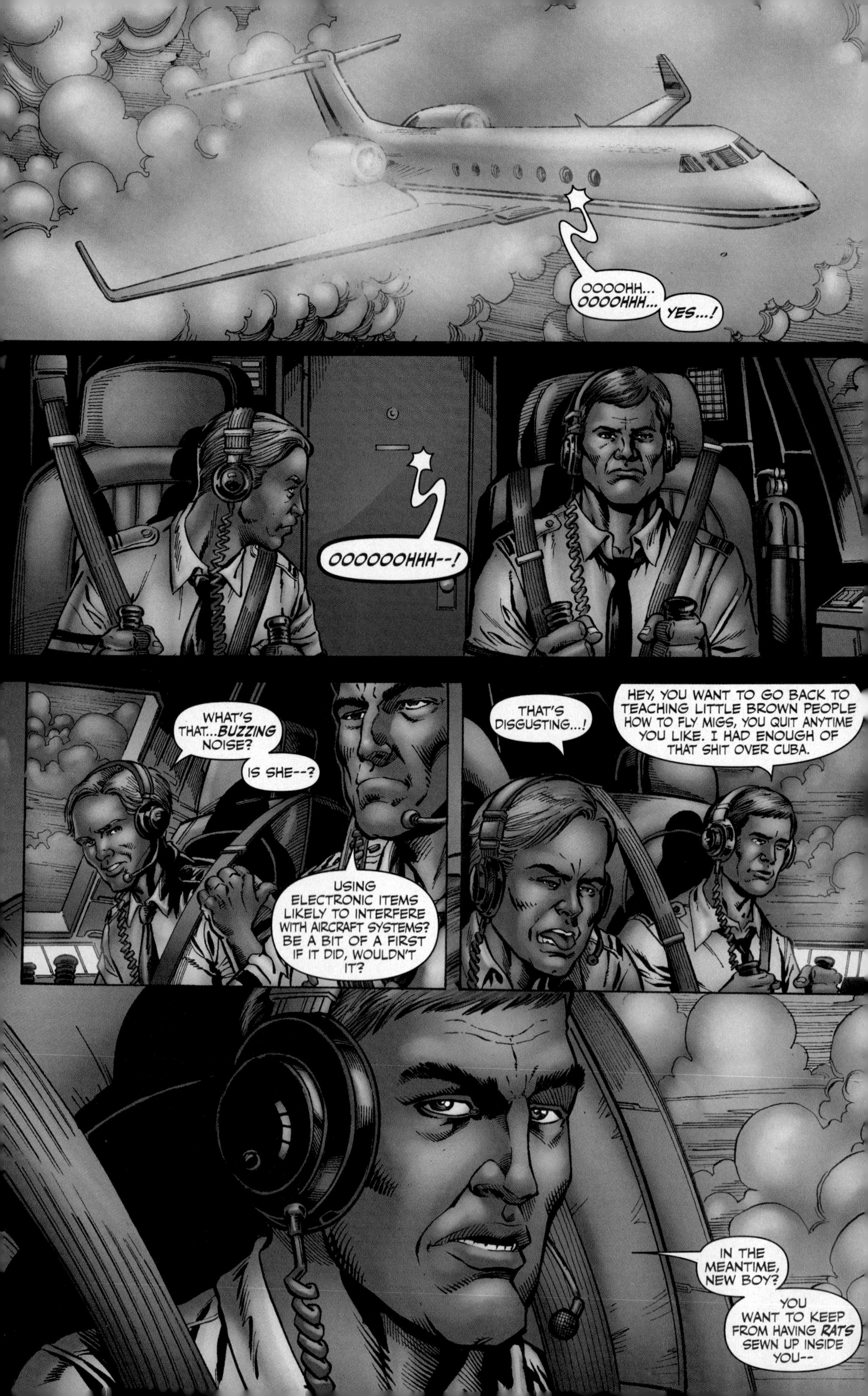

OOOOHH... OOOOHHH...
YES...!
OOOOOOHHH--!
WHAT'S THAT...BUZZING NOISE?
IS SHE--?
USING ELECTRONIC ITEMS LIKELY TO INTERFERE WITH AIRCRAFT SYSTEMS? BE A BIT OF A FIRST IF IT DID, WOULDN'T IT?
THAT'S DISGUSTING...!
HEY, YOU WANT TO GO BACK TO TEACHING LITTLE BROWN PEOPLE HOW TO FLY MIGS, YOU QUIT ANYTIME YOU LIKE. I HAD ENOUGH OF THAT SHIT OVER CUBA.
IN THE MEANTIME, NEW BOY?
YOU WANT TO KEEP FROM HAVING RATS SEWN UP INSIDE YOU--

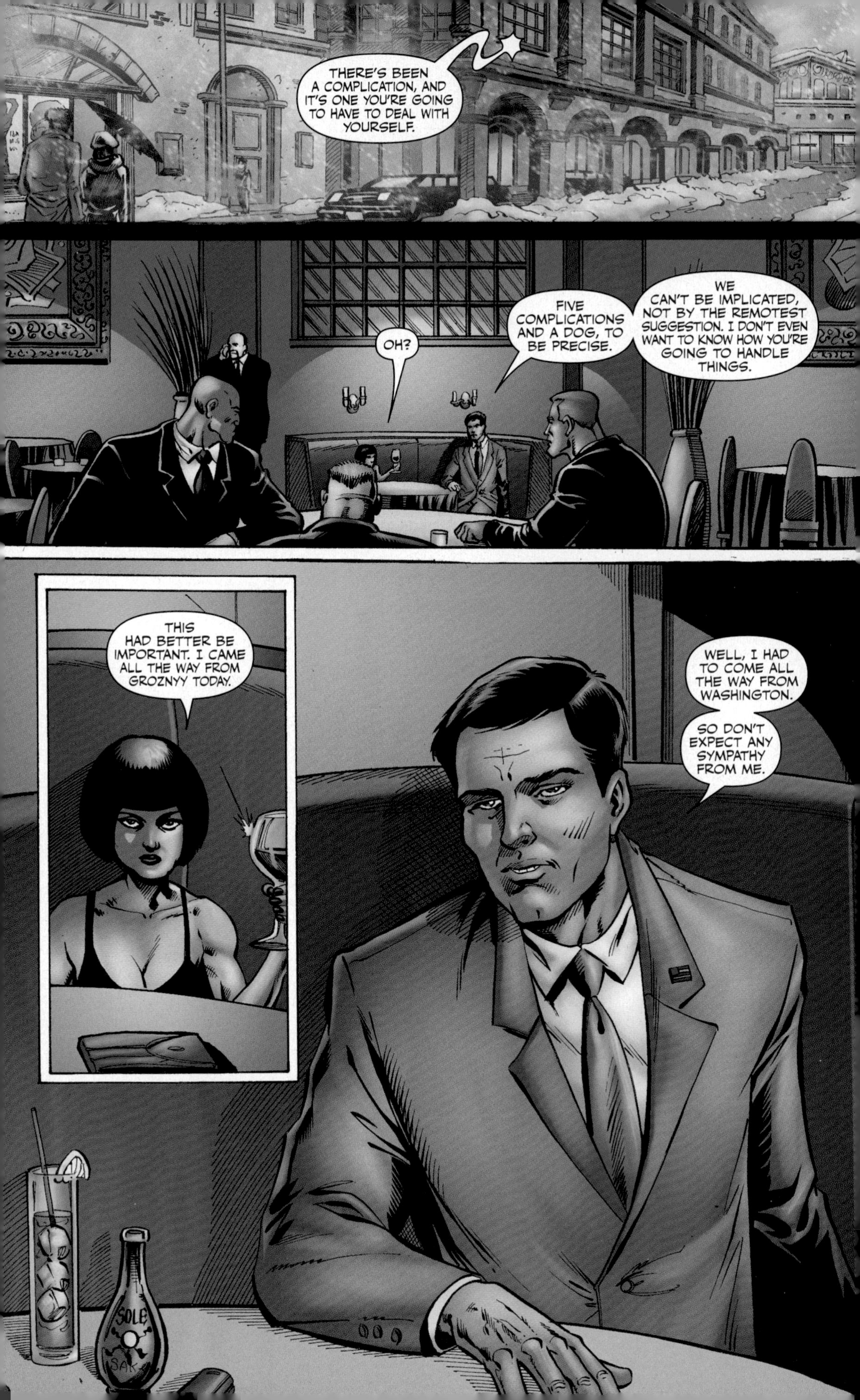
THERE'S BEEN A COMPLICATION, AND IT'S ONE YOU'RE GOING TO HAVE TO DEAL WITH YOURSELF.
OH?
FIVE COMPLICATIONS AND A DOG, TO BE PRECISE.
WE CAN'T BE IMPLICATED, NOT BY THE REMOTEST SUGGESTION. I DON'T EVEN WANT TO KNOW HOW YOU'RE GOING TO HANDLE THINGS.
THIS HAD BETTER BE IMPORTANT. I CAME ALL THE WAY FROM GROZNYY TODAY.
WELL, I HAD TO COME ALL THE WAY FROM WASHINGTON.
SO DON'T EXPECT ANY SYMPATHY FROM ME.

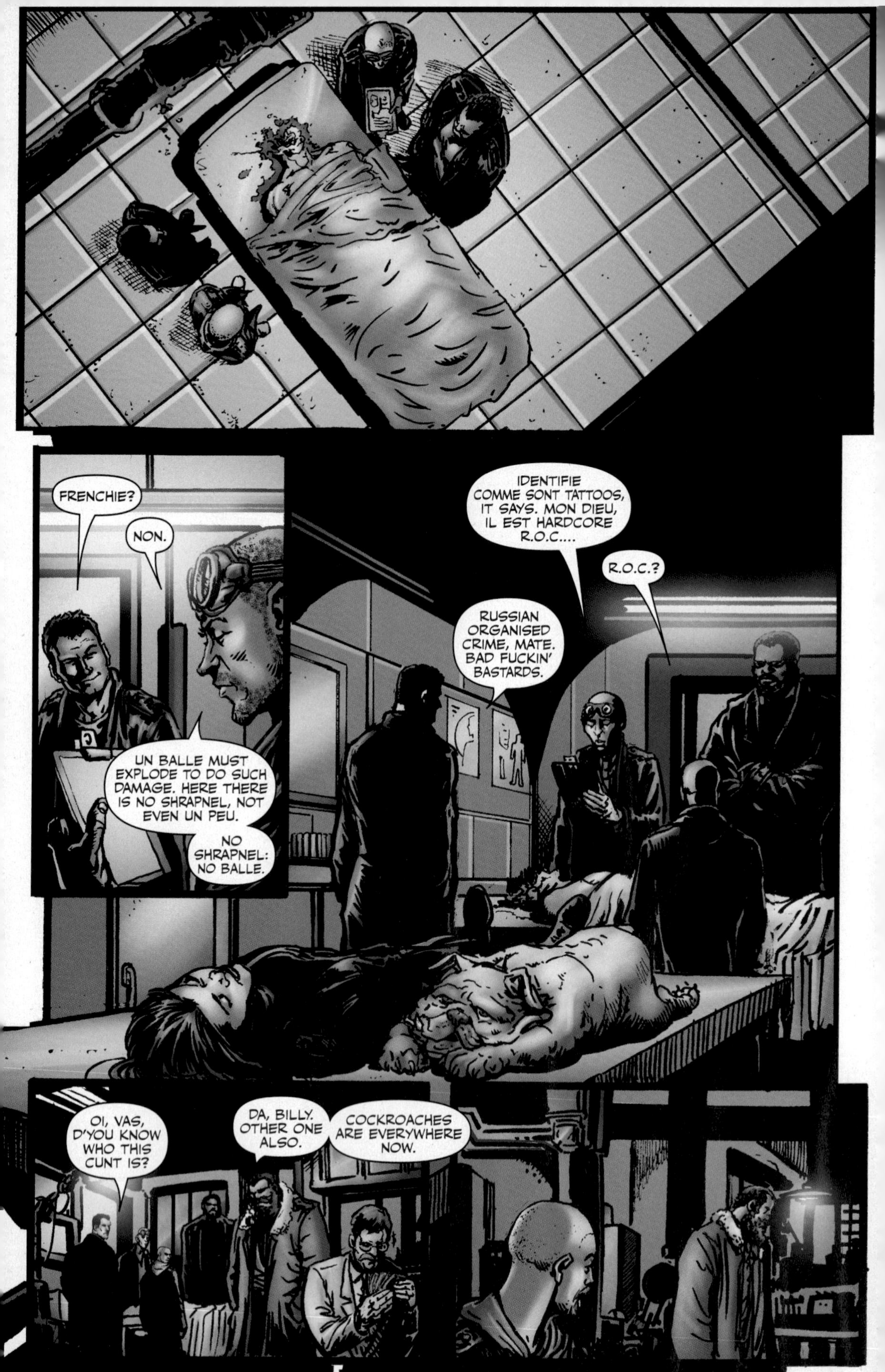
FRENCHIE?
NON.
IDENTIFIE COMME SONT TATTOOS, IT SAYS. MON DIEU, IL EST HARDCORE R.O.C....
R.O.C.?
RUSSIAN ORGANISED CRIME, MATE. BAD FUCKIN' BASTARDS.
UN BALLE MUST EXPLODE TO DO SUCH DAMAGE. HERE THERE IS NO SHRAPNEL, NOT EVEN UN PEU.
NO SHRAPNEL: NO BALLE.
OI, VAS, D'YOU KNOW WHO THIS CUNT IS?
DA, BILLY. OTHER ONE ALSO.
COCKROACHES ARE EVERYWHERE NOW.

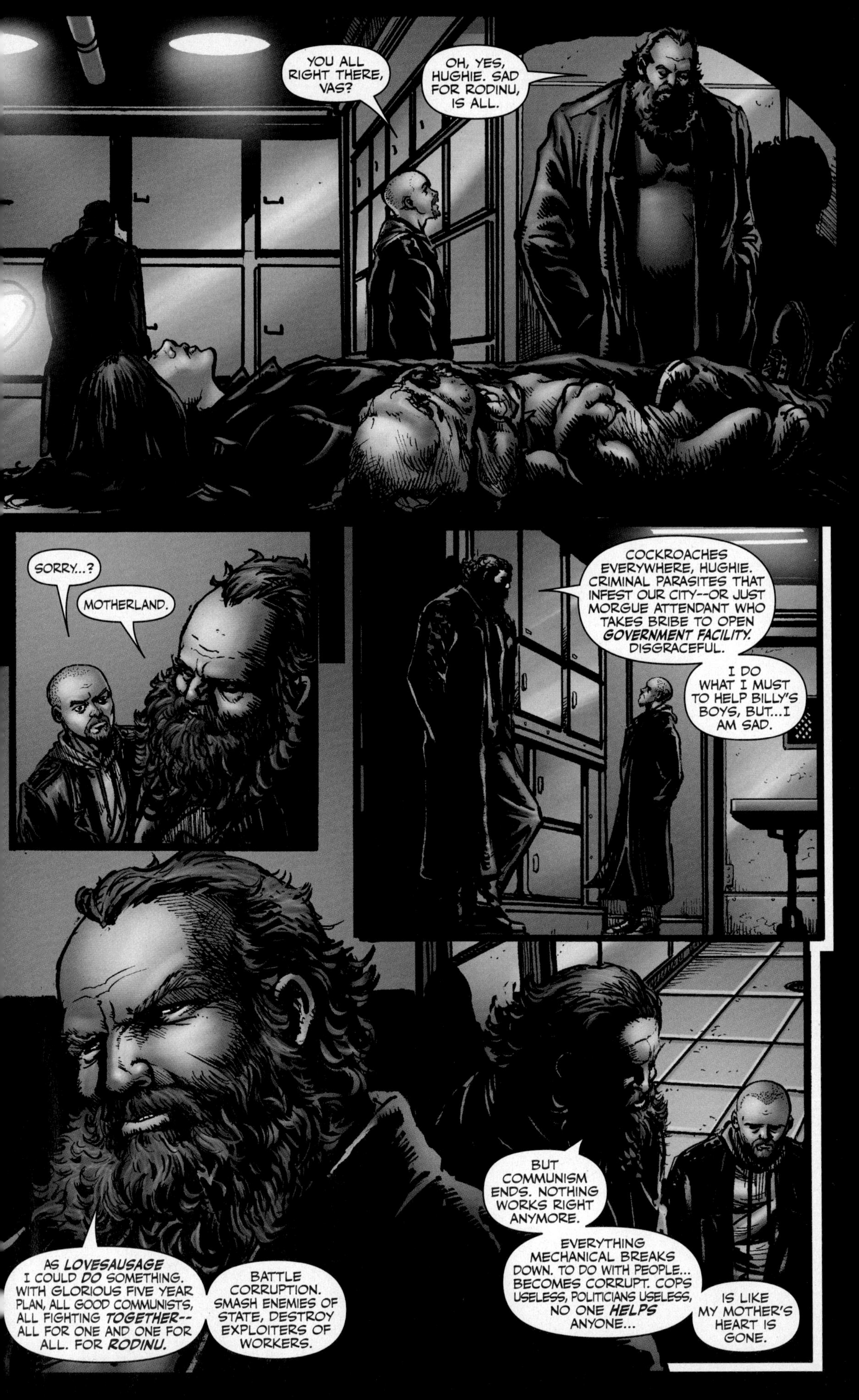

YOU ALL RIGHT THERE, VAS?
OH, YES, HUGHIE. SAD FOR RODINU, IS ALL.
SORRY...?
MOTHERLAND.
COCKROACHES EVERYWHERE, HUGHIE. CRIMINAL PARASITES THAT INFEST OUR CITY--OR JUST MORGUE ATTENDANT WHO TAKES BRIBE TO OPEN *GOVERNMENT FACILITY.* DISGRACEFUL.
I DO WHAT I MUST TO HELP BILLY'S BOYS, BUT...I AM SAD.
AS *LOVESAUSAGE* I COULD *DO* SOMETHING. WITH GLORIOUS FIVE YEAR PLAN, ALL GOOD COMMUNISTS, ALL FIGHTING *TOGETHER*-- ALL FOR ONE AND ONE FOR ALL. FOR *RODINU.*
BATTLE CORRUPTION. SMASH ENEMIES OF STATE, DESTROY EXPLOITERS OF WORKERS.
BUT COMMUNISM ENDS. NOTHING WORKS RIGHT ANYMORE.
EVERYTHING MECHANICAL BREAKS DOWN. TO DO WITH PEOPLE... BECOMES CORRUPT. COPS USELESS, POLITICIANS USELESS, NO ONE *HELPS* ANYONE...
IS LIKE MY MOTHER'S HEART IS GONE.

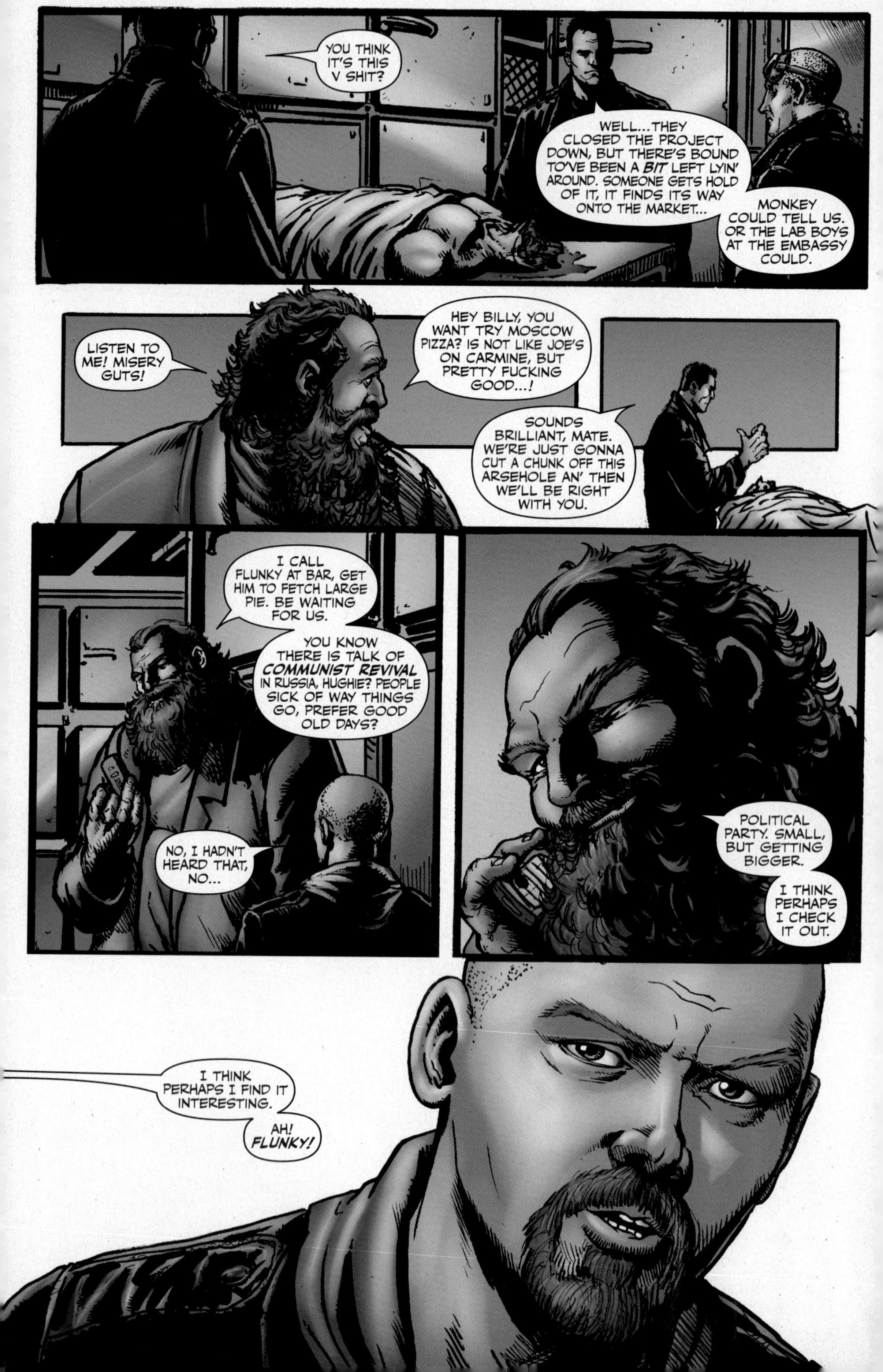
YOU THINK IT'S THIS V SHIT?
WELL...THEY CLOSED THE PROJECT DOWN, BUT THERE'S BOUND TO'VE BEEN A *BIT* LEFT LYIN' AROUND. SOMEONE GETS HOLD OF IT, IT FINDS ITS WAY ONTO THE MARKET...
MONKEY COULD TELL US. OR THE LAB BOYS AT THE EMBASSY COULD.
LISTEN TO ME! MISERY GUTS!
HEY BILLY, YOU WANT TRY MOSCOW PIZZA? IS NOT LIKE JOE'S ON CARMINE, BUT PRETTY FUCKING GOOD...!
SOUNDS BRILLIANT, MATE. WE'RE JUST GONNA CUT A CHUNK OFF THIS ARSEHOLE AN' THEN WE'LL BE RIGHT WITH YOU.
I CALL FLUNKY AT BAR, GET HIM TO FETCH LARGE PIE. BE WAITING FOR US.
YOU KNOW THERE IS TALK OF *COMMUNIST REVIVAL* IN RUSSIA, HUGHIE? PEOPLE SICK OF WAY THINGS GO, PREFER GOOD OLD DAYS?
NO, I HADN'T HEARD THAT, NO...
POLITICAL PARTY. SMALL, BUT GETTING BIGGER.
I THINK PERHAPS I CHECK IT OUT.
I THINK PERHAPS I FIND IT INTERESTING.
AH! *FLUNKY!*

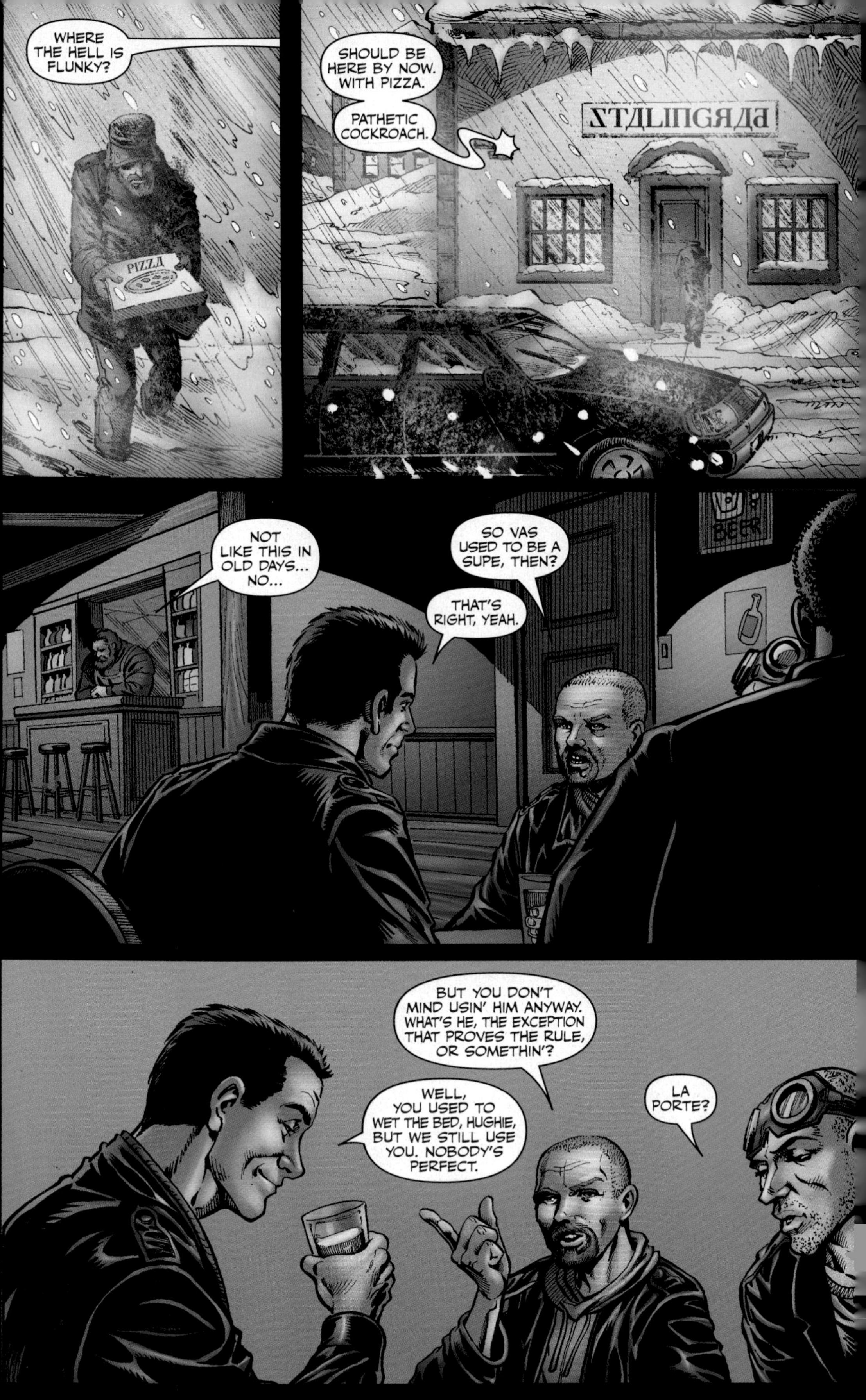
WHERE THE HELL IS FLUNKY?
SHOULD BE HERE BY NOW. WITH PIZZA.
PATHETIC COCKROACH.
PIZZA
STALINGRAD
NOT LIKE THIS IN OLD DAYS... NO...
SO VAS USED TO BE A SUPE, THEN?
THAT'S RIGHT, YEAH.
BUT YOU DON'T MIND USIN' HIM ANYWAY. WHAT'S HE, THE EXCEPTION THAT PROVES THE RULE, OR SOMETHIN'?
WELL, YOU USED TO WET THE BED, HUGHIE, BUT WE STILL USE YOU. NOBODY'S PERFECT.
LA PORTE?

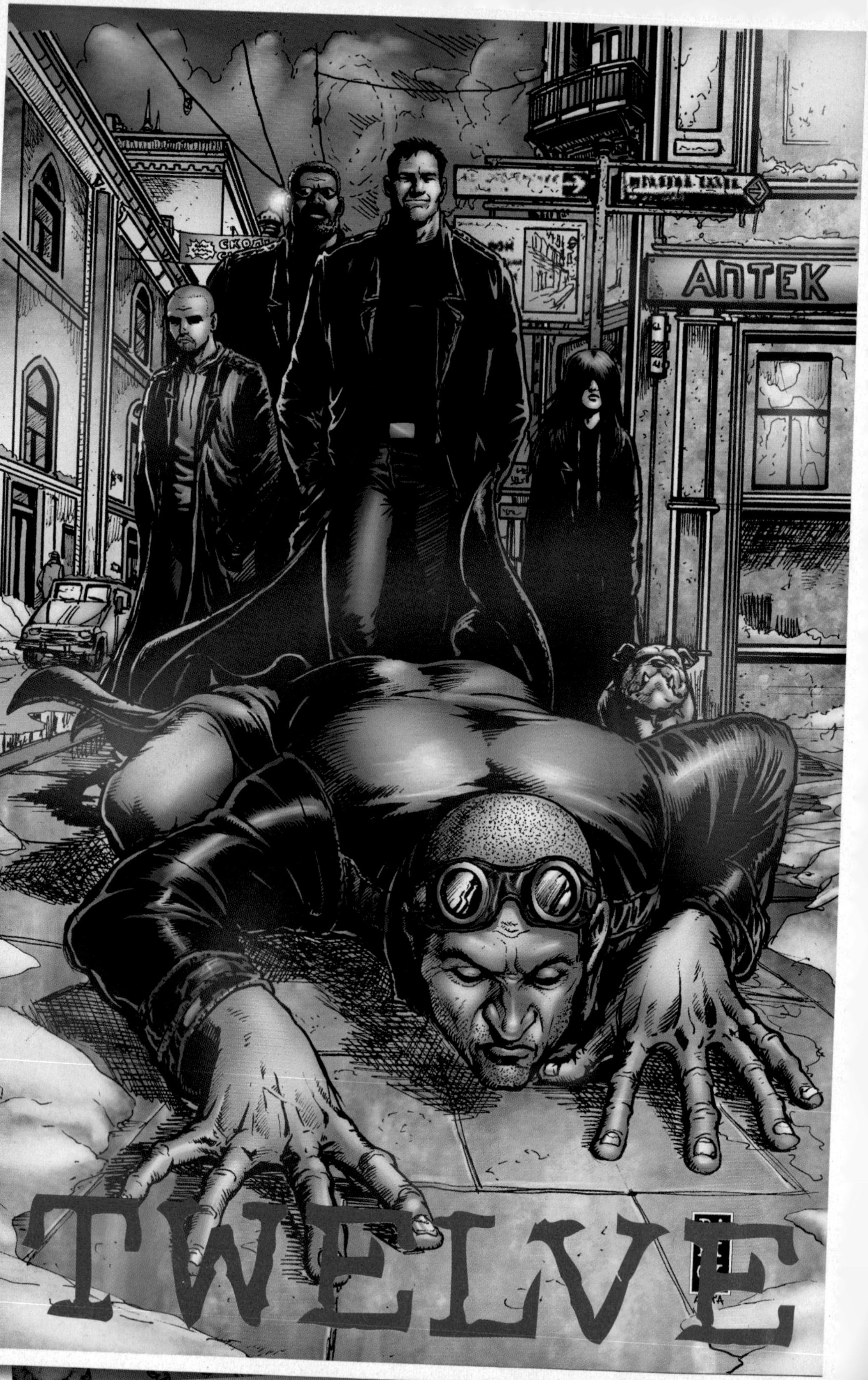
АПТЕК
TWELVE

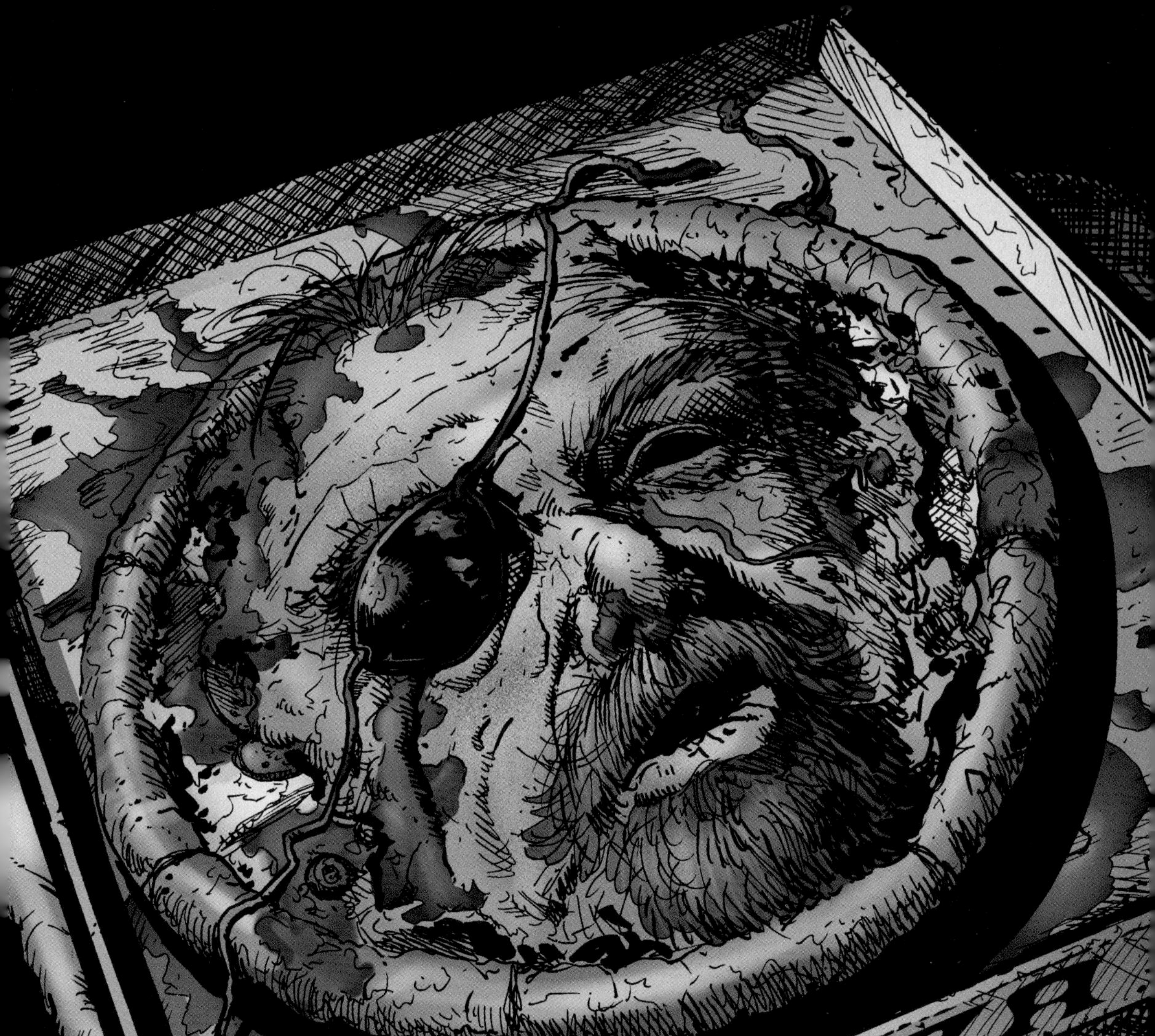

PIZZA

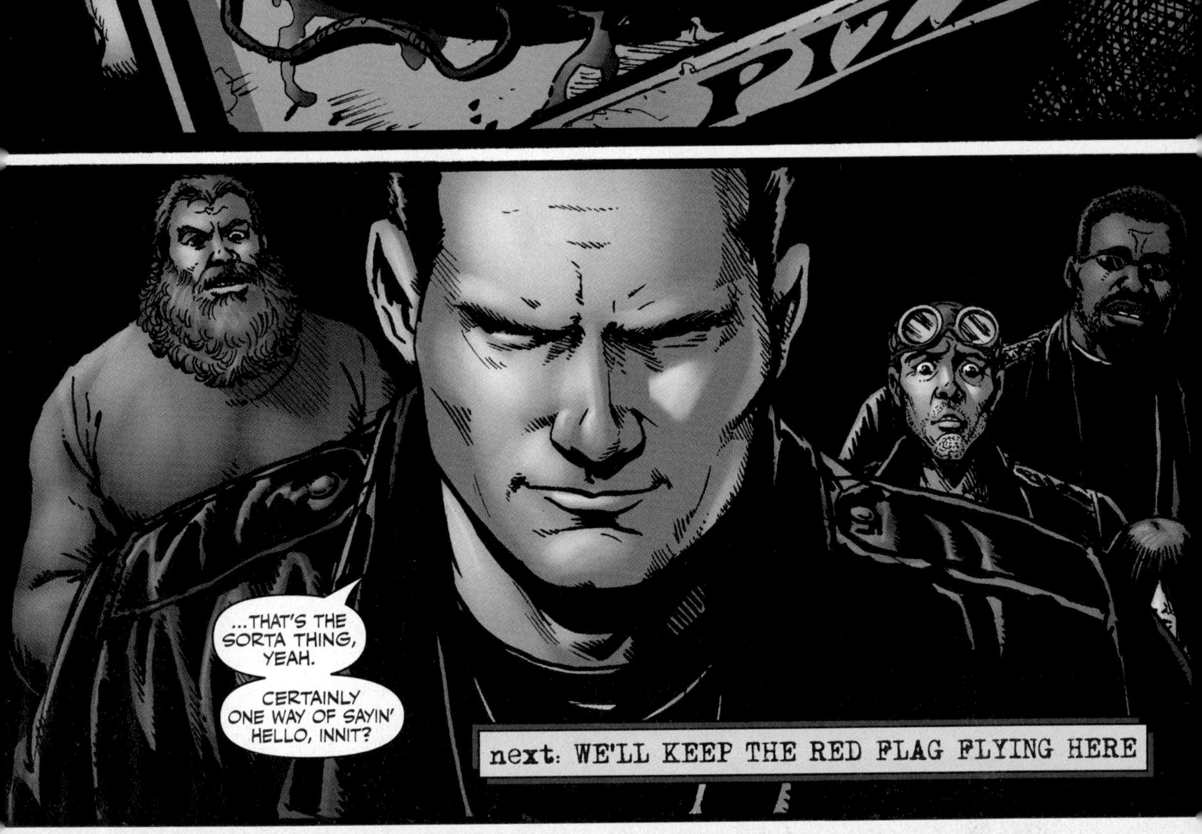

...THAT'S THE SORTA THING, YEAH.
CERTAINLY ONE WAY OF SAYIN' HELLO, INNIT?
next: WE'LL KEEP THE RED FLAG FLYING HERE

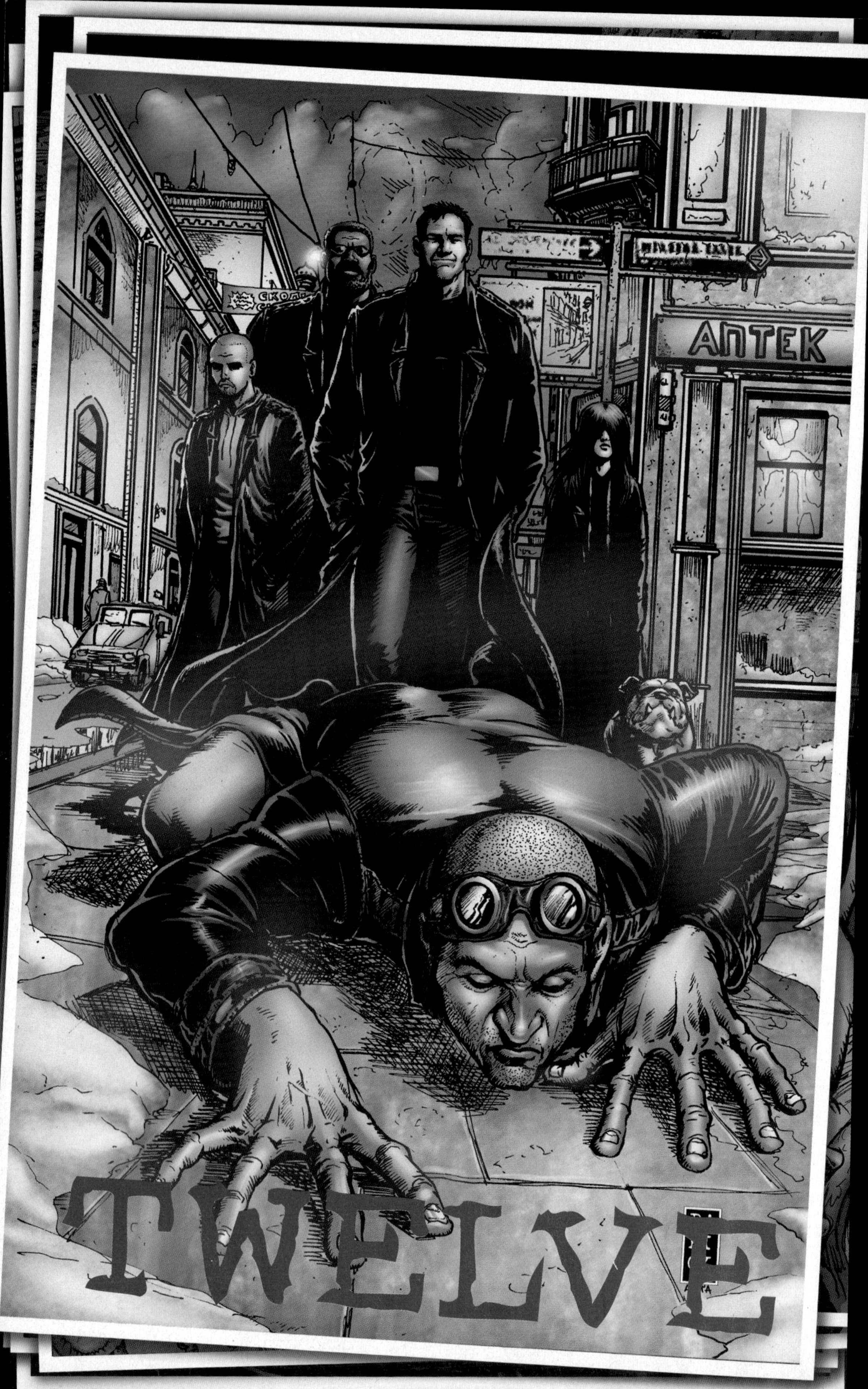
АПТЕК
TWELVE

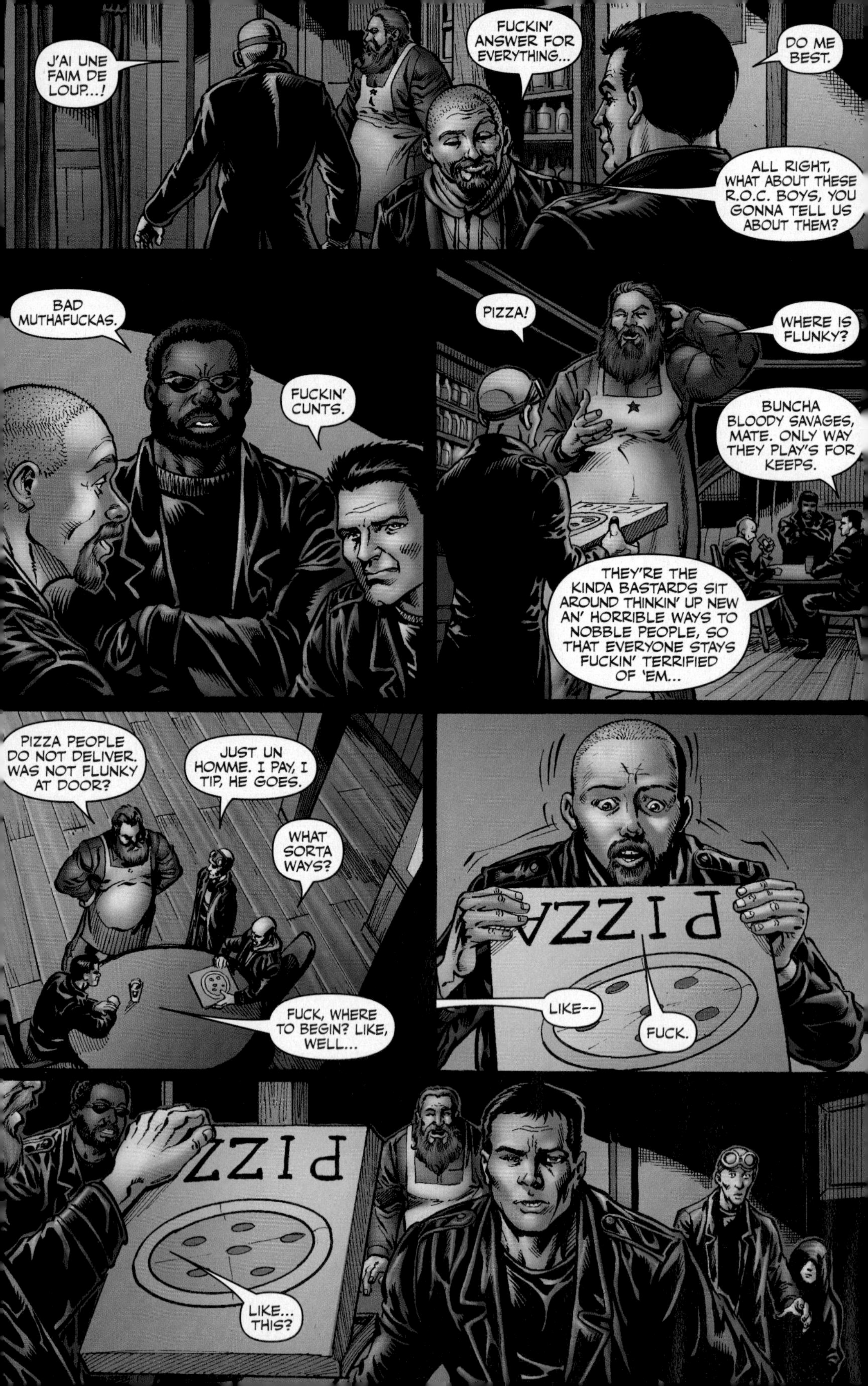
J'AI UNE FAIM DE LOUP...!
FUCKIN' ANSWER FOR EVERYTHING...
DO ME BEST.
ALL RIGHT, WHAT ABOUT THESE R.O.C. BOYS, YOU GONNA TELL US ABOUT THEM?
BAD MUTHAFUCKAS.
FUCKIN' CUNTS.
PIZZA!
WHERE IS FLUNKY?
BUNCHA BLOODY SAVAGES, MATE. ONLY WAY THEY PLAY'S FOR KEEPS.
PIZZA
THEY'RE THE KINDA BASTARDS SIT AROUND THINKIN' UP NEW AN' HORRIBLE WAYS TO NOBBLE PEOPLE, SO THAT EVERYONE STAYS FUCKIN' TERRIFIED OF 'EM...
PIZZA PEOPLE DO NOT DELIVER. WAS NOT FLUNKY AT DOOR?
JUST UN HOMME. I PAY, I TIP, HE GOES.
WHAT SORTA WAYS?
FUCK, WHERE TO BEGIN? LIKE, WELL...
PIZZA
LIKE--
FUCK.
PIZZ
LIKE... THIS?

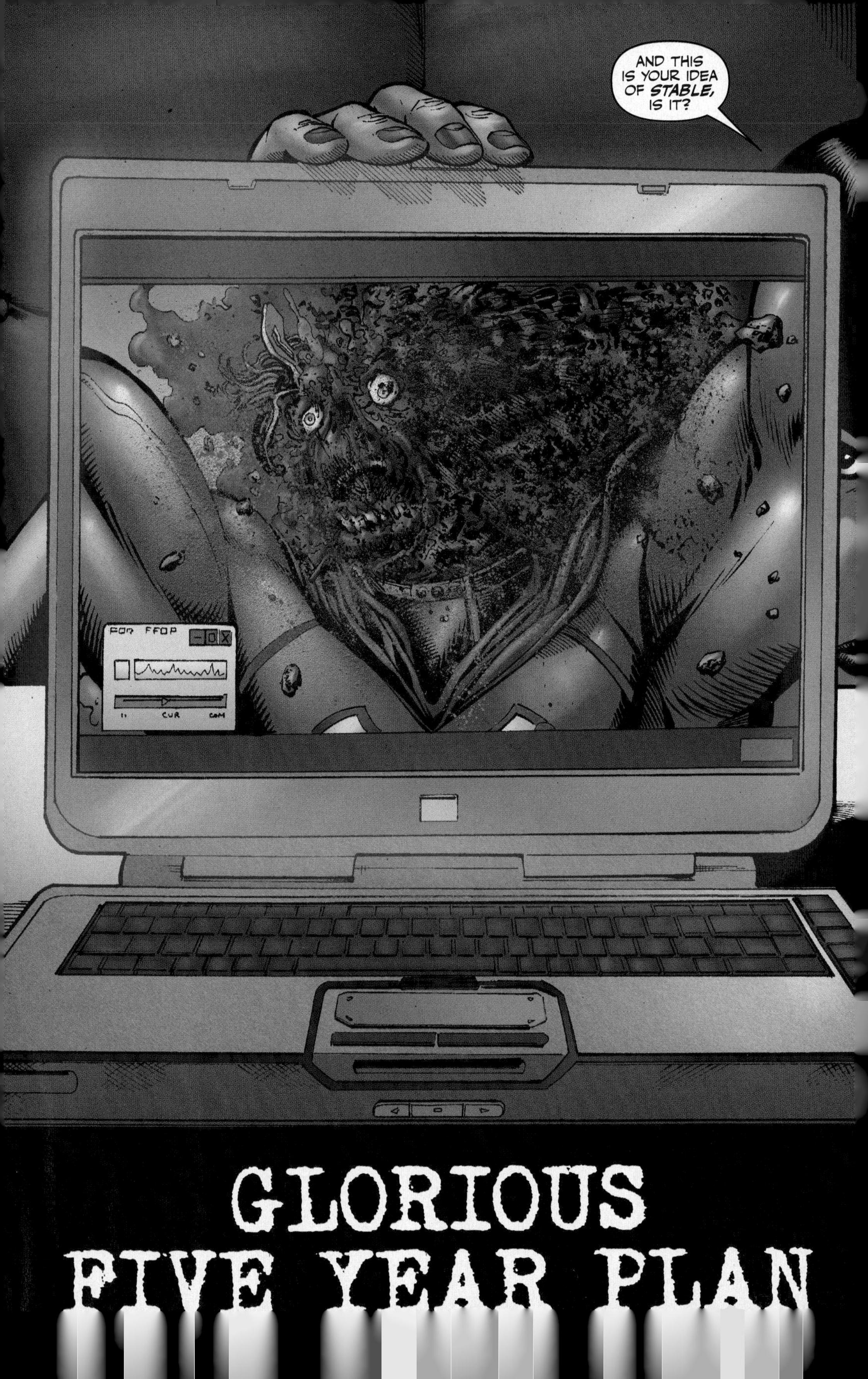
AND THIS IS YOUR IDEA OF *STABLE,* IS IT?

GLORIOUS FIVE YEAR PLAN

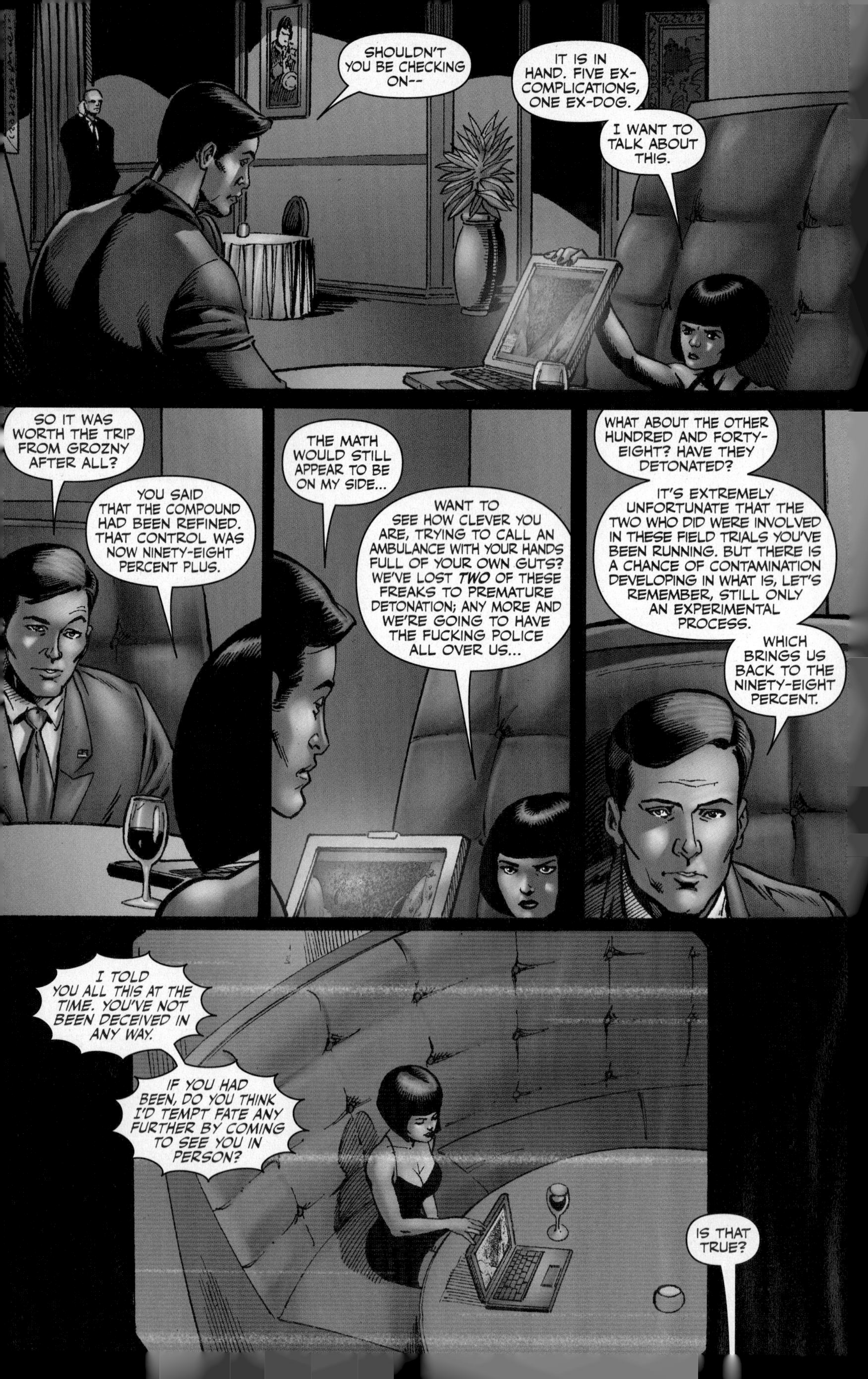
SHOULDN'T YOU BE CHECKING ON--
IT IS IN HAND. FIVE EX-COMPLICATIONS, ONE EX-DOG.
I WANT TO TALK ABOUT THIS.
SO IT WAS WORTH THE TRIP FROM GROZNY AFTER ALL?
YOU SAID THAT THE COMPOUND HAD BEEN REFINED. THAT CONTROL WAS NOW NINETY-EIGHT PERCENT PLUS.
THE MATH WOULD STILL APPEAR TO BE ON MY SIDE...
WANT TO SEE HOW CLEVER YOU ARE, TRYING TO CALL AN AMBULANCE WITH YOUR HANDS FULL OF YOUR OWN GUTS? WE'VE LOST TWO OF THESE FREAKS TO PREMATURE DETONATION; ANY MORE AND WE'RE GOING TO HAVE THE FUCKING POLICE ALL OVER US...
WHAT ABOUT THE OTHER HUNDRED AND FORTY-EIGHT? HAVE THEY DETONATED?
IT'S EXTREMELY UNFORTUNATE THAT THE TWO WHO DID WERE INVOLVED IN THESE FIELD TRIALS YOU'VE BEEN RUNNING. BUT THERE IS A CHANCE OF CONTAMINATION DEVELOPING IN WHAT IS, LET'S REMEMBER, STILL ONLY AN EXPERIMENTAL PROCESS.
WHICH BRINGS US BACK TO THE NINETY-EIGHT PERCENT.
I TOLD YOU ALL THIS AT THE TIME. YOU'VE NOT BEEN DECEIVED IN ANY WAY.
IF YOU HAD BEEN, DO YOU THINK I'D TEMPT FATE ANY FURTHER BY COMING TO SEE YOU IN PERSON?
IS THAT TRUE?

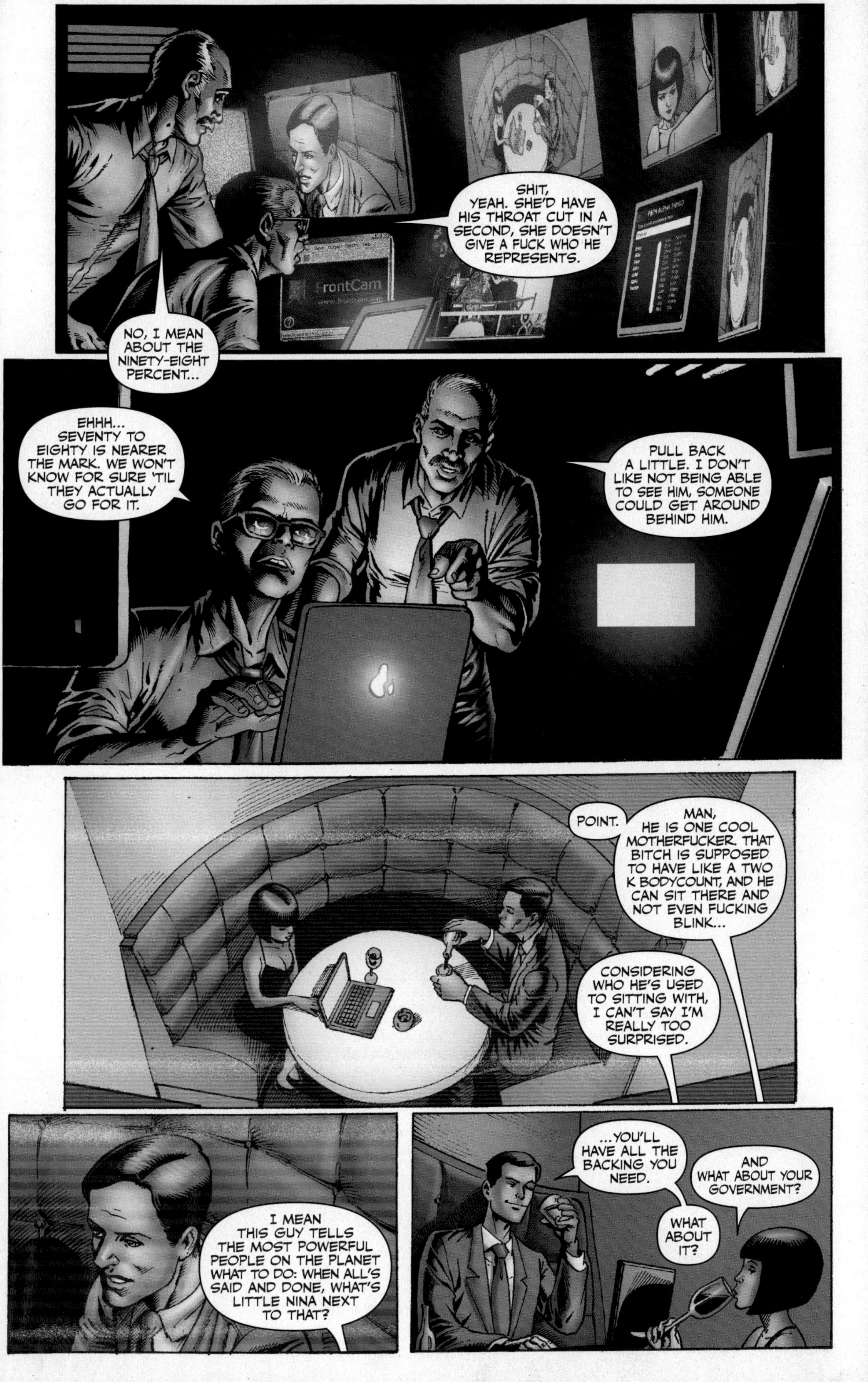
SHIT, YEAH. SHE'D HAVE HIS THROAT CUT IN A SECOND, SHE DOESN'T GIVE A FUCK WHO HE REPRESENTS.
FrontCam
NO, I MEAN ABOUT THE NINETY-EIGHT PERCENT...
EHHH... SEVENTY TO EIGHTY IS NEARER THE MARK. WE WON'T KNOW FOR SURE 'TIL THEY ACTUALLY GO FOR IT.
PULL BACK A LITTLE. I DON'T LIKE NOT BEING ABLE TO SEE HIM, SOMEONE COULD GET AROUND BEHIND HIM.
POINT.
MAN, HE IS ONE COOL MOTHERFUCKER. THAT BITCH IS SUPPOSED TO HAVE LIKE A TWO K BODYCOUNT, AND HE CAN SIT THERE AND NOT EVEN FUCKING BLINK...
CONSIDERING WHO HE'S USED TO SITTING WITH, I CAN'T SAY I'M REALLY TOO SURPRISED.
I MEAN THIS GUY TELLS THE MOST POWERFUL PEOPLE ON THE PLANET WHAT TO DO: WHEN ALL'S SAID AND DONE, WHAT'S LITTLE NINA NEXT TO THAT?
...YOU'LL HAVE ALL THE BACKING YOU NEED.
AND WHAT ABOUT YOUR GOVERNMENT?
WHAT ABOUT IT?

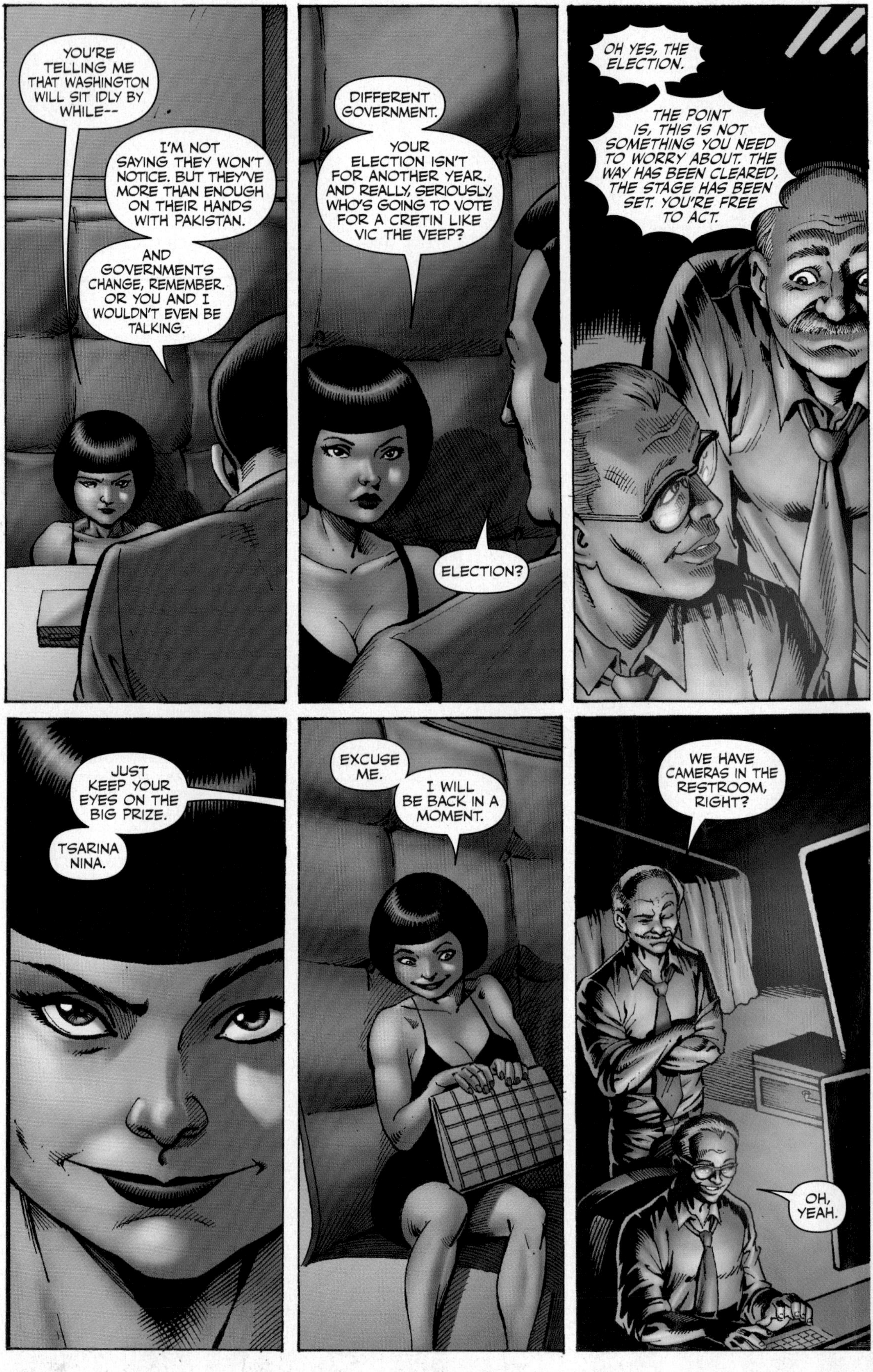
YOU'RE TELLING ME THAT WASHINGTON WILL SIT IDLY BY WHILE--
I'M NOT SAYING THEY WON'T NOTICE. BUT THEY'VE MORE THAN ENOUGH ON THEIR HANDS WITH PAKISTAN.
AND GOVERNMENTS CHANGE, REMEMBER. OR YOU AND I WOULDN'T EVEN BE TALKING.
DIFFERENT GOVERNMENT.
YOUR ELECTION ISN'T FOR ANOTHER YEAR. AND REALLY, SERIOUSLY, WHO'S GOING TO VOTE FOR A CRETIN LIKE VIC THE VEEP?
ELECTION?
OH YES, THE ELECTION.
THE POINT IS, THIS IS NOT SOMETHING YOU NEED TO WORRY ABOUT. THE WAY HAS BEEN CLEARED, THE STAGE HAS BEEN SET. YOU'RE FREE TO ACT.
JUST KEEP YOUR EYES ON THE BIG PRIZE.
TSARINA NINA.
EXCUSE ME.
I WILL BE BACK IN A MOMENT.
WE HAVE CAMERAS IN THE RESTROOM, RIGHT?
OH, YEAH.

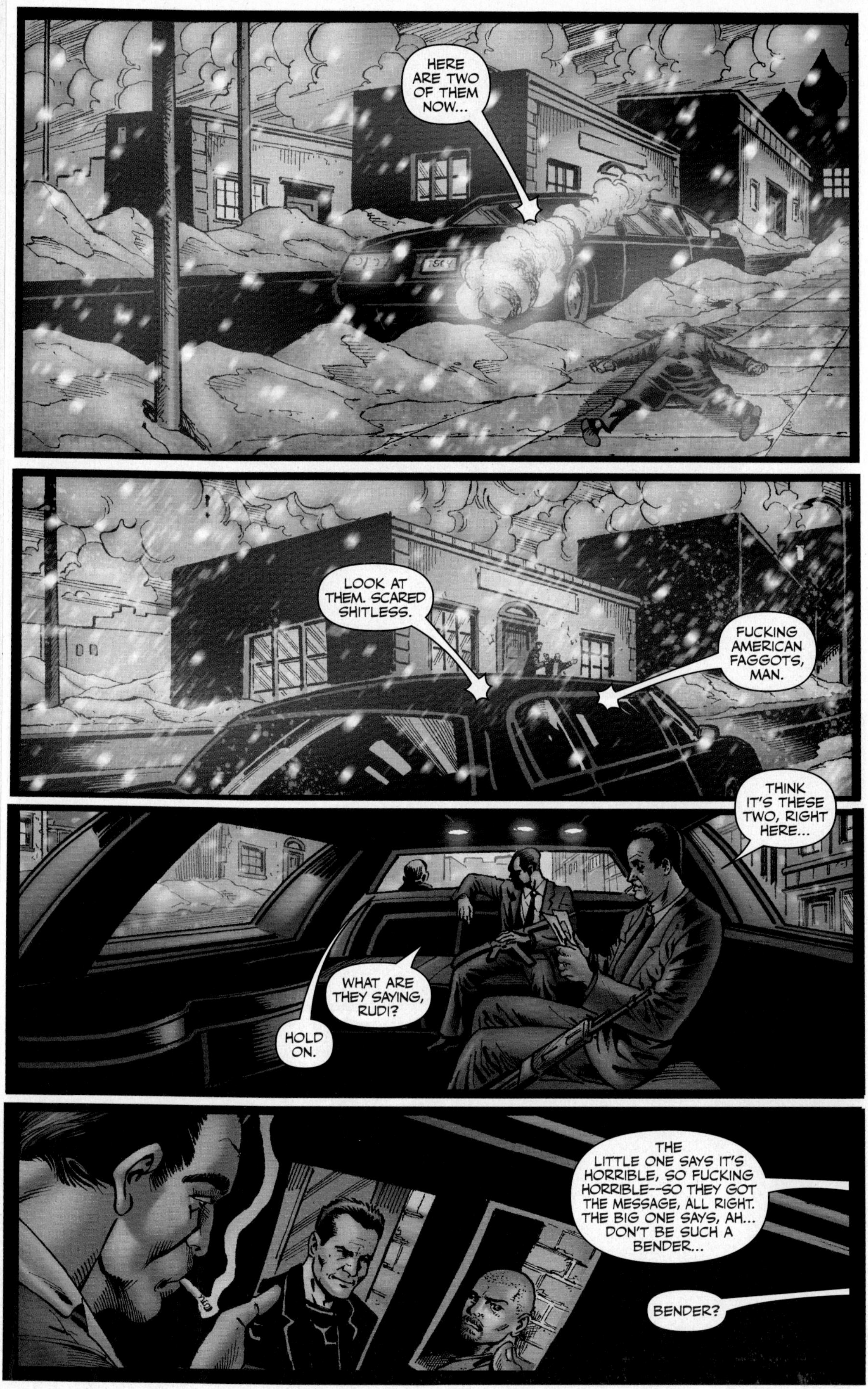
HERE ARE TWO OF THEM NOW...
LOOK AT THEM. SCARED SHITLESS.
FUCKING AMERICAN FAGGOTS, MAN.
THINK IT'S THESE TWO, RIGHT HERE...
WHAT ARE THEY SAYING, RUDI?
HOLD ON.
THE LITTLE ONE SAYS IT'S HORRIBLE, SO FUCKING HORRIBLE--SO THEY GOT THE MESSAGE, ALL RIGHT. THE BIG ONE SAYS, AH... DON'T BE SUCH A BENDER...
BENDER?

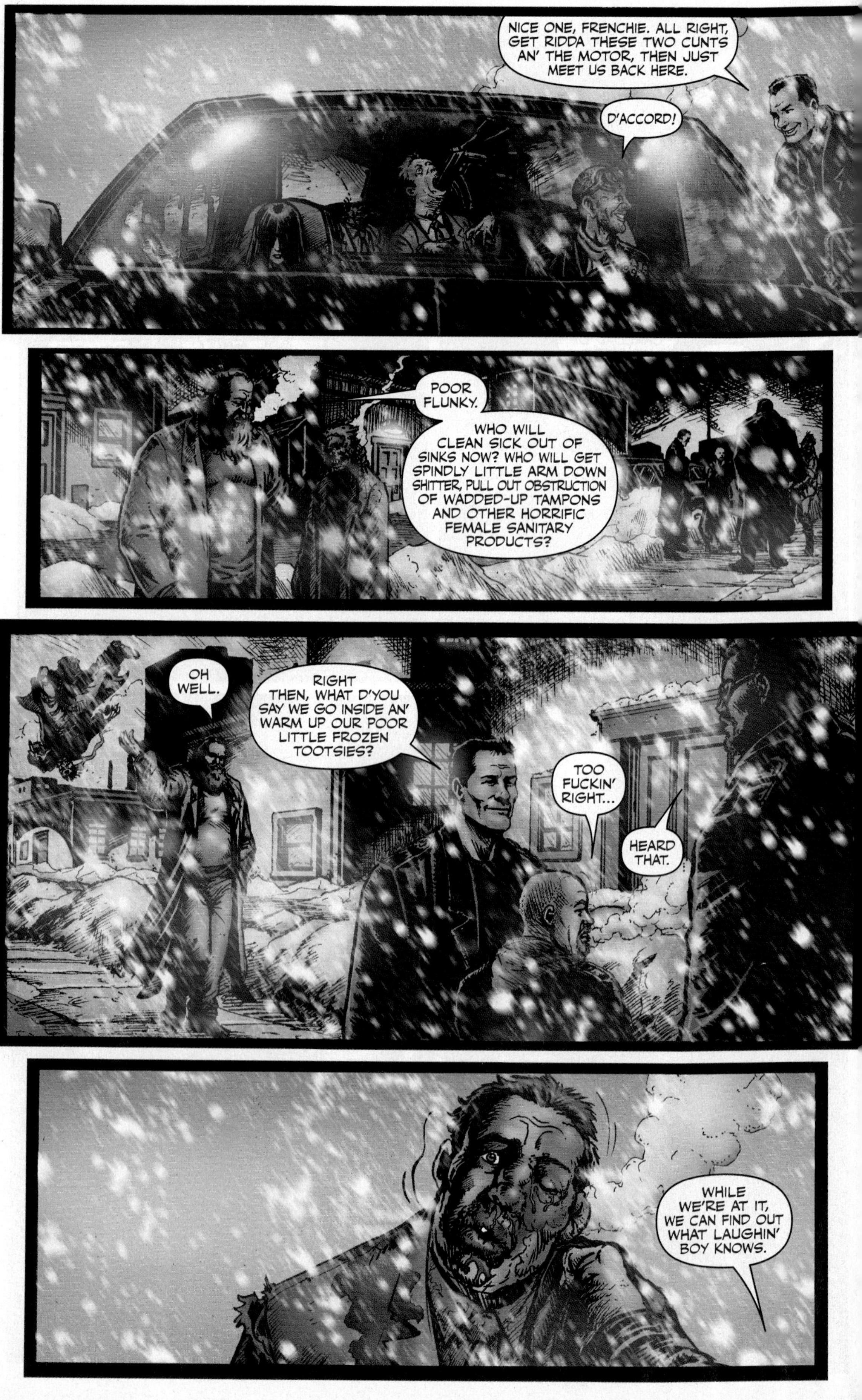

NICE ONE, FRENCHIE. ALL RIGHT, GET RIDDA THESE TWO CUNTS AN' THE MOTOR, THEN JUST MEET US BACK HERE.
D'ACCORD!
POOR FLUNKY.
WHO WILL CLEAN SICK OUT OF SINKS NOW? WHO WILL GET SPINDLY LITTLE ARM DOWN SHITTER, PULL OUT OBSTRUCTION OF WADDED-UP TAMPONS AND OTHER HORRIFIC FEMALE SANITARY PRODUCTS?
OH WELL.
RIGHT THEN, WHAT D'YOU SAY WE GO INSIDE AN' WARM UP OUR POOR LITTLE FROZEN TOOTSIES?
TOO FUCKIN' RIGHT...
HEARD THAT.
WHILE WE'RE AT IT, WE CAN FIND OUT WHAT LAUGHIN' BOY KNOWS.

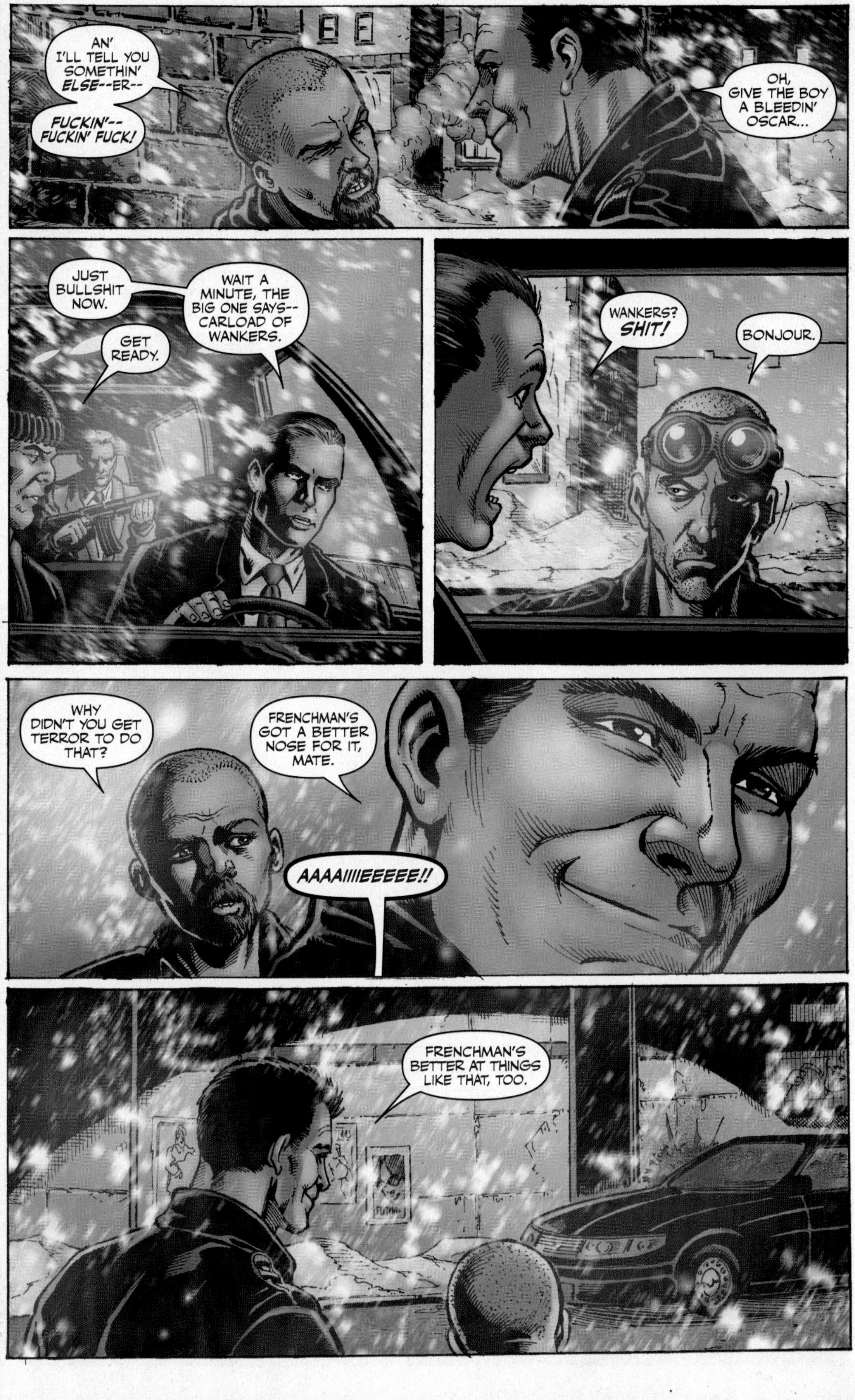
AN' I'LL TELL YOU SOMETHIN' ELSE--ER--
FUCKIN'-- FUCKIN' FUCK!
OH, GIVE THE BOY A BLEEDIN' OSCAR...
JUST BULLSHIT NOW.
WAIT A MINUTE, THE BIG ONE SAYS-- CARLOAD OF WANKERS.
GET READY.
WANKERS? SHIT!
BONJOUR.
WHY DIDN'T YOU GET TERROR TO DO THAT?
FRENCHMAN'S GOT A BETTER NOSE FOR IT, MATE.
AAAAIIIIIEEEEE!!
FRENCHMAN'S BETTER AT THINGS LIKE THAT, TOO.

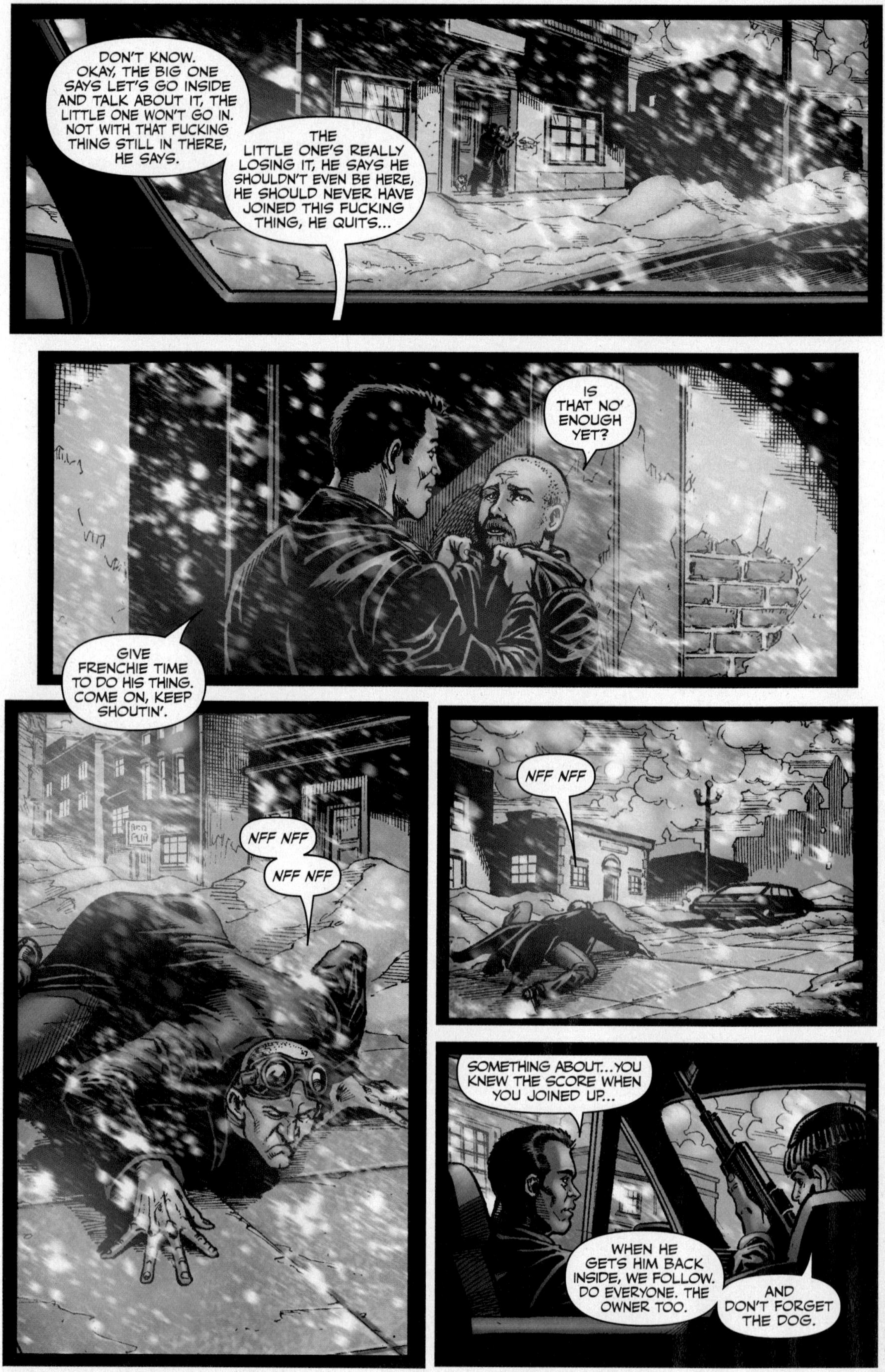
DON'T KNOW. OKAY, THE BIG ONE SAYS LET'S GO INSIDE AND TALK ABOUT IT, THE LITTLE ONE WON'T GO IN. NOT WITH THAT FUCKING THING STILL IN THERE, HE SAYS.
THE LITTLE ONE'S REALLY LOSING IT, HE SAYS HE SHOULDN'T EVEN BE HERE, HE SHOULD NEVER HAVE JOINED THIS FUCKING THING, HE QUITS...
IS THAT NO' ENOUGH YET?
GIVE FRENCHIE TIME TO DO HIS THING. COME ON, KEEP SHOUTIN'.
NFF NFF
NFF NFF
NFF NFF
SOMETHING ABOUT...YOU KNEW THE SCORE WHEN YOU JOINED UP...
WHEN HE GETS HIM BACK INSIDE, WE FOLLOW. DO EVERYONE. THE OWNER TOO.
AND DON'T FORGET THE DOG.

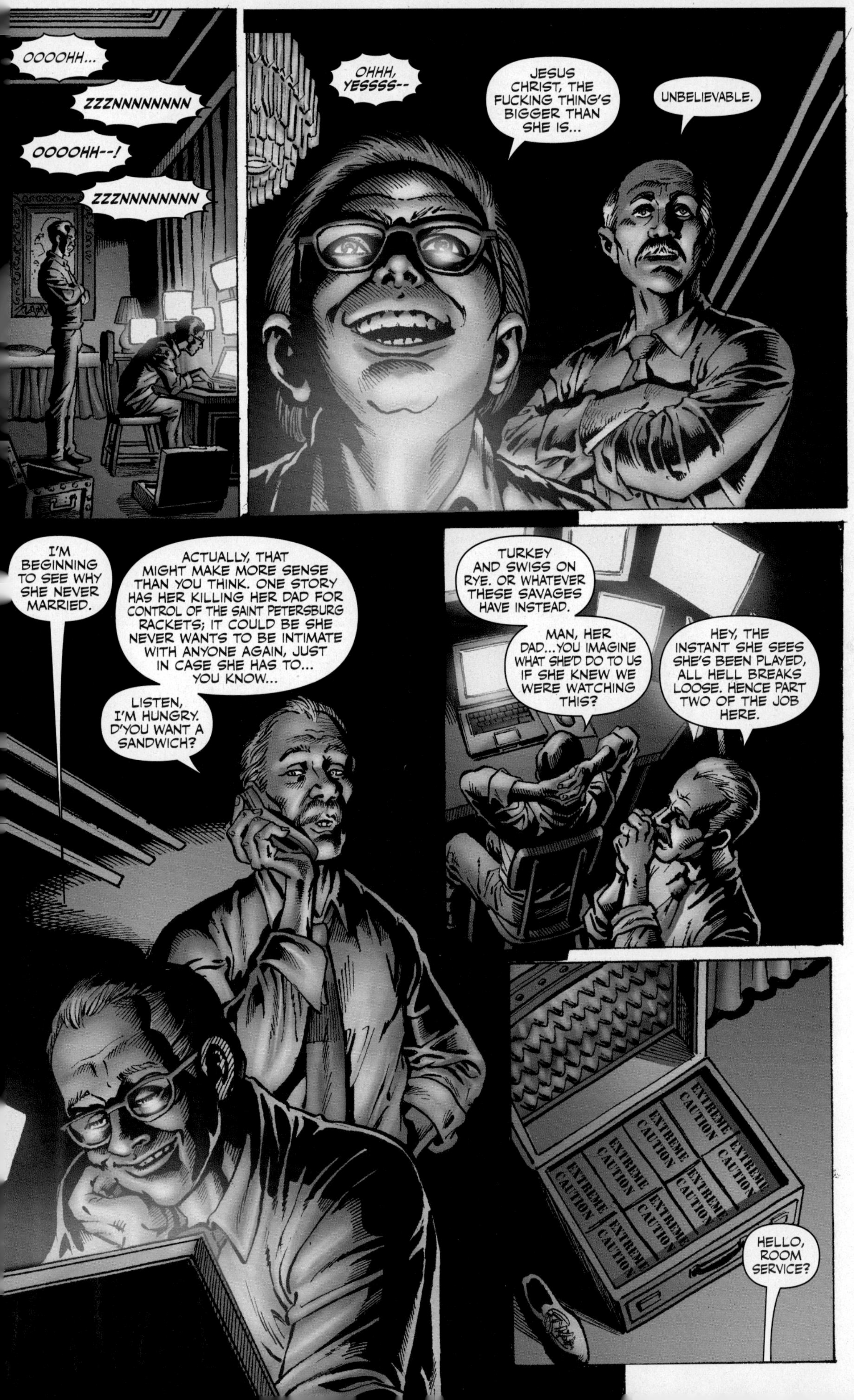
OOOOHH...
ZZZNNNNNNNN
OOOOHH--!
ZZZNNNNNNNN
OHHH, YESSSS--
JESUS CHRIST, THE FUCKING THING'S BIGGER THAN SHE IS...
UNBELIEVABLE.
I'M BEGINNING TO SEE WHY SHE NEVER MARRIED.
ACTUALLY, THAT MIGHT MAKE MORE SENSE THAN YOU THINK. ONE STORY HAS HER KILLING HER DAD FOR CONTROL OF THE SAINT PETERSBURG RACKETS; IT COULD BE SHE NEVER WANTS TO BE INTIMATE WITH ANYONE AGAIN, JUST IN CASE SHE HAS TO... YOU KNOW...
LISTEN, I'M HUNGRY. D'YOU WANT A SANDWICH?
TURKEY AND SWISS ON RYE. OR WHATEVER THESE SAVAGES HAVE INSTEAD.
MAN, HER DAD...YOU IMAGINE WHAT SHE'D DO TO US IF SHE KNEW WE WERE WATCHING THIS?
HEY, THE INSTANT SHE SEES SHE'S BEEN PLAYED, ALL HELL BREAKS LOOSE. HENCE PART TWO OF THE JOB HERE.
EXTREME CAUTION
HELLO, ROOM SERVICE?

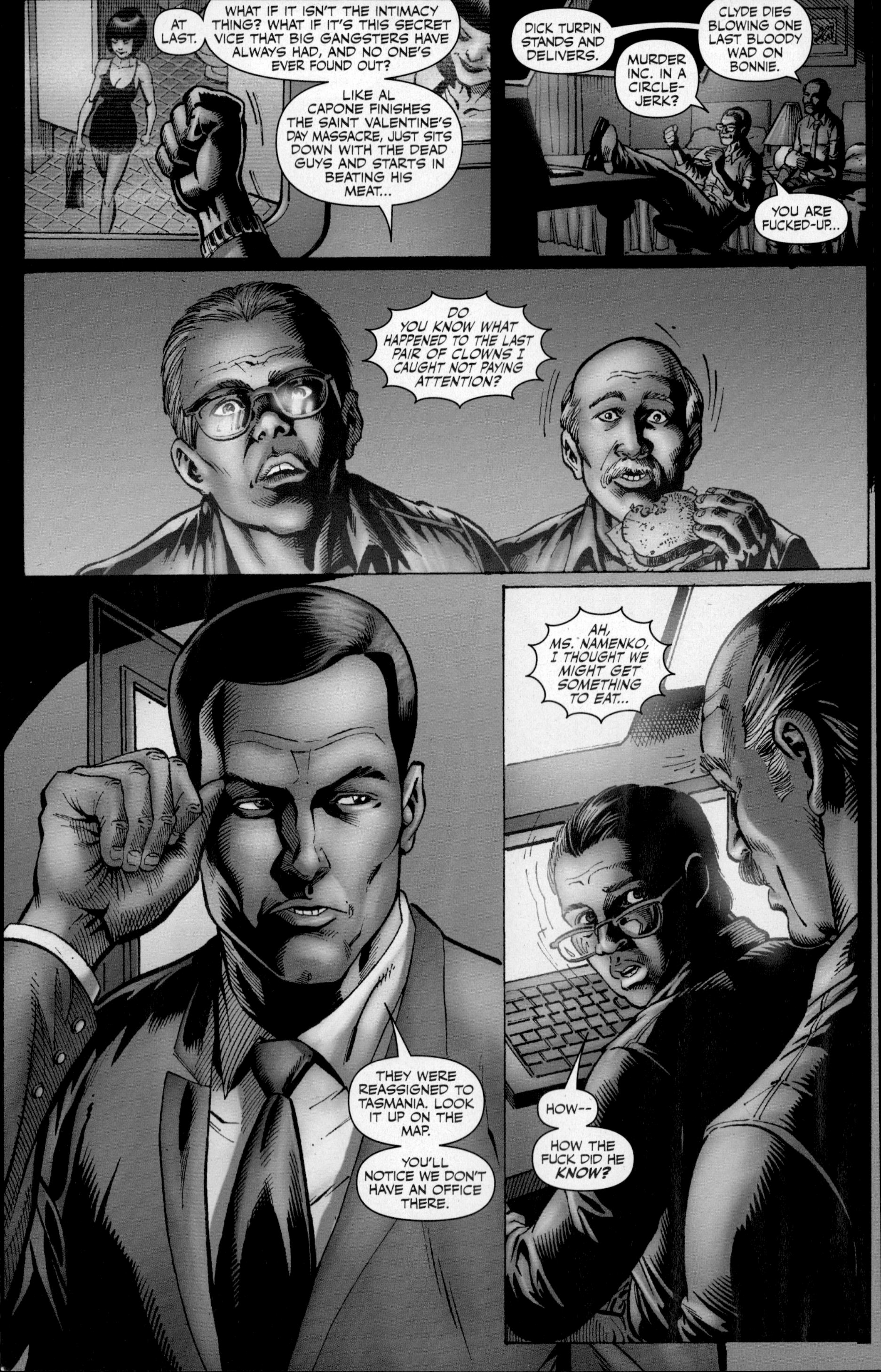
AT LAST.
WHAT IF IT ISN'T THE INTIMACY THING? WHAT IF IT'S THIS SECRET VICE THAT BIG GANGSTERS HAVE ALWAYS HAD, AND NO ONE'S EVER FOUND OUT?
LIKE AL CAPONE FINISHES THE SAINT VALENTINE'S DAY MASSACRE, JUST SITS DOWN WITH THE DEAD GUYS AND STARTS IN BEATING HIS MEAT...
DICK TURPIN STANDS AND DELIVERS.
CLYDE DIES BLOWING ONE LAST BLOODY WAD ON BONNIE.
MURDER INC. IN A CIRCLE-JERK?
YOU ARE FUCKED-UP...
DO YOU KNOW WHAT HAPPENED TO THE LAST PAIR OF CLOWNS I CAUGHT NOT PAYING ATTENTION?
THEY WERE REASSIGNED TO TASMANIA. LOOK IT UP ON THE MAP.
YOU'LL NOTICE WE DON'T HAVE AN OFFICE THERE.
AH, MS. NAMENKO, I THOUGHT WE MIGHT GET SOMETHING TO EAT...
HOW--
HOW THE FUCK DID HE *KNOW?*

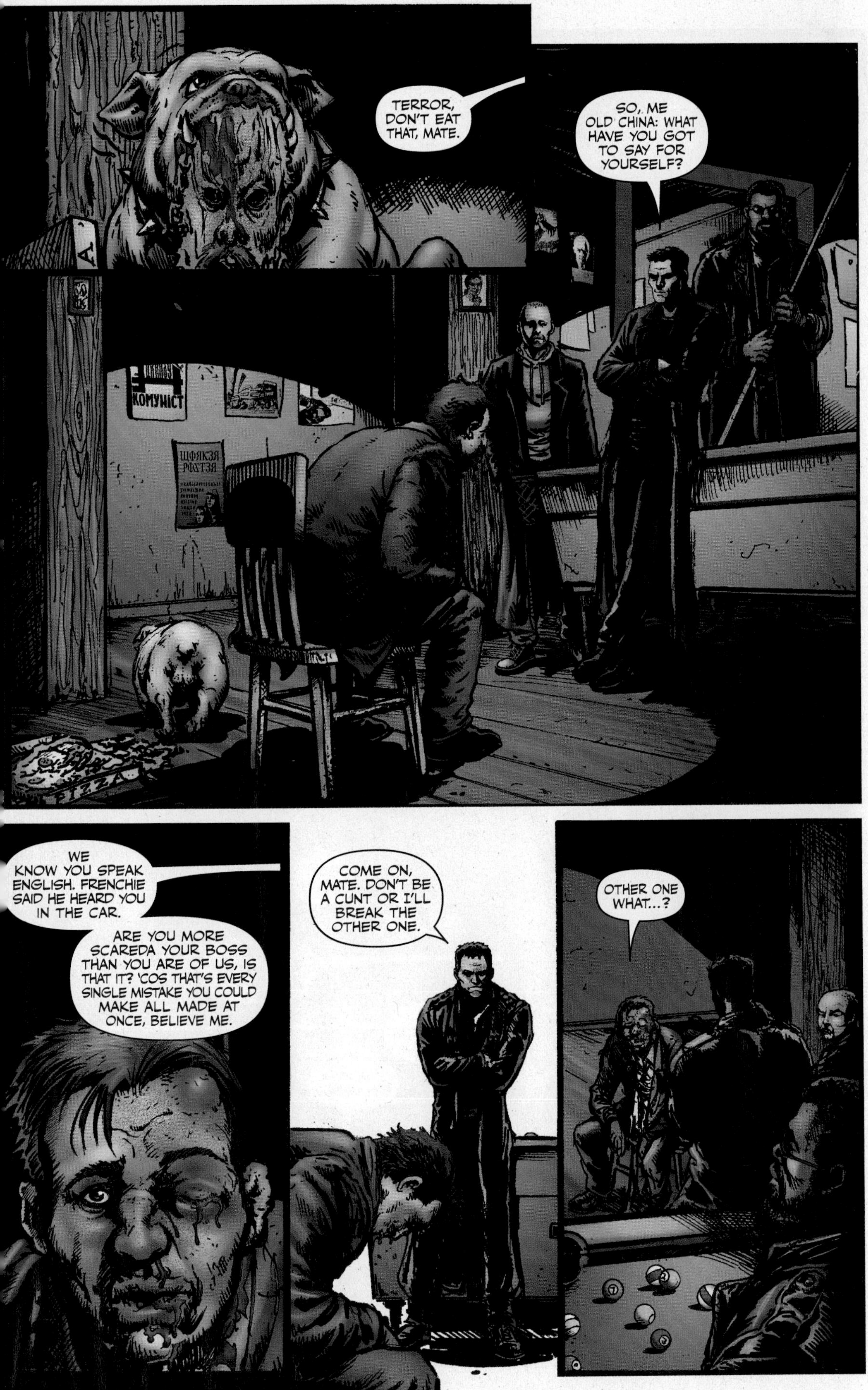
TERROR, DON'T EAT THAT, MATE.
SO, ME OLD CHINA: WHAT HAVE YOU GOT TO SAY FOR YOURSELF?
КОМУНІСТ
WE KNOW YOU SPEAK ENGLISH. FRENCHIE SAID HE HEARD YOU IN THE CAR.
ARE YOU MORE SCAREDA YOUR BOSS THAN YOU ARE OF US, IS THAT IT? 'COS THAT'S EVERY SINGLE MISTAKE YOU COULD MAKE ALL MADE AT ONCE, BELIEVE ME.
COME ON, MATE. DON'T BE A CUNT OR I'LL BREAK THE OTHER ONE.
OTHER ONE WHAT...?

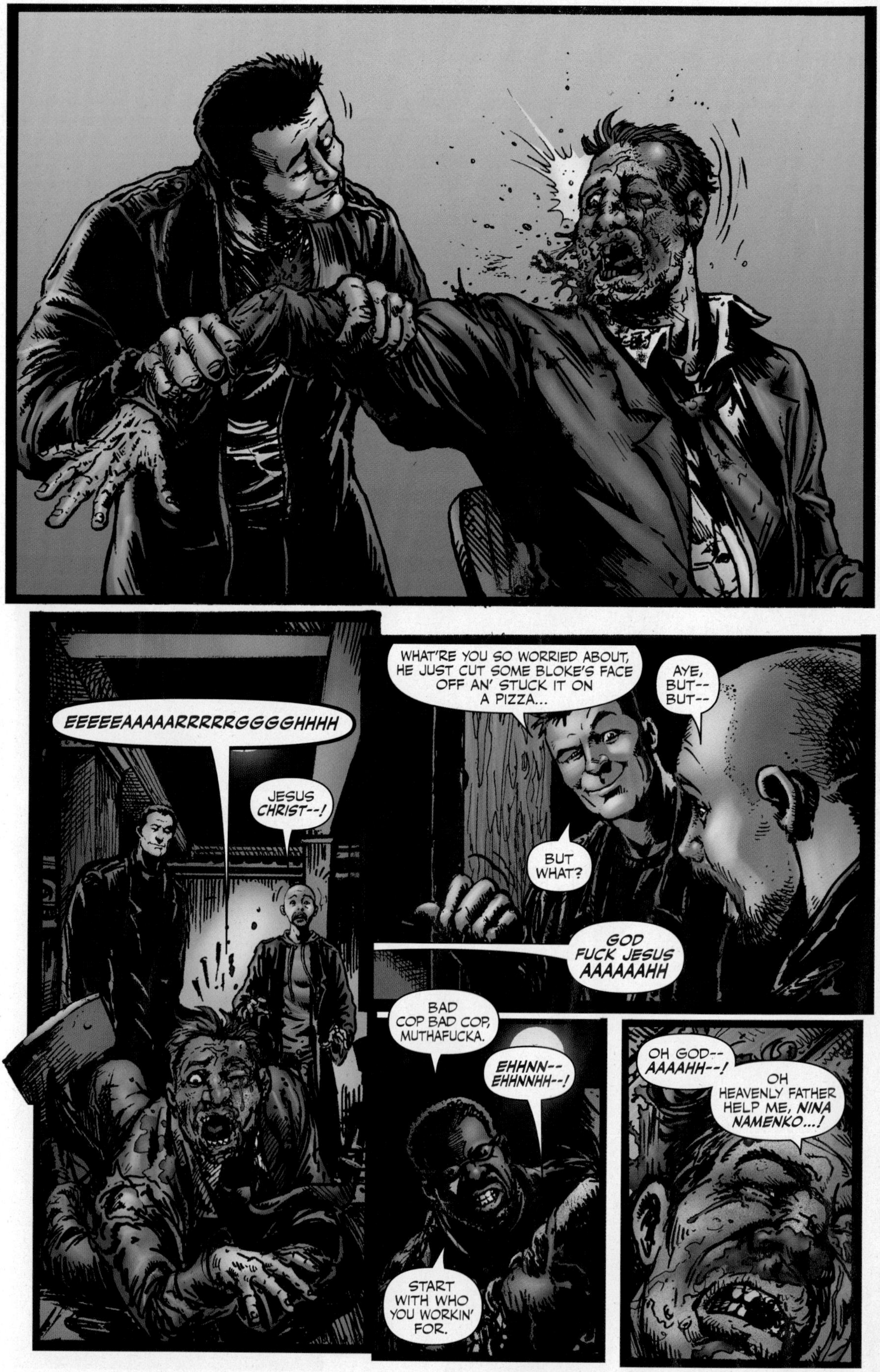

EEEEEAAAAARRRRRGGGGHHHH
JESUS CHRIST--!
WHAT'RE YOU SO WORRIED ABOUT, HE JUST CUT SOME BLOKE'S FACE OFF AN' STUCK IT ON A PIZZA...
AYE, BUT-- BUT--
BUT WHAT?
GOD FUCK JESUS AAAAAAHH
BAD COP BAD COP, MUTHAFUCKA.
EHHNN-- EHHNNHH--!
START WITH WHO YOU WORKIN' FOR.
OH GOD-- AAAAHH--!
OH HEAVENLY FATHER HELP ME, NINA NAMENKO...!

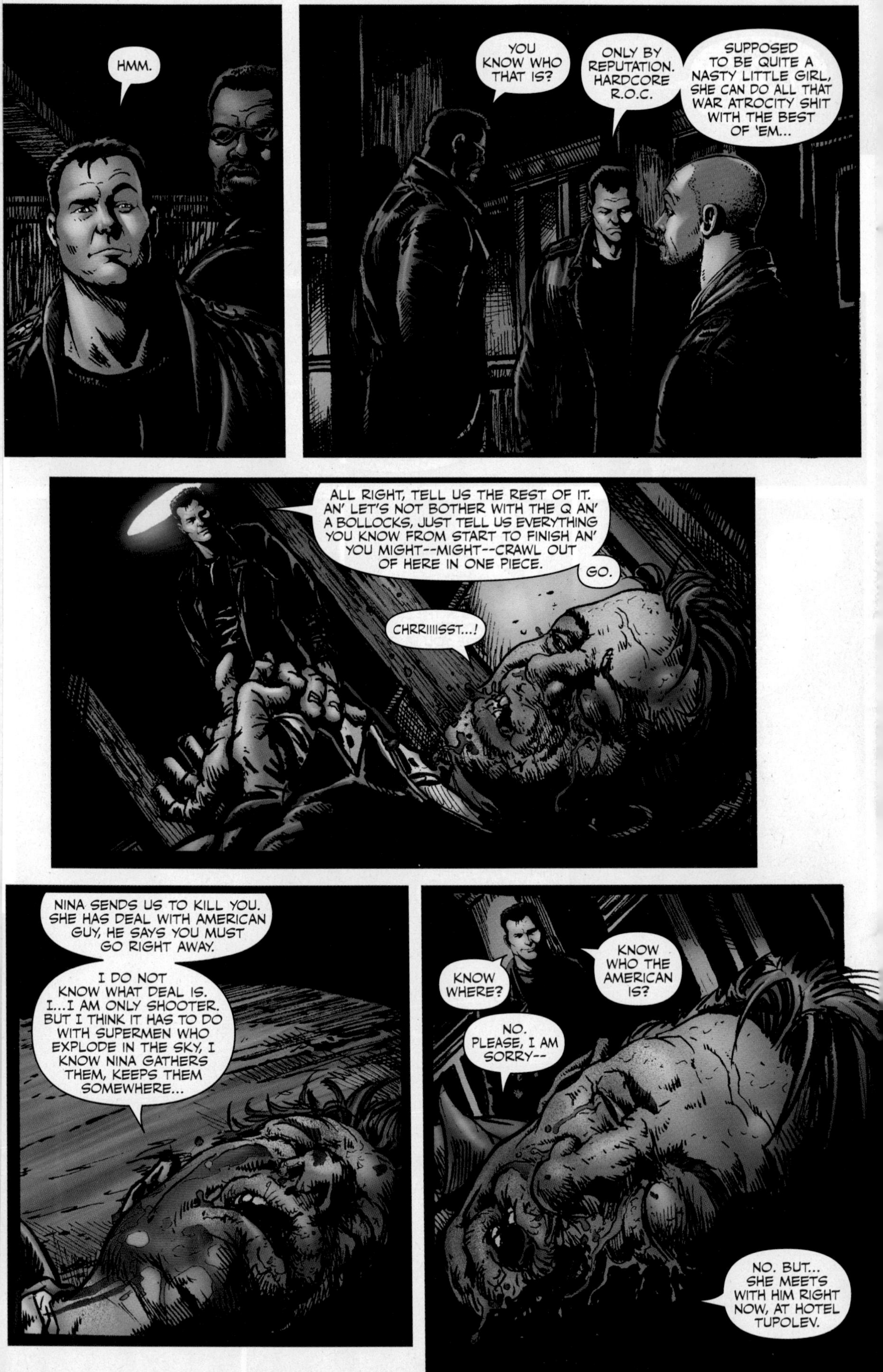
HMM.
YOU KNOW WHO THAT IS?
ONLY BY REPUTATION. HARDCORE R.O.C.
SUPPOSED TO BE QUITE A NASTY LITTLE GIRL, SHE CAN DO ALL THAT WAR ATROCITY SHIT WITH THE BEST OF 'EM...
ALL RIGHT, TELL US THE REST OF IT. AN' LET'S NOT BOTHER WITH THE Q AN' A BOLLOCKS, JUST TELL US EVERYTHING YOU KNOW FROM START TO FINISH AN' YOU MIGHT--MIGHT--CRAWL OUT OF HERE IN ONE PIECE.
GO.
CHRRIIIISST...!
NINA SENDS US TO KILL YOU. SHE HAS DEAL WITH AMERICAN GUY, HE SAYS YOU MUST GO RIGHT AWAY.
I DO NOT KNOW WHAT DEAL IS. I...I AM ONLY SHOOTER. BUT I THINK IT HAS TO DO WITH SUPERMEN WHO EXPLODE IN THE SKY, I KNOW NINA GATHERS THEM, KEEPS THEM SOMEWHERE...
KNOW WHO THE AMERICAN IS?
KNOW WHERE?
NO. PLEASE, I AM SORRY--
NO. BUT... SHE MEETS WITH HIM RIGHT NOW, AT HOTEL TUPOLEV.

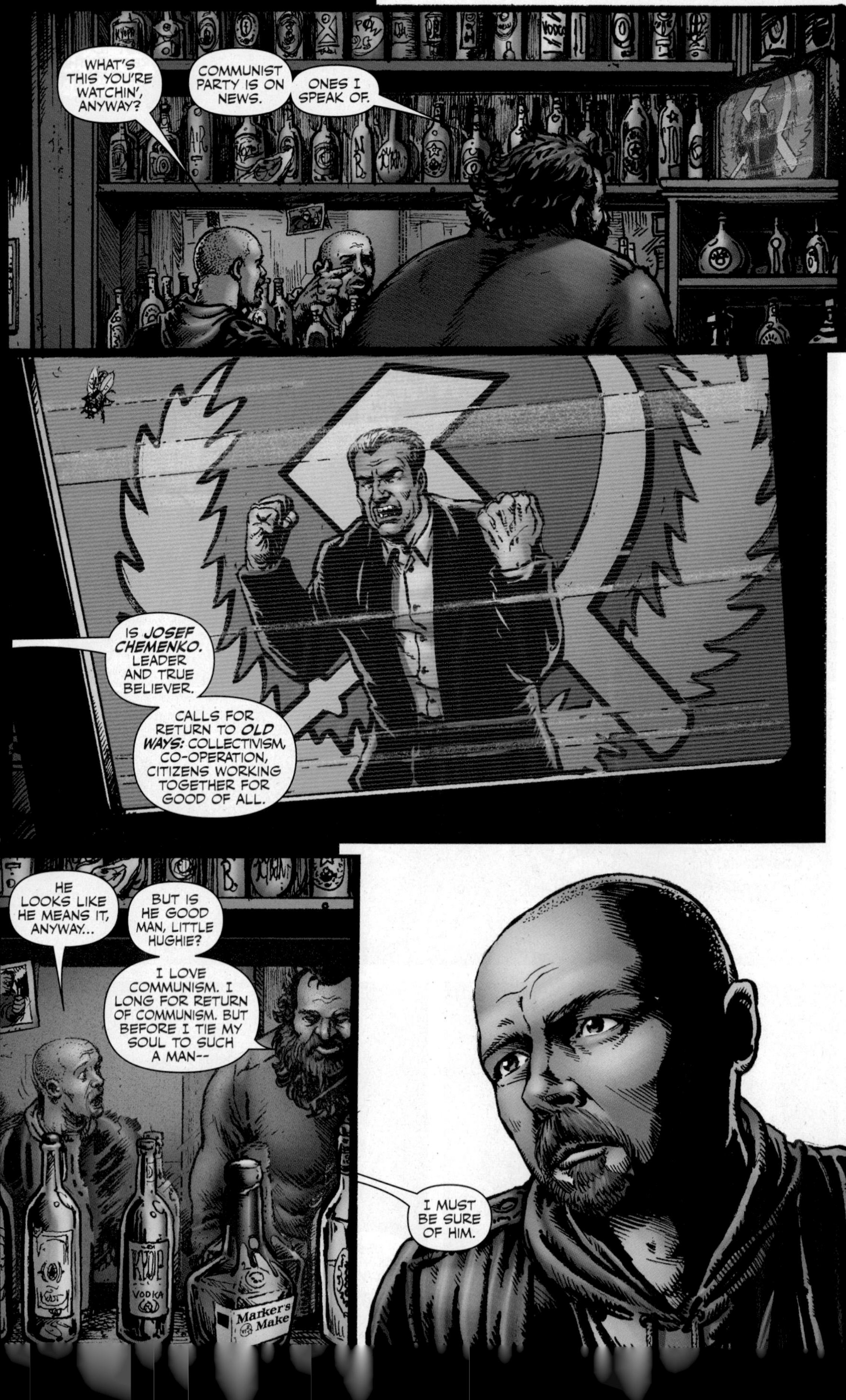

WHAT'S THIS YOU'RE WATCHIN', ANYWAY?
COMMUNIST PARTY IS ON NEWS.
ONES I SPEAK OF.
IS JOSEF CHEMENKO. LEADER AND TRUE BELIEVER.
CALLS FOR RETURN TO OLD WAYS: COLLECTIVISM, CO-OPERATION, CITIZENS WORKING TOGETHER FOR GOOD OF ALL.
HE LOOKS LIKE HE MEANS IT, ANYWAY...
BUT IS HE GOOD MAN, LITTLE HUGHIE?
I LOVE COMMUNISM. I LONG FOR RETURN OF COMMUNISM. BUT BEFORE I TIE MY SOUL TO SUCH A MAN--
I MUST BE SURE OF HIM.

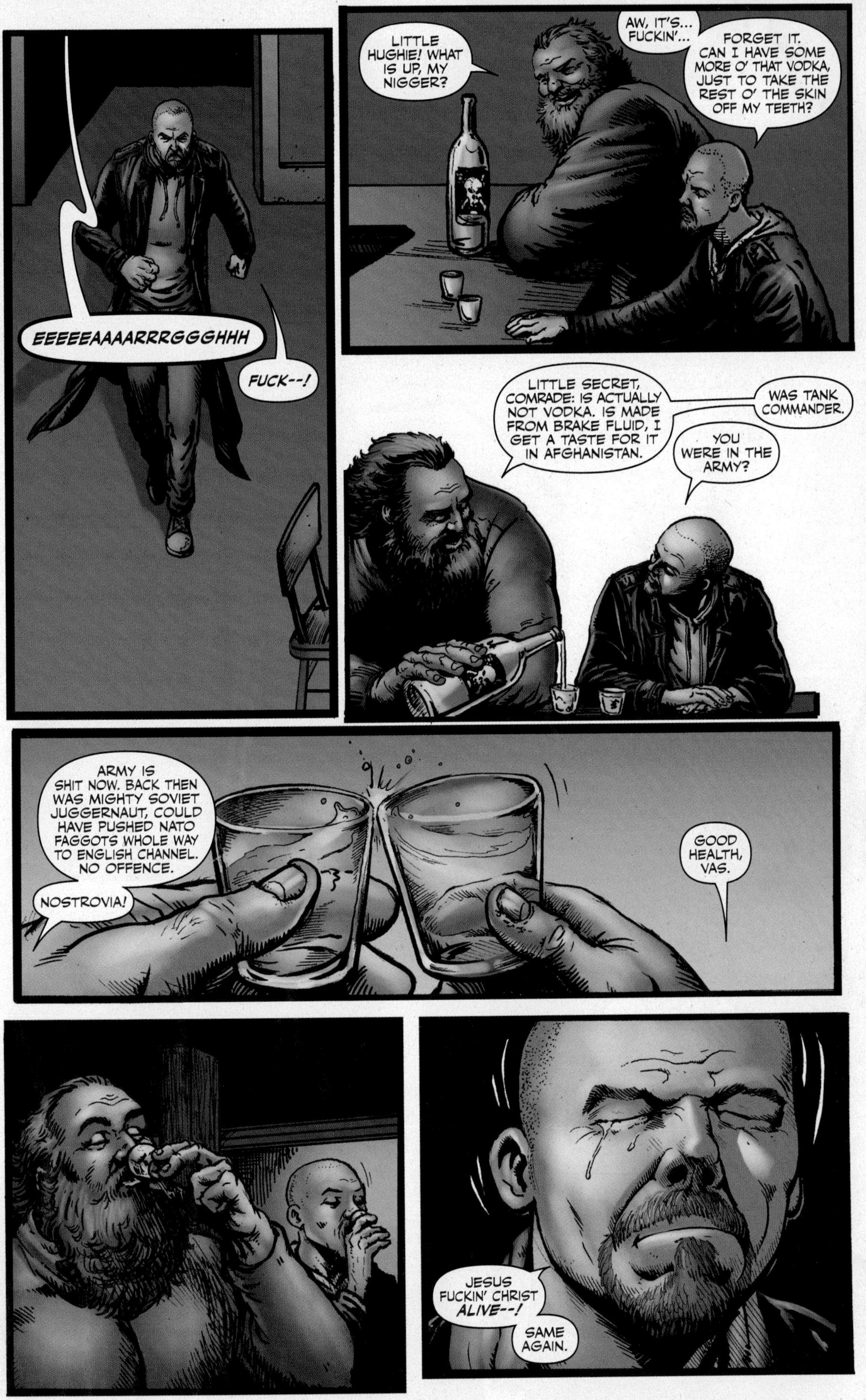
EEEEEAAAARRRGGGHHH
FUCK--!
LITTLE HUGHIE! WHAT IS UP, MY NIGGER?
AW, IT'S... FUCKIN'...
FORGET IT. CAN I HAVE SOME MORE O' THAT VODKA, JUST TO TAKE THE REST O' THE SKIN OFF MY TEETH?
LITTLE SECRET, COMRADE: IS ACTUALLY NOT VODKA. IS MADE FROM BRAKE FLUID, I GET A TASTE FOR IT IN AFGHANISTAN.
YOU WERE IN THE ARMY?
WAS TANK COMMANDER.
ARMY IS SHIT NOW. BACK THEN WAS MIGHTY SOVIET JUGGERNAUT, COULD HAVE PUSHED NATO FAGGOTS WHOLE WAY TO ENGLISH CHANNEL. NO OFFENCE.
NOSTROVIA!
GOOD HEALTH, VAS.
JESUS FUCKIN' CHRIST ALIVE--!
SAME AGAIN.

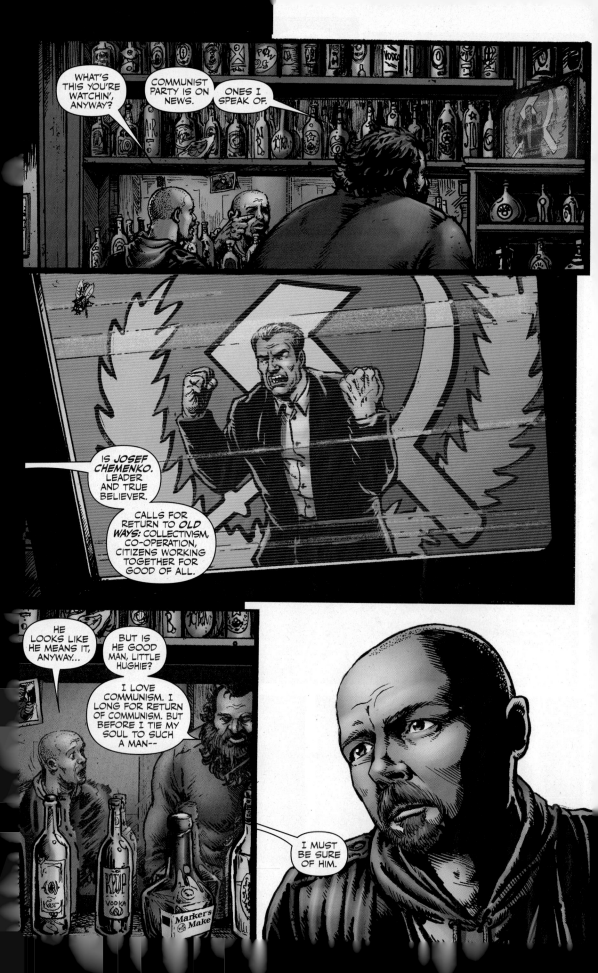

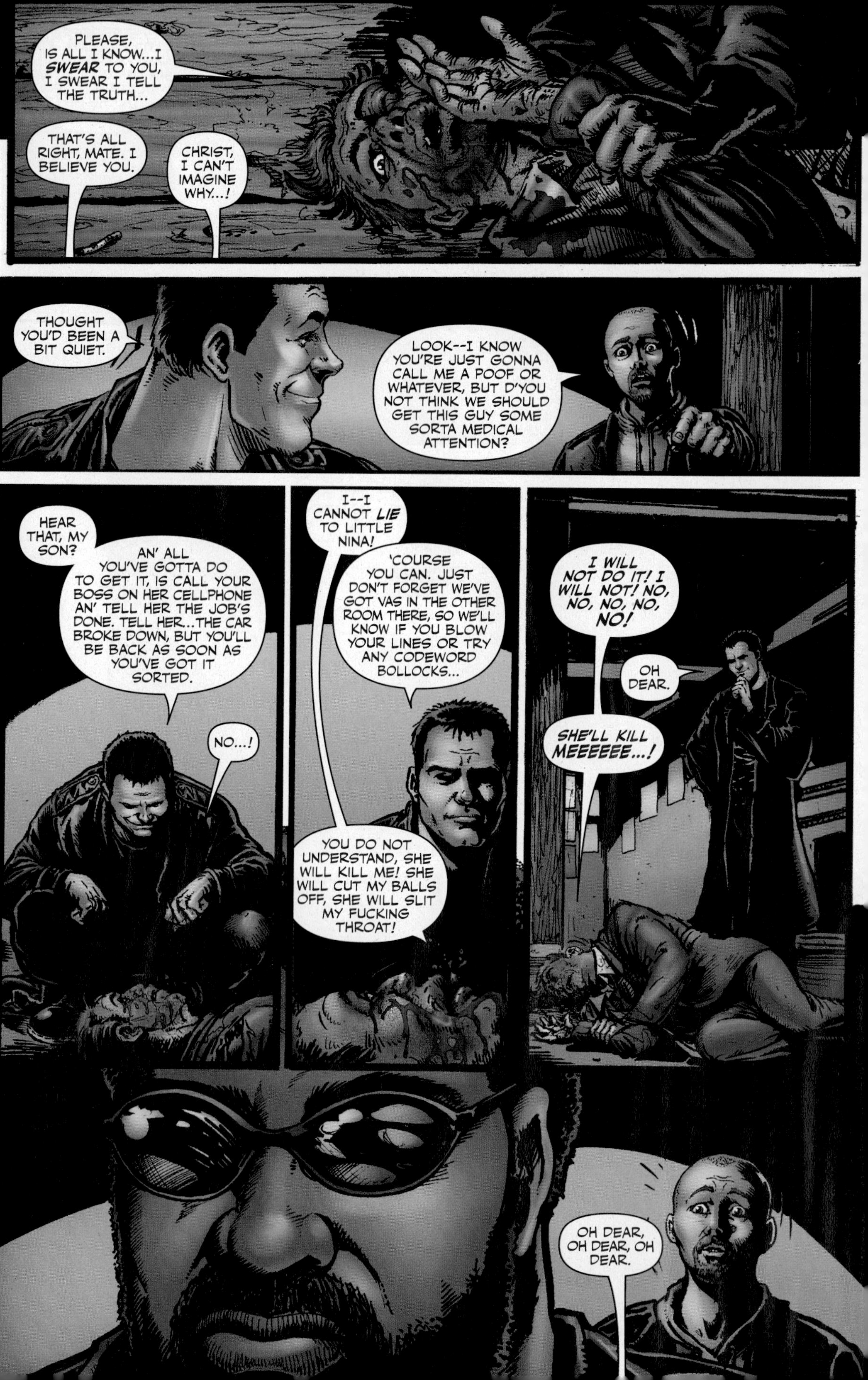
PLEASE, IS ALL I KNOW...I SWEAR TO YOU, I SWEAR I TELL THE TRUTH...
THAT'S ALL RIGHT, MATE. I BELIEVE YOU.
CHRIST, I CAN'T IMAGINE WHY...!
THOUGHT YOU'D BEEN A BIT QUIET.
LOOK--I KNOW YOU'RE JUST GONNA CALL ME A POOF OR WHATEVER, BUT D'YOU NOT THINK WE SHOULD GET THIS GUY SOME SORTA MEDICAL ATTENTION?
HEAR THAT, MY SON?
AN' ALL YOU'VE GOTTA DO TO GET IT, IS CALL YOUR BOSS ON HER CELLPHONE AN' TELL HER THE JOB'S DONE. TELL HER...THE CAR BROKE DOWN, BUT YOU'LL BE BACK AS SOON AS YOU'VE GOT IT SORTED.
NO...!
I--I CANNOT LIE TO LITTLE NINA!
'COURSE YOU CAN. JUST DON'T FORGET WE'VE GOT VAS IN THE OTHER ROOM THERE, SO WE'LL KNOW IF YOU BLOW YOUR LINES OR TRY ANY CODEWORD BOLLOCKS...
YOU DO NOT UNDERSTAND, SHE WILL KILL ME! SHE WILL CUT MY BALLS OFF, SHE WILL SLIT MY FUCKING THROAT!
I WILL NOT DO IT! I WILL NOT! NO, NO, NO, NO, NO!
OH DEAR.
SHE'LL KILL MEEEEEE...!
OH DEAR, OH DEAR, OH DEAR.

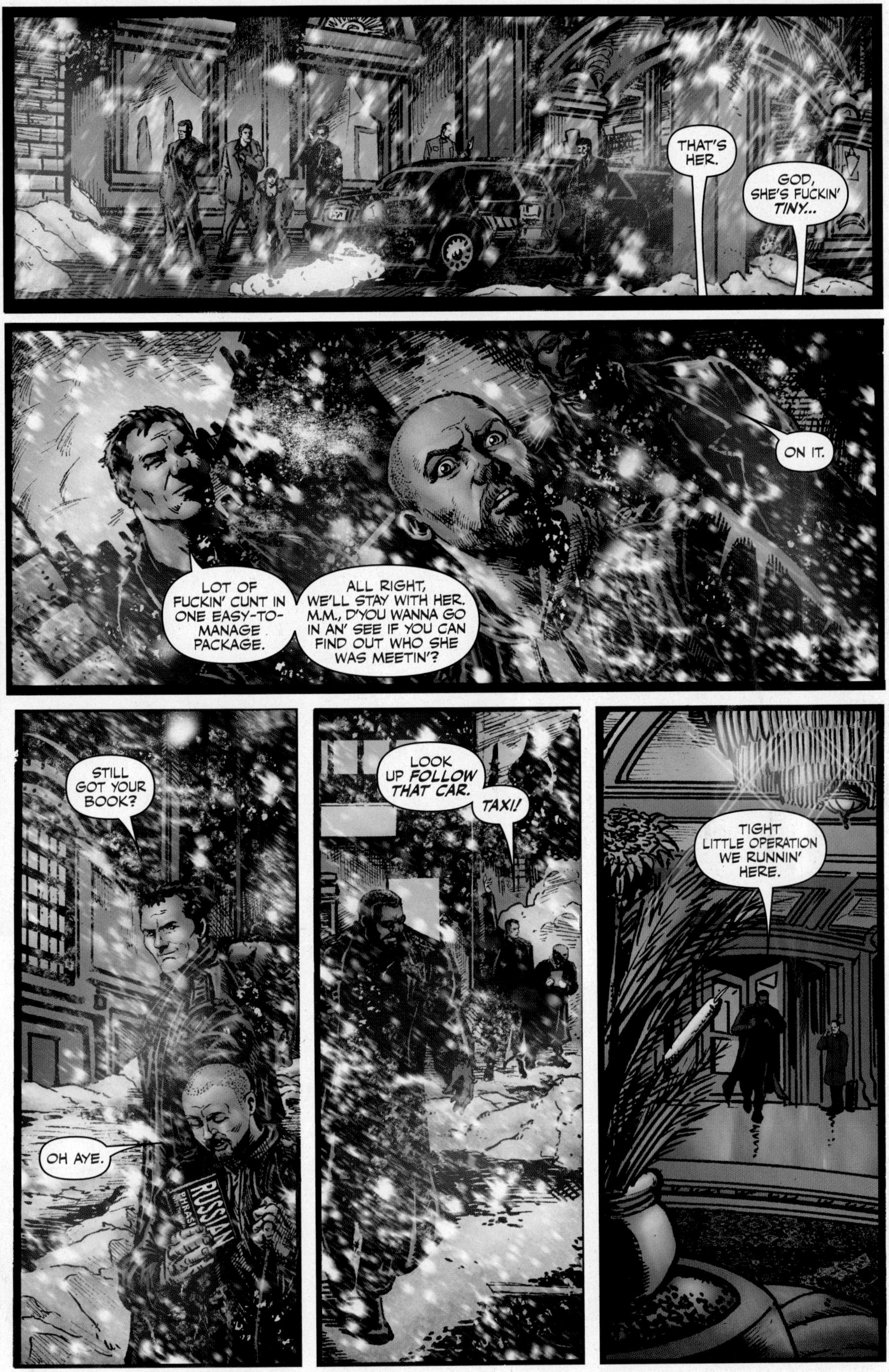
THAT'S HER.
GOD, SHE'S FUCKIN' TINY...
ON IT.
LOT OF FUCKIN' CUNT IN ONE EASY-TO-MANAGE PACKAGE.
ALL RIGHT, WE'LL STAY WITH HER. M.M., D'YOU WANNA GO IN AN' SEE IF YOU CAN FIND OUT WHO SHE WAS MEETIN'?
STILL GOT YOUR BOOK?
OH AYE.
RUSSIAN
LOOK UP FOLLOW THAT CAR.
TAXI!
TIGHT LITTLE OPERATION WE RUNNIN' HERE.

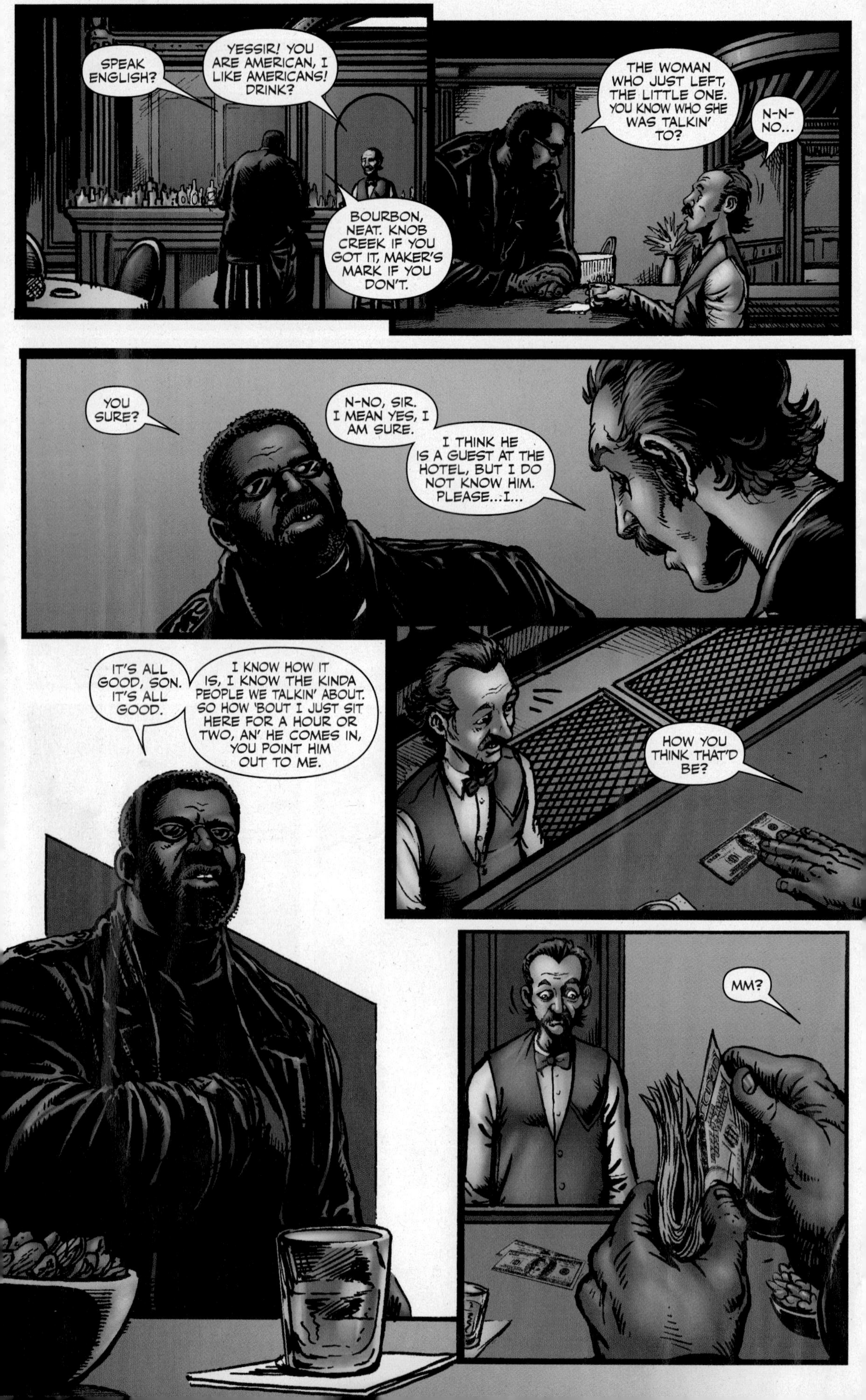
SPEAK ENGLISH?
YESSIR! YOU ARE AMERICAN, I LIKE AMERICANS! DRINK?
BOURBON, NEAT. KNOB CREEK IF YOU GOT IT, MAKER'S MARK IF YOU DON'T.
THE WOMAN WHO JUST LEFT, THE LITTLE ONE. YOU KNOW WHO SHE WAS TALKIN' TO?
N-N-NO...
YOU SURE?
N-NO, SIR. I MEAN YES, I AM SURE.
I THINK HE IS A GUEST AT THE HOTEL, BUT I DO NOT KNOW HIM. PLEASE...I...
IT'S ALL GOOD, SON. IT'S ALL GOOD.
I KNOW HOW IT IS, I KNOW THE KINDA PEOPLE WE TALKIN' ABOUT. SO HOW 'BOUT I JUST SIT HERE FOR A HOUR OR TWO, AN' HE COMES IN, YOU POINT HIM OUT TO ME.
HOW YOU THINK THAT'D BE?
MM?

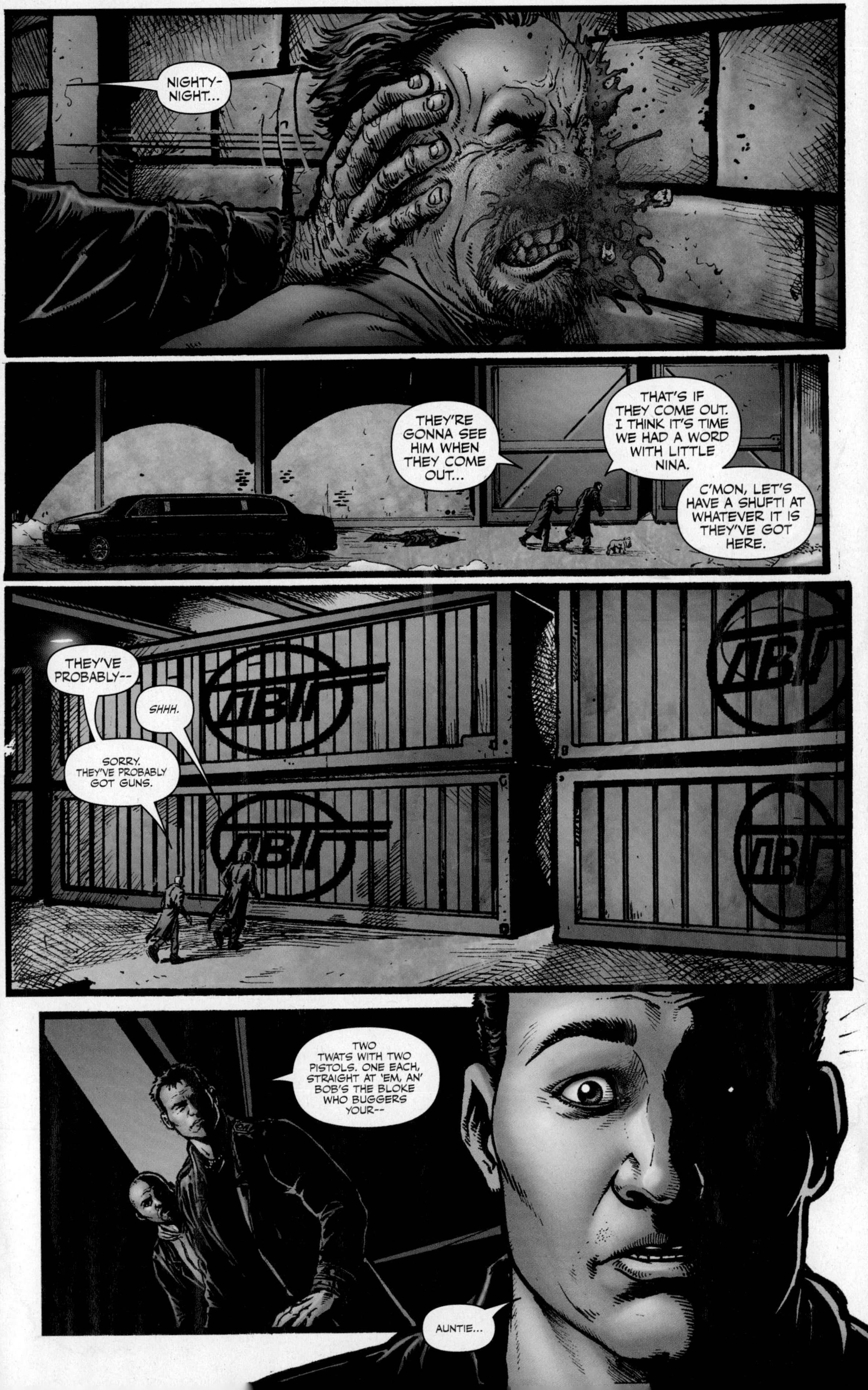
NIGHTY-NIGHT...
THEY'RE GONNA SEE HIM WHEN THEY COME OUT...
THAT'S IF THEY COME OUT. I THINK IT'S TIME WE HAD A WORD WITH LITTLE NINA.
C'MON, LET'S HAVE A SHUFTI AT WHATEVER IT IS THEY'VE GOT HERE.
THEY'VE PROBABLY--
SHHH.
SORRY. THEY'VE PROBABLY GOT GUNS.
TWO TWATS WITH TWO PISTOLS. ONE EACH, STRAIGHT AT 'EM, AN' BOB'S THE BLOKE WHO BUGGERS YOUR--
AUNTIE...

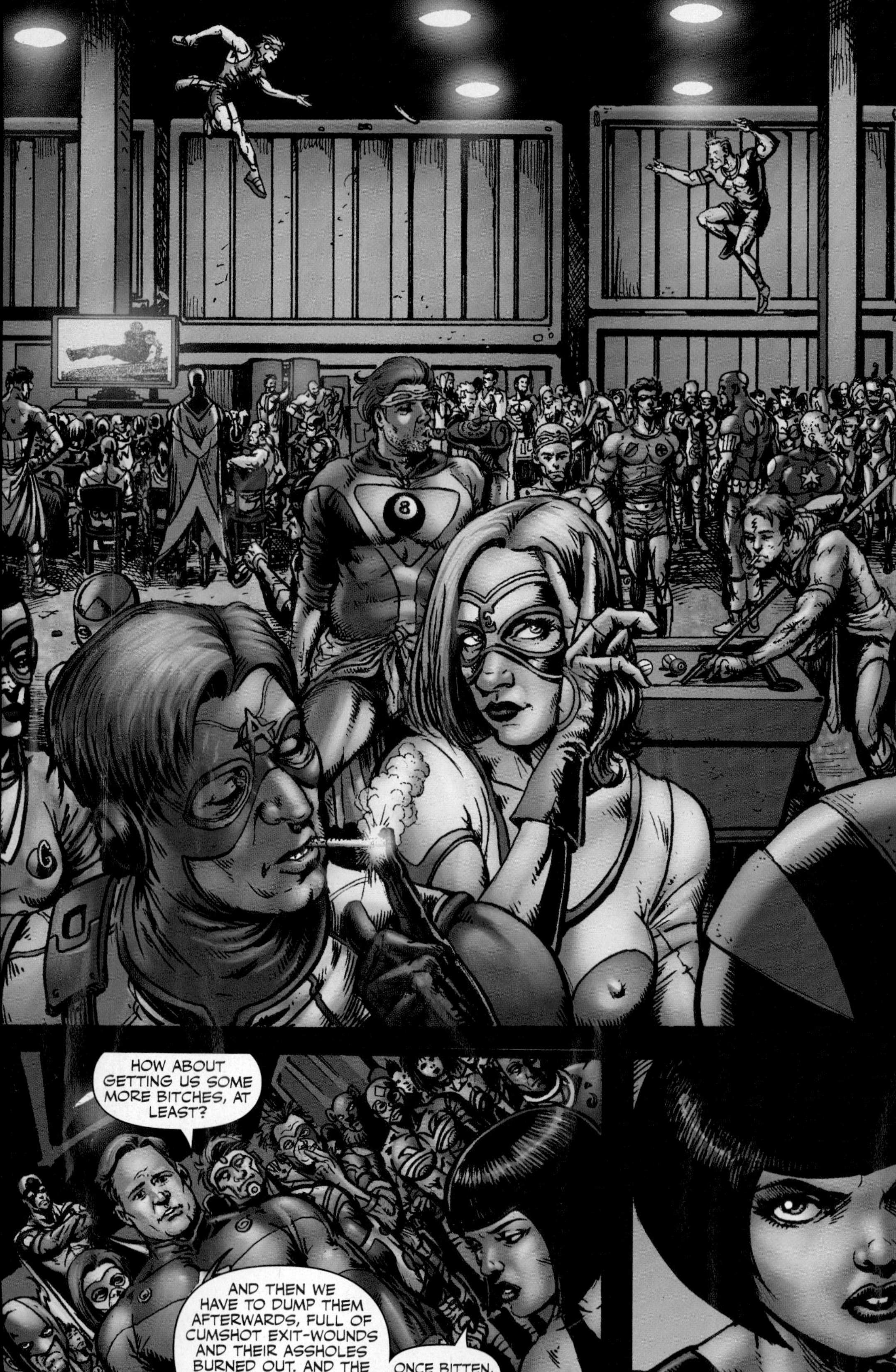
HOW ABOUT GETTING US SOME MORE BITCHES, AT LEAST?
AND THEN WE HAVE TO DUMP THEM AFTERWARDS, FULL OF CUMSHOT EXIT-WOUNDS AND THEIR ASSHOLES BURNED OUT. AND THE COPS SAY, WHERE THE FUCK ARE THEY ALL COMING FROM?
ONCE BITTEN, TWICE SHY.

...BUT FOR CHRIST'S SAKE, HOW MUCH LONGER?

SOON.

YOU HAVE ANY IDEA JUST HOW FUCKING BORING IT IS HERE...?

YOU HAVE ANY IDEA HOW MUCH MONEY IS ACCUMULATING IN YOUR BANK ACCOUNT?

SOON.

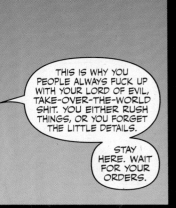

THIS IS WHY YOU PEOPLE ALWAYS FUCK UP WITH YOUR LORD OF EVIL, TAKE-OVER-THE-WORLD SHIT. YOU EITHER RUSH THINGS, OR YOU FORGET THE LITTLE DETAILS.

STAY HERE. WAIT FOR YOUR ORDERS.

LEG IT.

AND DO NOT EVER CALL ME AGAIN.

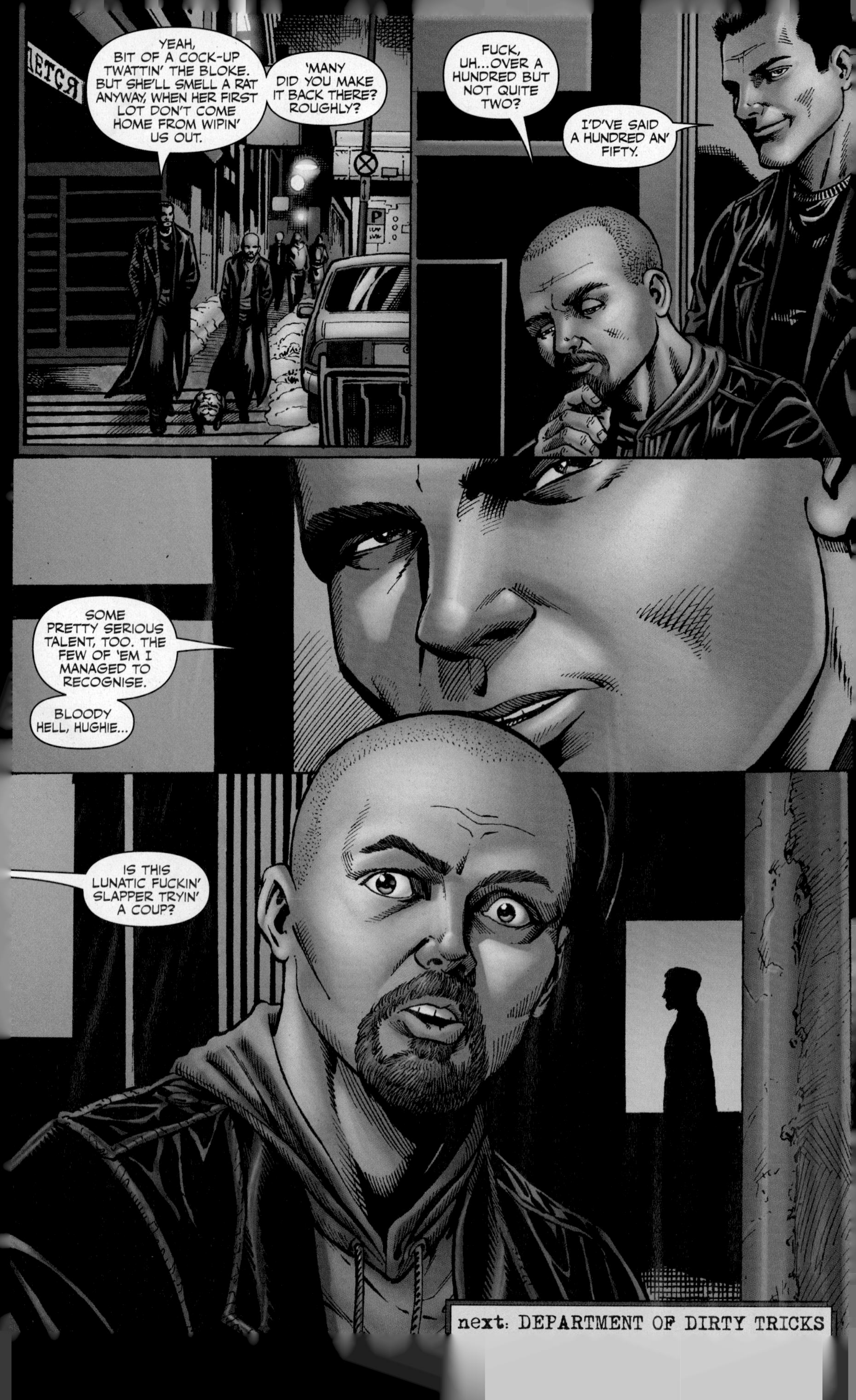
YEAH, BIT OF A COCK-UP TWATTIN' THE BLOKE. BUT SHE'LL SMELL A RAT ANYWAY, WHEN HER FIRST LOT DON'T COME HOME FROM WIPIN' US OUT.
'MANY DID YOU MAKE IT BACK THERE? ROUGHLY?
FUCK, UH...OVER A HUNDRED BUT NOT QUITE TWO?
I'D'VE SAID A HUNDRED AN' FIFTY.
SOME PRETTY SERIOUS TALENT, TOO. THE FEW OF 'EM I MANAGED TO RECOGNISE.
BLOODY HELL, HUGHIE...
IS THIS LUNATIC FUCKIN' SLAPPER TRYIN' A COUP?
next: DEPARTMENT OF DIRTY TRICKS

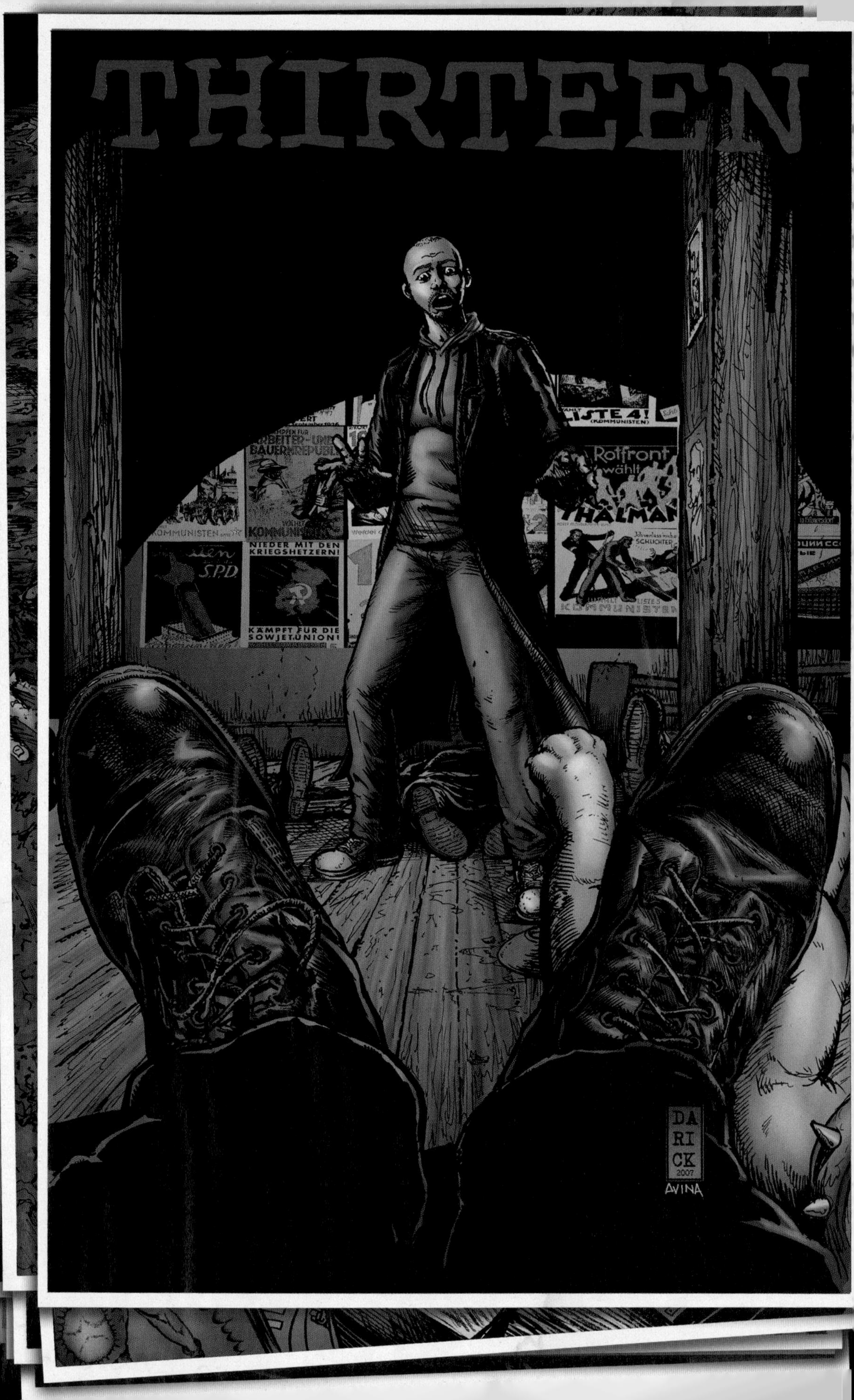
THIRTEEN
LISTE 4!
(KOMMUNISTEN)
Rotfront
wählt
THÄLMAN
BAUERNREPUBLI
KOMMUNISTEN
S.P.D.
NIEDER MIT DEN
KRIEGSHETZERN!
KÄMPFT FÜR DIE
SOWJETUNION!
KOMMUNISTEN
DA
RI
CK
2007
AVINA

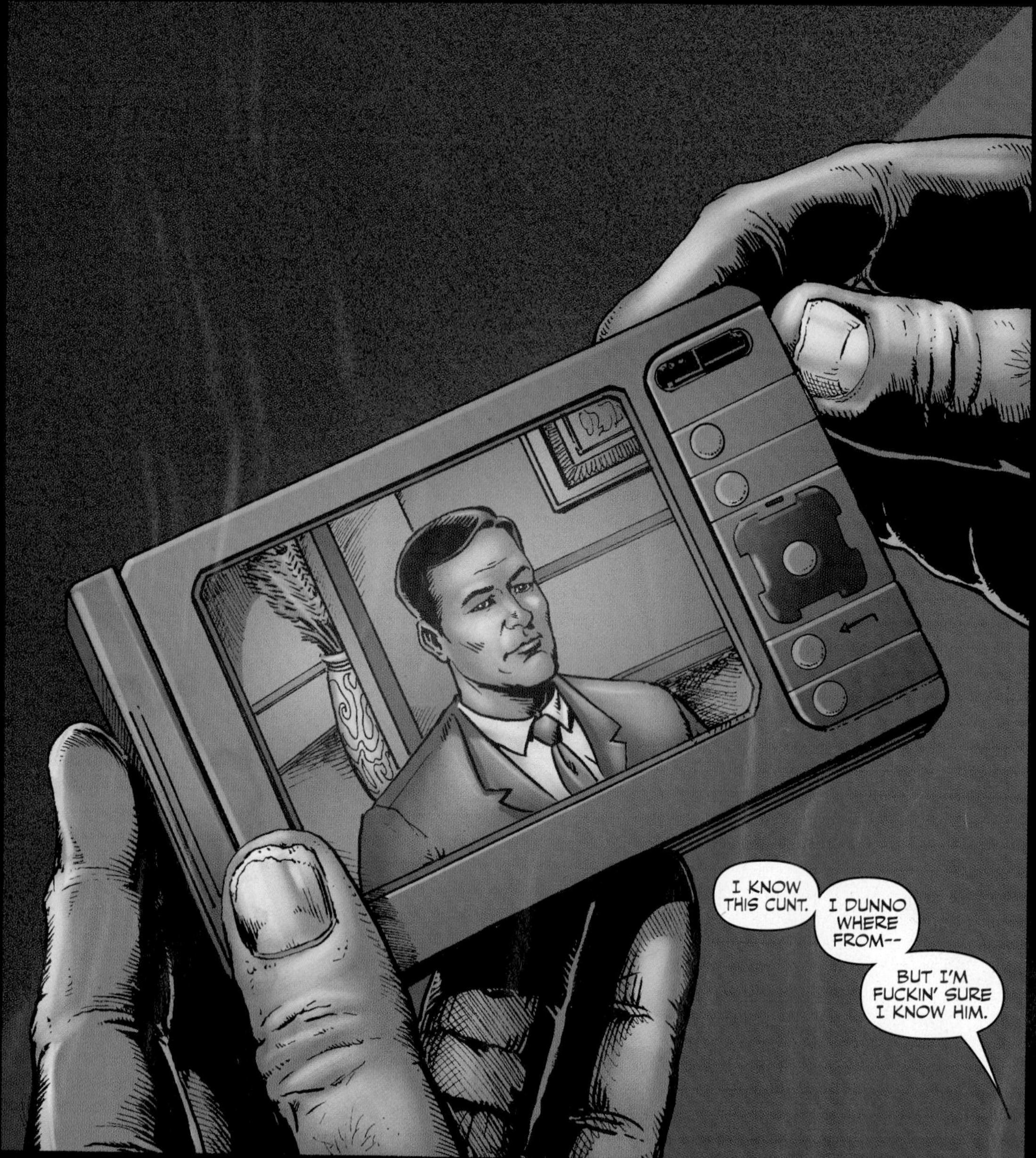
I KNOW THIS CUNT.
I DUNNO WHERE FROM--
BUT I'M FUCKIN' SURE I KNOW HIM.

GLORIOUS FIVE YEAR PLAN

part three

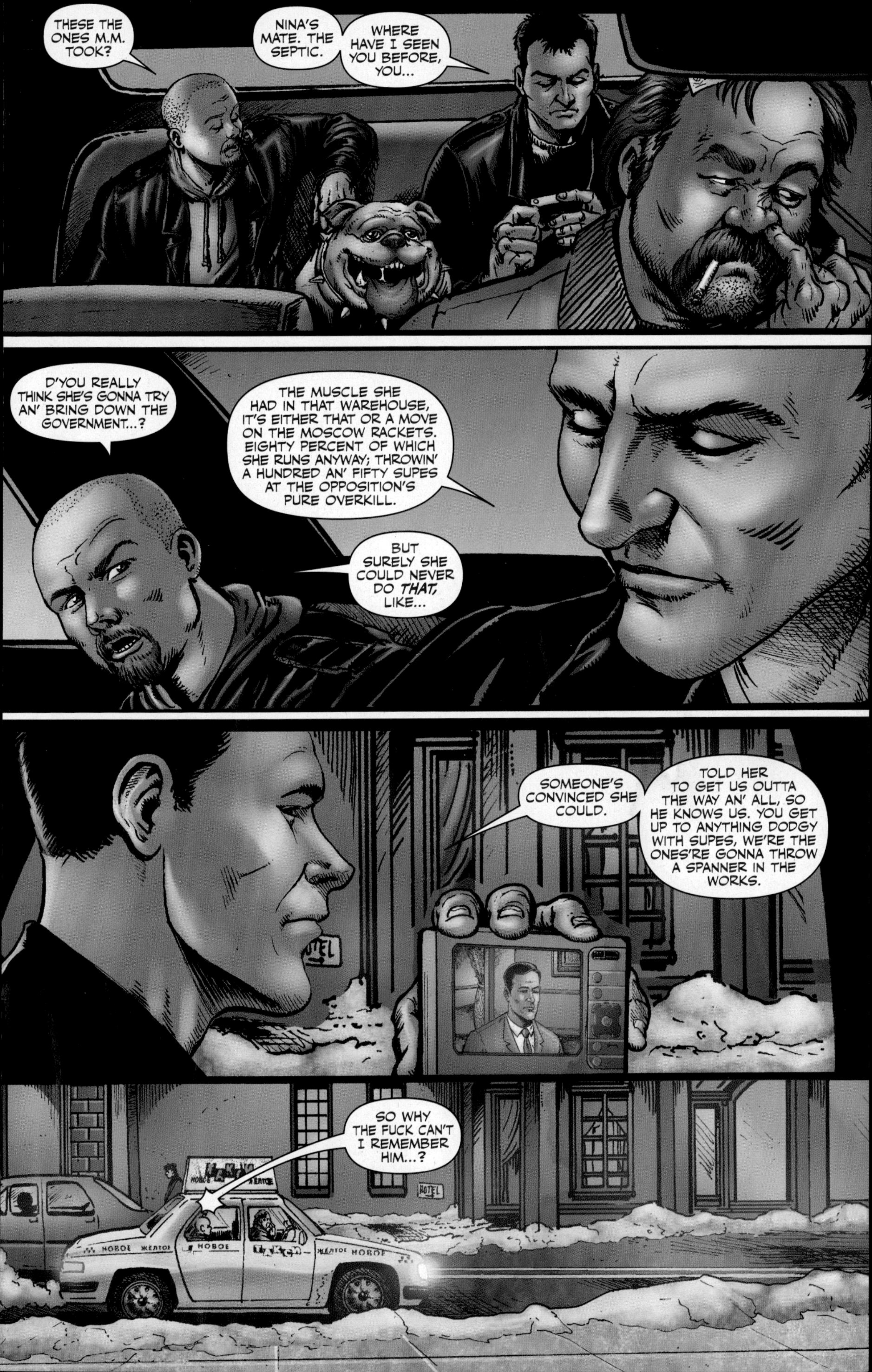
THESE THE ONES M.M. TOOK?
NINA'S MATE. THE SEPTIC.
WHERE HAVE I SEEN YOU BEFORE, YOU...
D'YOU REALLY THINK SHE'S GONNA TRY AN' BRING DOWN THE GOVERNMENT...?
THE MUSCLE SHE HAD IN THAT WAREHOUSE, IT'S EITHER THAT OR A MOVE ON THE MOSCOW RACKETS. EIGHTY PERCENT OF WHICH SHE RUNS ANYWAY; THROWIN' A HUNDRED AN' FIFTY SUPES AT THE OPPOSITION'S PURE OVERKILL.
BUT SURELY SHE COULD NEVER DO *THAT,* LIKE...
SOMEONE'S CONVINCED SHE COULD.
TOLD HER TO GET US OUTTA THE WAY AN' ALL, SO HE KNOWS US. YOU GET UP TO ANYTHING DODGY WITH SUPES, WE'RE THE ONES'RE GONNA THROW A SPANNER IN THE WORKS.
SO WHY THE FUCK CAN'T I REMEMBER HIM...?
HOTEL
НОВОЕ ЖЕЛТОЕ

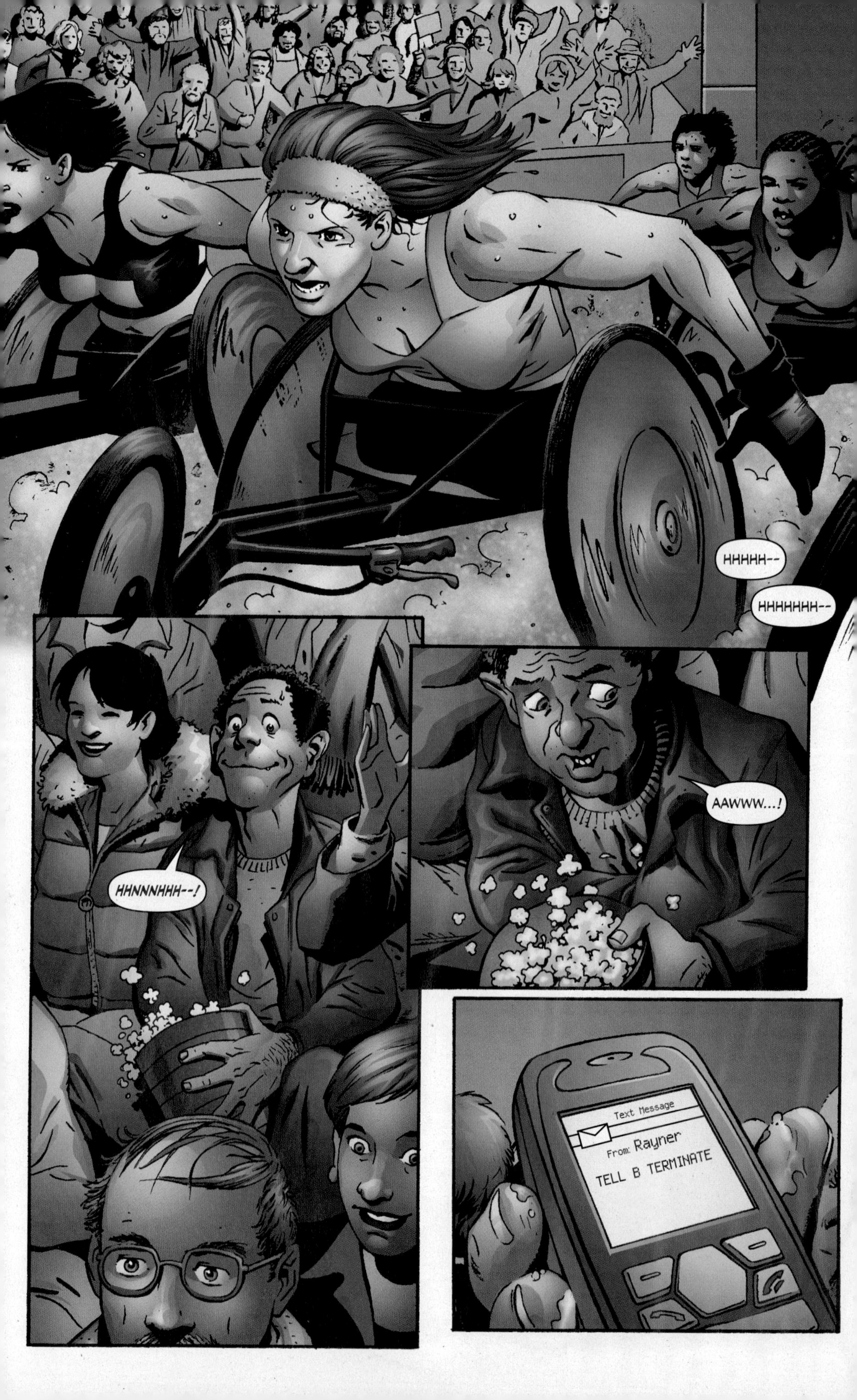
HHHHH--
HHHHHHH--
HHNNNHHH--!
AAWWW...!
Text Message
From: Rayner
TELL B TERMINATE

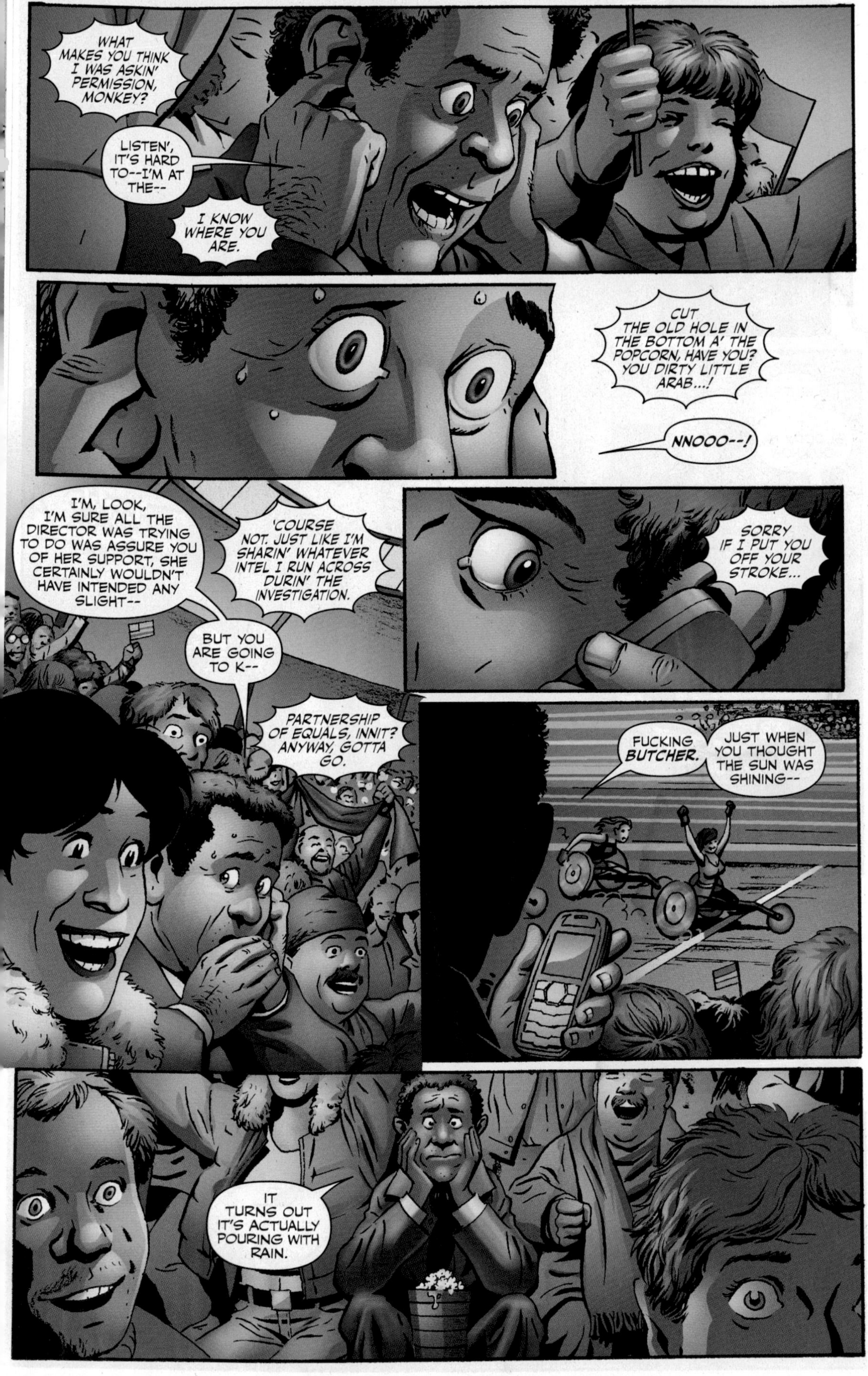
WHAT MAKES YOU THINK I WAS ASKIN' PERMISSION, MONKEY?
LISTEN', IT'S HARD TO--I'M AT THE--
I KNOW WHERE YOU ARE.
CUT THE OLD HOLE IN THE BOTTOM A' THE POPCORN, HAVE YOU? YOU DIRTY LITTLE ARAB...!
NNOOO--!
I'M, LOOK, I'M SURE ALL THE DIRECTOR WAS TRYING TO DO WAS ASSURE YOU OF HER SUPPORT, SHE CERTAINLY WOULDN'T HAVE INTENDED ANY SLIGHT--
'COURSE NOT. JUST LIKE I'M SHARIN' WHATEVER INTEL I RUN ACROSS DURIN' THE INVESTIGATION.
BUT YOU ARE GOING TO K--
PARTNERSHIP OF EQUALS, INNIT? ANYWAY, GOTTA GO.
SORRY IF I PUT YOU OFF YOUR STROKE...
FUCKING BUTCHER.
JUST WHEN YOU THOUGHT THE SUN WAS SHINING--
IT TURNS OUT IT'S ACTUALLY POURING WITH RAIN.

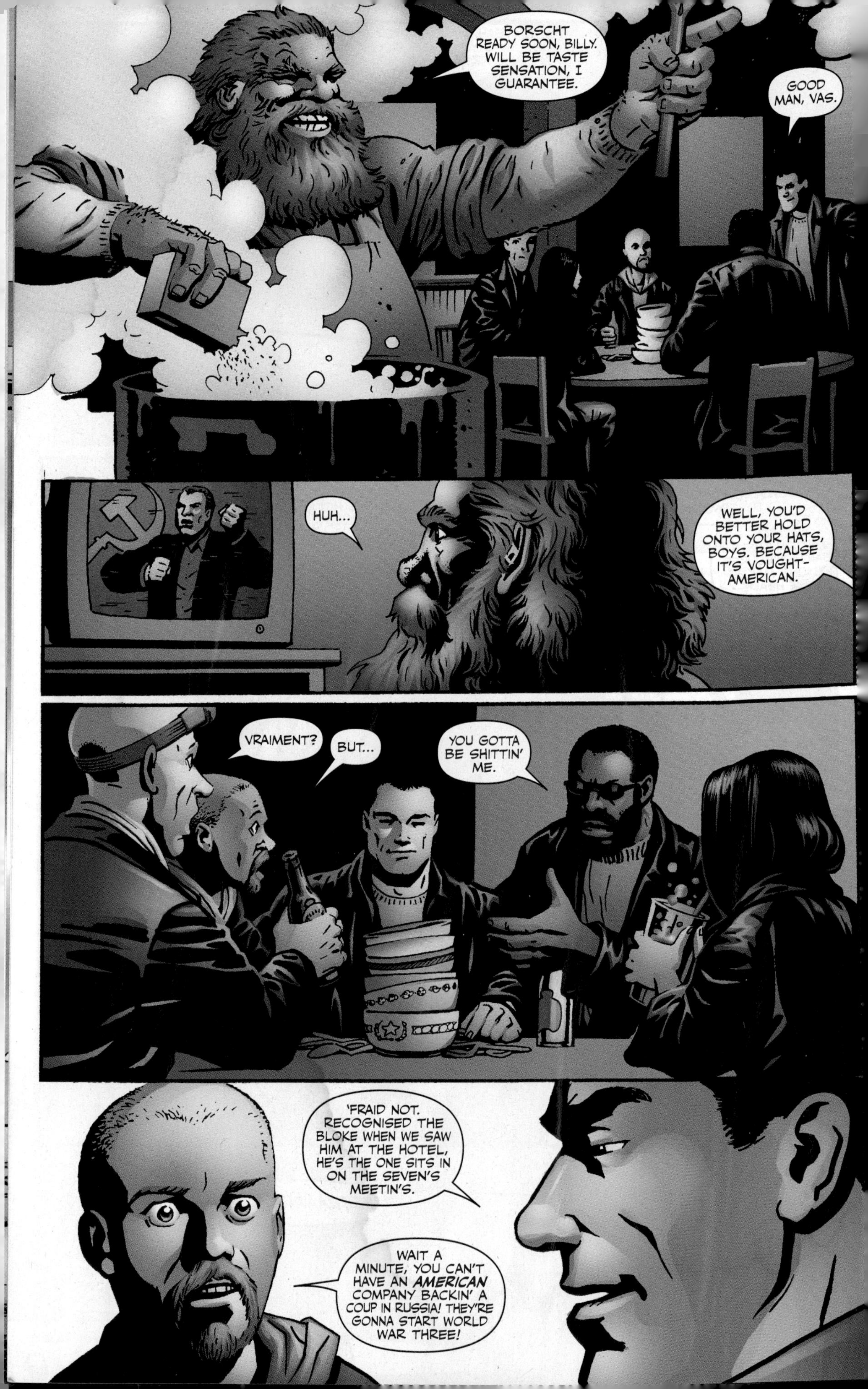
BORSCHT READY SOON, BILLY. WILL BE TASTE SENSATION, I GUARANTEE.
GOOD MAN, VAS.
HUH...
WELL, YOU'D BETTER HOLD ONTO YOUR HATS, BOYS. BECAUSE IT'S VOUGHT-AMERICAN.
VRAIMENT?
BUT...
YOU GOTTA BE SHITTIN' ME.
'FRAID NOT. RECOGNISED THE BLOKE WHEN WE SAW HIM AT THE HOTEL, HE'S THE ONE SITS IN ON THE SEVEN'S MEETIN'S.
WAIT A MINUTE, YOU CAN'T HAVE AN *AMERICAN* COMPANY BACKIN' A COUP IN RUSSIA! THEY'RE GONNA START WORLD WAR THREE!

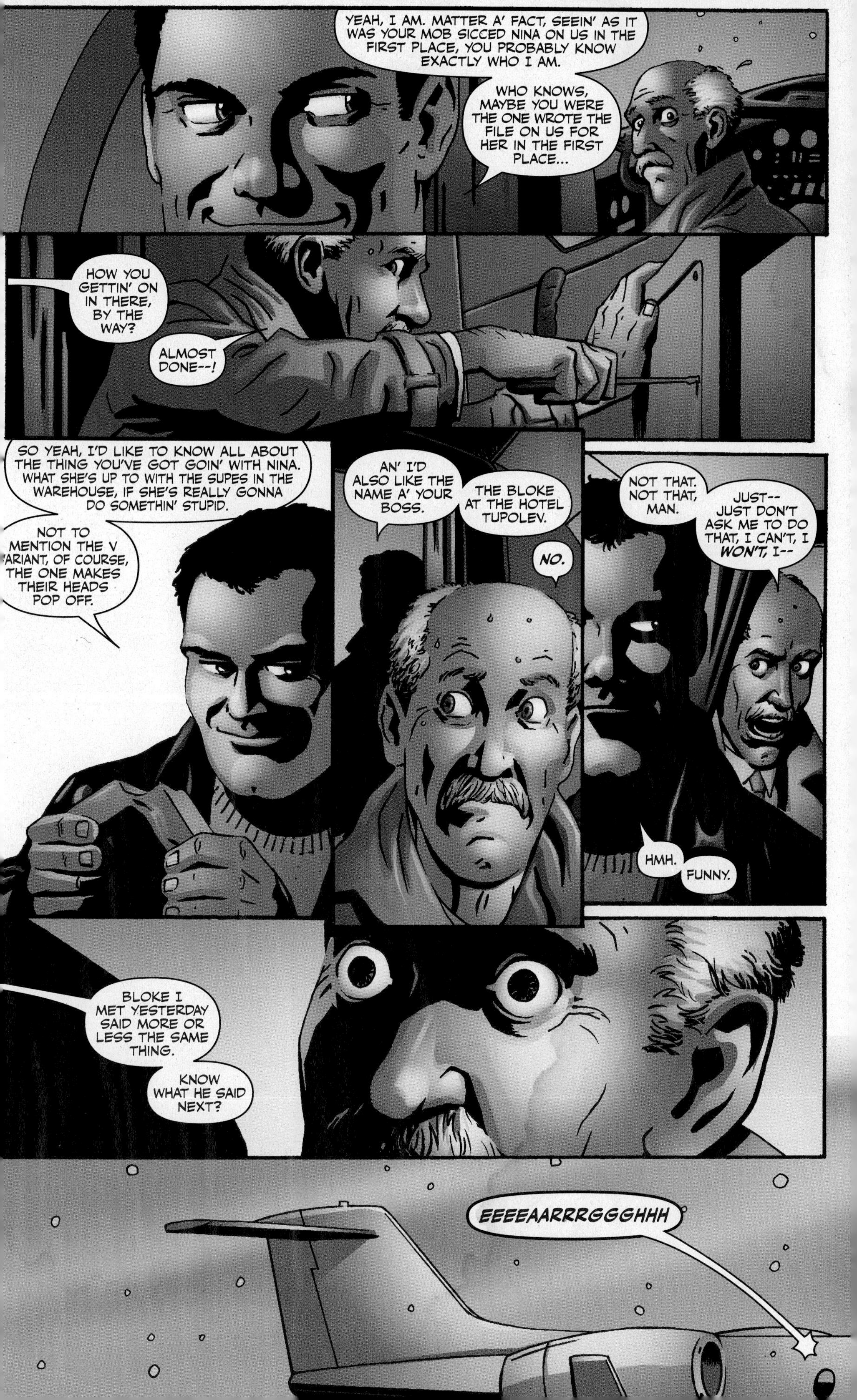
YEAH, I AM. MATTER A' FACT, SEEIN' AS IT WAS YOUR MOB SICCED NINA ON US IN THE FIRST PLACE, YOU PROBABLY KNOW EXACTLY WHO I AM.
WHO KNOWS, MAYBE YOU WERE THE ONE WROTE THE FILE ON US FOR HER IN THE FIRST PLACE...
HOW YOU GETTIN' ON IN THERE, BY THE WAY?
ALMOST DONE--!
SO YEAH, I'D LIKE TO KNOW ALL ABOUT THE THING YOU'VE GOT GOIN' WITH NINA. WHAT SHE'S UP TO WITH THE SUPES IN THE WAREHOUSE, IF SHE'S REALLY GONNA DO SOMETHIN' STUPID.
NOT TO MENTION THE V ARIANT, OF COURSE, THE ONE MAKES THEIR HEADS POP OFF.
AN' I'D ALSO LIKE THE NAME A' YOUR BOSS.
THE BLOKE AT THE HOTEL TUPOLEV.
NO.
NOT THAT. NOT THAT, MAN.
JUST-- JUST DON'T ASK ME TO DO THAT, I CAN'T, I WON'T, I--
HMH.
FUNNY.
BLOKE I MET YESTERDAY SAID MORE OR LESS THE SAME THING.
KNOW WHAT HE SAID NEXT?
EEEEAARRRGGGHHH

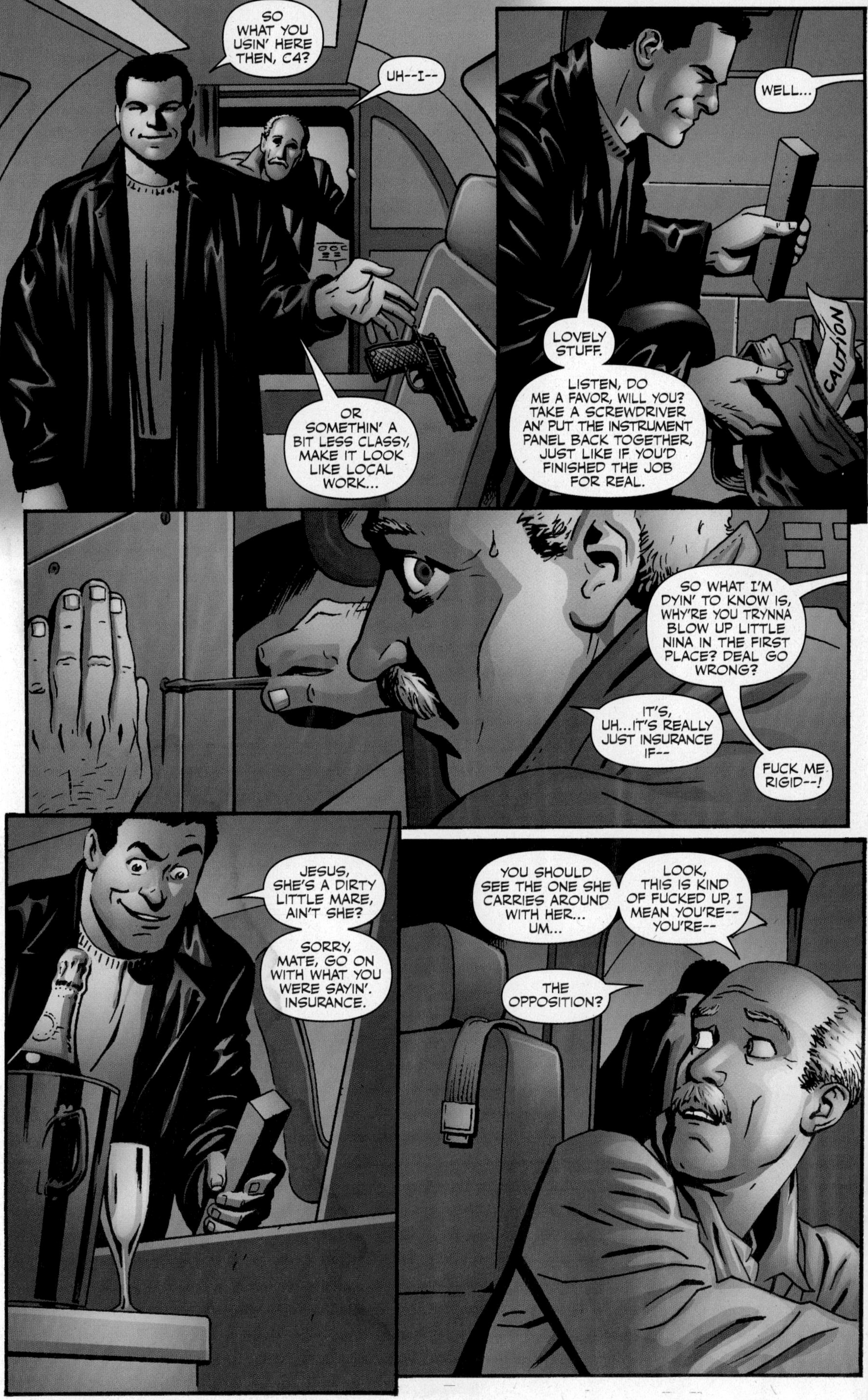

SO WHAT YOU USIN' HERE THEN, C4?
UH--I--
OR SOMETHIN' A BIT LESS CLASSY, MAKE IT LOOK LIKE LOCAL WORK...
WELL...
LOVELY STUFF.
LISTEN, DO ME A FAVOR, WILL YOU? TAKE A SCREWDRIVER AN' PUT THE INSTRUMENT PANEL BACK TOGETHER, JUST LIKE IF YOU'D FINISHED THE JOB FOR REAL.
CAUTION
SO WHAT I'M DYIN' TO KNOW IS, WHY'RE YOU TRYNNA BLOW UP LITTLE NINA IN THE FIRST PLACE? DEAL GO WRONG?
IT'S, UH...IT'S REALLY JUST INSURANCE IF--
FUCK ME RIGID--!
JESUS, SHE'S A DIRTY LITTLE MARE, AIN'T SHE?
SORRY, MATE, GO ON WITH WHAT YOU WERE SAYIN'. INSURANCE.
YOU SHOULD SEE THE ONE SHE CARRIES AROUND WITH HER... UM...
LOOK, THIS IS KIND OF FUCKED UP, I MEAN YOU'RE-- YOU'RE--
THE OPPOSITION?

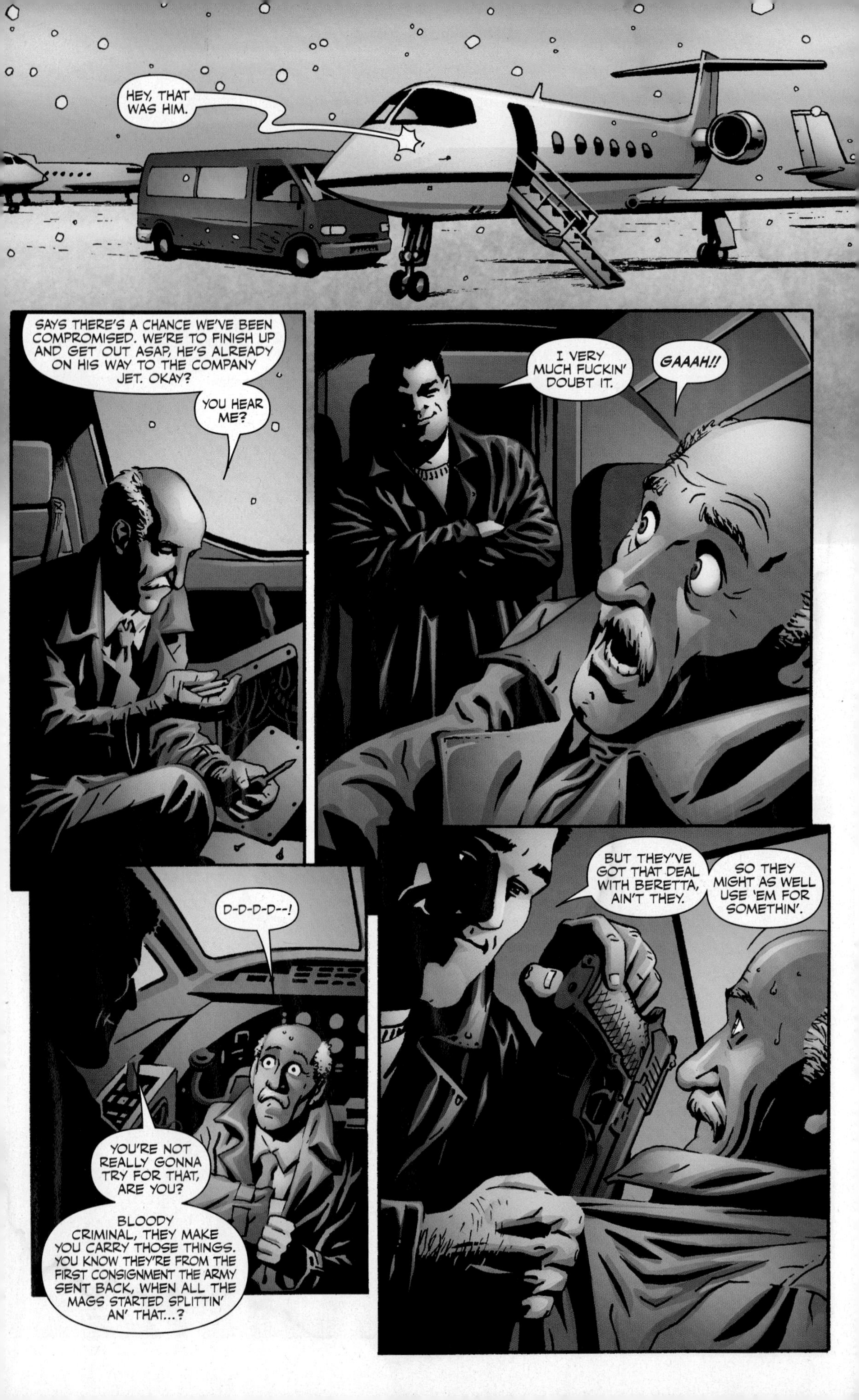
HEY, THAT WAS HIM.
SAYS THERE'S A CHANCE WE'VE BEEN COMPROMISED. WE'RE TO FINISH UP AND GET OUT ASAP, HE'S ALREADY ON HIS WAY TO THE COMPANY JET. OKAY?
YOU HEAR ME?
I VERY MUCH FUCKIN' DOUBT IT.
GAAAH!!
D-D-D-D--!
YOU'RE NOT REALLY GONNA TRY FOR THAT, ARE YOU?
BLOODY CRIMINAL, THEY MAKE YOU CARRY THOSE THINGS. YOU KNOW THEY'RE FROM THE FIRST CONSIGNMENT THE ARMY SENT BACK, WHEN ALL THE MAGS STARTED SPLITTIN' AN' THAT...?
BUT THEY'VE GOT THAT DEAL WITH BERETTA, AIN'T THEY.
SO THEY MIGHT AS WELL USE 'EM FOR SOMETHIN'.

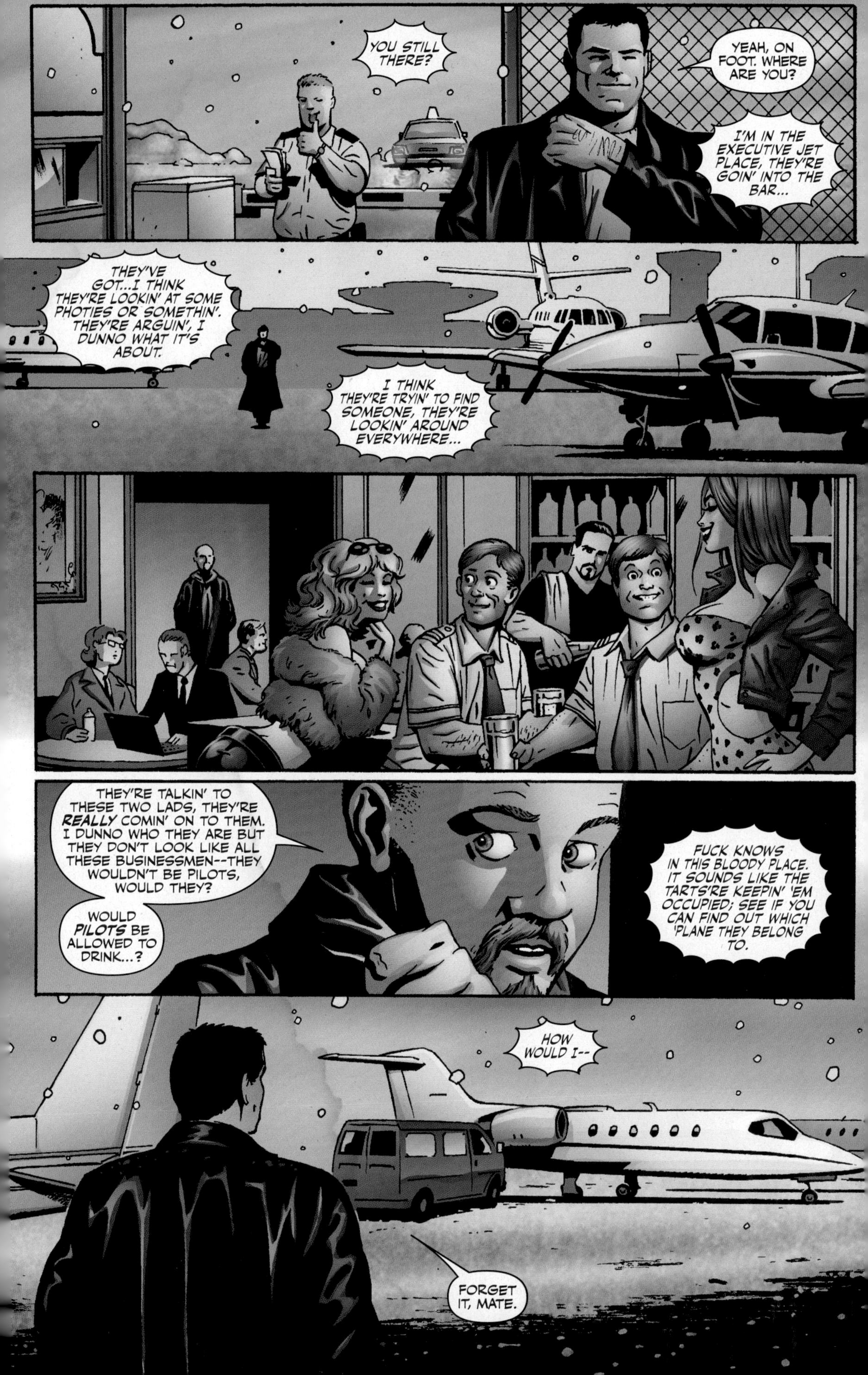
YOU STILL THERE?
YEAH, ON FOOT. WHERE ARE YOU?
I'M IN THE EXECUTIVE JET PLACE, THEY'RE GOIN' INTO THE BAR...
THEY'VE GOT...I THINK THEY'RE LOOKIN' AT SOME PHOTIES OR SOMETHIN'. THEY'RE ARGUIN', I DUNNO WHAT IT'S ABOUT.
I THINK THEY'RE TRYIN' TO FIND SOMEONE, THEY'RE LOOKIN' AROUND EVERYWHERE...
THEY'RE TALKIN' TO THESE TWO LADS, THEY'RE REALLY COMIN' ON TO THEM. I DUNNO WHO THEY ARE BUT THEY DON'T LOOK LIKE ALL THESE BUSINESSMEN--THEY WOULDN'T BE PILOTS, WOULD THEY?
WOULD PILOTS BE ALLOWED TO DRINK...?
FUCK KNOWS IN THIS BLOODY PLACE. IT SOUNDS LIKE THE TARTS'RE KEEPIN' 'EM OCCUPIED; SEE IF YOU CAN FIND OUT WHICH 'PLANE THEY BELONG TO.
HOW WOULD I--
FORGET IT, MATE.

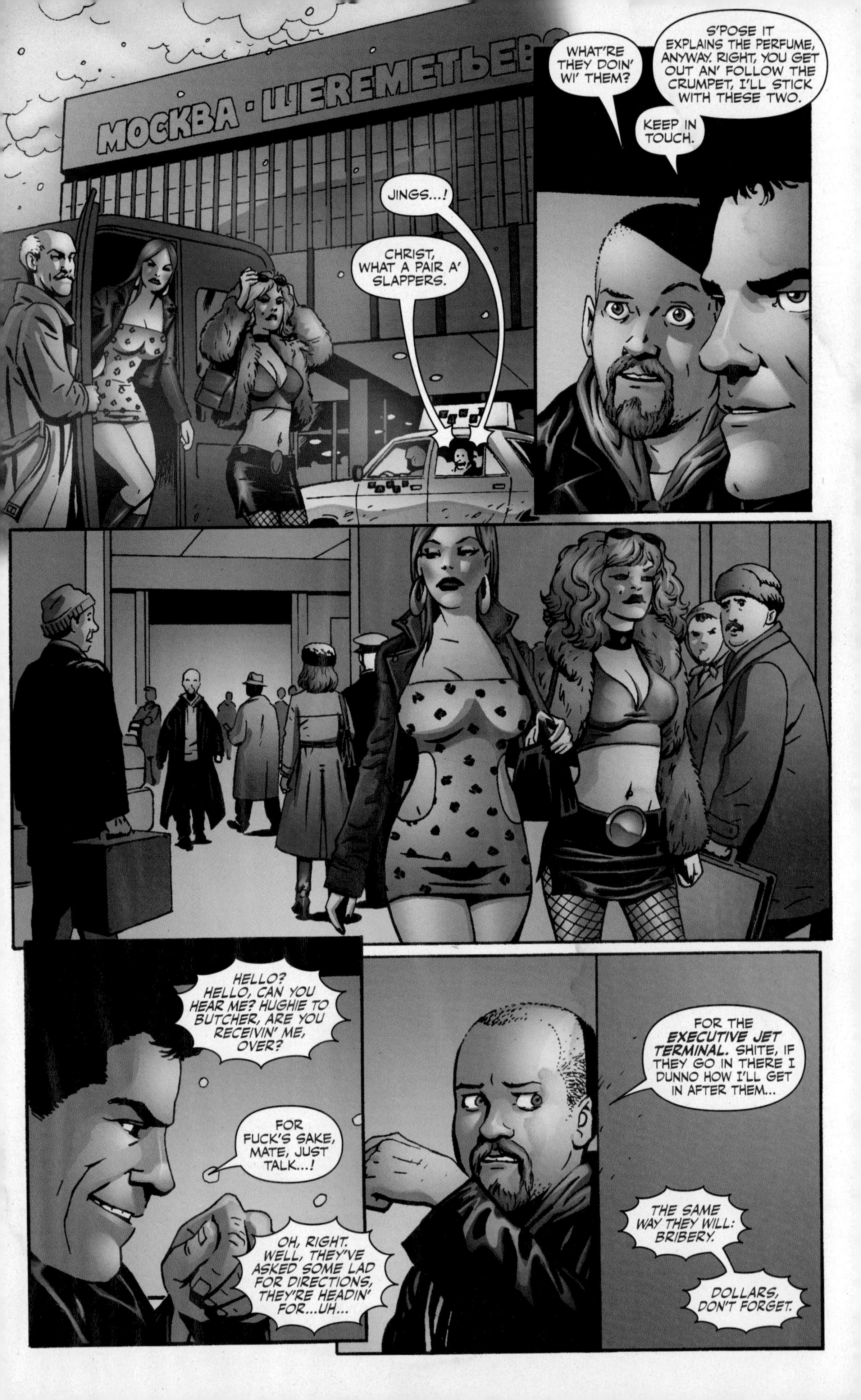
МОСКВА · ШЕРЕМЕТЬЕВО
JINGS...!
CHRIST, WHAT A PAIR A' SLAPPERS.
WHAT'RE THEY DOIN' WI' THEM?
S'POSE IT EXPLAINS THE PERFUME, ANYWAY. RIGHT, YOU GET OUT AN' FOLLOW THE CRUMPET, I'LL STICK WITH THESE TWO.
KEEP IN TOUCH.
HELLO? HELLO, CAN YOU HEAR ME? HUGHIE TO BUTCHER, ARE YOU RECEIVIN' ME, OVER?
FOR FUCK'S SAKE, MATE, JUST TALK...!
OH, RIGHT. WELL, THEY'VE ASKED SOME LAD FOR DIRECTIONS, THEY'RE HEADIN' FOR...UH...
FOR THE ***EXECUTIVE JET TERMINAL.*** SHITE, IF THEY GO IN THERE I DUNNO HOW I'LL GET IN AFTER THEM...
THE SAME WAY THEY WILL: BRIBERY.
DOLLARS, DON'T FORGET.

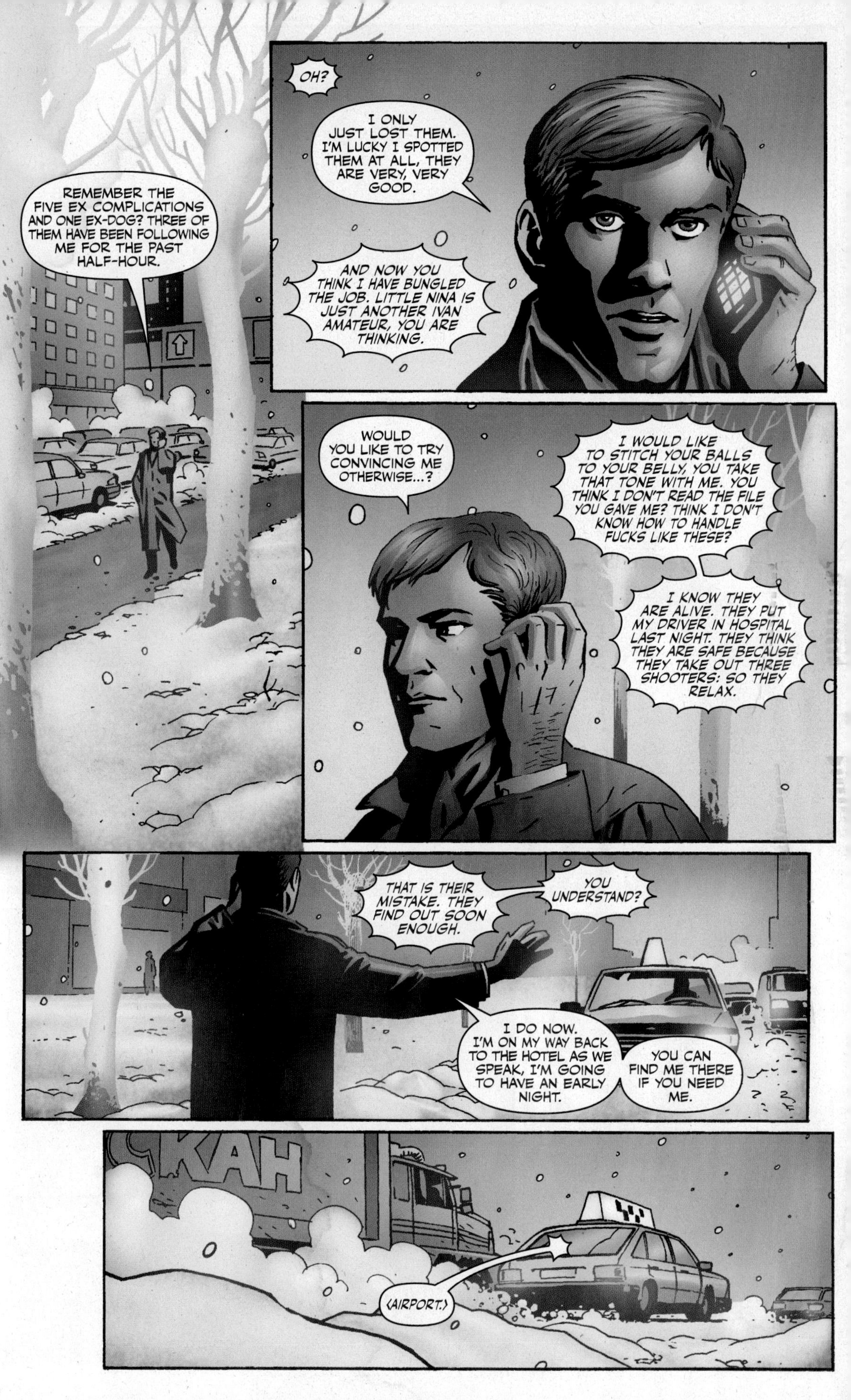
REMEMBER THE FIVE EX COMPLICATIONS AND ONE EX-DOG? THREE OF THEM HAVE BEEN FOLLOWING ME FOR THE PAST HALF-HOUR.
OH?
I ONLY JUST LOST THEM. I'M LUCKY I SPOTTED THEM AT ALL, THEY ARE VERY, VERY GOOD.
AND NOW YOU THINK I HAVE BUNGLED THE JOB. LITTLE NINA IS JUST ANOTHER IVAN AMATEUR, YOU ARE THINKING.
WOULD YOU LIKE TO TRY CONVINCING ME OTHERWISE...?
I WOULD LIKE TO STITCH YOUR BALLS TO YOUR BELLY, YOU TAKE THAT TONE WITH ME. YOU THINK I DON'T READ THE FILE YOU GAVE ME? THINK I DON'T KNOW HOW TO HANDLE FUCKS LIKE THESE?
I KNOW THEY ARE ALIVE. THEY PUT MY DRIVER IN HOSPITAL LAST NIGHT. THEY THINK THEY ARE SAFE BECAUSE THEY TAKE OUT THREE SHOOTERS: SO THEY RELAX.
THAT IS THEIR MISTAKE. THEY FIND OUT SOON ENOUGH.
YOU UNDERSTAND?
I DO NOW. I'M ON MY WAY BACK TO THE HOTEL AS WE SPEAK, I'M GOING TO HAVE AN EARLY NIGHT.
YOU CAN FIND ME THERE IF YOU NEED ME.
KAH
‹AIRPORT.›

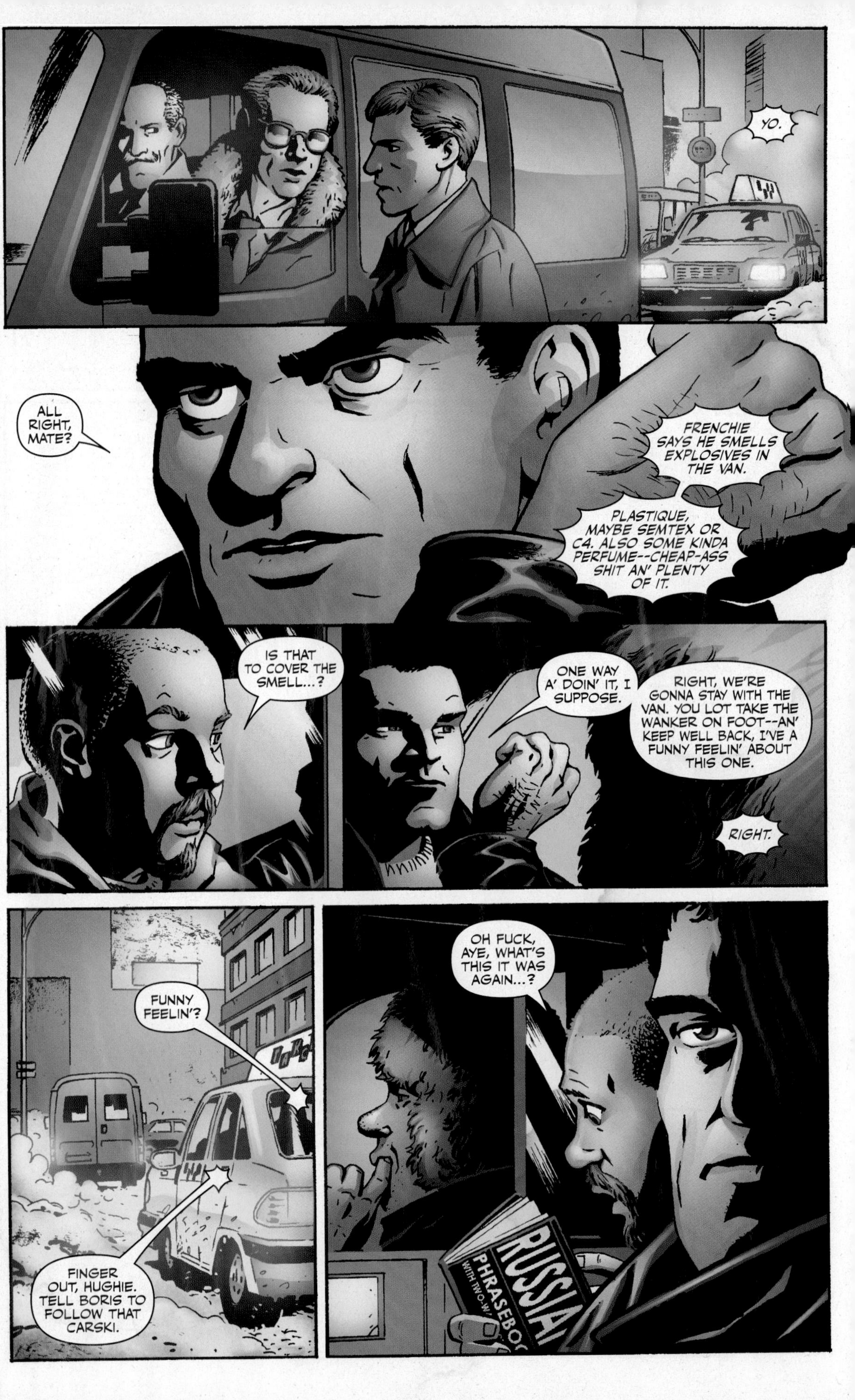

YO.
ALL RIGHT, MATE?
FRENCHIE SAYS HE SMELLS EXPLOSIVES IN THE VAN.
PLASTIQUE, MAYBE SEMTEX OR C4. ALSO SOME KINDA PERFUME--CHEAP-ASS SHIT AN' PLENTY OF IT.
IS THAT TO COVER THE SMELL...?
ONE WAY A' DOIN' IT, I SUPPOSE.
RIGHT, WE'RE GONNA STAY WITH THE VAN. YOU LOT TAKE THE WANKER ON FOOT--AN' KEEP WELL BACK, I'VE A FUNNY FEELIN' ABOUT THIS ONE.
RIGHT.
FUNNY FEELIN'?
FINGER OUT, HUGHIE. TELL BORIS TO FOLLOW THAT CARSKI.
OH FUCK, AYE, WHAT'S THIS IT WAS AGAIN...?
RUSSIAN PHRASEBO

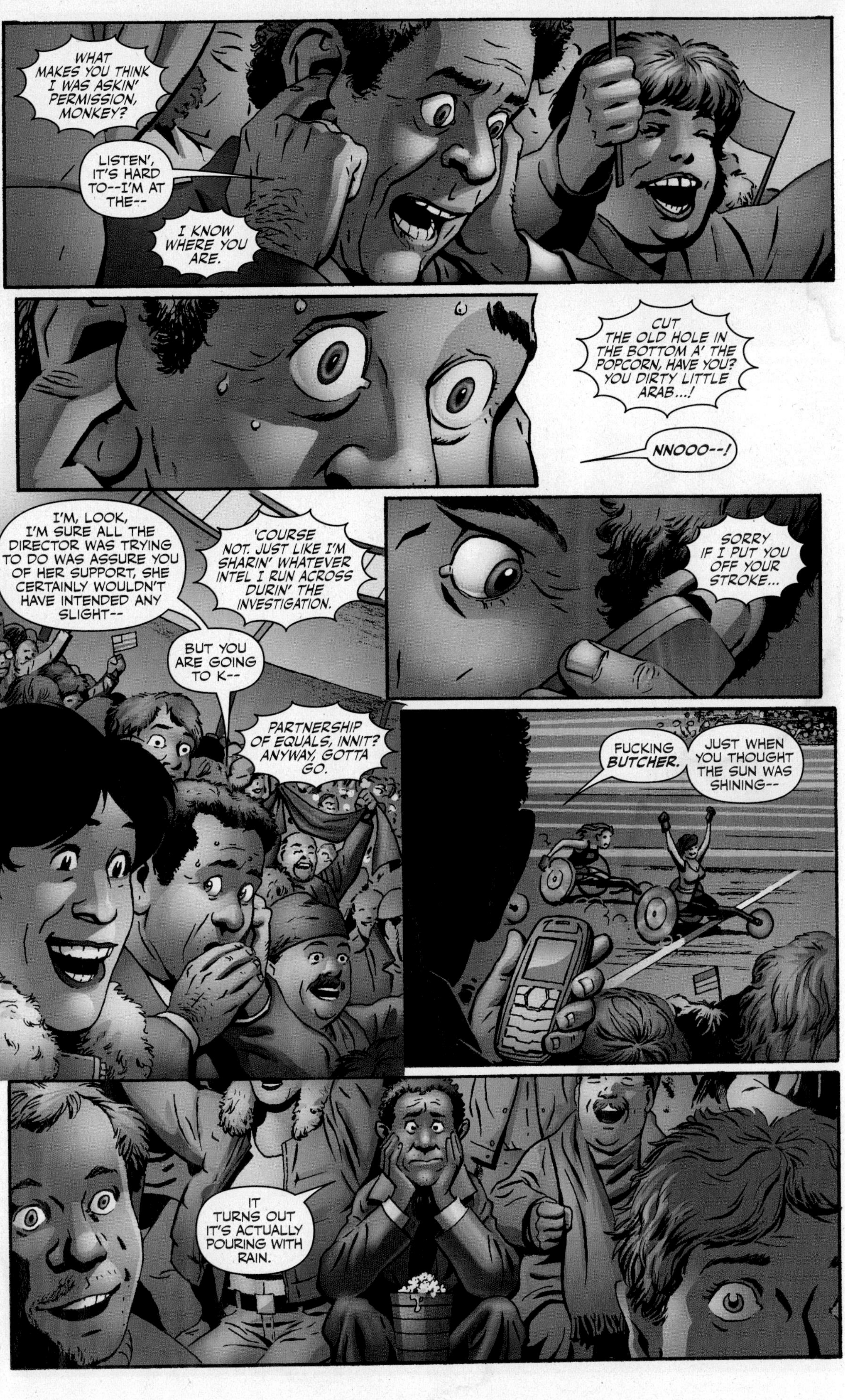
WHAT MAKES YOU THINK I WAS ASKIN' PERMISSION, MONKEY?
LISTEN', IT'S HARD TO--I'M AT THE--
I KNOW WHERE YOU ARE.
CUT THE OLD HOLE IN THE BOTTOM A' THE POPCORN, HAVE YOU? YOU DIRTY LITTLE ARAB...!
NNOOO--!
I'M, LOOK, I'M SURE ALL THE DIRECTOR WAS TRYING TO DO WAS ASSURE YOU OF HER SUPPORT, SHE CERTAINLY WOULDN'T HAVE INTENDED ANY SLIGHT--
'COURSE NOT. JUST LIKE I'M SHARIN' WHATEVER INTEL I RUN ACROSS DURIN' THE INVESTIGATION.
BUT YOU ARE GOING TO K--
PARTNERSHIP OF EQUALS, INNIT? ANYWAY, GOTTA GO.
SORRY IF I PUT YOU OFF YOUR STROKE...
FUCKING BUTCHER.
JUST WHEN YOU THOUGHT THE SUN WAS SHINING--
IT TURNS OUT IT'S ACTUALLY POURING WITH RAIN.

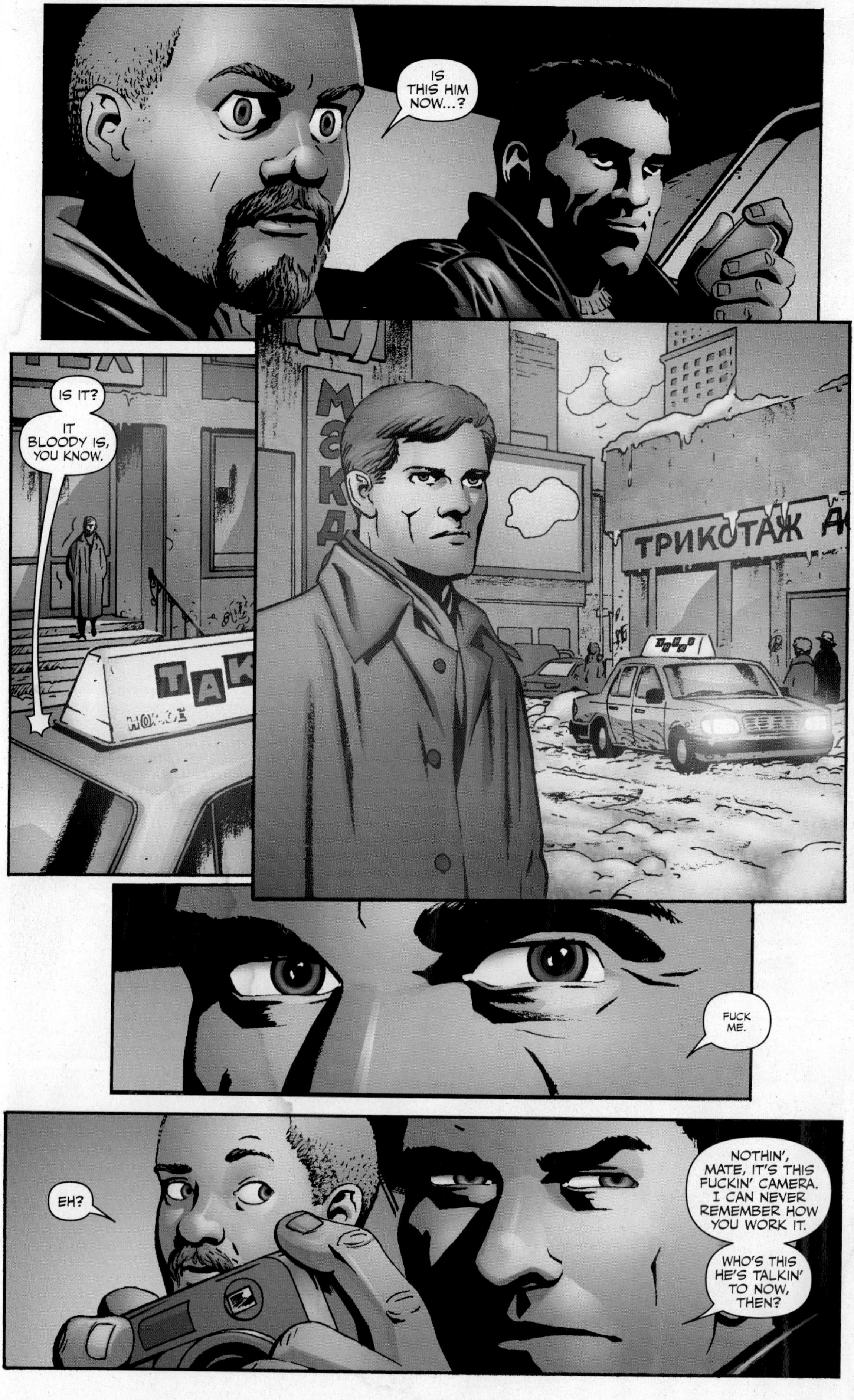
IS THIS HIM NOW...?
IS IT?
IT BLOODY IS, YOU KNOW.
ТРИКОТАЖ
FUCK ME.
EH?
NOTHIN', MATE, IT'S THIS FUCKIN' CAMERA. I CAN NEVER REMEMBER HOW YOU WORK IT.
WHO'S THIS HE'S TALKIN' TO NOW, THEN?

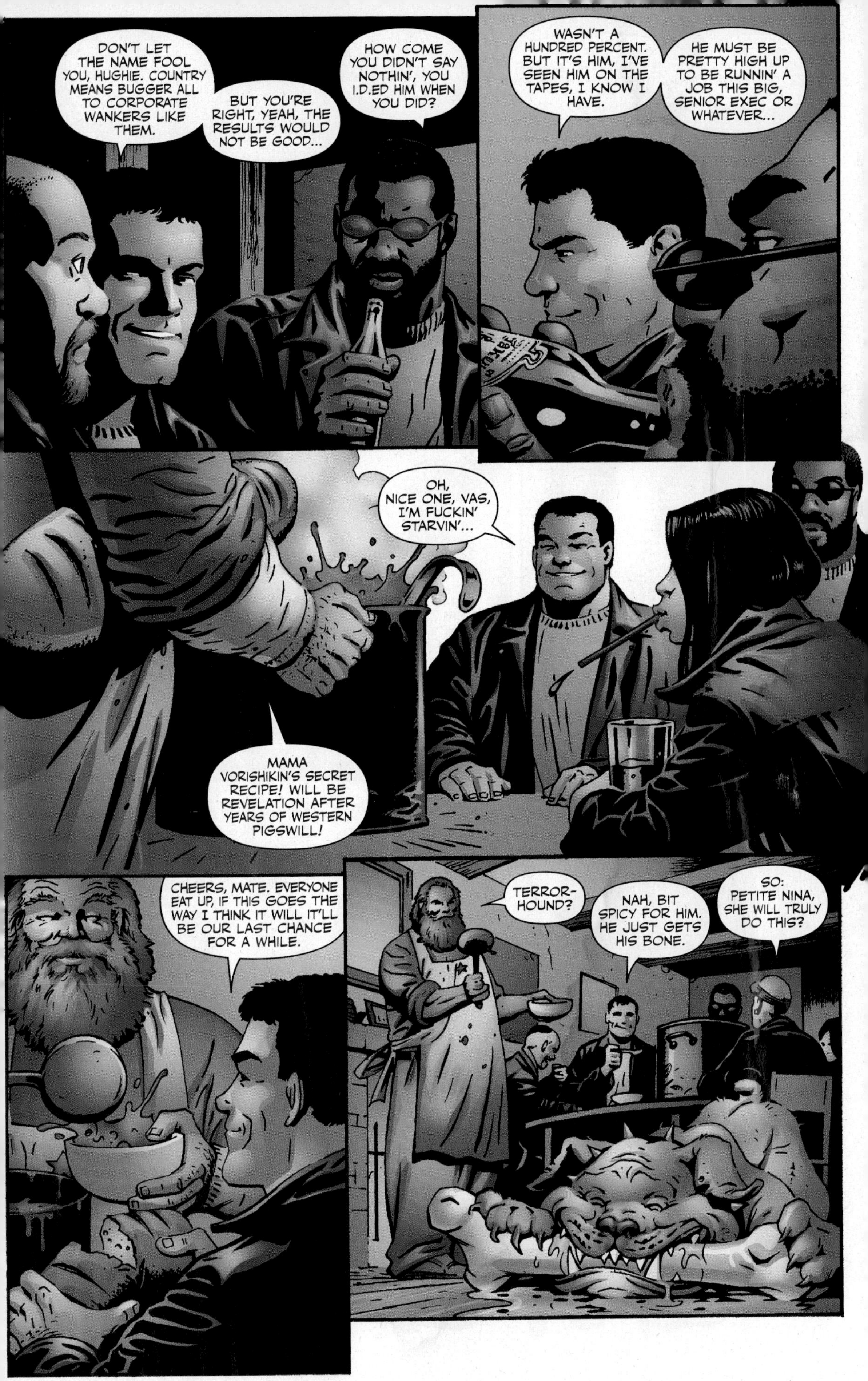
DON'T LET THE NAME FOOL YOU, HUGHIE. COUNTRY MEANS BUGGER ALL TO CORPORATE WANKERS LIKE THEM.
BUT YOU'RE RIGHT, YEAH, THE RESULTS WOULD NOT BE GOOD...
HOW COME YOU DIDN'T SAY NOTHIN', YOU I.D.ED HIM WHEN YOU DID?
WASN'T A HUNDRED PERCENT. BUT IT'S HIM, I'VE SEEN HIM ON THE TAPES, I KNOW I HAVE.
HE MUST BE PRETTY HIGH UP TO BE RUNNIN' A JOB THIS BIG, SENIOR EXEC OR WHATEVER...
OH, NICE ONE, VAS, I'M FUCKIN' STARVIN'...
MAMA VORISHIKIN'S SECRET RECIPE! WILL BE REVELATION AFTER YEARS OF WESTERN PIGSWILL!
CHEERS, MATE. EVERYONE EAT UP, IF THIS GOES THE WAY I THINK IT WILL IT'LL BE OUR LAST CHANCE FOR A WHILE.
TERROR-HOUND?
NAH, BIT SPICY FOR HIM. HE JUST GETS HIS BONE.
SO: PETITE NINA, SHE WILL TRULY DO THIS?

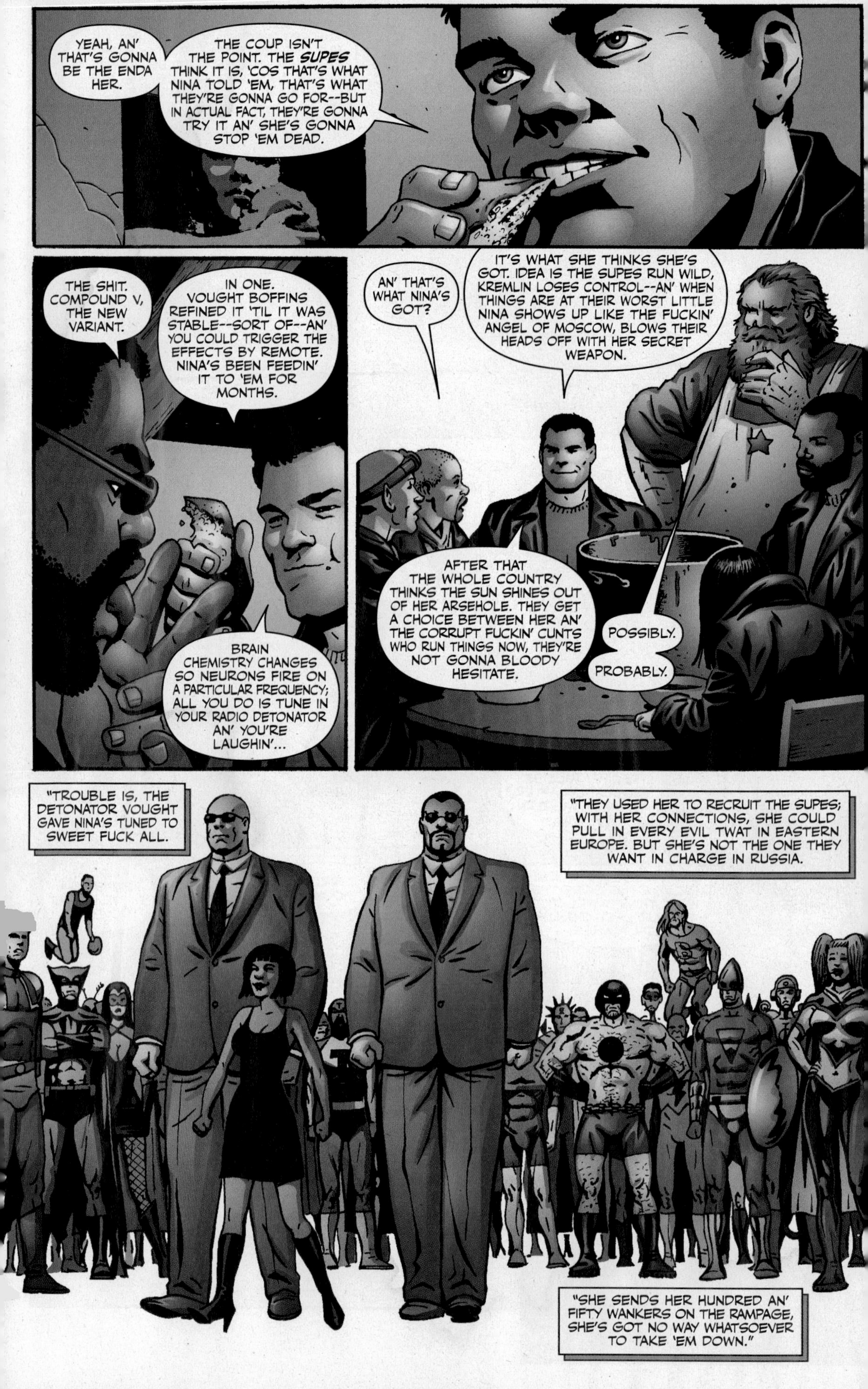
YEAH, AN' THAT'S GONNA BE THE ENDA HER.
THE COUP ISN'T THE POINT. THE *SUPES* THINK IT IS, 'COS THAT'S WHAT NINA TOLD 'EM, THAT'S WHAT THEY'RE GONNA GO FOR--BUT IN ACTUAL FACT, THEY'RE GONNA TRY IT AN' SHE'S GONNA STOP 'EM DEAD.
THE SHIT. COMPOUND V, THE NEW VARIANT.
IN ONE. VOUGHT BOFFINS REFINED IT 'TIL IT WAS STABLE--SORT OF--AN' YOU COULD TRIGGER THE EFFECTS BY REMOTE. NINA'S BEEN FEEDIN' IT TO 'EM FOR MONTHS.
BRAIN CHEMISTRY CHANGES SO NEURONS FIRE ON A PARTICULAR FREQUENCY; ALL YOU DO IS TUNE IN YOUR RADIO DETONATOR AN' YOU'RE LAUGHIN'...
AN' THAT'S WHAT NINA'S GOT?
IT'S WHAT SHE THINKS SHE'S GOT. IDEA IS THE SUPES RUN WILD, KREMLIN LOSES CONTROL--AN' WHEN THINGS ARE AT THEIR WORST LITTLE NINA SHOWS UP LIKE THE FUCKIN' ANGEL OF MOSCOW, BLOWS THEIR HEADS OFF WITH HER SECRET WEAPON.
AFTER THAT THE WHOLE COUNTRY THINKS THE SUN SHINES OUT OF HER ARSEHOLE. THEY GET A CHOICE BETWEEN HER AN' THE CORRUPT FUCKIN' CUNTS WHO RUN THINGS NOW, THEY'RE NOT GONNA BLOODY HESITATE.
POSSIBLY.
PROBABLY.
"TROUBLE IS, THE DETONATOR VOUGHT GAVE NINA'S TUNED TO SWEET FUCK ALL.
"THEY USED HER TO RECRUIT THE SUPES; WITH HER CONNECTIONS, SHE COULD PULL IN EVERY EVIL TWAT IN EASTERN EUROPE. BUT SHE'S NOT THE ONE THEY WANT IN CHARGE IN RUSSIA.
"SHE SENDS HER HUNDRED AN' FIFTY WANKERS ON THE RAMPAGE, SHE'S GOT NO WAY WHATSOEVER TO TAKE 'EM DOWN."

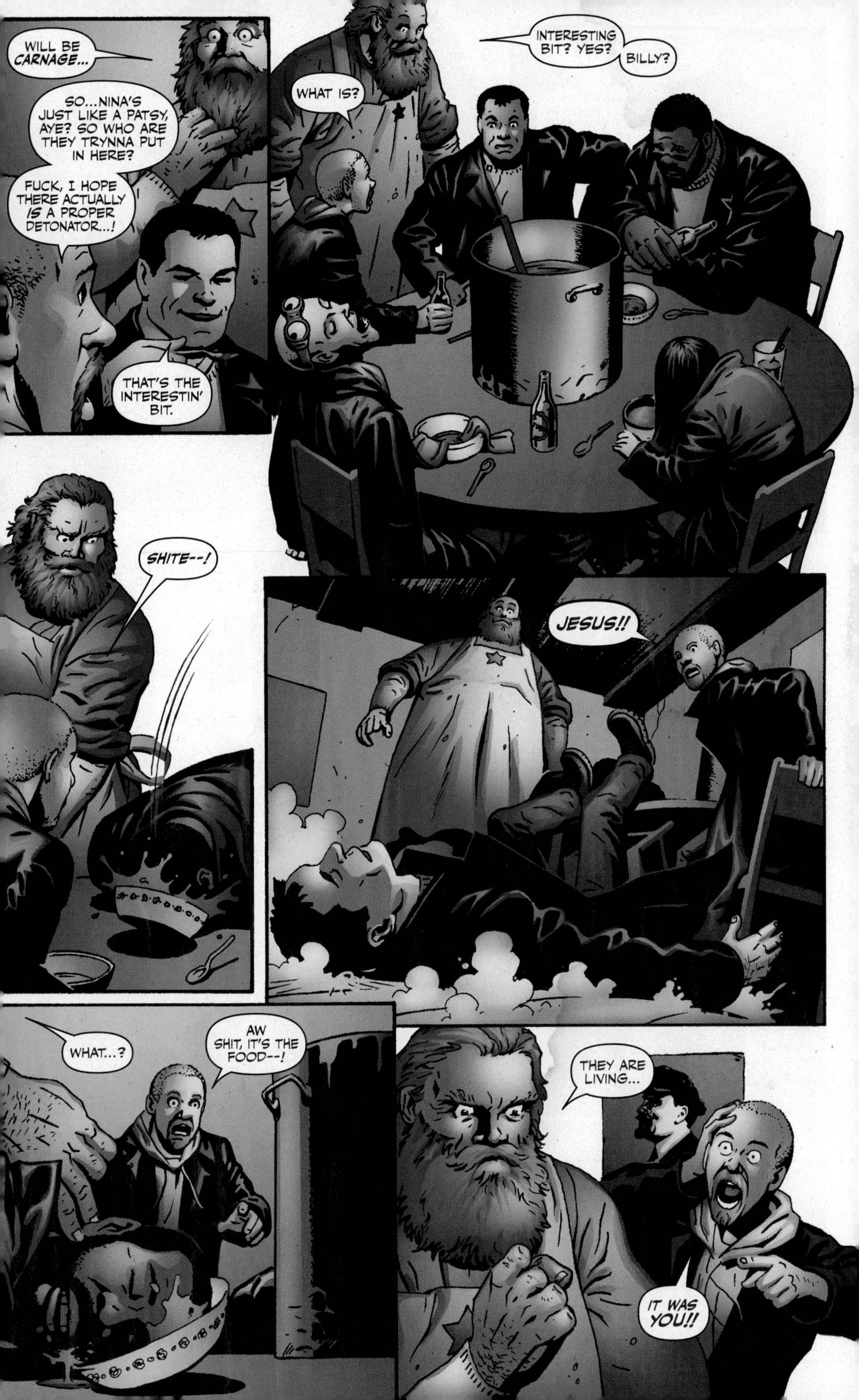
WILL BE CARNAGE...
SO...NINA'S JUST LIKE A PATSY, AYE? SO WHO ARE THEY TRYNNA PUT IN HERE?
FUCK, I HOPE THERE ACTUALLY IS A PROPER DETONATOR...!
THAT'S THE INTERESTIN' BIT.
WHAT IS?
INTERESTING BIT? YES?
BILLY?
SHITE--!
JESUS!!
WHAT...?
AW SHIT, IT'S THE FOOD--!
THEY ARE LIVING...
IT WAS YOU!!

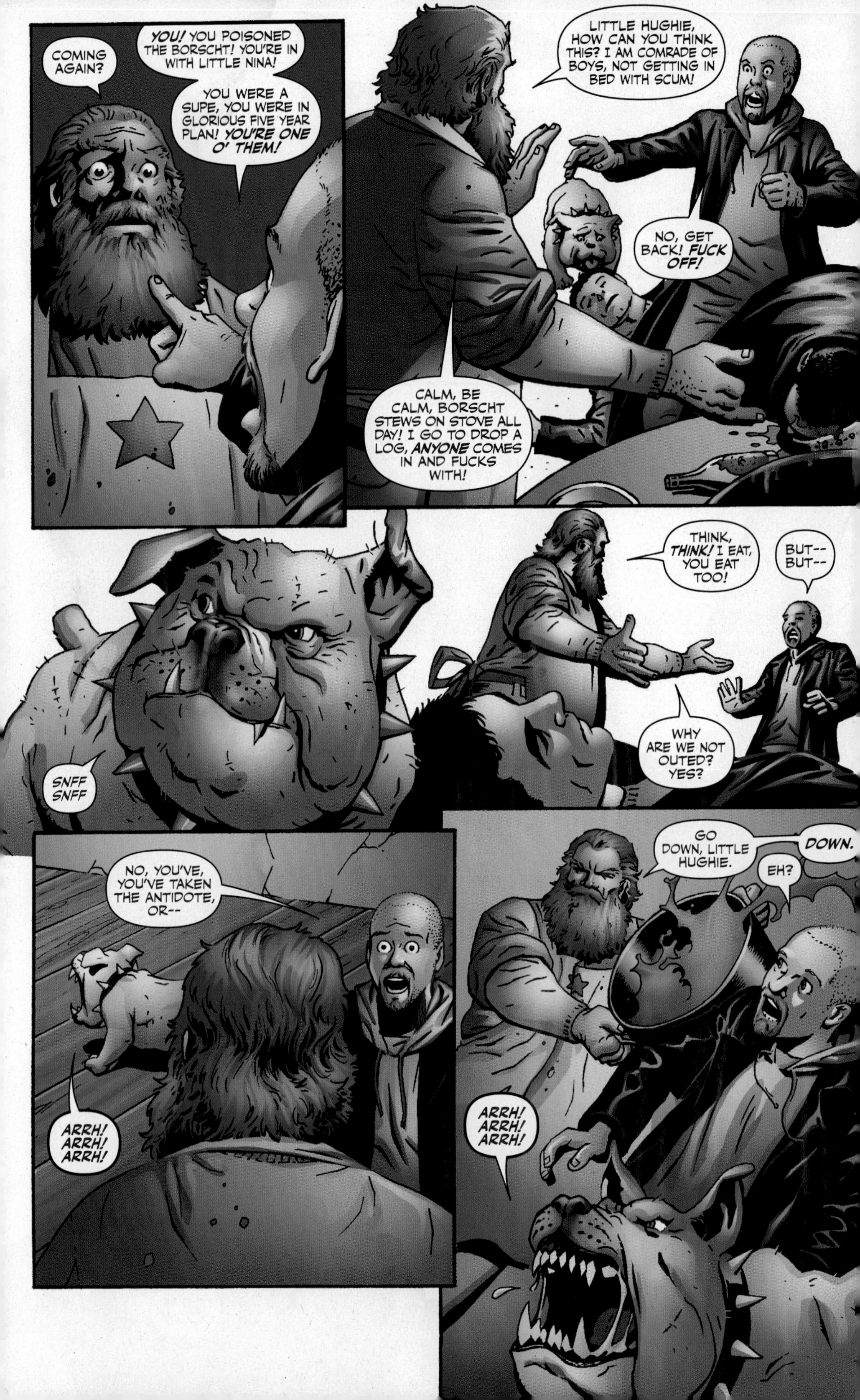
COMING AGAIN?
YOU! YOU POISONED THE BORSCHT! YOU'RE IN WITH LITTLE NINA!
YOU WERE A SUPE, YOU WERE IN GLORIOUS FIVE YEAR PLAN! YOU'RE ONE O' THEM!
LITTLE HUGHIE, HOW CAN YOU THINK THIS? I AM COMRADE OF BOYS, NOT GETTING IN BED WITH SCUM!
NO, GET BACK! FUCK OFF!
CALM, BE CALM, BORSCHT STEWS ON STOVE ALL DAY! I GO TO DROP A LOG, ANYONE COMES IN AND FUCKS WITH!
SNFF SNFF
THINK, THINK! I EAT, YOU EAT TOO!
BUT-- BUT--
WHY ARE WE NOT OUTED? YES?
NO, YOU'VE, YOU'VE TAKEN THE ANTIDOTE, OR--
ARRH! ARRH! ARRH!
GO DOWN, LITTLE HUGHIE.
DOWN.
EH?
ARRH! ARRH! ARRH!

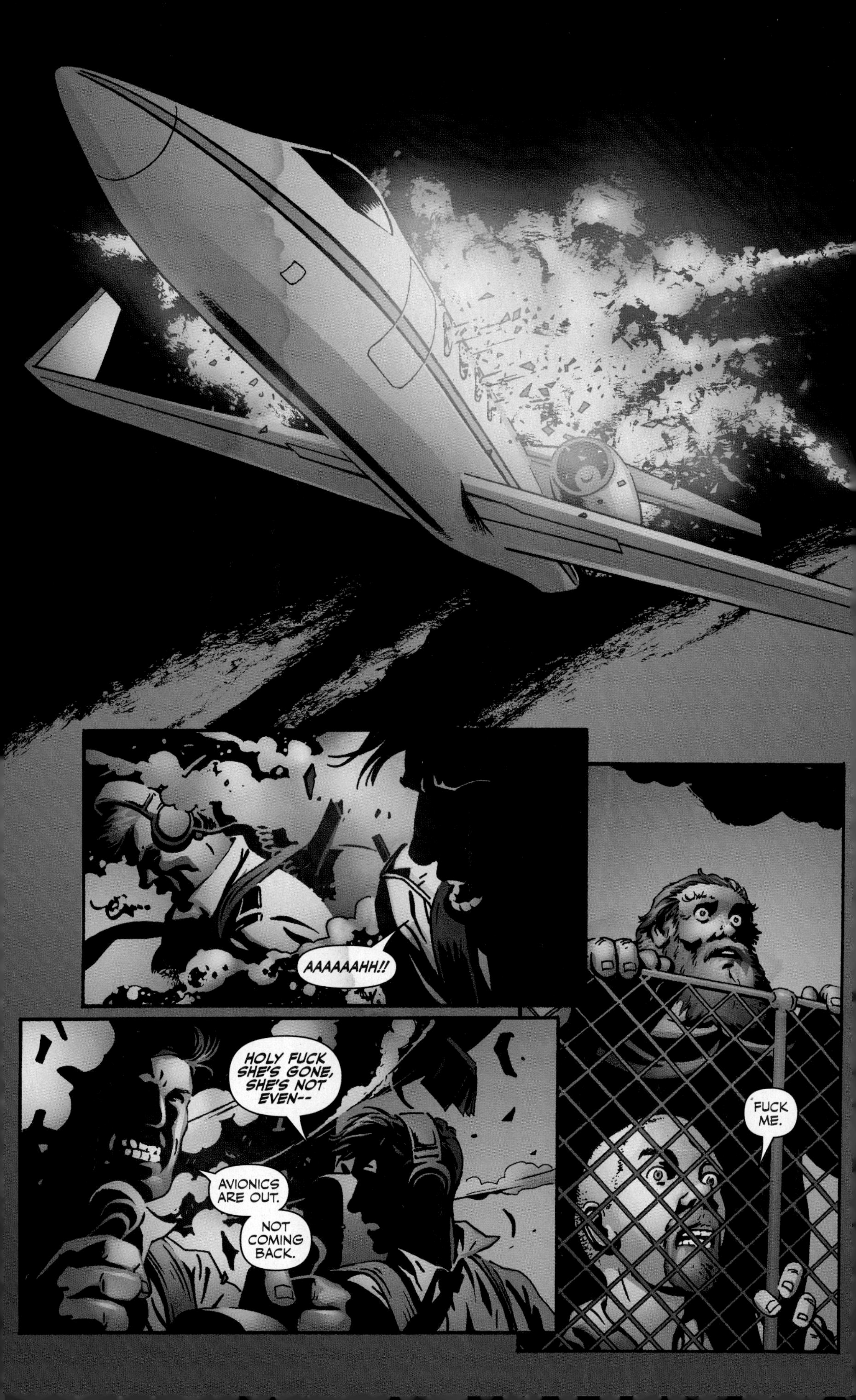
AAAAAAHH!!
HOLY FUCK SHE'S GONE, SHE'S NOT EVEN--
AVIONICS ARE OUT.
NOT COMING BACK.
FUCK ME.

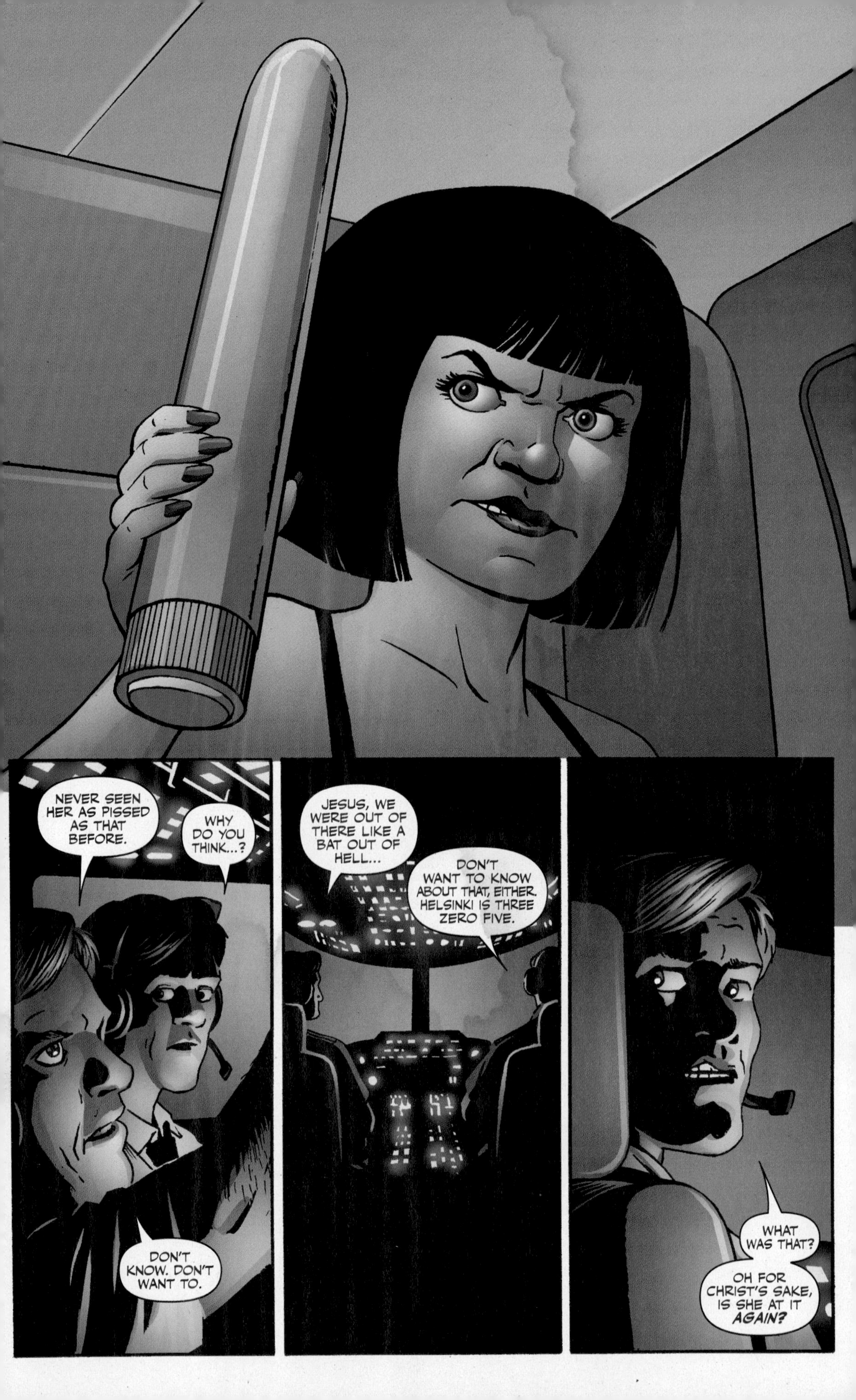
NEVER SEEN HER AS PISSED AS THAT BEFORE.
WHY DO YOU THINK...?
DON'T KNOW. DON'T WANT TO.
JESUS, WE WERE OUT OF THERE LIKE A BAT OUT OF HELL...
DON'T WANT TO KNOW ABOUT THAT, EITHER. HELSINKI IS THREE ZERO FIVE.
WHAT WAS THAT?
OH FOR CHRIST'S SAKE, IS SHE AT IT *AGAIN?*

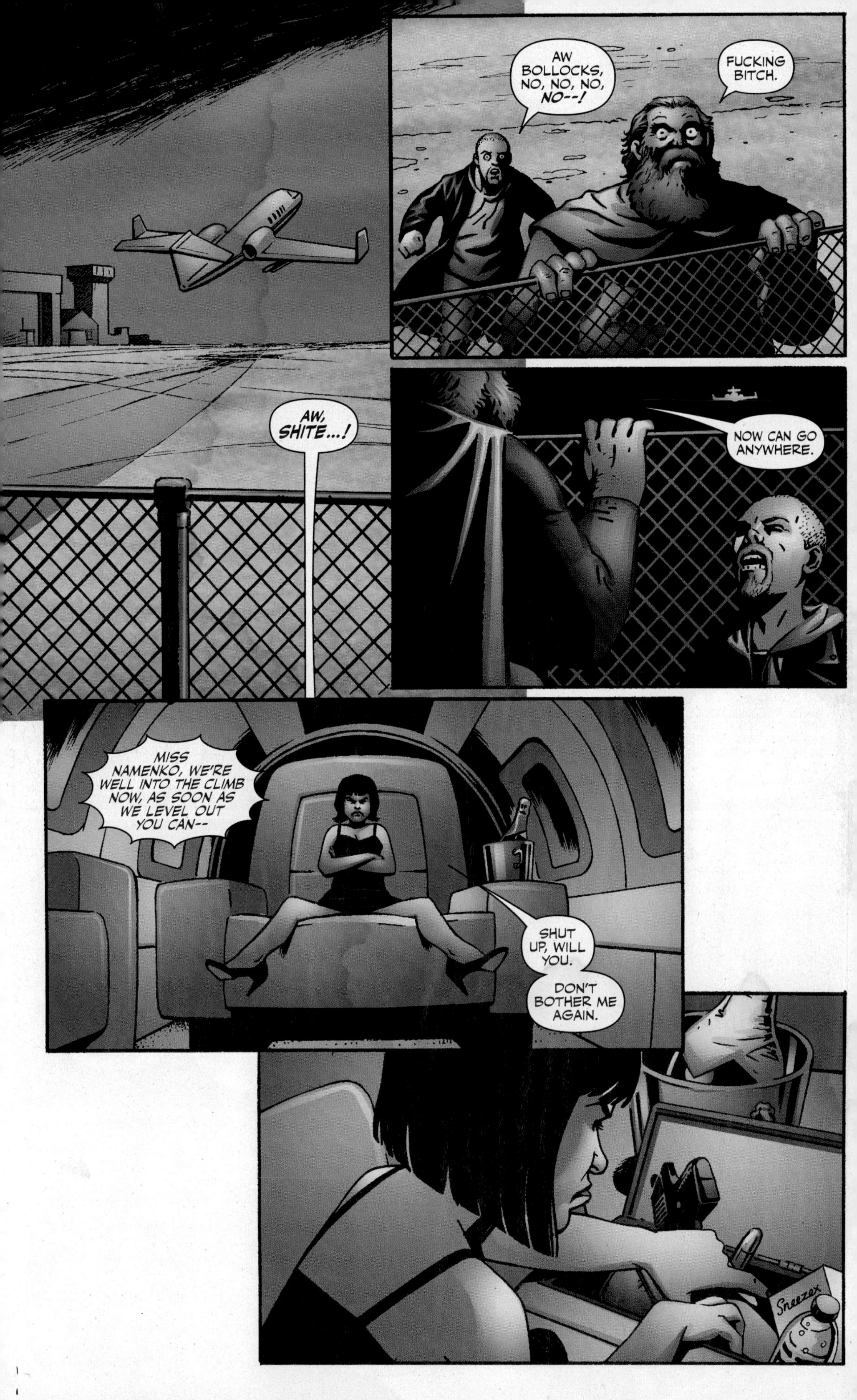
AW BOLLOCKS, NO, NO, NO, NO--!
FUCKING BITCH.
AW, SHITE...!
NOW CAN GO ANYWHERE.
MISS NAMENKO, WE'RE WELL INTO THE CLIMB NOW, AS SOON AS WE LEVEL OUT YOU CAN--
SHUT UP, WILL YOU.
DON'T BOTHER ME AGAIN.
Sneezex

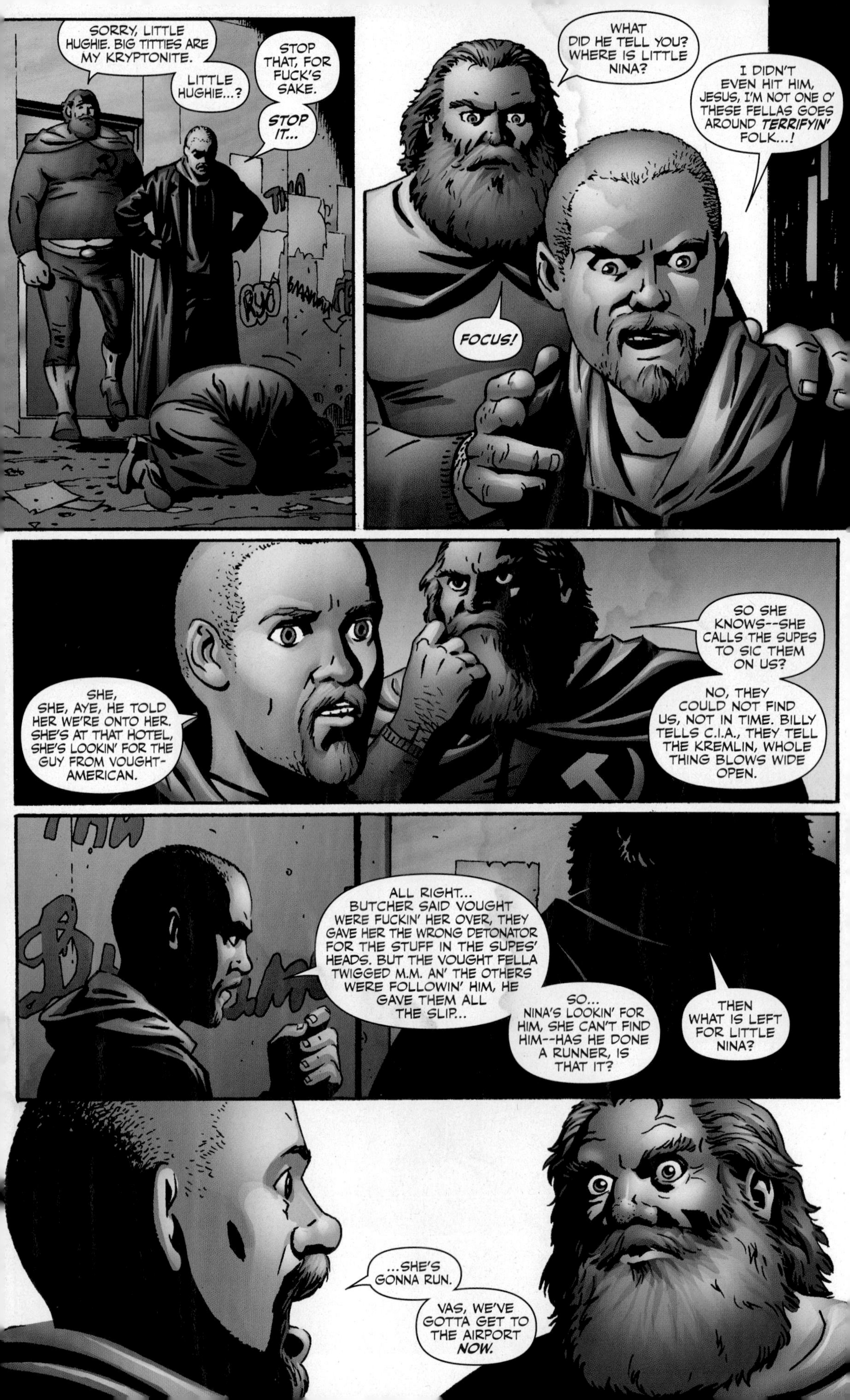
SORRY, LITTLE HUGHIE. BIG TITTIES ARE MY KRYPTONITE.
LITTLE HUGHIE...?
STOP THAT, FOR FUCK'S SAKE.
STOP IT...
WHAT DID HE TELL YOU? WHERE IS LITTLE NINA?
I DIDN'T EVEN HIT HIM, JESUS, I'M NOT ONE O' THESE FELLAS GOES AROUND TERRIFYIN' FOLK...!
FOCUS!
SHE, SHE, AYE, HE TOLD HER WE'RE ONTO HER. SHE'S AT THAT HOTEL, SHE'S LOOKIN' FOR THE GUY FROM VOUGHT-AMERICAN.
SO SHE KNOWS--SHE CALLS THE SUPES TO SIC THEM ON US?
NO, THEY COULD NOT FIND US, NOT IN TIME. BILLY TELLS C.I.A., THEY TELL THE KREMLIN, WHOLE THING BLOWS WIDE OPEN.
ALL RIGHT... BUTCHER SAID VOUGHT WERE FUCKIN' HER OVER, THEY GAVE HER THE WRONG DETONATOR FOR THE STUFF IN THE SUPES' HEADS. BUT THE VOUGHT FELLA TWIGGED M.M. AN' THE OTHERS WERE FOLLOWIN' HIM, HE GAVE THEM ALL THE SLIP...
SO... NINA'S LOOKIN' FOR HIM, SHE CAN'T FIND HIM--HAS HE DONE A RUNNER, IS THAT IT?
THEN WHAT IS LEFT FOR LITTLE NINA?
...SHE'S GONNA RUN.
VAS, WE'VE GOTTA GET TO THE AIRPORT NOW.

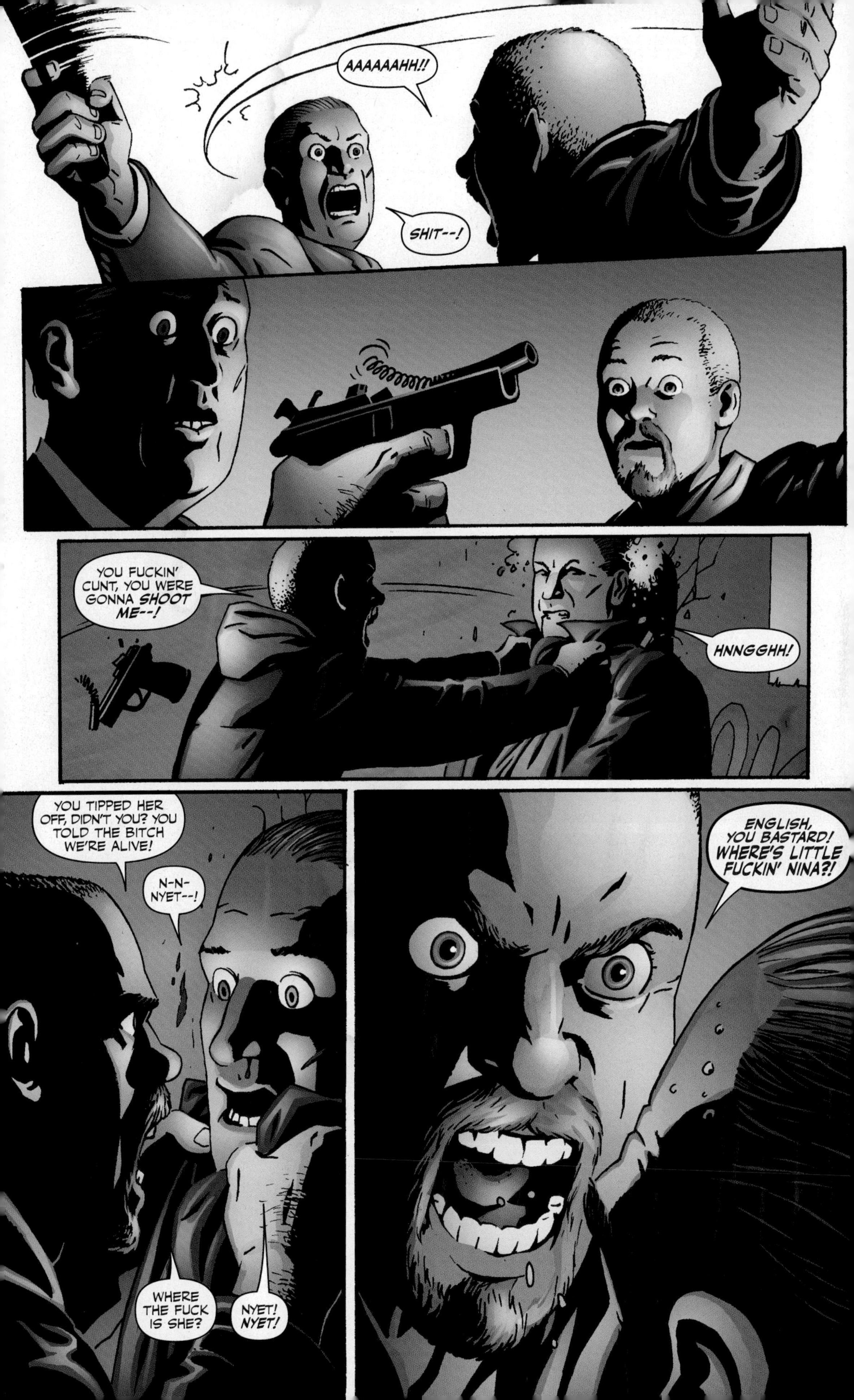

AAAAAAHH!!
SHIT--!
YOU FUCKIN' CUNT, YOU WERE GONNA SHOOT ME--!
HNNGGHH!
YOU TIPPED HER OFF, DIDN'T YOU? YOU TOLD THE BITCH WE'RE ALIVE!
N-N-NYET--!
WHERE THE FUCK IS SHE?
NYET! NYET!
ENGLISH, YOU BASTARD! WHERE'S LITTLE FUCKIN' NINA?!

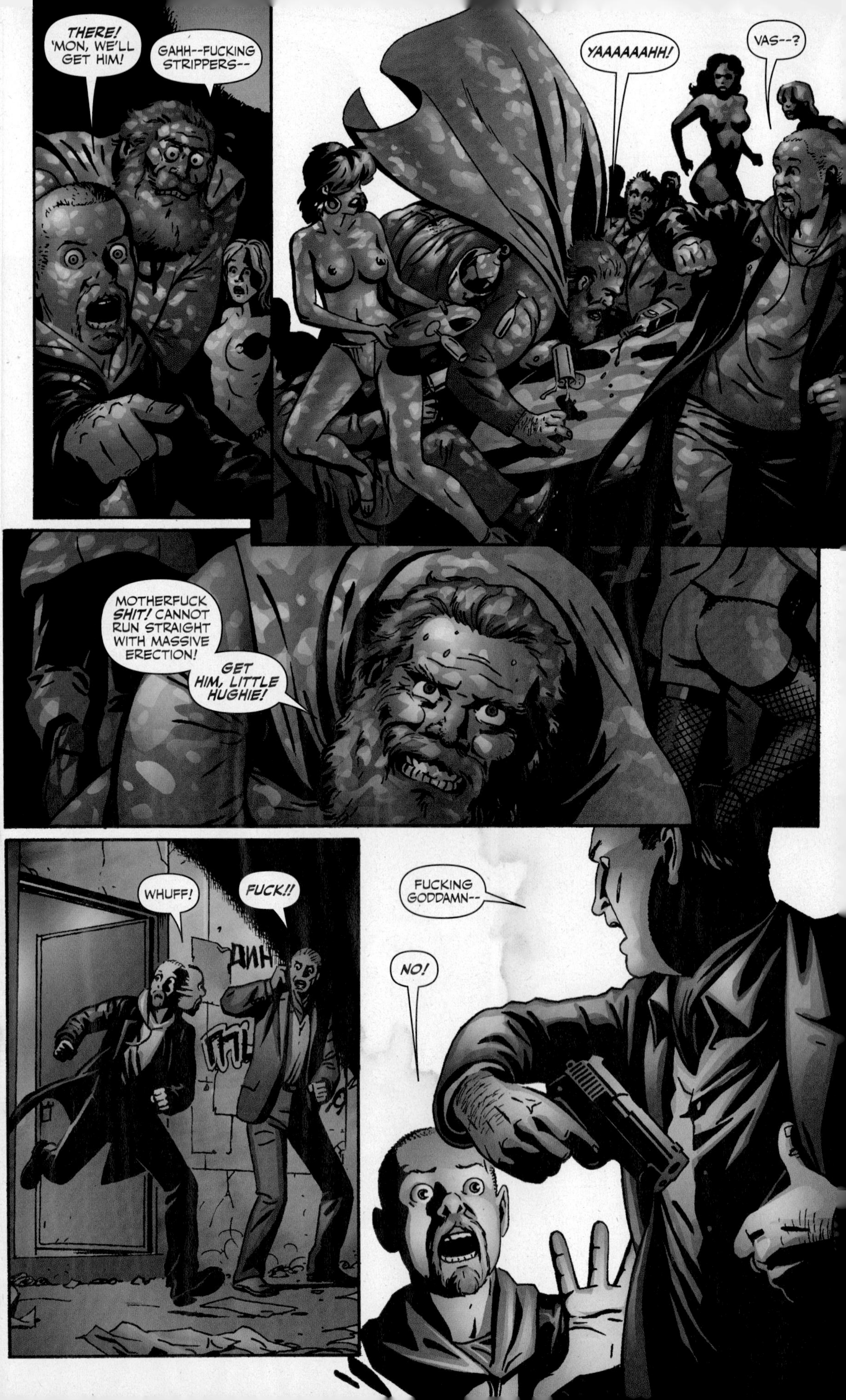
THERE! 'MON, WE'LL GET HIM!
GAHH--FUCKING STRIPPERS--
YAAAAAAHH!
VAS--?
MOTHERFUCK SHIT! CANNOT RUN STRAIGHT WITH MASSIVE ERECTION!
GET HIM, LITTLE HUGHIE!
WHUFF!
FUCK!!
FUCKING GODDAMN--
NO!

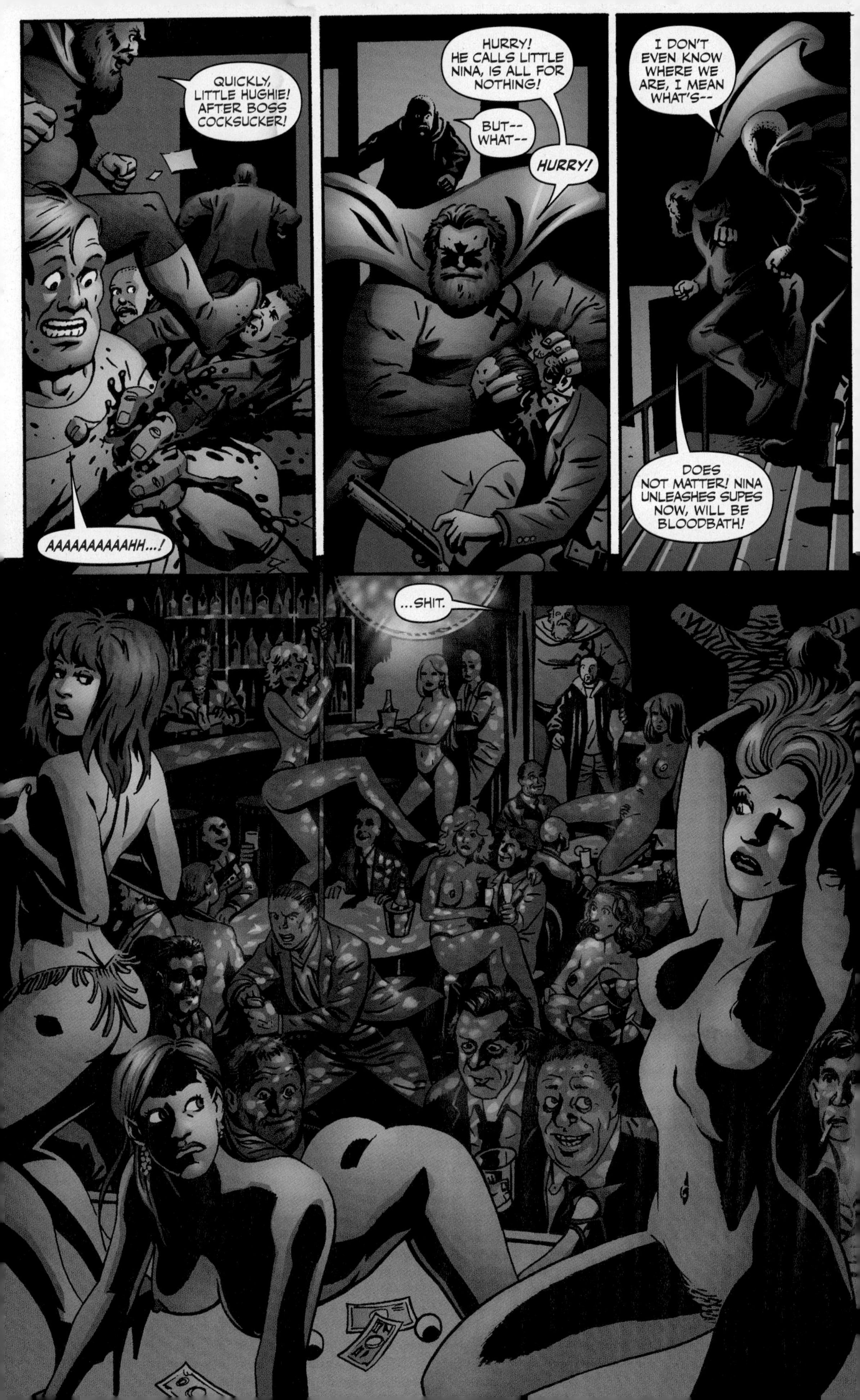
QUICKLY, LITTLE HUGHIE! AFTER BOSS COCKSUCKER!
AAAAAAAAAAHH...!
HURRY! HE CALLS LITTLE NINA, IS ALL FOR NOTHING!
BUT-- WHAT--
HURRY!
I DON'T EVEN KNOW WHERE WE ARE, I MEAN WHAT'S--
DOES NOT MATTER! NINA UNLEASHES SUPES NOW, WILL BE BLOODBATH!
...SHIT.

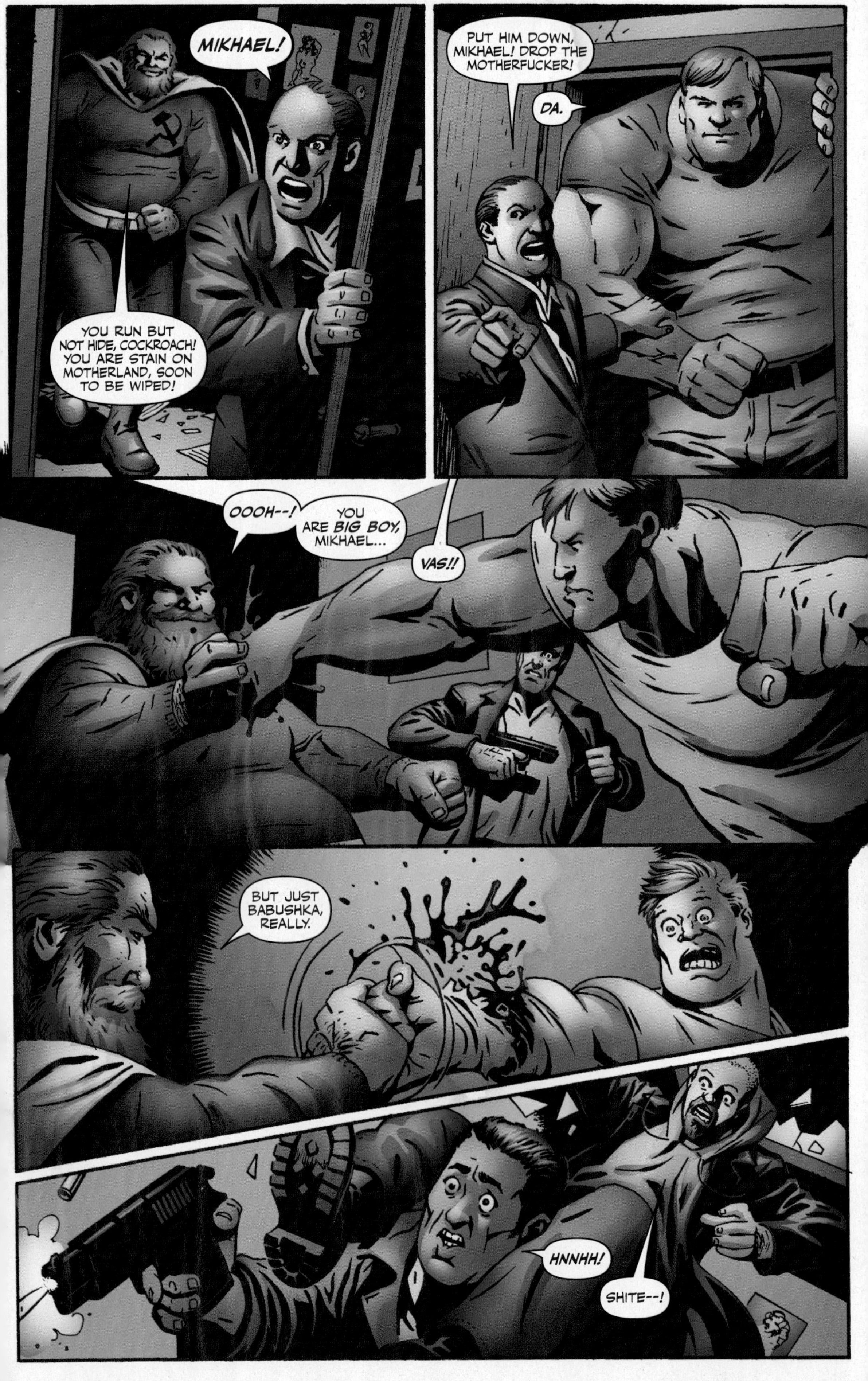
MIKHAEL!
YOU RUN BUT NOT HIDE, COCKROACH! YOU ARE STAIN ON MOTHERLAND, SOON TO BE WIPED!
PUT HIM DOWN, MIKHAEL! DROP THE MOTHERFUCKER!
DA.
OOOH--!
YOU ARE BIG BOY, MIKHAEL...
VAS!!
BUT JUST BABUSHKA, REALLY.
HNNHH!
SHITE--!

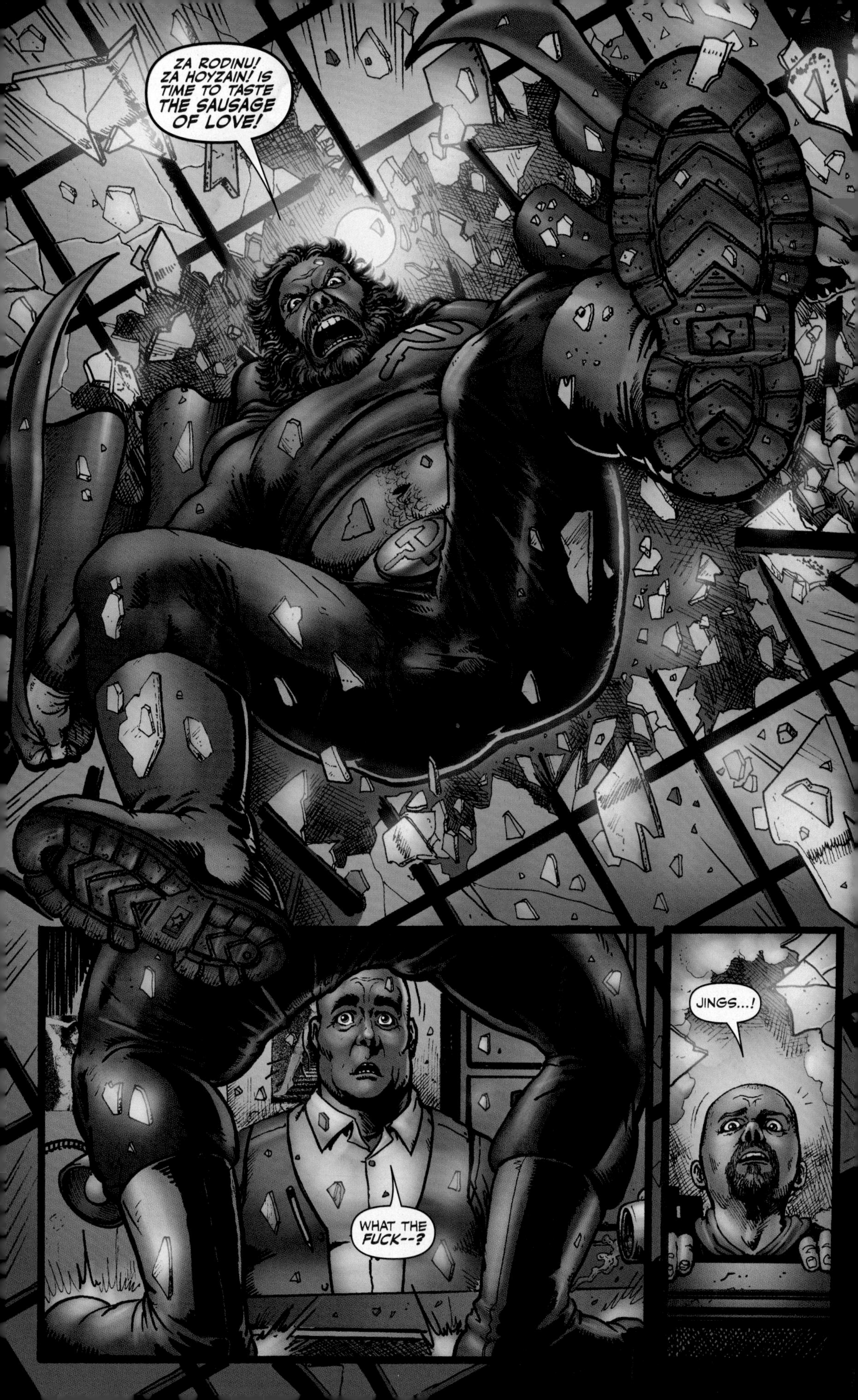
ZA RODINU! ZA HOYZAIN! IS TIME TO TASTE THE SAUSAGE OF LOVE!
WHAT THE FUCK--?
JINGS...!

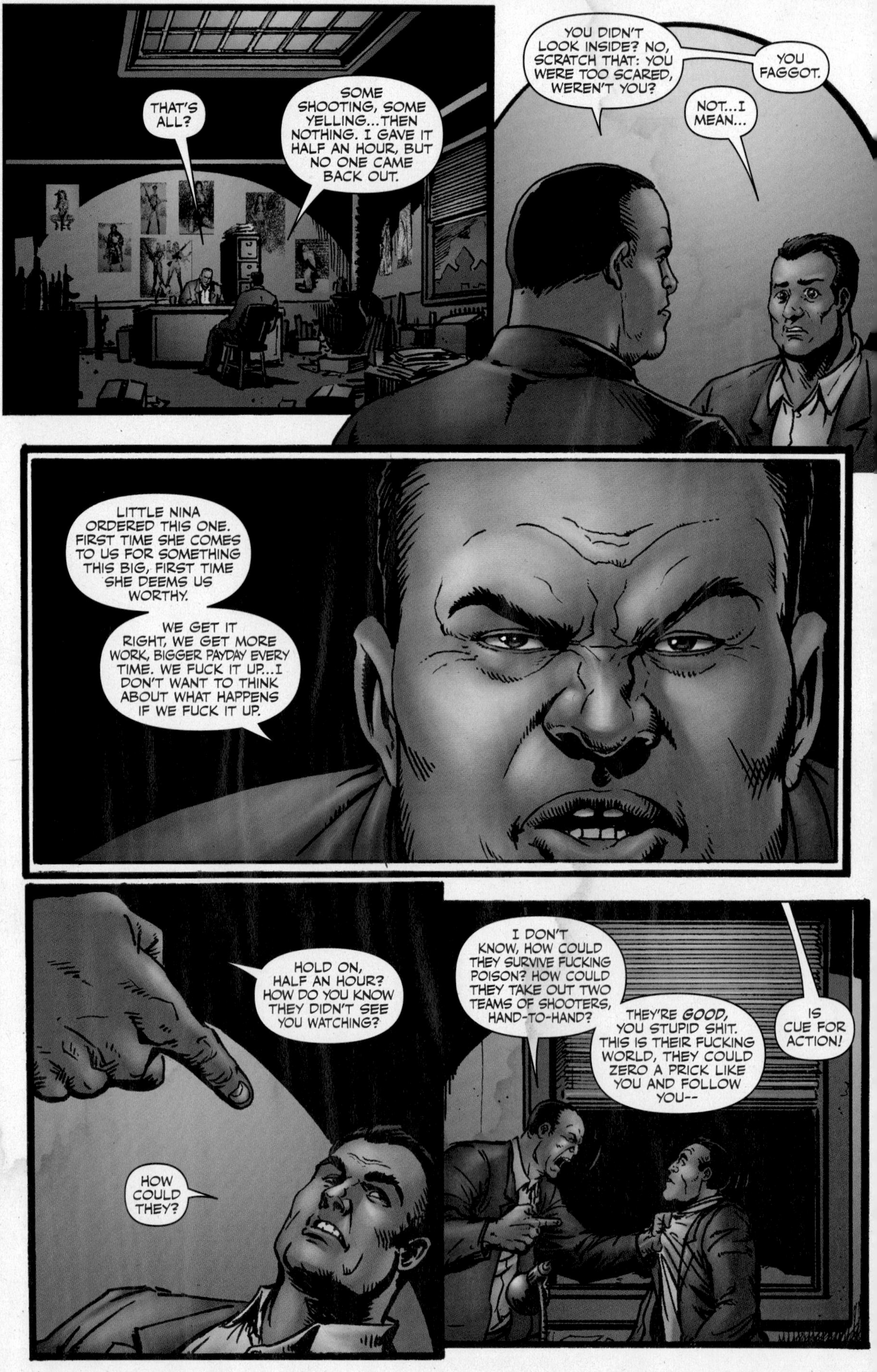
THAT'S ALL?
SOME SHOOTING, SOME YELLING...THEN NOTHING. I GAVE IT HALF AN HOUR, BUT NO ONE CAME BACK OUT.
YOU DIDN'T LOOK INSIDE? NO, SCRATCH THAT: YOU WERE TOO SCARED, WEREN'T YOU?
YOU FAGGOT.
NOT...I MEAN...
LITTLE NINA ORDERED THIS ONE. FIRST TIME SHE COMES TO US FOR SOMETHING THIS BIG, FIRST TIME SHE DEEMS US WORTHY.
WE GET IT RIGHT, WE GET MORE WORK, BIGGER PAYDAY EVERY TIME. WE FUCK IT UP...I DON'T WANT TO THINK ABOUT WHAT HAPPENS IF WE FUCK IT UP.
HOLD ON, HALF AN HOUR? HOW DO YOU KNOW THEY DIDN'T SEE YOU WATCHING?
HOW COULD THEY?
I DON'T KNOW, HOW COULD THEY SURVIVE FUCKING POISON? HOW COULD THEY TAKE OUT TWO TEAMS OF SHOOTERS, HAND-TO-HAND?
THEY'RE *GOOD,* YOU STUPID SHIT. THIS IS THEIR FUCKING WORLD, THEY COULD ZERO A PRICK LIKE YOU AND FOLLOW YOU--
IS CUE FOR ACTION!

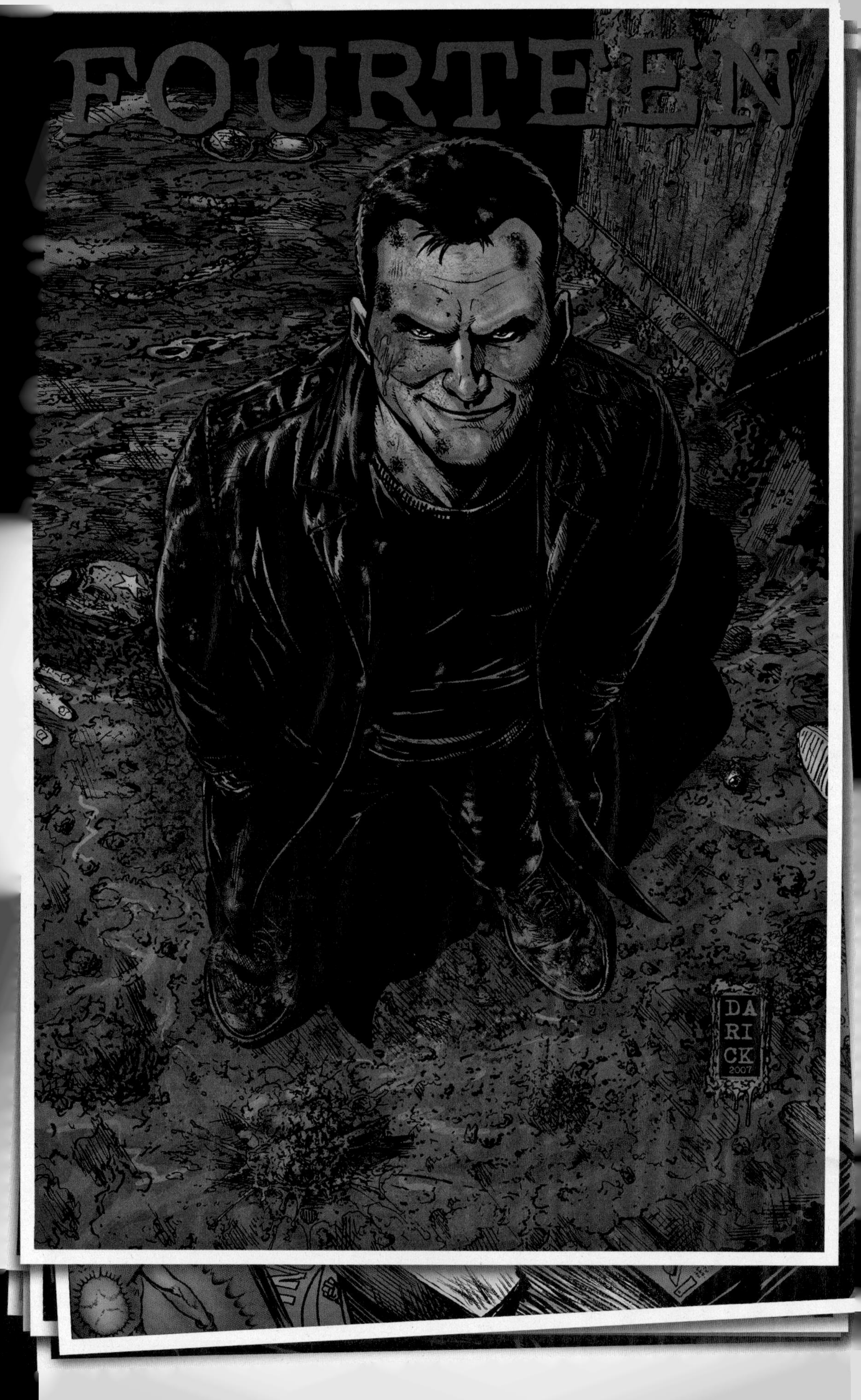
FOURTEEN
DA
RI
CK
2007

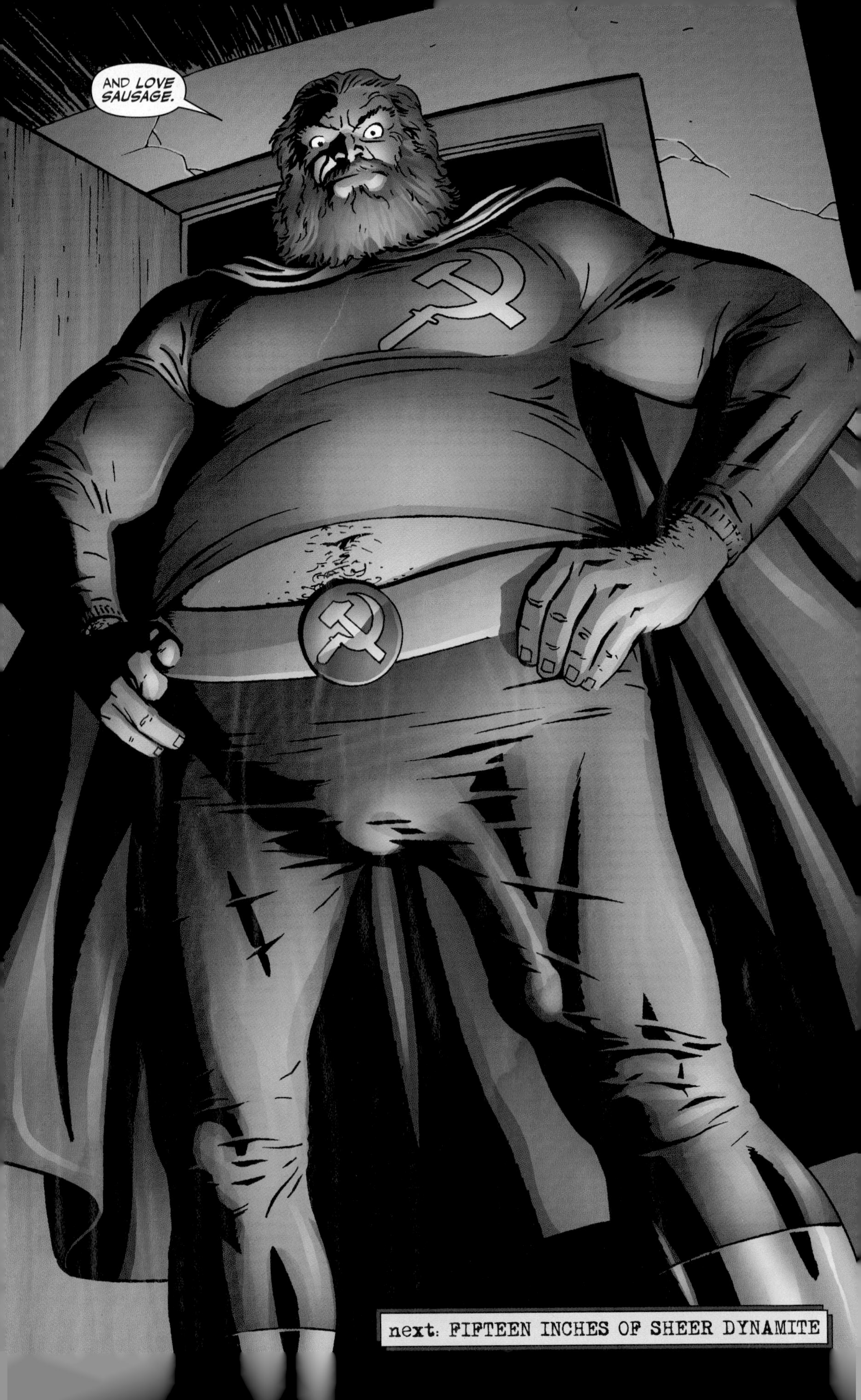
AND LOVE SAUSAGE.
next: FIFTEEN INCHES OF SHEER DYNAMITE

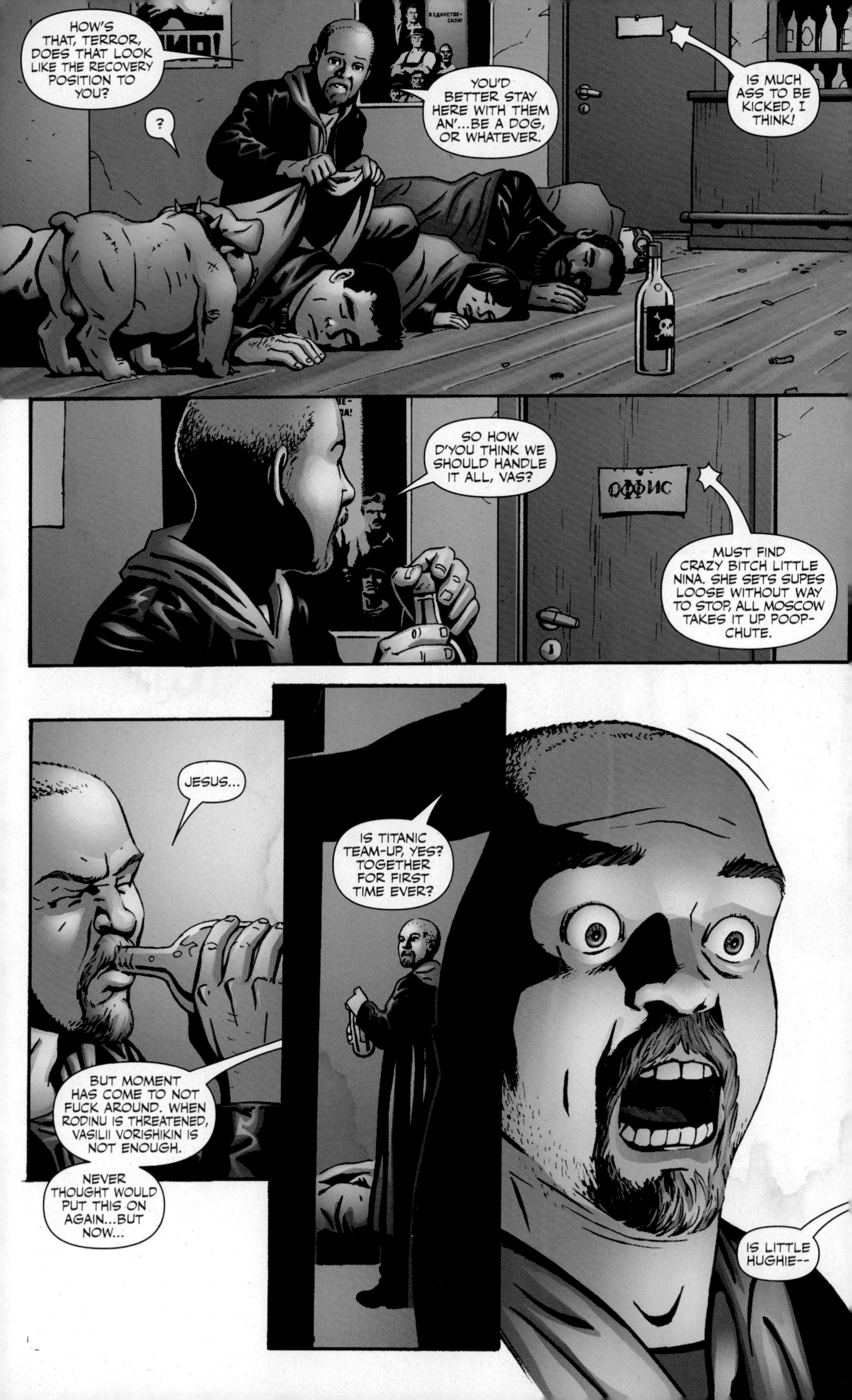
HOW'S THAT, TERROR, DOES THAT LOOK LIKE THE RECOVERY POSITION TO YOU?
?
YOU'D BETTER STAY HERE WITH THEM AN'...BE A DOG, OR WHATEVER.
IS MUCH ASS TO BE KICKED, I THINK!
SO HOW D'YOU THINK WE SHOULD HANDLE IT ALL, VAS?
ОФФИС
MUST FIND CRAZY BITCH LITTLE NINA. SHE SETS SUPES LOOSE WITHOUT WAY TO STOP, ALL MOSCOW TAKES IT UP POOP-CHUTE.
JESUS...
BUT MOMENT HAS COME TO NOT FUCK AROUND. WHEN RODINU IS THREATENED, VASILII VORISHIKIN IS NOT ENOUGH.
NEVER THOUGHT WOULD PUT THIS ON AGAIN...BUT NOW...
IS TITANIC TEAM-UP, YES? TOGETHER FOR FIRST TIME EVER?
IS LITTLE HUGHIE--

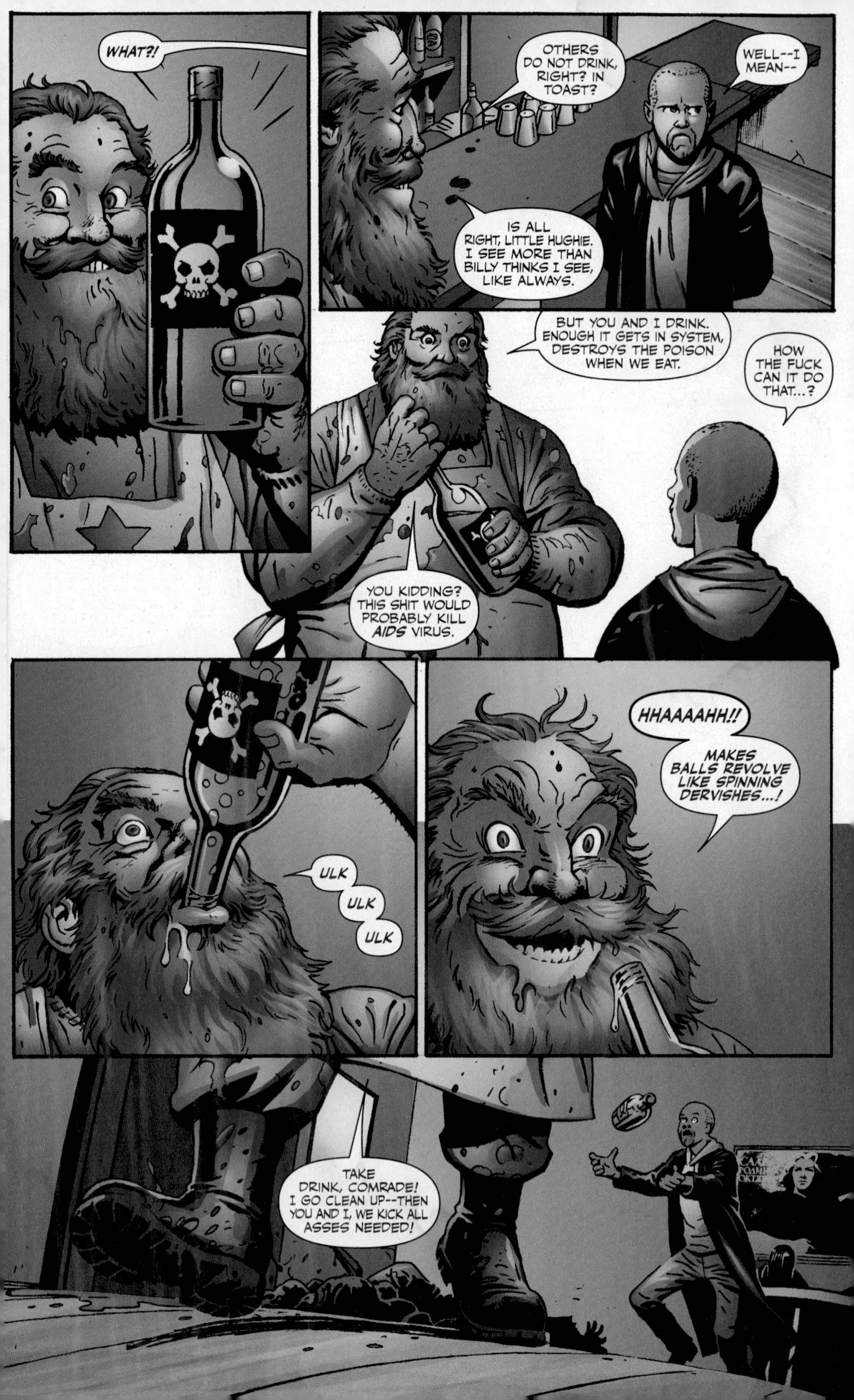
WHAT?!
OTHERS DO NOT DRINK, RIGHT? IN TOAST?
WELL--I MEAN--
IS ALL RIGHT, LITTLE HUGHIE. I SEE MORE THAN BILLY THINKS I SEE, LIKE ALWAYS.
BUT YOU AND I DRINK. ENOUGH IT GETS IN SYSTEM, DESTROYS THE POISON WHEN WE EAT.
HOW THE FUCK CAN IT DO THAT...?
YOU KIDDING? THIS SHIT WOULD PROBABLY KILL AIDS VIRUS.
ULK
ULK
ULK
HHAAAAHH!!
MAKES BALLS REVOLVE LIKE SPINNING DERVISHES...!
TAKE DRINK, COMRADE! I GO CLEAN UP--THEN YOU AND I, WE KICK ALL ASSES NEEDED!

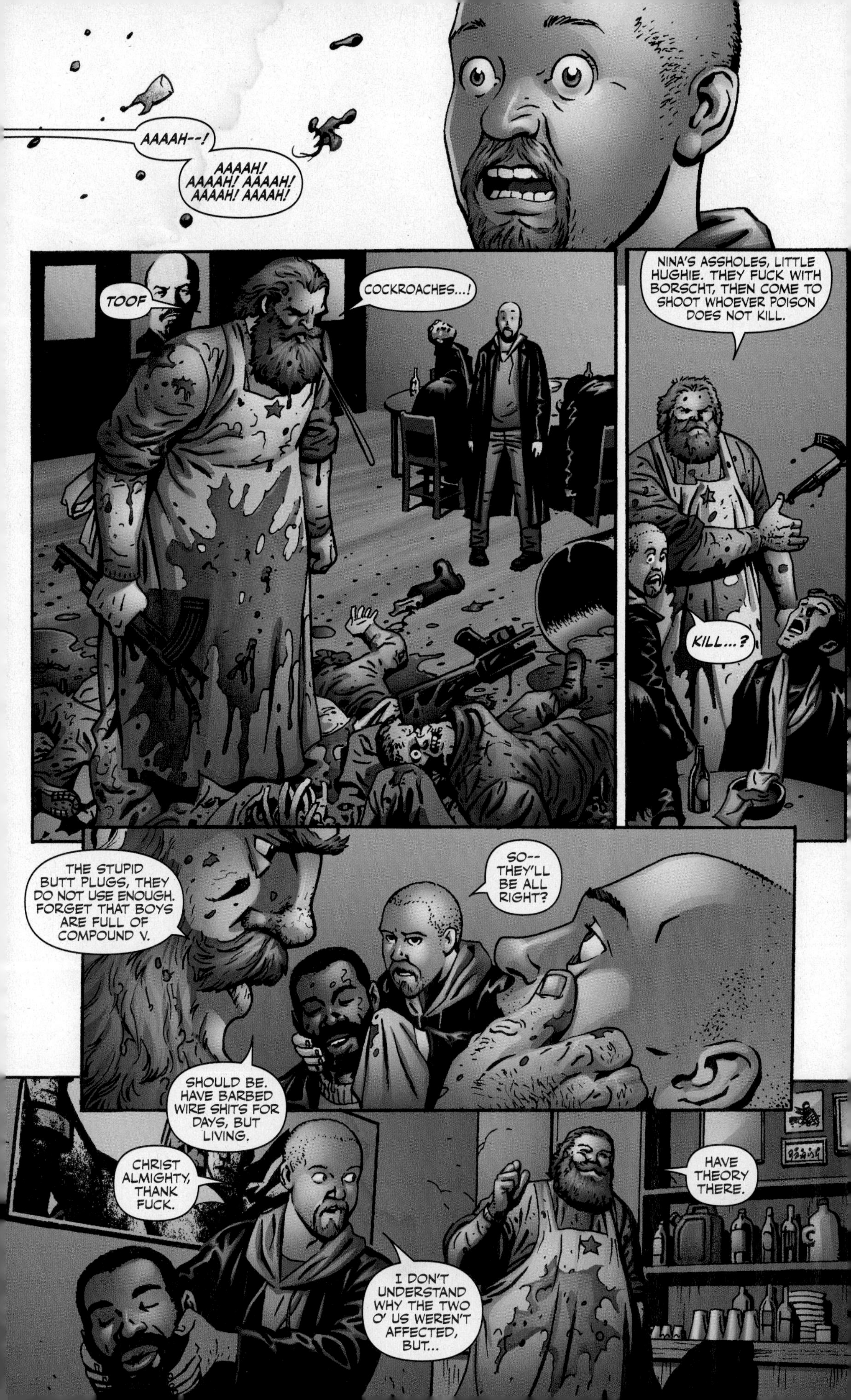
AAAAH--!
AAAAH! AAAAH! AAAAH! AAAAH! AAAAH!
TOOF
COCKROACHES...!
NINA'S ASSHOLES, LITTLE HUGHIE. THEY FUCK WITH BORSCHT, THEN COME TO SHOOT WHOEVER POISON DOES NOT KILL.
KILL...?
THE STUPID BUTT PLUGS, THEY DO NOT USE ENOUGH. FORGET THAT BOYS ARE FULL OF COMPOUND V.
SO-- THEY'LL BE ALL RIGHT?
SHOULD BE. HAVE BARBED WIRE SHITS FOR DAYS, BUT LIVING.
CHRIST ALMIGHTY, THANK FUCK.
I DON'T UNDERSTAND WHY THE TWO O' US WEREN'T AFFECTED, BUT...
HAVE THEORY THERE.

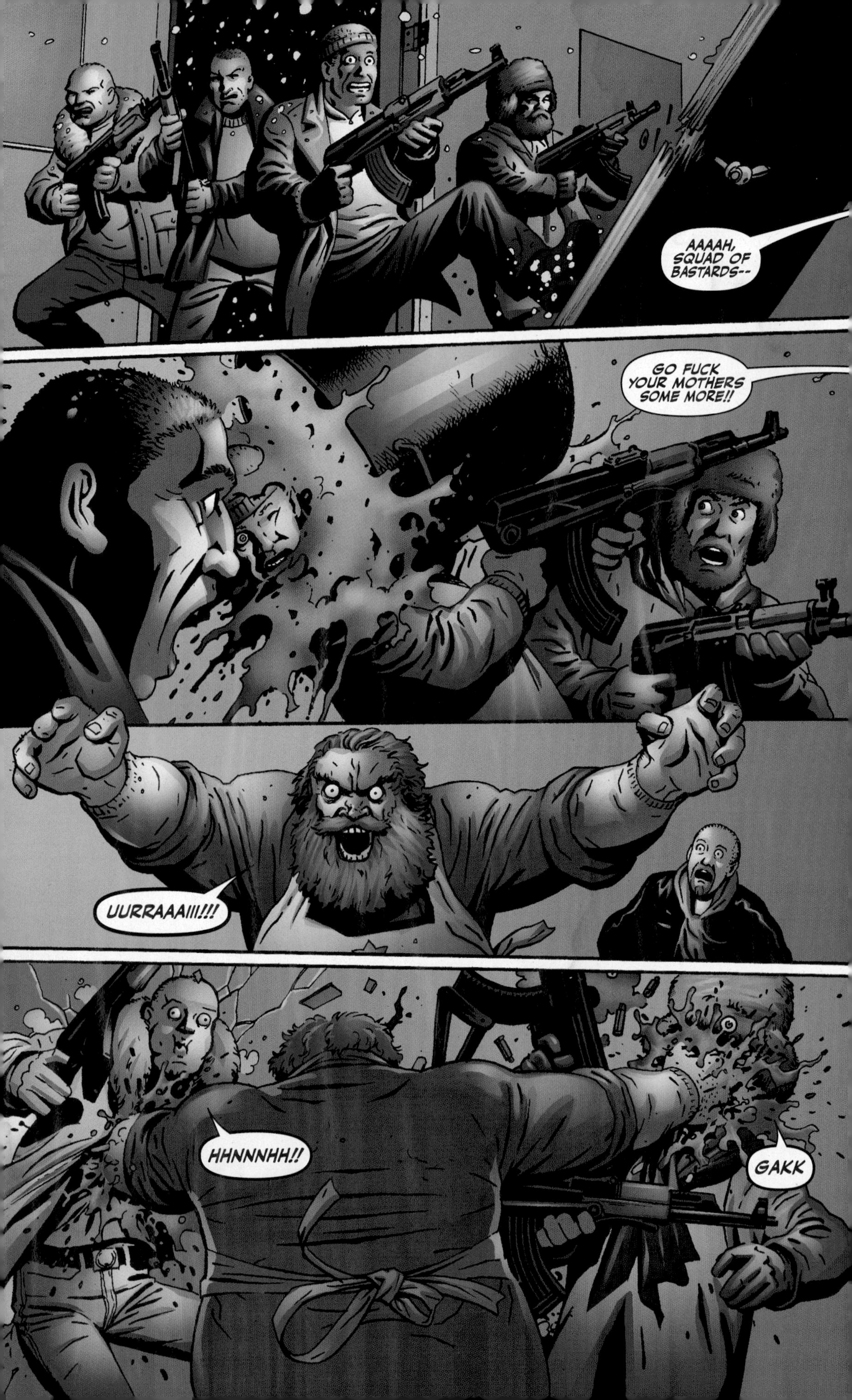
AAAAH, SQUAD OF BASTARDS--
GO FUCK YOUR MOTHERS SOME MORE!!
UURRAAAIII!!!
HHNNNHH!!
GAKK

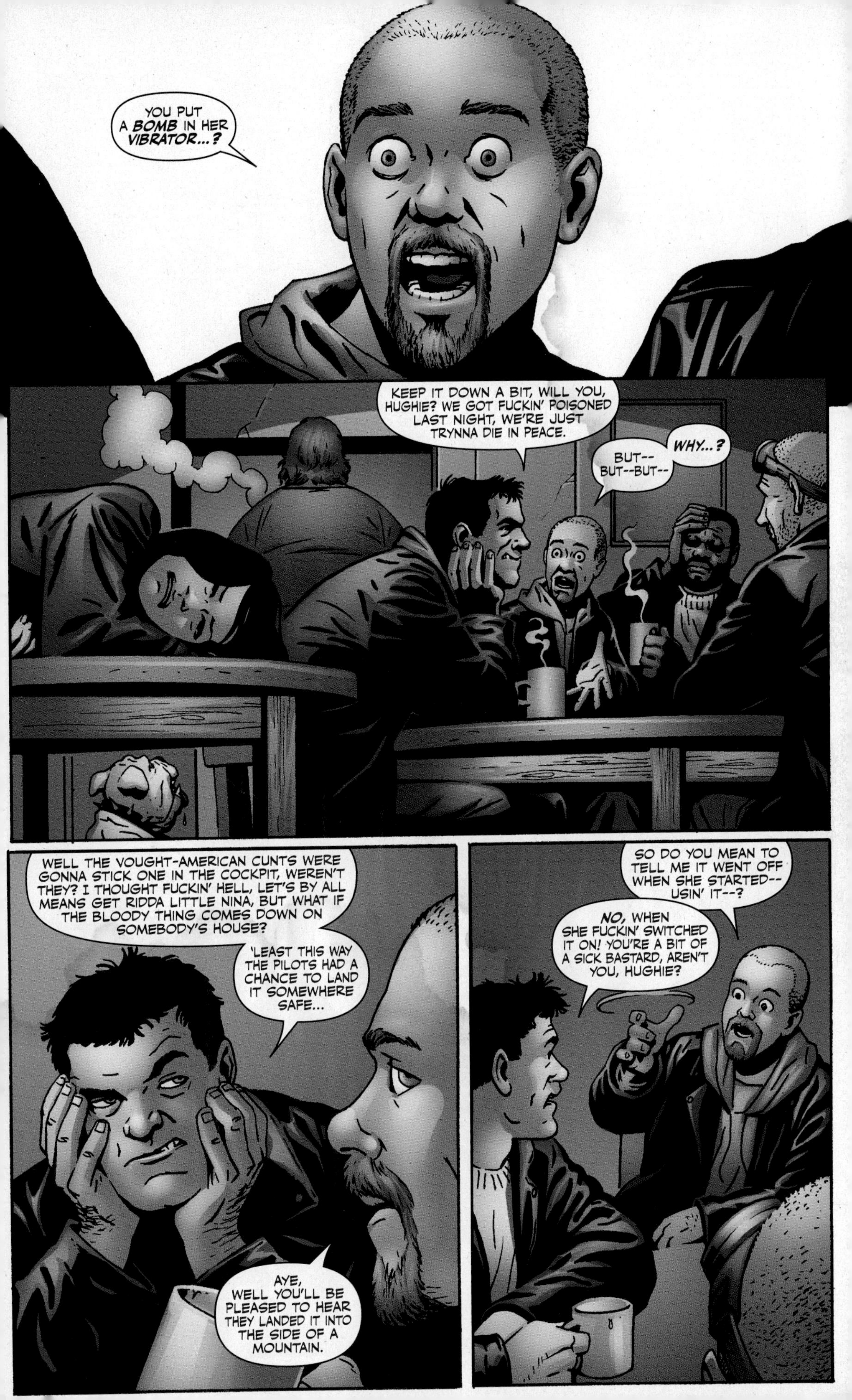
YOU PUT A BOMB IN HER VIBRATOR...?
KEEP IT DOWN A BIT, WILL YOU, HUGHIE? WE GOT FUCKIN' POISONED LAST NIGHT, WE'RE JUST TRYNNA DIE IN PEACE.
BUT-- BUT--BUT--
WHY...?
WELL THE VOUGHT-AMERICAN CUNTS WERE GONNA STICK ONE IN THE COCKPIT, WEREN'T THEY? I THOUGHT FUCKIN' HELL, LET'S BY ALL MEANS GET RIDDA LITTLE NINA, BUT WHAT IF THE BLOODY THING COMES DOWN ON SOMEBODY'S HOUSE?
'LEAST THIS WAY THE PILOTS HAD A CHANCE TO LAND IT SOMEWHERE SAFE...
AYE, WELL YOU'LL BE PLEASED TO HEAR THEY LANDED IT INTO THE SIDE OF A MOUNTAIN.
SO DO YOU MEAN TO TELL ME IT WENT OFF WHEN SHE STARTED-- USIN' IT--?
NO, WHEN SHE FUCKIN' SWITCHED IT ON! YOU'RE A BIT OF A SICK BASTARD, AREN'T YOU, HUGHIE?

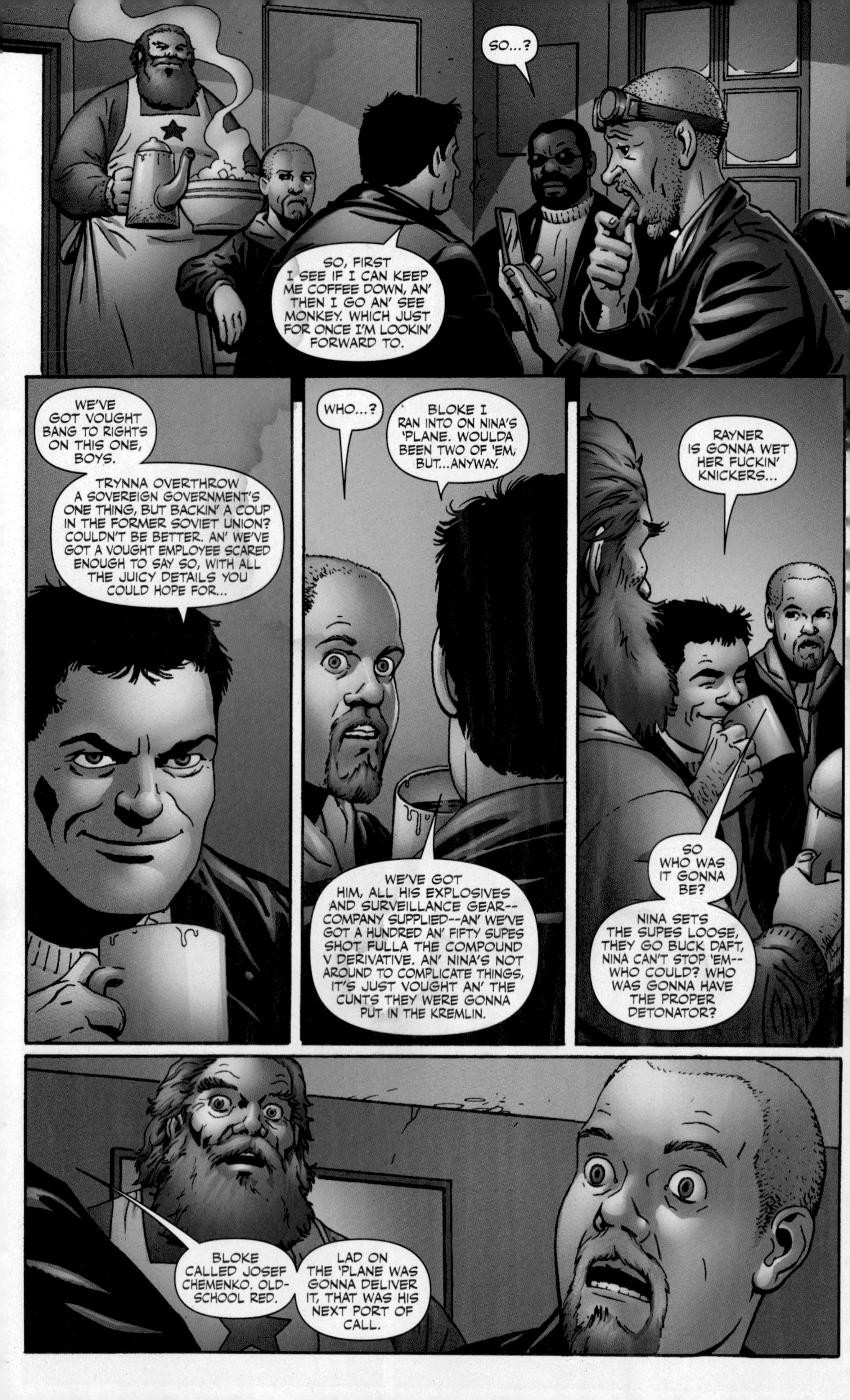

SO...?
SO, FIRST I SEE IF I CAN KEEP ME COFFEE DOWN, AN' THEN I GO AN' SEE MONKEY. WHICH JUST FOR ONCE I'M LOOKIN' FORWARD TO.
WE'VE GOT VOUGHT BANG TO RIGHTS ON THIS ONE, BOYS.
TRYNNA OVERTHROW A SOVEREIGN GOVERNMENT'S ONE THING, BUT BACKIN' A COUP IN THE FORMER SOVIET UNION? COULDN'T BE BETTER. AN' WE'VE GOT A VOUGHT EMPLOYEE SCARED ENOUGH TO SAY SO, WITH ALL THE JUICY DETAILS YOU COULD HOPE FOR...
WHO...?
BLOKE I RAN INTO ON NINA'S 'PLANE. WOULDA BEEN TWO OF 'EM, BUT...ANYWAY.
WE'VE GOT HIM, ALL HIS EXPLOSIVES AND SURVEILLANCE GEAR--COMPANY SUPPLIED--AN' WE'VE GOT A HUNDRED AN' FIFTY SUPES SHOT FULLA THE COMPOUND V DERIVATIVE. AN' NINA'S NOT AROUND TO COMPLICATE THINGS, IT'S JUST VOUGHT AN' THE CUNTS THEY WERE GONNA PUT IN THE KREMLIN.
RAYNER IS GONNA WET HER FUCKIN' KNICKERS...
SO WHO WAS IT GONNA BE?
NINA SETS THE SUPES LOOSE, THEY GO BUCK DAFT, NINA CAN'T STOP 'EM--WHO COULD? WHO WAS GONNA HAVE THE PROPER DETONATOR?
BLOKE CALLED JOSEF CHEMENKO. OLD-SCHOOL RED.
LAD ON THE 'PLANE WAS GONNA DELIVER IT, THAT WAS HIS NEXT PORT OF CALL.

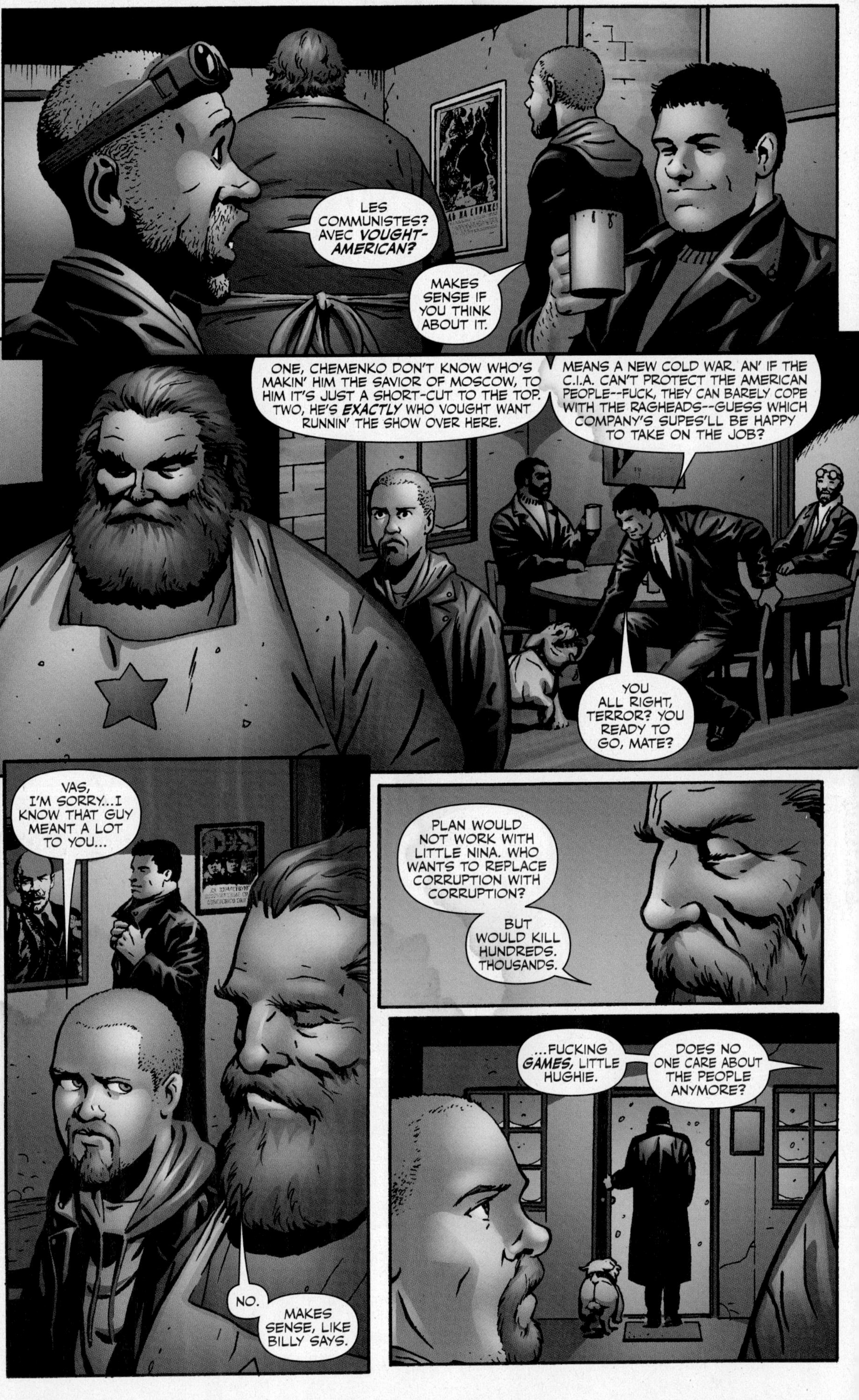
LES COMMUNISTES? AVEC *VOUGHT-AMERICAN?*
MAKES SENSE IF YOU THINK ABOUT IT.
ONE, CHEMENKO DON'T KNOW WHO'S MAKIN' HIM THE SAVIOR OF MOSCOW, TO HIM IT'S JUST A SHORT-CUT TO THE TOP. TWO, HE'S *EXACTLY* WHO VOUGHT WANT RUNNIN' THE SHOW OVER HERE.
MEANS A NEW COLD WAR. AN' IF THE C.I.A. CAN'T PROTECT THE AMERICAN PEOPLE--FUCK, THEY CAN BARELY COPE WITH THE RAGHEADS--GUESS WHICH COMPANY'S SUPES'LL BE HAPPY TO TAKE ON THE JOB?
YOU ALL RIGHT, TERROR? YOU READY TO GO, MATE?
VAS, I'M SORRY...I KNOW THAT GUY MEANT A LOT TO YOU...
NO.
MAKES SENSE, LIKE BILLY SAYS.
PLAN WOULD NOT WORK WITH LITTLE NINA. WHO WANTS TO REPLACE CORRUPTION WITH CORRUPTION?
BUT WOULD KILL HUNDREDS. THOUSANDS.
...FUCKING *GAMES,* LITTLE HUGHIE.
DOES NO ONE CARE ABOUT THE PEOPLE ANYMORE?

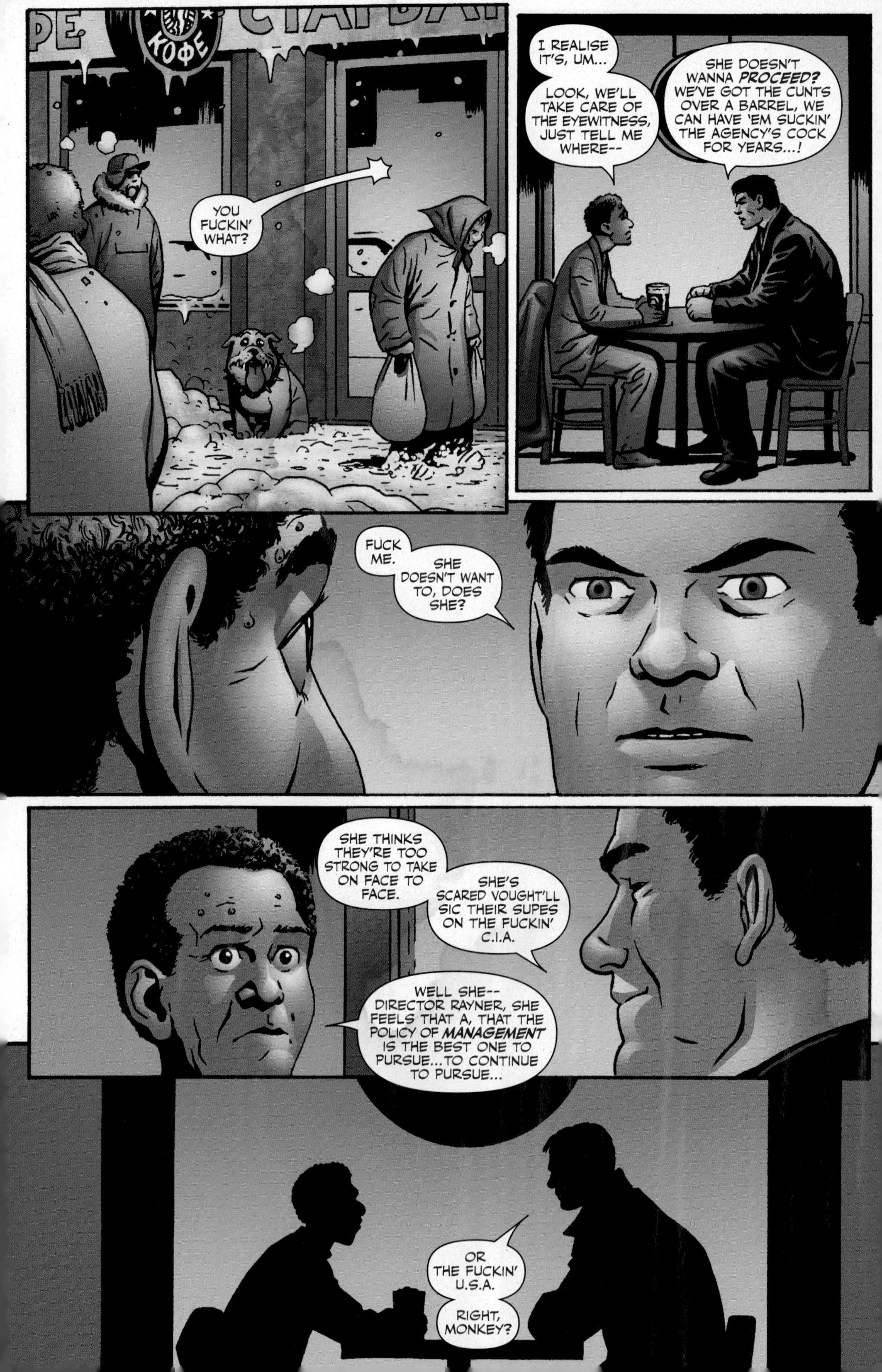

КОФЕ
YOU FUCKIN' WHAT?
I REALISE IT'S, UM...
LOOK, WE'LL TAKE CARE OF THE EYEWITNESS, JUST TELL ME WHERE--
SHE DOESN'T WANNA *PROCEED?* WE'VE GOT THE CUNTS OVER A BARREL, WE CAN HAVE 'EM SUCKIN' THE AGENCY'S COCK FOR YEARS...!
FUCK ME.
SHE DOESN'T WANT TO, DOES SHE?
SHE THINKS THEY'RE TOO STRONG TO TAKE ON FACE TO FACE.
SHE'S SCARED VOUGHT'LL SIC THEIR SUPES ON THE FUCKIN' C.I.A.
WELL SHE-- DIRECTOR RAYNER, SHE FEELS THAT A, THAT THE POLICY OF *MANAGEMENT* IS THE BEST ONE TO PURSUE...TO CONTINUE TO PURSUE...
OR THE FUCKIN' U.S.A.
RIGHT, MONKEY?

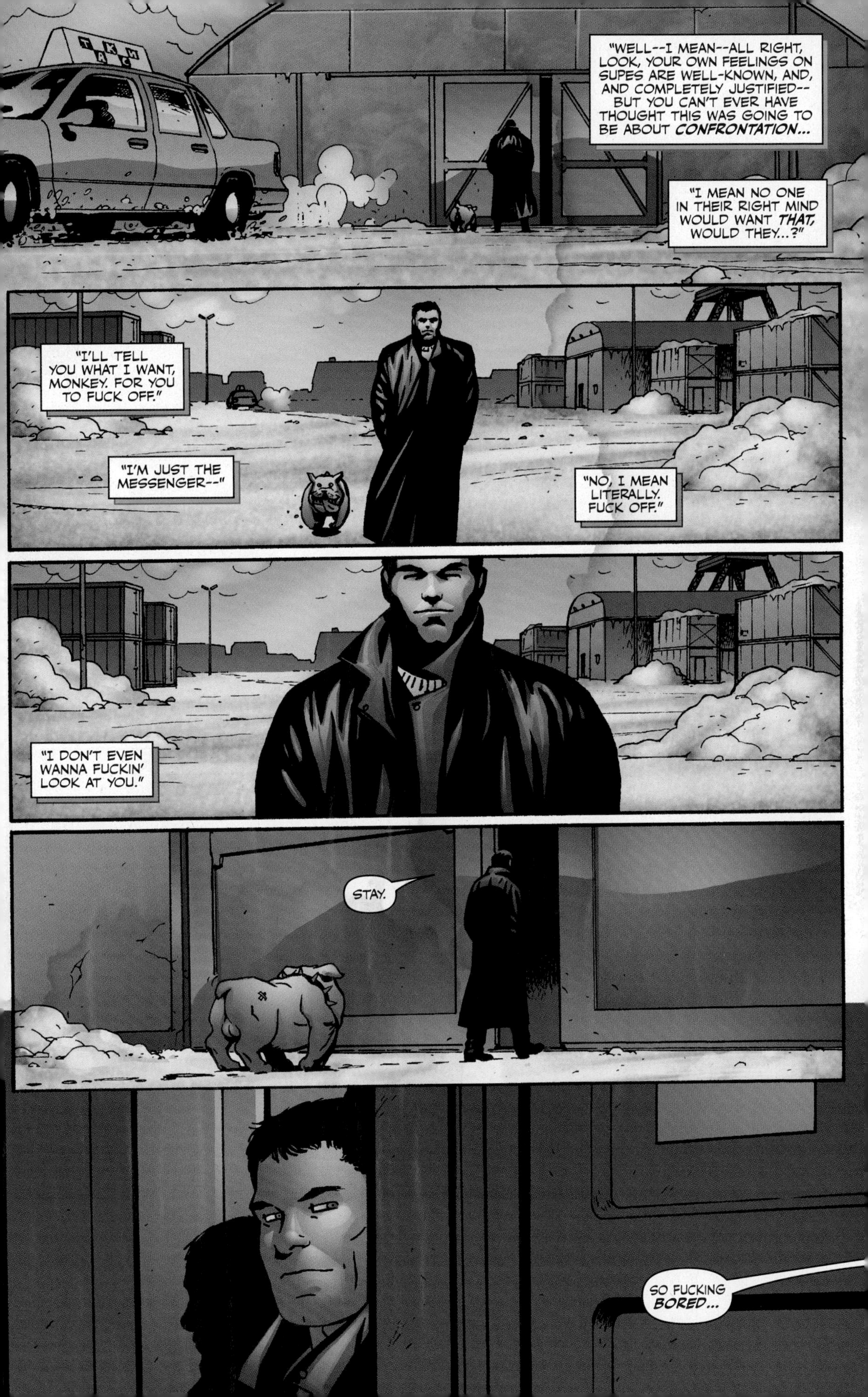

"WELL--I MEAN--ALL RIGHT, LOOK, YOUR OWN FEELINGS ON SUPES ARE WELL-KNOWN, AND, AND COMPLETELY JUSTIFIED-- BUT YOU CAN'T EVER HAVE THOUGHT THIS WAS GOING TO BE ABOUT *CONFRONTATION...*
"I MEAN NO ONE IN THEIR RIGHT MIND WOULD WANT *THAT,* WOULD THEY...?"
"I'LL TELL YOU WHAT I WANT, MONKEY. FOR YOU TO FUCK OFF."
"I'M JUST THE MESSENGER--"
"NO, I MEAN LITERALLY. FUCK OFF."
"I DON'T EVEN WANNA FUCKIN' LOOK AT YOU."
STAY.
SO FUCKING *BORED...*

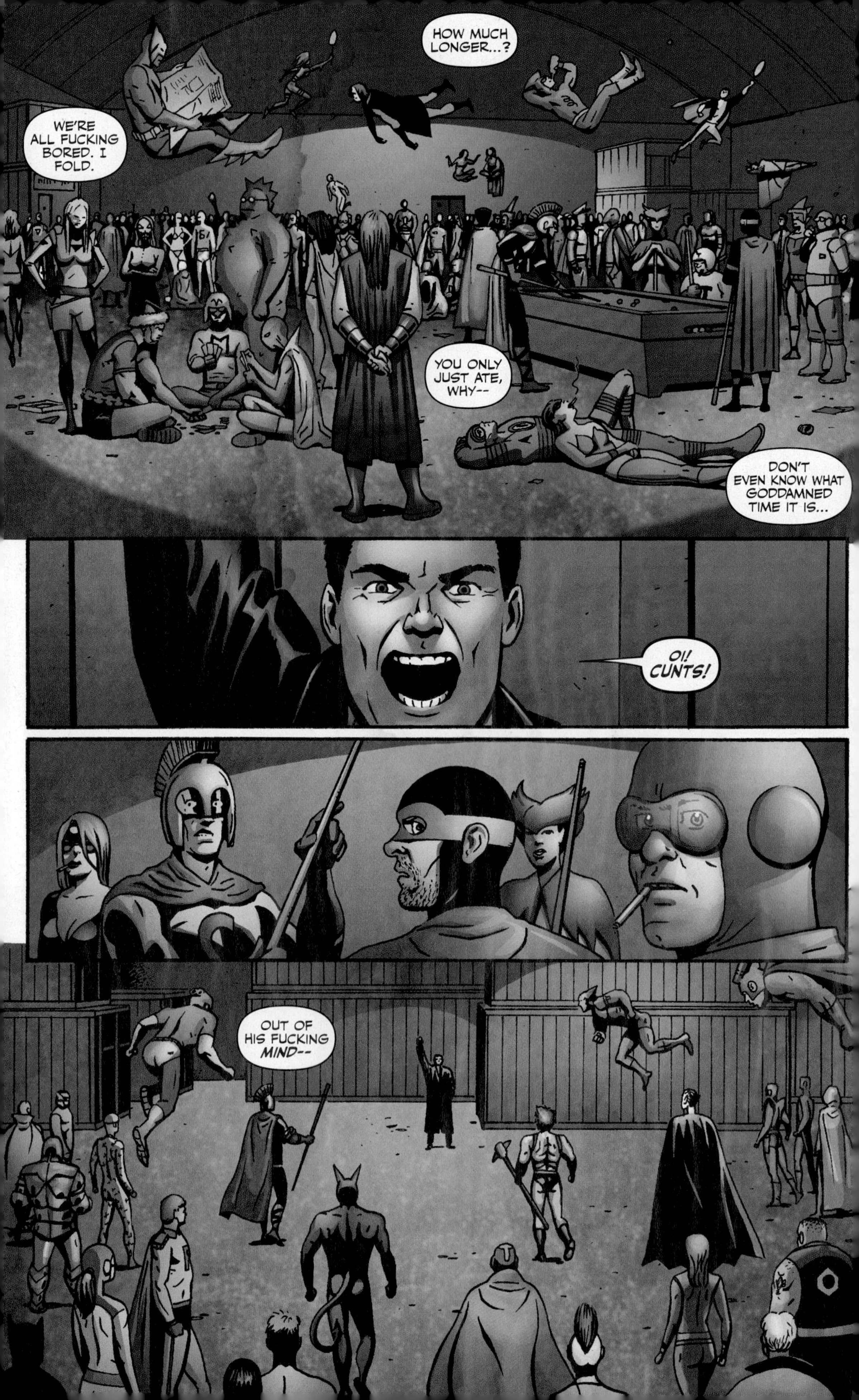
WE'RE ALL FUCKING BORED. I FOLD.
HOW MUCH LONGER...?
YOU ONLY JUST ATE, WHY--
DON'T EVEN KNOW WHAT GODDAMNED TIME IT IS...
OI! CUNTS!
OUT OF HIS FUCKING MIND--

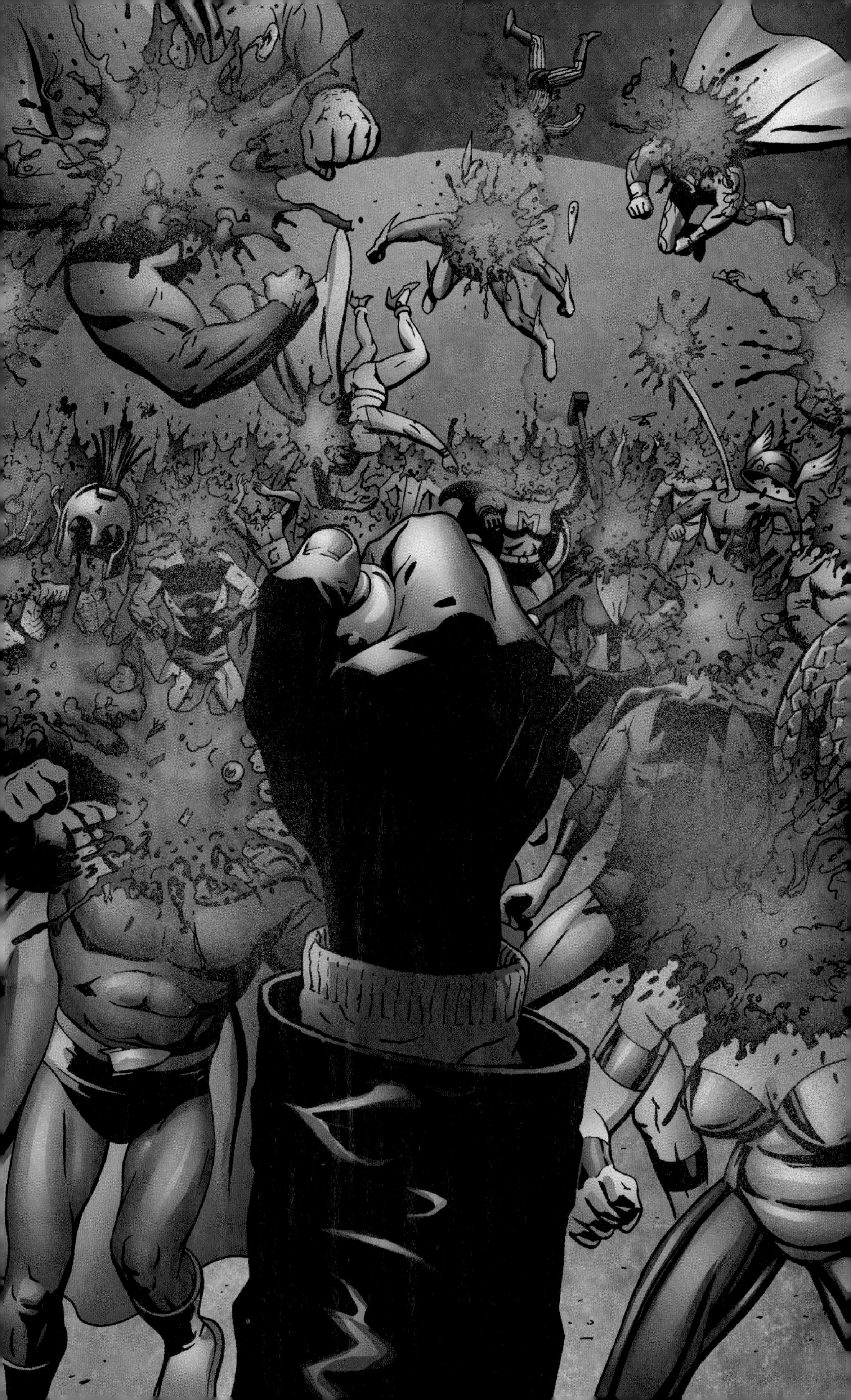

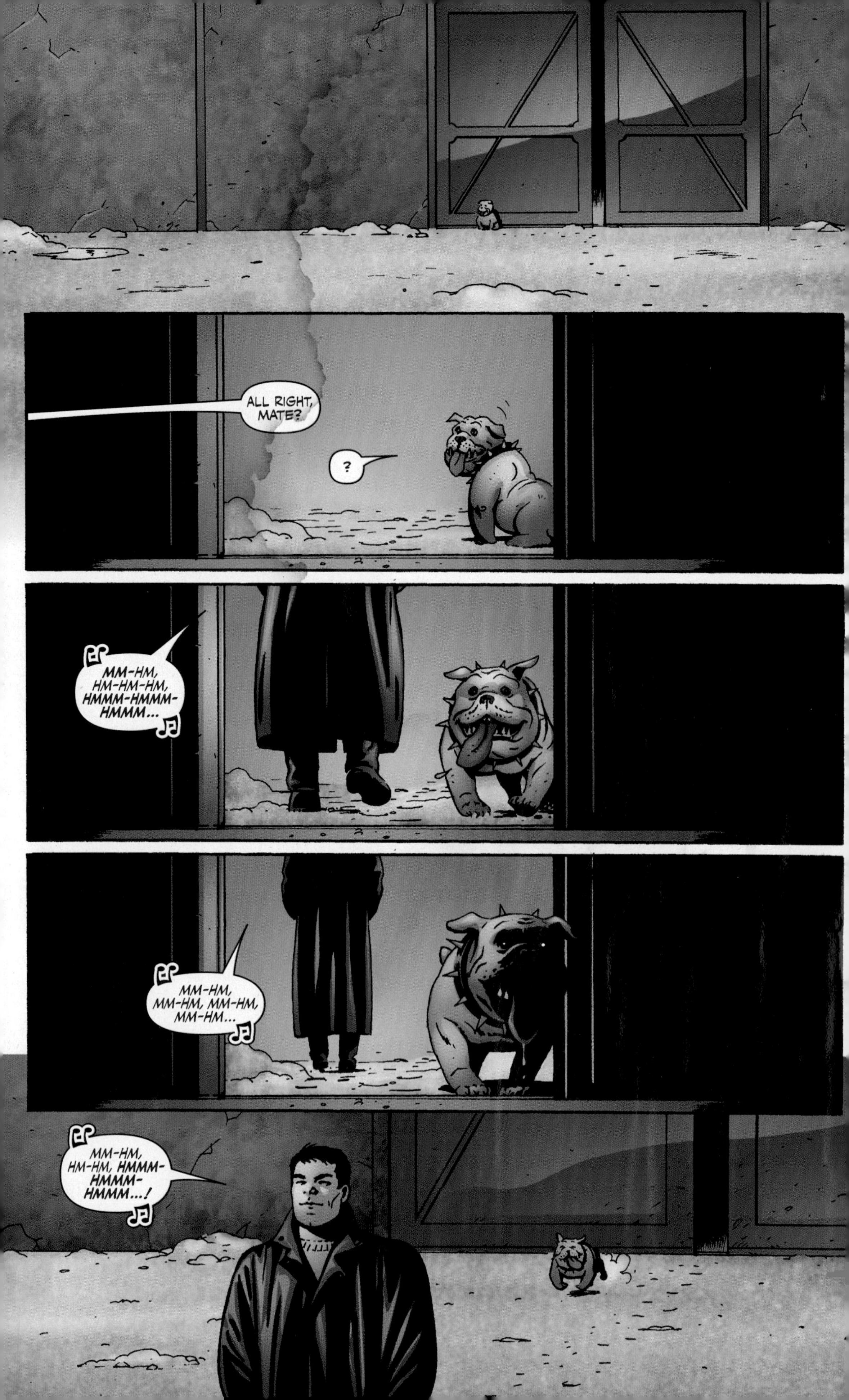
ALL RIGHT, MATE?
?
MM-HM, HM-HM-HM, HMMM-HMMM-HMMM...
MM-HM, MM-HM, MM-HM, MM-HM...
MM-HM, HM-HM, HMMM-HMMM-HMMM...!

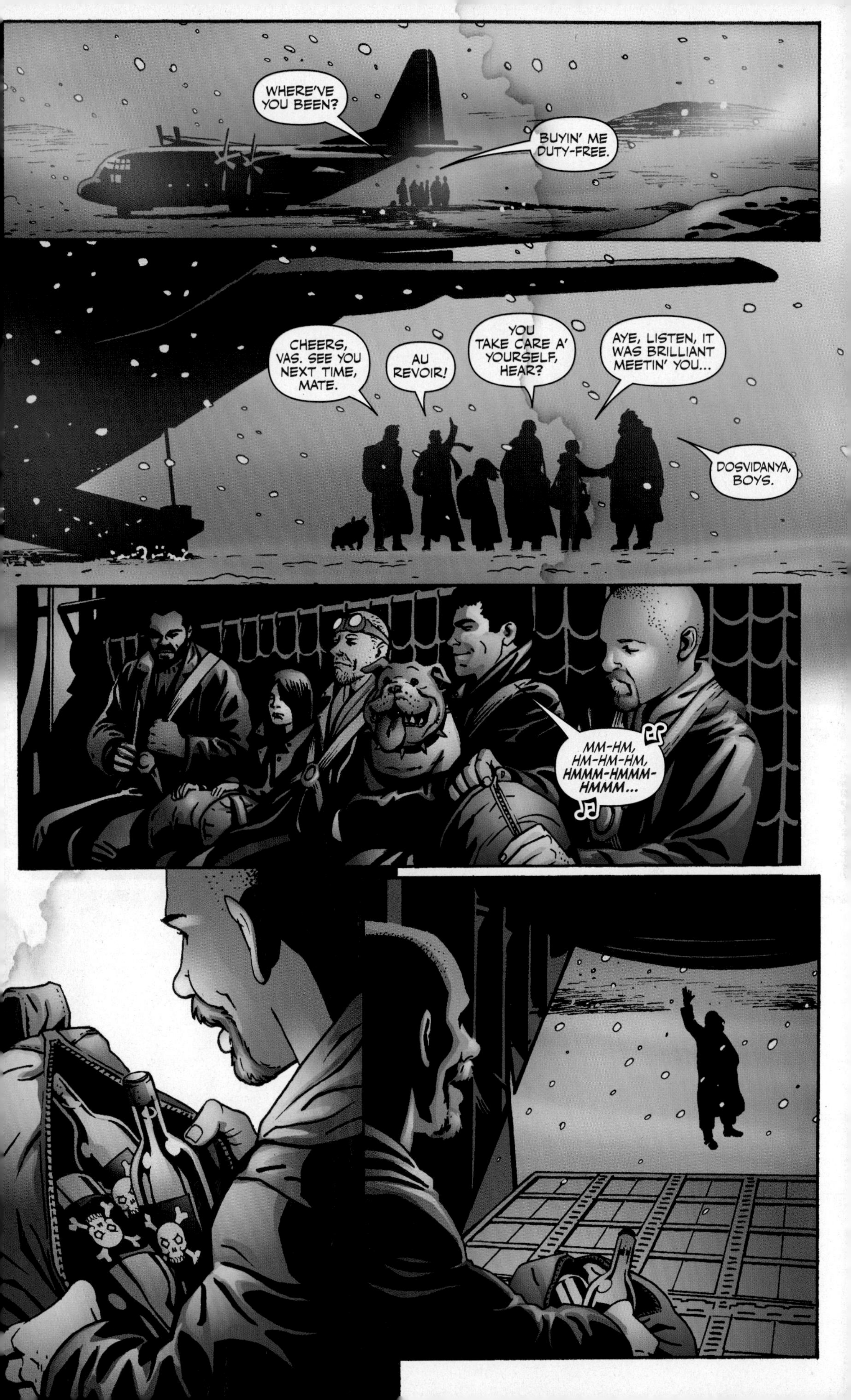
WHERE'VE YOU BEEN?
BUYIN' ME DUTY-FREE.
CHEERS, VAS. SEE YOU NEXT TIME, MATE.
AU REVOIR!
YOU TAKE CARE A' YOURSELF, HEAR?
AYE, LISTEN, IT WAS BRILLIANT MEETIN' YOU...
DOSVIDANYA, BOYS.
MM-HM, HM-HM-HM, HMMM-HMMM-HMMM...

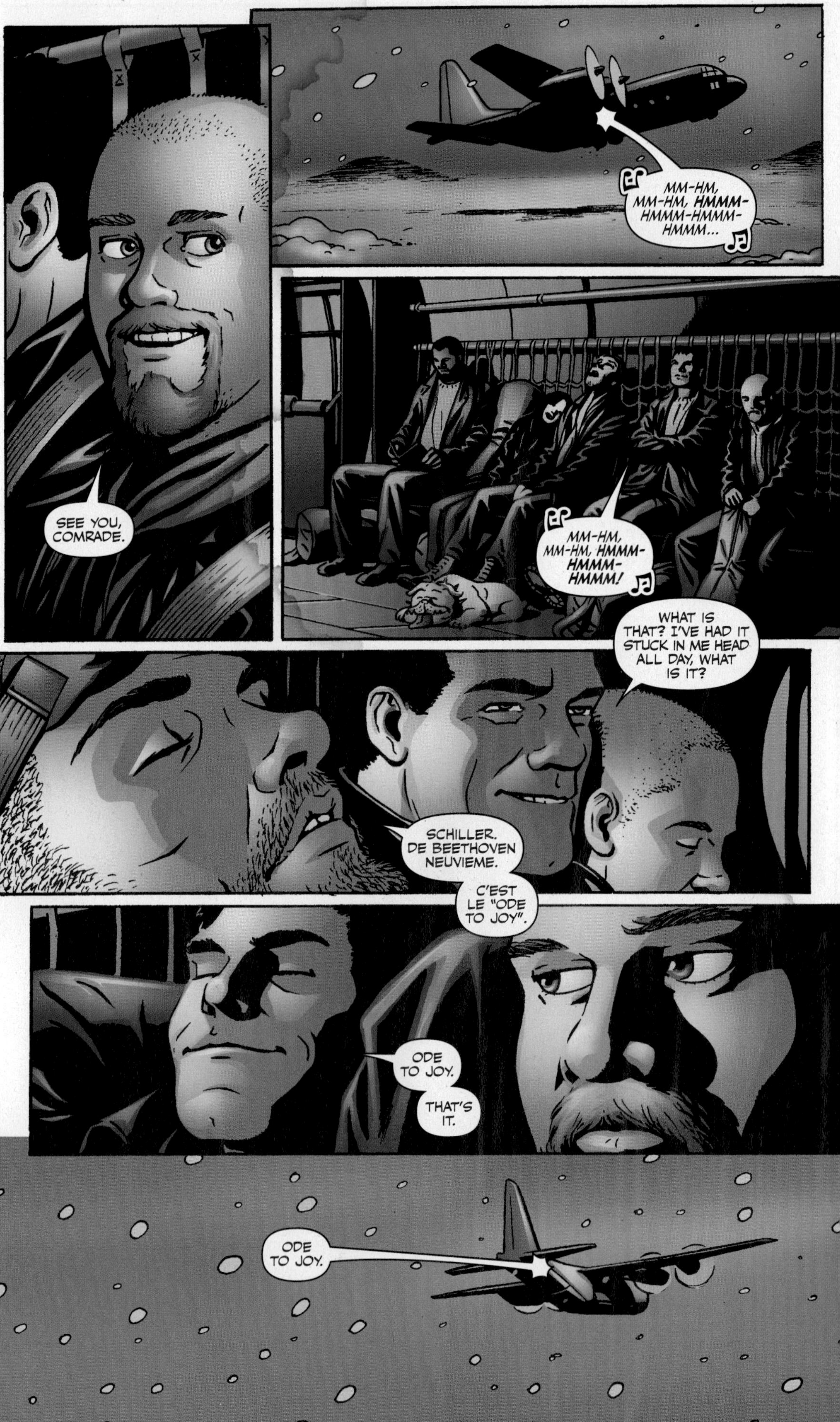
MM-HM, MM-HM, HMMM-HMMM-HMMM-HMMM...
SEE YOU, COMRADE.
MM-HM, MM-HM, HMMM-HMMM-HMMM!
WHAT IS THAT? I'VE HAD IT STUCK IN ME HEAD ALL DAY, WHAT IS IT?
SCHILLER. DE BEETHOVEN NEUVIEME.
C'EST LE "ODE TO JOY".
ODE TO JOY.
THAT'S IT.
ODE TO JOY.

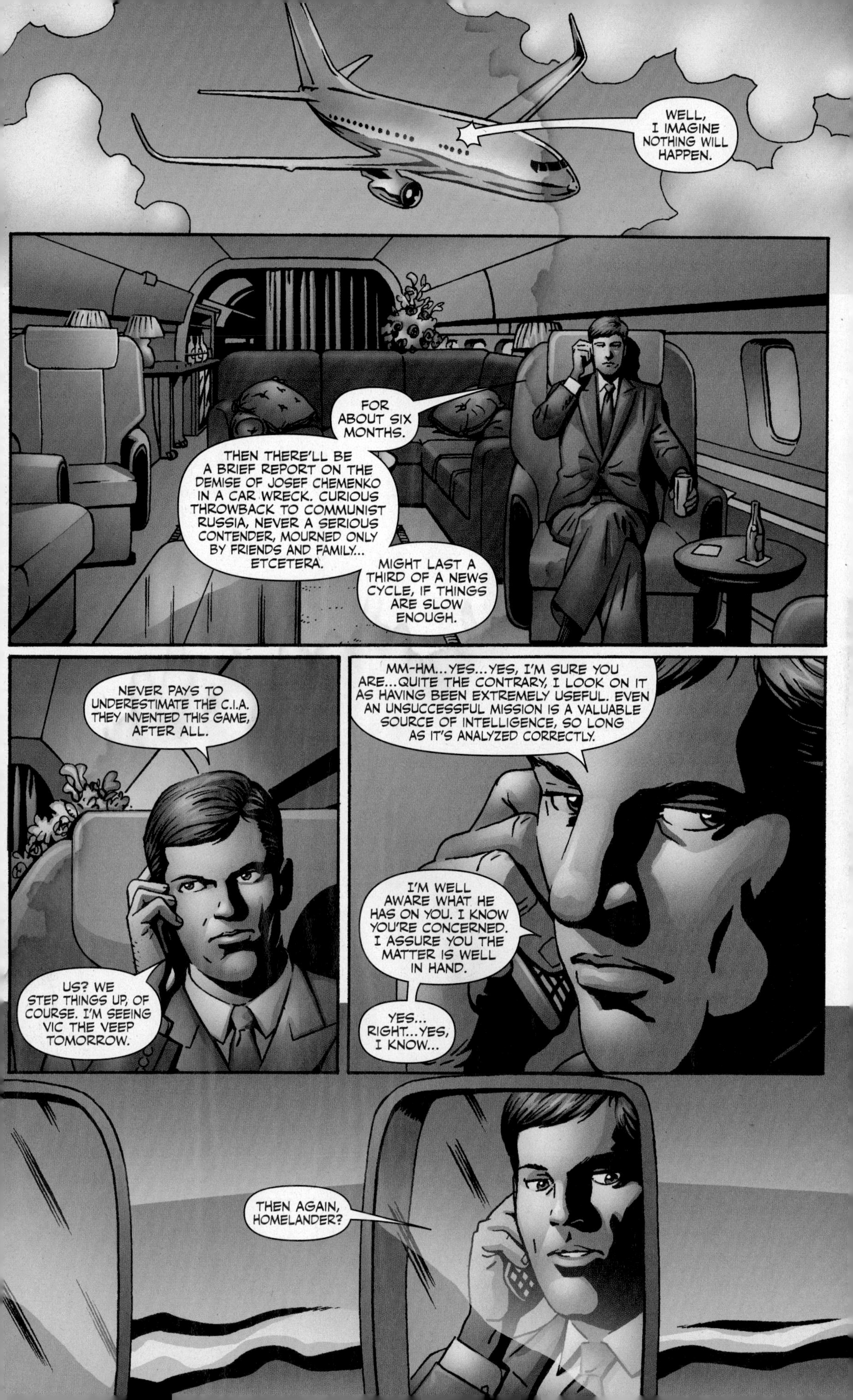
WELL, I IMAGINE NOTHING WILL HAPPEN.
FOR ABOUT SIX MONTHS.
THEN THERE'LL BE A BRIEF REPORT ON THE DEMISE OF JOSEF CHEMENKO IN A CAR WRECK. CURIOUS THROWBACK TO COMMUNIST RUSSIA, NEVER A SERIOUS CONTENDER, MOURNED ONLY BY FRIENDS AND FAMILY... ETCETERA.
MIGHT LAST A THIRD OF A NEWS CYCLE, IF THINGS ARE SLOW ENOUGH.
NEVER PAYS TO UNDERESTIMATE THE C.I.A. THEY INVENTED THIS GAME, AFTER ALL.
US? WE STEP THINGS UP, OF COURSE. I'M SEEING VIC THE VEEP TOMORROW.
MM-HM...YES...YES, I'M SURE YOU ARE...QUITE THE CONTRARY, I LOOK ON IT AS HAVING BEEN EXTREMELY USEFUL. EVEN AN UNSUCCESSFUL MISSION IS A VALUABLE SOURCE OF INTELLIGENCE, SO LONG AS IT'S ANALYZED CORRECTLY.
I'M WELL AWARE WHAT HE HAS ON YOU. I KNOW YOU'RE CONCERNED. I ASSURE YOU THE MATTER IS WELL IN HAND.
YES... RIGHT...YES, I KNOW...
THEN AGAIN, HOMELANDER?

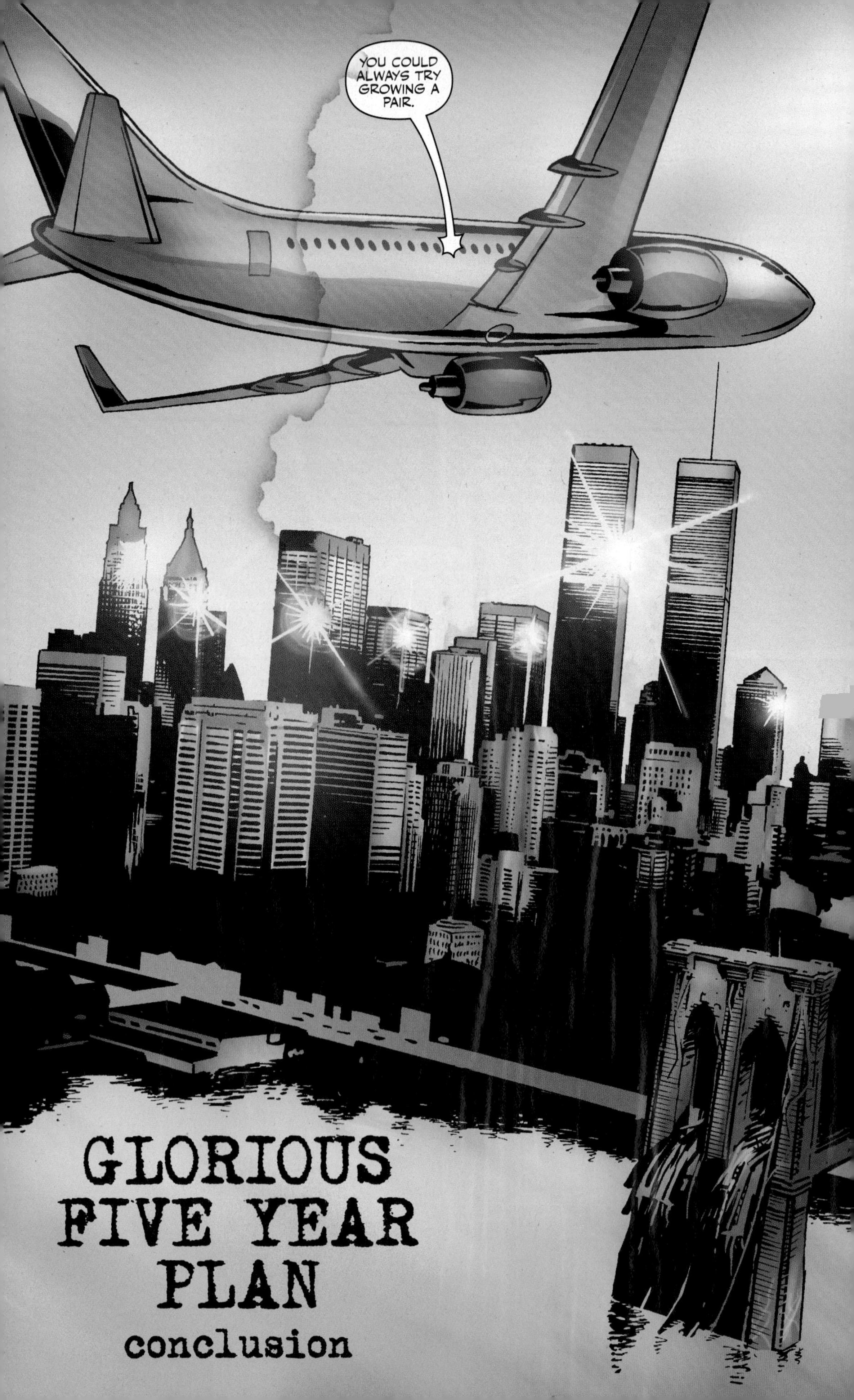
YOU COULD ALWAYS TRY GROWING A PAIR.
GLORIOUS FIVE YEAR PLAN
conclusion

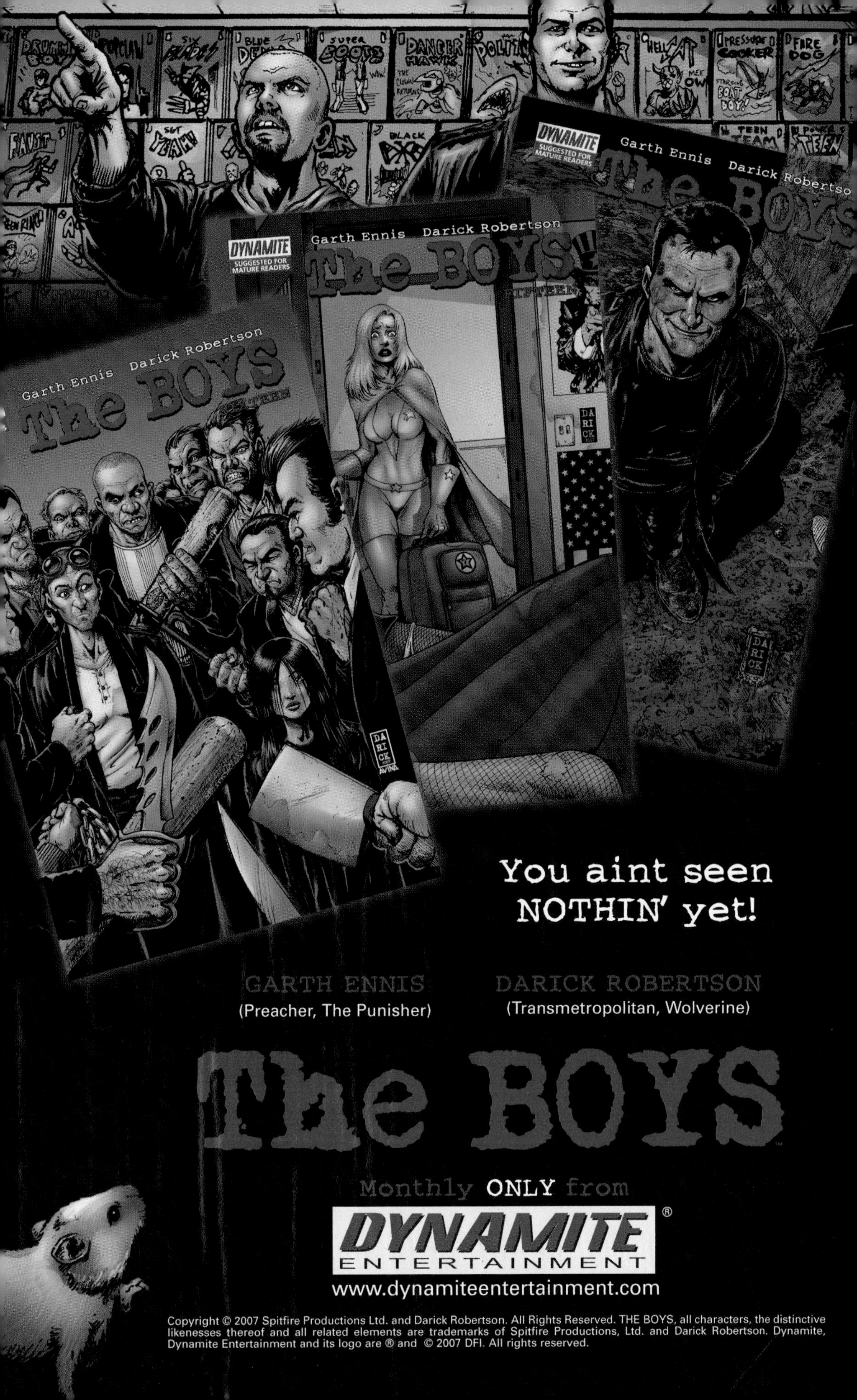
DYNAMITE
SUGGESTED FOR MATURE READERS
Garth Ennis Darick Robertson
The BOYS
DYNAMITE
SUGGESTED FOR MATURE READERS
Garth Ennis Darick Robertson
The BOYS
Garth Ennis Darick Robertson
The BOYS
You aint seen NOTHIN' yet!
GARTH ENNIS
(Preacher, The Punisher)
DARICK ROBERTSON
(Transmetropolitan, Wolverine)
The BOYS
Monthly ONLY from
DYNAMITE ENTERTAINMENT
www.dynamiteentertainment.com

The BOYS™

VOLUME ONE: THE NAME OF THE GAME

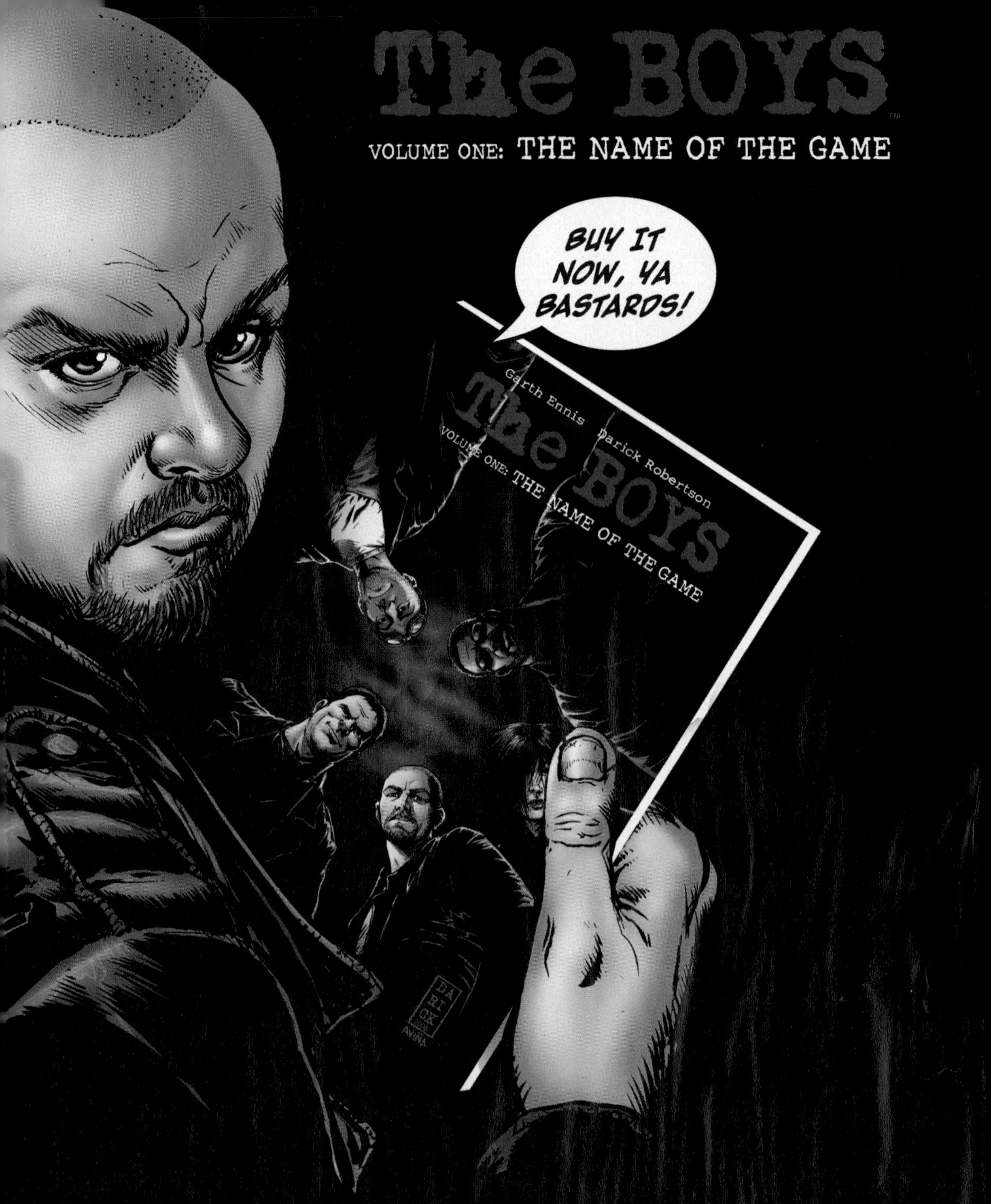
BUY IT NOW, YA BASTARDS!
Garth Ennis
Darick Robertson
The BOYS
VOLUME ONE: THE NAME OF THE GAME

written by
GARTH ENNIS
(Preacher, Punisher)

art and cover by
DARICK ROBERTSON
(Transmetropolitan, Wolverine)

This collection features:
Issues 1-6 of the smash-hit series, a complete cover gallery, concept art and sketches, and an introduction by Simon (Shaun of the Dead, Hot Fuzz) Pegg!

ONLY from

DYNAMITE® ENTERTAINMENT

information • exclusives • interviews • forums• contests • downloads • more
WWW.DYNAMITEENTERTAINMENT.COM

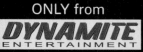

"EPIC AND EMOTIONAL, SPARE YET RICH, THE LONE RANGER IS WORTH ITS WEIGHT IN (HI-YO) SILVER. A-" - ENTERTAINMENT WEEKLY

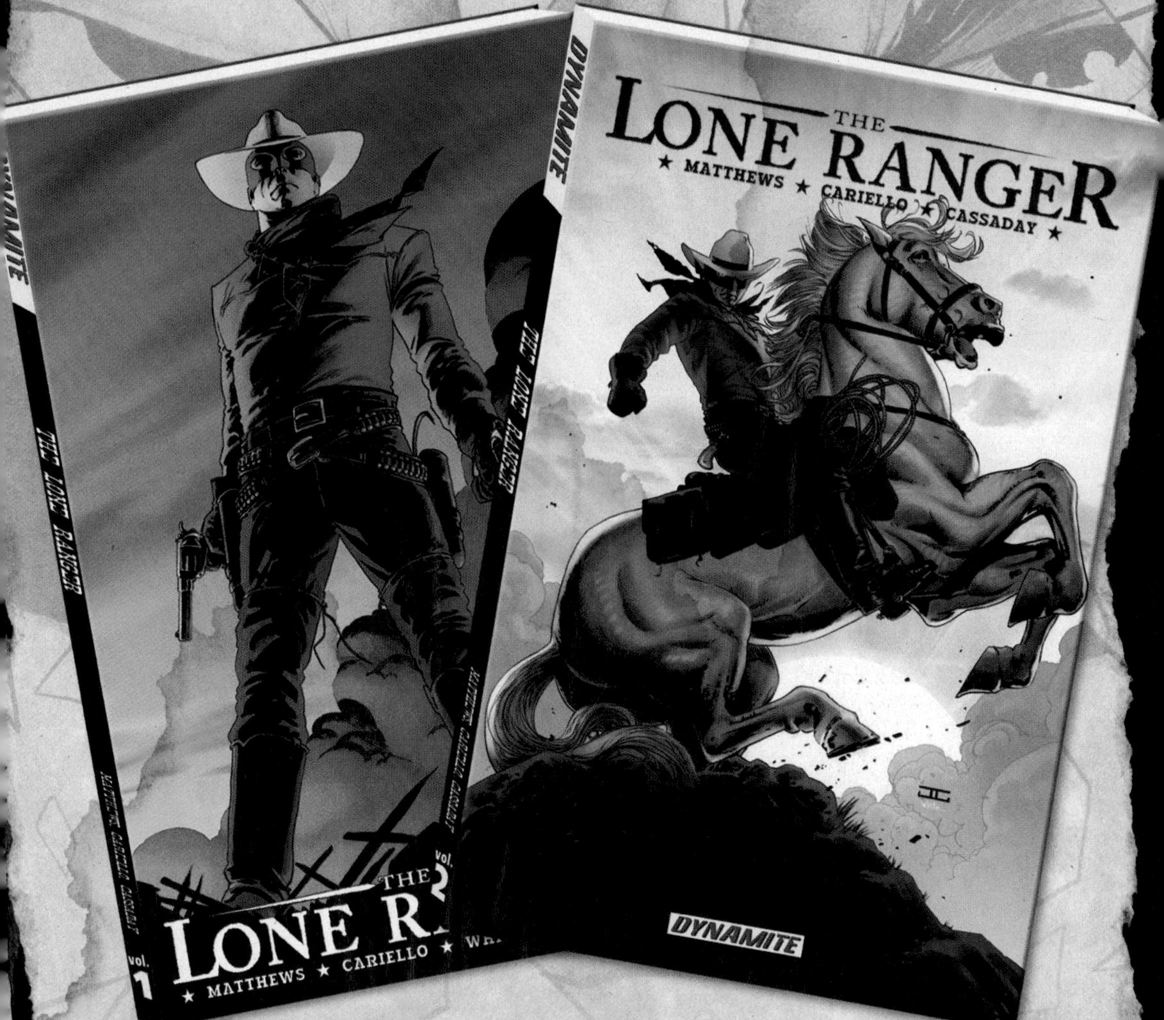
DYNAMITE
THE LONE RANGER
MATTHEWS ★ CARIELLO ★ CASSADAY
vol. 1
THE LONE RANGER
DYNAMITE

BRETT MATTHEWS • SERGIO CARIELLO • JOHN CASSADAY • DYNAMITE

THE LONE RANGER VOLUME 1: NOW & FOREVER HARDCOVER

- Issues one through six of Dynamite's The Lone Ranger
- A complete gallery featuring all of John Cassaday's covers for these issues
- A look into the sketchbooks of Sergio Cariello and John Cassaday
- DVD-Style Commentary of issue one by Brett Matthews

THE LONE RANGER VOLUME 2: LINES NOT CROSSED HARDCOVER

- Issues seven through eleven of Dynamite's The Lone Ranger
- A complete gallery featuring all of John Cassaday's covers for these issues

EXCLUSIVE • PREVIEWS • INTERVIEWS • CONTESTS • DOWNLOADS • FORUMS • MORE

WWW.DYNAMITEENTERTAINMENT.COM

THE DYNAMITE ENTERTAINMENT COLLECTION

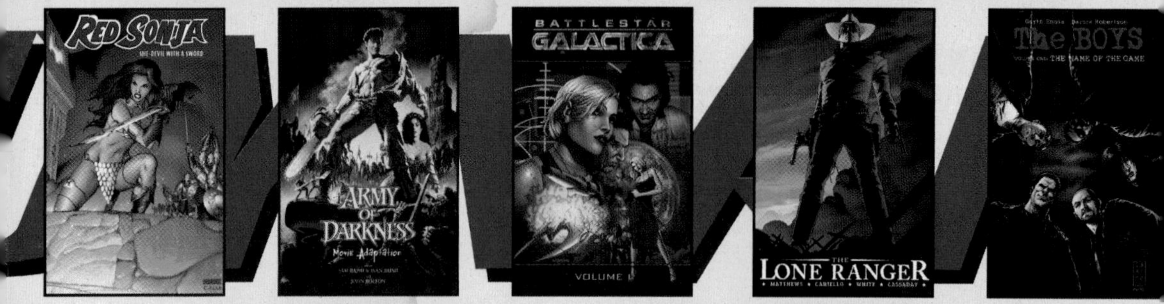
RED SONJA
SHE-DEVIL WITH A SWORD
ARMY OF DARKNESS
Movie Adaptation
BATTLESTAR GALACTICA
VOLUME 1
THE LONE RANGER
MATTHEWS • CARIELLO • WHITE • CASSADAY
The BOYS
THE NAME OF THE GAME

CURRENTLY AVAILABLE AND UPCOMING COLLECTIONS FROM DYNAMITE ENTERTAINMENT!

- ADVENTURES OF RED SONJA Vol. 1
  Softcover (ISBN: 1-933305-07-X)
- ADVENTURES OF RED SONJA Vol. 2
  Softcover (ISBN: 1-933305-12-6)
- ADVENTURES OF RED SONJA Vol. 3
  Softcover (ISBN: 1-933305-98-3)
- ARMY OF DARKNESS: MOVIE ADAPTATION
  Softcover (ISBN: 1-933305-17-7)
- ARMY OF DARKNESS: ASHES TO ASHES
  Softcover (ISBN: 0-9749638-9-5)
- ARMY OF DARKNESS: SHOP 'TIL YOU DROP DEAD
  Softcover (ISBN: 1-933305-26-6)
- ARMY OF DARKNESS vs. RE-ANIMATOR
  Softcover (ISBN: 1-933305-13-4)
- ARMY OF DARKNESS: OLD SCHOOL & MORE
  Softcover (ISBN: 1-933305-18-5)
- ARMY OF DARKNESS: ASH vs. THE CLASSIC MONSTERS
  Softcover (ISBN: 1-933305-41-X)
- BAD BOY 10TH ANNIVERSARY
  Hardcover (ISBN: 1-933305-54-1
- BORDERLINE Vol. 1
  Softcover (ISBN: 1-933305-05-3)
- BORDERLINE Vol. 2
  Softcover (ISBN: 1-933305-47-9)
- THE BOYS Vol. 1: THE NAME OF THE GAME
  Softcover (ISBN: 1-933305-46-0)
- THE BOYS Vol. 2: GET SOME
  Softcover (ISBN: 1-933305-68-1)
- CLASSIC BATTLESTAR GALACTICA Vol. 1
  Softcover (ISBN: 1-933305-45-2)
- CLASSIC BSG Vol. 2: CYLON APOCALYPSE
  Softcover (ISBN: 1-933305-55-X)
- DARKMAN vs. ARMY OF DARKNESS Vol. 1
  Softcover (ISBN: 1-933305-48-7)
- DREADSTAR THE DEFINITIVE COLLECTION Vol. 1
  Hardcover (ISBN: 0-9749638-0-1)
  Part 1 Softcover (ISBN: 0-9749638-1-X)
  Part 2 Softcover (ISBN: 0-9749638-2-8)
- DREADSTAR THE BEGINNING
  Hardcover (ISBN: 1-933305-10-X)
- EDUARDO RISSO'S TALES OF TERROR
  Softcover (ISBN: 1-933305-23-1)
- HIGHLANDER Vol. 1
  Hardcover (ISBN: 1-933305-31-2)
  Softcover (ISBN: 1-933305-32-0)
- HIGHLANDER Vol. 2
  Softcover (ISBN: 1-933305-59-2)
- KID KOSMOS: COSMIC GUARD
  Softcover (ISBN: 1-933305-02-9)
- KID KOSMOS: KIDNAPPED
  Softcover (ISBN: 1-933305-29-0)
- THE LONE RANGER Vol.1: NOW AND FOREVER
  Hardcover (ISBN: 1-933305-39-8)
  Softcover (ISBN: 1-933305-40-1)
- MONSTER WAR
  Softcover (ISBN: 1-933305-30-4)
- NEW BATTLESTAR GALACTICA Vol. 1
  Hardcover (ISBN: 1-933305-33-9)
  Softcover (ISBN: 1-933305-34-7)
- NEW BATTLESTAR GALACTICA Vol. 2
  Hardcover (ISBN: 1-933305-53-3)
  Softcover (ISBN: 1-933305-49-5)
- NEW BATTLESTAR GALACTICA Vol. 3
  Hardcover (ISBN: 1-933305-57-6)
  Softcover (ISBN: 1-933305-58-4)
- NEW BATTLESTAR GALACTICA: ZAREK
  Softcover (ISBN: 1-933305-50-9)
- ESSENTIAL PAINKILLER JANE
  Softcover (ISBN: 1-933305-97-5)
- PAINKILLER JANE Vol. 1
  Softcover (ISBN: 1-933305-42-8)
- PAINKILLER JANE Vol. 2
  Softcover (ISBN: 1-933305-65-7)
- RAISE THE DEAD
  Hardcover (ISBN: 1-933305-56-8)
- RED SONJA: SHE-DEVIL WITH A SWORD Vol. 1
  Hardcover (ISBN: 1-933305-36-3)
  Softcover (ISBN: 1-933305-11-8)
- RED SONJA vs. THULSA DOOM
  Softcover (ISBN: 1-933305-96-7)
- RED SONJA: SHE-DEVIL WITH A SWORD Vol. 2
  Hardcover (ISBN: 1-933305-44-4)
  Softcover (ISBN: 1-933305-43-6)
- SAVAGE RED SONJA: QUEEN OF THE FROZEN WASTES Hardcover (ISBN: 1-933305-37-1)
  Softcover (ISBN: 1-933305-38-X)
- RED SONJA: SHE-DEVIL WITH A SWORD Vol. 3
  Hardcover (ISBN: 1-933305-51-7)
  Softcover (ISBN: 1-933305-52-5)
- RED SONJA: TRAVELS
  Softcover (ISBN: 1-933305-20-7)
- RED SONJA: SHE-DEVIL WITH A SWORD Vol. 4
  Hardcover (ISBN: 1-933305-64-9)
  Softcover (ISBN: 1-933305-63-0)
- SCOUT Vol. 1
  Softcover (ISBN: 1-933305-95-9)
- SCOUT Vol. 2
  Softcover (ISBN: 1-933305-60-6)
- SIX FROM SIRIUS
  Softcover (ISBN: 1-933305-03-7)
- STREET MAGIK
  Softcover (ISBN: 1-933305-47-9)
- XENA Vol. 1: CONTEST OF PANTHEONS
  Softcover (ISBN: 1-933305-35-5)
- XENA Vol. 2: DARK XENA
  Softcover (ISBN: 1-933305-61-4)

information • previews • interviews • contests downloads • forums • podcasts • and more

WWW.DYNAMITEENTERTAINMENT.COM